LEADERS OF THE WORLD
General Editor: **ROBERT MAXWELL, M.C.**

Y. V. ANDROPOV

Speeches and Writings
Second Enlarged Edition

LEADERS OF THE WORLD

General Editor: ROBERT MAXWELL, M.C.

Yuri Vladimirovich Andropov

Y. V. ANDROPOV

General Secretary of the CPSU Central Committee and
President of the Presidium of the USSR Supreme Soviet.

Speeches and Writings

Second Enlarged Edition

PERGAMON PRESS

OXFORD · NEW YORK · TORONTO · SYDNEY · PARIS · FRANKFURT

U.K.	Pergamon Press Ltd., Headington Hill Hall, Oxford OX3 0BW, England
U.S.A.	Pergamon Press Inc., Maxwell House, Fairview Park, Elmsford, New York 10523, U.S.A.
CANADA	Pergamon Press Canada Ltd., Suite 104, 150 Consumers Road, Willowdale, Ontario M2J 1P9, Canada
AUSTRALIA	Pergamon Press (Aust.) Pty. Ltd., PO Box 544, Potts Point, N.S.W. 2011, Australia
FRANCE	Pergamon Press SARL, 24 rue des Ecoles, 75240 Paris, Cedex 05, France
FEDERAL REPUBLIC OF GERMANY	Pergamon Press GmbH, Hammerweg 6, D-6242 Kronberg-Taunus, Federal Republic of Germany

Selection, arrangement and translation copyright
© 1983 VAAP, Moscow

First edition 1983
Second enlarged edition 1983

Library of Congress Cataloging in Publication Data
Andropov, IU. V. (IUriĭ Vladimirovich), 1914-
Speeches and writings.
Translated from the Russian. —(Leaders of the world)
1. Soviet Union—Politics and government—1953-
—Addresses, essays, lectures. 2. Communism—Soviet
Union—Addresses, essays, lectures. I. Title.
DK275.A53A5   1983   324.247075'092'4
82-22408

British Library Cataloguing in Publication Data
Andropov, Y. V.
Speeches and writings. —(Leaders of the world)
1. Soviet Union—History—1953—Sources
2. Soviet Union—Politics and government—Sources
I. Title
947.085'3'092419   DK274
ISBN 0 08 031287 X

PUBLISHER'S NOTE TO READERS

As is well known, Pergamon Press have for some time been publishing books by senior Soviet politicians (Politbureau members) for the purpose of enabling interested English-speaking readers to know their views and opinions about international and domestic affairs.

The views expressed in this book are those of the author and not necessarily those of the Publisher.

Printed in Great Britain by A. Wheaton & Co., Exeter.

To Readers in the British Isles

In our age of space communication and mass information media as fast as lightning, the book has still retained its significance. In particular, it serves the peoples well as a vehicle of circumstantial and thorough acquaintance with one another.

I hope this collection of my speeches, articles and interviews published by Pergamon Press will help you learn more about the life of the Soviet people today and how they intend to resolve the problems facing our country.

You may note that we take pride in our achievements in various fields. At the same time, you will see that we do not rest on our oars; that we are aware of and critically assess our shortcomings; that we continually seek to perfect our society; that we are furthering its all-round progress, in particular by developing Soviet democracy.

Although the Soviet and British peoples live under different political and social systems, this fact cannot and must not be a barrier separating them, especially in today's situation where mankind must be saved from nuclear catastrophe.

I am obliged to say that we regard the deployment in the British Isles of American medium-range nuclear missiles, in addition to the U.S. nuclear bases existing there and the nuclear weapons of Great Britain itself, as a factor upsetting the balance of forces in Europe, and a considerable increase in danger to the security of the Soviet people. Should such deployment take place, we shall have no option other than to take counter measures.

Can the danger of nuclear war be averted? Our answer is a clear "Yes". This, however, requires an honest and fair deal between West and East, reckoning with the lawful interests of both sides to end the arms race, primarily in the nuclear field, and reduce the level of these armaments on the principles of parity and equal security. It is important to be fully aware of the disastrous consequences of nuclear war and finally draw a practical conclusion to this effect.

The Soviet Union believes that a nuclear tragedy should not be allowed to occur on earth. We have peaceful intentions; we are deeply concerned for the security of our socialist state and our allies; we are in favour of a mutual freeze on all nuclear arsenals. You probably know also of the Soviet Union's solemn pledge not to be the first to resort to nuclear arms. We call upon other nuclear powers to follow suit.

The conclusion of a treaty on mutual renunciation of armed force and maintaining peaceful relations between the member nations of the Warsaw Treaty and the North Atlantic Alliance could erect an effective barrier to war. Unfortunately, the Western governments have so far shown no desire to agree to this. It is high time that they did.

The peoples of the Soviet Union and Great Britain are long-standing partners in politics, commerce, culture and science. They shed their blood in the common battle against Nazi Germany, when our soldiers, seamen and airmen fought side by side for mankind's peaceful future.

It will be recalled that Winston Churchill, who never concealed his hostility to our political system, spoke with admiration of the Soviet people's heroic exploits in the Second World War. He called on our two nations to live "under the bright sun of victorious peace" in a situation of "loyal friendship and sympathy".

It is useful to recall these words today, when those willing to provoke a conflict between our two nations, to make them forget their record of friendship and co-operation and their common vital interests are actively at work. Today our peoples, and all mankind for that matter, have a formidable common enemy — the danger of world thermonuclear war that would take a toll of hundreds of millions of human lives and wipe out whole countries and peoples. To do away with this danger is the central task of present-day politics and the public activity of the peoples.

I wish all readers a life of peace, happiness and prosperity.

Yuri V. Andropov

Moscow, August 1983

Soviet Preface

This collection of selected speeches and writings of Yuri V. Andropov, General Secretary of the Central Committee of the CPSU, President of the Presidium of the Supreme Soviet of the USSR, covers the period of his work in leading Party and government posts from 1942 to June 1983.

The book opens with the report "The USSR: Sixty Years", which sums up the main results of the implementation in the Soviet Union of the Leninist policy towards nationalities and outlines the tasks to be fulfilled in this field at the stage of developed socialism. All the other items are presented in chronological order.

Yuri Andropov brings into focus the problems involved in the exercise by the Communist Party of the Soviet Union of its guiding and leading role as the political vanguard organizing and educating the masses, and the problems of solidifying the indissoluble unity of the Party and people. He describes the many-sided activities of the Central Committee of the CPSU and its Politbureau in the guidance of communist construction. Yuri Andropov emphasizes that the main content of the activities of the Party and people at the present stage is the perfection of developed socialism, that the Soviet Union has just entered this long historical stage of gradual transition to communism.

He discusses in detail the main sphere of the Soviet people's activities — the economy. Examining the full spectrum of economic policy planned by the Party on scientific lines, the author attaches first priority to enhancing the efficiency of production and its intensification, and to improving the guidance of the economy — management, planning, the economic mechanism, the mobilization of latent reserves in the national economy.

The general line of the economic policy of the CPSU is to advance the well-being of the Soviet people, and to provide favourable material prerequisites for further stimulation of their spiritual, cultural life and their social activity.

The author concentrates on the key problem which is crucial to the rapid rate of progress of Soviet society and which can be solved effectively with minimum inputs of work and resources. This is the problem of measures to strengthen Party, state and labour discipline, to enhance the responsibility of executives at all levels, and to encourage the creativity and initiative of the masses.

"We are making and will continue to make progress", Yuri Andropov says. "However, to make progress, to provide still better conditions for living, means first and foremost to work better."

Considerable space is devoted to the socio-political and ideological unity of Soviet society, and the continued flourishing and integration of the Soviet Union's nations and national minorities, which constitute a new historical community of men — the Soviet people.

The author discusses the theoretical and practical problems of socialist statehood, of developing the political system of Soviet society, of perfecting socialist democracy and the machinery of state, of enhancing the activity of work collectives, of reinforcing people's control, of consolidating the legal foundation of the affairs of state and society.

Yuri Andropov's views reflect the principal aspects of the foreign policy of the CPSU and the Soviet state, and the activities of the Party and government in defending the achievements of socialism, in maintaining the Soviet Union's defence capability at a modern level, and in frustrating the plans of the United States and NATO to achieve military superiority over the USSR and the member nations of the Warsaw Treaty.

He describes the class character of the foreign policy of the CPSU and the Soviet state and shows that the core of the Party's international policy is, as in the past, the principle of proletarian, socialist internationalism, which is the basis for deepening the Soviet Union's fraternal relations with socialist countries, and for strengthening the unity and cohesion of the world communist movement. He attaches high priority to implementing the Leninist principle of peaceful coexistence of states belonging to different social systems, the line pursued by the CPSU and the Soviet state to promote cooperation with the developing countries which have freed themselves from colonial oppression, and to support national liberation movements.

The author vividly describes the Soviet Union's consistent and stubborn efforts to preserve peace and firmly guarantee the security of nations.

Individual items deal with the pressing problems involved in the implementation of the Leninist principles of selection, placement and education of cadres, of improving the Party's organizational, ideological and political work, the problems of intra-Party life, and the style and methods of Party guidance of society.

This material shows the consistency of the strategic and political line of the CPSU. It helps Party organizations to assess their work critically, to organize it in the light of the historical experience of revolutionary struggle, and the construction of socialism and communism.

A few items are abridged.

Contents

Introduction
By Robert Maxwell
General Editor of the "Leaders of the World Series"

Most people on earth have recently asked themselves whether the election of Mr Yuri Andropov is a good thing for world peace and prosperity or otherwise. There is really no answer to this question until we have witnessed the results of his leadership during the next few years. Very little is known of Mr Andropov in the Western world. If we are to understand him and the policies he will try to pursue it may be helpful to examine a selection of his speeches and writings (including his very latest pronouncements in Moscow and Prague) which bear so much on the major issue of peace or war in our time and on relations between East and West, North and South. It is for this reason that I am glad to make this volume available in the Leaders of the World Series.

In retrospect it is clear that Yuri Andropov's speech given in Moscow in April 1982 on the occasion of a ceremonial meeting commemorating the 112th anniversary of Lenin's birth published in this volume entitled "Leninism: the Mainspring of the Revolutionary Energy and Creativity of the Masses" was given after it had been agreed by Mr Brezhnev and the Politburo that Mr Andropov should succeed Mr Brezhnev, and it may well be that Mr Andropov had been carrying out many of the functions of Mr Brezhnev prior to his death. One can in a sense regard this as his inaugural speech.

Andropov replies frankly to criticisms of the Soviet Union's role in other Socialist countries and to the debate on "models of socialism". He shows himself to be dismissive of the idea of Western democratic pluralism. Andropov clearly states his attitude, amongst other points, to Soviet society's advance towards communism. In his estimation the possibilities of the USSR have increased enormously.

He emphasises that the Soviet Union today has a vast economic potential, which has doubled during the last ten years alone. He discusses the improvements in the working people's standard of living, the development of industry and the programme of advancing agriculture, and the increasing production of consumer goods. At the same time, Andropov frankly highlights some of the weaknesses and failings within the Soviet economy and agriculture.

Andropov emphasises that the Soviet Union's willingness "to have a constructive dialogue with the United States" but lambasts the US approach to the latest round of nuclear arms limitation talks, highlighting what he sees as their delaying tactics to avoid any serious talks concerning the declared deployment of new missiles by NATO in Europe. Andropov urges the need for all negotiations to be conducted on the basis of the principles of parity and equal security and in an uncompromising statement indicates his intention to guarantee the defence capability of the USSR at a sufficient level to ensure its security.

Everybody is agreed that neither we nor the Soviet Union want war. What is at issue is not the level of Soviet or Western nuclear and non-nuclear armed forces but reconciling Soviet and Western estimates of what their own security demands.

Since Mr Andropov became the new leader of the Soviet Union he has devoted a great deal of his time to impose himself on the World stage as a careful and energetic leader and "dove of peace". He has suggested a summit meeting with President Reagan. He has serious offers for the reduction of armaments, both nuclear and conventional, for the prohibition of nuclear weapons tests, for a non-aggression pact with NATO, and for a ban on all weapons in outer space. Mr Andropov would like to avoid war, as do all members of NATO and the Warsaw Pact. Towards this end he has proposed that an agreement be reached between the two blocs binding the two sides against first use of both nuclear and conventional armaments. Mr Andropov has also proposed to dismantle sufficient of his nuclear weapons to balance those held by Britain and France if the Europeans will forego the planned installation this year of US Cruise and Pershing missiles.

The Warsaw Pact Meeting Political Declaration which I have published as an addendum to this book makes a series of proposals as follows: the USSR and US should freeze their long-range nuclear arsenals at present levels; all nuclear powers should promise not to use their nuclear weapons first; conventions should be drafted at the 40-nation Geneva disarmament conference to: prohibit all tests of nuclear weapons; eliminate all chemical weapons; outlaw the neutron bomb; talks on naval disarmament, limits on the deployment of warships and naval confidence-building measures should be started; talk on limiting sales of conventional weapons should be resumed; NATO and the Warsaw pact should agree on measures to limit military spending; nuclear free zones should be established in northern Europe and in the Balkans; steps should be taken towards dismantling all foreign military bases and withdrawing troops from foreign territories; NATO and Warsaw pact should sign a treaty renouncing the use of force against each other; this could later be extended to other countries; agreements on arms control should be properly verified, where necessary by 'international procedures'.

Mr Andropov, however, is opposed to unilateral disarmament. He said: "We are in favour of searching for a sound basis for a solution to the most complicated problems acceptable to both sides . . . primarily of course to curbing the arms race, both nuclear and conventional. However, no-one can expect us to disarm unilaterally. We are not naïve, we are not demanding unilateral disarmament of the West, we are in favour of equality, respect for the interests of both side, an honest agreement. We are fully prepared for a fair deal."

Even the major political opponents of the Soviet Union such as Mr Reagan, Mr Weinberger, Mr Mitterand, Mrs Thatcher and Herr Kohl must accept that not all of Mr Andropov's proposals are for propaganda purposes. It is certainly not enough for Western leaders to be dismissive about Mr Andropov's overtures. The average voter of the Western world hears talk of peace from Mr Andropov, the head of one of the super powers; in the interest of our Western leaders not losing the confidence of a substantial number of their electorate these proposals cannot be ignored. They require careful consideration followed by constructive, detailed negotiations at a well-prepared summit later this year.

Like many people who read this volume, I do not agree with

everything Mr Andropov says or writes. I hope this volume (containing a selection of Mr Andropov's speeches and writings during the past 20 years as he worked his way to the top post in his country) will be useful for all those who need to know, understand, interpret and anticipate the broad outline of possible Soviet policies at home and abroad.

Oxford, January 1983

ROBERT MAXWELL
General Editor of the
"Leaders of the World Series"

The USSR: Sixty Years

**Report on the occasion of the 60th
anniversary of the USSR in the Kremlin
Palace of Congresses, 21 December 1982**

Dear comrades!
Esteemed guests!
Sixty years ago the peoples of this country, liberated by the victorious
October Revolution, joined of their own free will in the Union of
Soviet Socialist Republics.

Summing up the deliberations of the First unifying congress of the
Soviet Republics, which proclaimed the formation of the USSR,
Mikhail I. Kalinin[1] said: "For thousands of years mankind's best
minds have been struggling with theoretical problems in quests of
forms that would enable the peoples to live as friends and brothers,
without internecine strife and severe hardships. It is only today,
however, that the first stone has practically been laid in this direction."

The development of capitalism had failed to abolish ethnic oppression. On the contrary, ethnic oppression was supplemented and
aggravated by colonial oppression. Having enslaved hundreds of
millions of people, a handful of capitalist powers doomed them to a
life of misery and barred their ways to progress.

Marxism revealed for the first time ever an organic link between
the nationalities problem and the social, class nature of society, the
prevailing type of ownership. In other words, the roots of relations
between nations are embedded in the social soil. From here Marx and
Engels drew their fundamental conclusion: the abolition of social

---

[1] Mikhail I. Kalinin (1875–1946), Chairman of the Central Executive Committee of
the USSR from 1919, President of the Presidium of the Supreme Soviet of the USSR
from 1938 to 1946. [*Translator.*]

oppression is an indispensable prerequisite for the abolition of ethnic oppression. " . . . Victory of the proletariat over the *bourgeoisie*", Marx said, "is simultaneously a signal for the emancipation of all oppressed nations." The immortal slogan "Workers of the world unite!" proclaimed by the founders of Marxism has become a call for the working people's international struggle against all forms of enslavement, both social and ethnic.

In a new historical situation the cause of Marx and Engels was continued by Lenin. He took the lead in the revolutionary movement when the first lightnings of revolution flashed over Russia. In the country which was rightly called a "prison of nations" the nationalities problem was given high priority in the strategy and tactics planned by the Bolshevik Party.

Lenin focused his attention on the right of nations to self-determination as the sole dependable way of securing their real and firm *rapprochement*. It was only the right to self-determination that could be the ideological and political foundation for voluntary unity of all nations in the struggle to overthrow czarism, and to build a new society. That was how Lenin put this problem. That was the pivot of the Leninist Party's policy towards the nationalities problem.

The October Revolution placed political slogans and demands on the plane of daily organizing work. The realities of life, formidable economic, social, foreign policy and defence tasks, dictated the need for cohesion of nations, for a union of the Republics which had emerged from the ruins of the Russian Empire.

What looks obvious today was by no means so obvious in that stormy transitional period. The quests for concrete forms of statehood, for political institutions to embody the general ideas and prerequisites of a nationalities programme, aroused heated debates. Conflicting opinions ranged from a programme of loose, amorphous unification of the Republics in a confederation to a demand for their simple incorporation into the Russian Federation on the principle of autonomy. It took Lenin's genius and prestige to find and affirm the only correct path, that of socialist federalism.

What is the essence of the path indicated by Lenin? It may be briefly formulated as follows. This is an absolutely voluntary union of free nations as the guarantee of the maximum durability of a federation of socialist Republics. This is the complete equality of all nations, large and small, a consistent policy of abolishing not only their legal but also their actual inequality. This is the free development of each Republic, each nationality within the framework of their fraternal union. This is persistent cultivation of internationalist consciousness and steady efforts to bring all nations and national minorities of this country closer together.

In the year when the Soviet Union was formed Lenin wrote what vividly illustrated the course of his reflection on the nationalities problem. "Our experience of five years in solving the nationalities problem in a state containing such a multitude of nationalities as can be hardly found in other countries has strongly convinced us that the only correct attitude to the interests of nations in such cases would be to meet them to a maximum and to provide conditions that would rule out any possibility of conflicts on these grounds. Our experience [Lenin went on] has made us absolutely confident that only enormous attention to the interests of different nations removes the ground for conflicts, removes mutual distrust, removes apprehensions of any intrigues, creates trust, particularly among the workers and peasants speaking different languages, without which neither peaceful relations between peoples nor any successful development of all that is valuable in modern civilisation are absolutely impossible."

Lenin's behests, the Leninist principles of nationalities policy, are sacred to us. Relying on them and consistently implementing them in practice, we have built a powerful state—the Union of Soviet Socialist Republics, whose formation was not only a long step in the progress of socialism but also a major turning point in world history.

1. THE RESULTS OF SOVIET PROGRESS AND
THE TASKS IN THE NATIONALITIES POLICY

The path traversed by the Soviet Union over the last sixty years is equivalent to a whole epoch. History perhaps has never known such a spectacular advance from a condition of backwardness, misery and ruin to the grandeur of a modern great power with highly advanced culture and steadily growing welfare of the people.

What are the most significant results of our development?

—The historical correctness of the Marxist–Leninist theory to the effect that a solution to the nationalities problem can be found only on a class foundation has been fully confirmed. Ethnic discord, all kinds of racial and national inequality and oppression, have become a thing of the past along with the social antagonisms.

—It has been proved conclusively that the Communist Party with its scientifically planned policy is the leading and guiding force in the socialist solution of the nationalities problem, the guarantor of a correct solution.

—The backward ethnic provinces where feudal-patriarchal and even tribal relations often prevailed have ceased to exist.

—An integrated all Union national economic complex has formed on the basis of the dynamic economic growth of all the Republics according to a general state plan.

—The social structure in the Republics has changed qualitatively; in each of them there has emerged a modern working class, the peasants are following the new path of collective farming, a new intelligentsia has been raised, highly-qualified personnel have been trained in all areas of government and public activities.

—Multinational socialist culture has reached a flourishing stage on the basis of progressive traditions, an intensive exchange of cultural values.

—The socialist nations have matured and now they make up a new historical community of men—the Soviet people.

The interests of the Republics are being interlocked ever more closely, their mutual assistance and mutual ties directing the constructive efforts of Soviet nations and national minorities into a common channel are becoming ever more fruitful. The all-round development of each of the socialist nations in this country naturally results in their steadily increasing consolidation.

Each of the Union Republics—the Russian Federation, the Ukraine and Byelorussia, Uzbekistan and Kazakhstan, Georgia and Azerbaijan, Lithuania and Moldavia, Latvia and Kirghizia, Tadjikistan and Armenia, Turkmenia and Estonia—each, I emphasize this, of the Union Republics makes an indispensable contribution to the general advancement of the Soviet Union's economy and culture. This is not simply an arithmetic sum total but a multiple increase in our creative potentials.

All nations and national minorities living in the twenty autonomous Republics and eighteen autonomous regions and districts as one friendly family succesfully bring their potentialities into play. Millions of Germans, Poles, Koreans, Kurds and members of other nationalities are fully-fledged Soviet citizens for whom the Soviet Union has long been their homeland.

The peoples of this country feel especially warm gratitude to the Russian people. Without its selfless fraternal assistance the present achievements of any of the Republics would have been impossible. A factor of exceptional significance in the economic, political and cultural life of this country, in promoting the unity of all its nations and national minorities, in giving them access to the wealth of world civilization, is the Russian language, which has naturally become part and parcel of the life of millions of people of any nationality.

The new Constitution of the USSR has been a major milestone in consolidating the national state foundations of Soviet society. This outstanding document has not only summed up the results of earlier development but has also formulated the strong and stable political and legal foundations for the continued prosperity and consolidation of all nations of this country, both large and small.

The real qualitative changes which have taken place in relations between nations over the last sixty years is evidence that the nationalities problem in the form we inherited from the exploiter system has been successfully resolved finally and irreversibly. For the first time in history the multinational composition of a country's population has turned from a source of its weakness into a source of its strength and prosperity.

Speaking in this hall exactly ten years ago, Leonid Brezhnev described this very well in the following words: "In this country. . . there have developed relations without precedent in history which we rightly call the Leninist friendship of nations. This friendship is our invaluable property, one of the most significant achievements of socialism cherished by every Soviet citizen. We Soviet people will always cherish this friendship as the apple of our eye."

On this red-letter day we pay tribute to many generations of Soviet

people of all nationalities, men and women, workers and peasants, the intelligentsia, Party and government workers, servicemen of the Armed Forces, communists and unaffiliated people—all those who have built socialism, defended it in the most difficult war and translated the thousand-year-old dream of equality, friendship and brotherhood of nations into reality.

Reviewing the results of our efforts we naturally focus our attention on what still remains to be done, our ultimate goal is clear. This is, to use Lenin's words, "not only *rapprochement* between nations but their integration". The Party is well aware of the fact that the road to this goal is a long one. Here one should by no means forestall events, nor should one hold back processes which have come to a head.

Success in solving the nationalities problem does not mean at all that all problems generated by the very fact that numerous nations and national minorities live and work within the framework of a union state have been settled. This is hardly possible as long as nations and national distinctions exist. And they will survive for a long time, much longer than class distinctions will do.

This is why the efforts to perfect developed socialism—and this is precisely how we can define the main content of the activity of the Party and people at the present stage—must include a thoroughly planned nationalities policy based on scientific principles. I would like to dwell upon some of its tasks.

I have already mentioned what enormous benefits and advantages the people of this country, its Republics, have gained from their association in a single union. However, the opportunities offered by such association are far from being exhausted.

Let us take the economy. Modern productive forces demand integration even when it is a matter of different countries. All the more so, they demand close and skilful integration of efforts of different regions and Republics within the confines of one country. The most rational use of the natural and manpower resources, the climatic distinctions of each of the Republics, the most rational inclusion of this potential into that of the whole Union—this is what will yield the greatest benefits to every region, every nation and national minority, just as the country as a whole.

This is our position of principle. Our central and local planning and economic executive bodies will have to put in a good deal of work to carry it into effect. It will be necessary to continue improving the distribution of productive forces, regional specialization and co-operation, the schemes of economic ties and transportation. This task, of course, is not a simple one, but it is a pressing task, and its fulfilment holds out considerable advantages.

This whole country is now working to implement the Food Programme, which has clearly defined the concrete tasks facing all the Union Republics. Each of them will have to put forth substantial efforts to make a tangible contribution, and in the immediate future at that, to the all-important cause of securing uninterrupted food supplies to Soviet consumers.

As is known, the Food Programme refers to pressing tasks of first priority. Casting a look in perspective, however, one will certainly see that the continued development of our agro-industrial complex, just as the national economy as a whole for that matter, will require more detailed and consistent specialization of agriculture on a nation-wide scale.

There is yet another question. In a country so vast as ours a role of crucial significance is played by the transport services, which is an economic, political and, if you like, psychological role.

Without smoothly functioning transport services it is very difficult to ensure both the accelerated development of all the Republics and the further deepening of their economic co-operation. The transport services, however, are crucial not only to the fulfilment of strictly economic tasks. The development of the transport services and the road network brings villages closer to towns and will largely contribute, for instance, to permanent settlement of specialist manpower on the land. This will, of course, also help accomplish the great social task of securing rational and flexible use of manpower resources. Maintaining daily contacts between people throughout the Soviet Union, current ties between all Republics and regions of the country, the transport services help bring the achievements of socialist civilization in the broadest sense of the word within reach of all Soviet citizens.

Their association in a union has become one of the additional sources of not only the material but also the cultural wealth of the

Soviet people. In this area too, however, far from all opportunities are being utilized so far. It is mandatory to search for new ways and means of work meeting today's requirements and making the mutual enrichment of cultures still more fruitful, giving all citizens still broader access to the finest achievements of the culture of each Soviet nation. Radio and television broadcasting services, as, of course, other mass media, are called upon to play a steadily growing part in this noble work.

It should be borne in mind at the same time that the cultural heritage, traditions and customs of each nation contain not only what is good but also what is bad and outdated. Hence another task: not to conserve what is bad but to get rid of all that is obsolete, what runs counter to the principles of Soviet society, socialist morals, our communist ideals.

The realities of life show that the economic and cultural progress of all nations, large and small, is inevitably accompanied by the growth of their national self-awareness. This is a legitimate, objective process. It is important, however, that a nation's natural pride in its achievements should not turn into national arrogance or conceit, generate trends towards self-isolation, a disrespectful attitude to other nations and national minorities. Negative phenomena of this kind, however, are occasionally in evidence, and it would be wrong to attribute them to survivals of the past alone. They are nourished at times by our own errors in work as well. In this area there are no trifles, but everything is important: the attitude to language, to relics of the past, the interpretation of historical events, and the way we transform villages and towns, influencing the working and living conditions of their residents.

As as result of natural population migration each of our Republics tends to become even more multinational. This also holds true, to a varying extent, of every region and every city. This means that the Party and government bodies, all our local cadres, have an increasing role to play as vehicles of the Party's nationalities policy. Moreover, they have to carry the lofty principles of this policy into effect every day, promoting harmonious, brotherly relations between members of all nations, large and small, in work and in everyday life.

The Party has invariably paid enormous attention to the growth of the ethnic contingents of the Soviet working class, the leading force in our society. The results are here for all to see. Today the workers constitute the largest social group in all the Union Republics. However, in some of them the indigenous nationality should be more fully represented in the composition of the working class. Hence the task set by the 26th Congress of the CPSU: to widen and improve the training of skilled workers from among all nations and national minorities living in the Republics. This is dictated by the need for economic development. This is also important politically. The multi-national labour collectives, of workers first and foremost, are precisely the milieu where the spirit of internationalism is cultivated best of all, and the brotherhood and friendship of Soviet nations are strengthened the most.

Another highly important question is one of representation of working people in the Party and government bodies of the Republics and the Union as a whole This is not, of course, a matter of some formal representation quotas. An arithmetic approach to the solution of such problems would be irrelevant. However, it is necessary to work consistently for all nationalities existing in a given Republic to be duly represented in various Party and government echelons. Consideration of the moral and political qualities of personnel, attention and solicitude, great tact in their selection and placement are particularly indispensable in the conditions of the multinational Union and Autonomous Republics.

A permanent task of fundamental importance is education of all Soviet citizens in the spirit of mutual respect and friendship of all Soviet nations and national minorities, dedication to their great Soviet Motherland, internationalism and solidarity with the working people of foreign nations. This task is being fulfilled by all Party and YCL organizations, the Soviets and the trades unions, and our Armed Forces, which have always been a good school of internationalism. This should also be a matter of daily concern to all educational institutions of this country.

In the field of internationalist education, just as in all our ideological and mass-scale political work, we are confronted by immense tasks. A persuasive, concrete demonstration of our achievements, a profound analysis of new problems constantly generated by life,

ASW-A*

freshness of thought and word—such is the way to improve all our propaganda which should be more truthful and realistic, as well as interesting and understandable and hence more effective.

The continued development of friendship and co-operation among Soviet nations largely depends on efforts to deepen socialist democracy. The steadily widening involvement of the working people of all nationalities in the management of the affairs of society and state— such is the most condensed definition of the leading tendency in Soviet political life. The Party will do its utmost to make it grow stronger and develop.

It follows from the aforesaid that in mature socialist society the problems of relations between nations remain the order of the day. They demand special concern and constant attention from the Communist Party. The Party must thoroughly analyse them, outline ways of solving them, creatively enriching the Leninist principles of the nationalities policy with the practical experience of developed socialism.

We boldly speak of existing problems and outstanding tasks because we are firmly confident that we can measure up to these problems and tasks, that we can and must solve them. Determined action rather than loud words—this is what we need today to make the great and powerful Union of Soviet Socialist Republics stronger still. I am confident that all those present in this audience, all our Party and the entire Soviet people, think as much.

2. THE USSR: THE BULWARK OF THE GREAT CAUSE OF PEACE AND FREEDOM OF NATIONS

On the very same day, 30 December 1922, that the Declaration and Treaty of the Formation of the USSR were adopted in Moscow the Soviet delegation at the Lausanne Conference declared on Lenin's instructions that the Soviet Republics guided as they were by the interests of universal peace deemed it "their imperative duty . . . to contribute with all their forces to establishing a régime of political equality between races, respect for the right of nations to self-determination and to complete political and economic independence of all states."

That was a simple and clear expression of the essence of the fundamentally new foreign policy that the world's first socialist country had started to pursue consistently on the international scene.

As new socialist countries came into being, international relations of a perfectly new type began to take shape. They are based on ideological unity, common goals, comradely co-operation—with complete respect for the interests, distinctions and traditions of each of these countries. They are based on the principle of socialist internationalism.

In developing these relations the socialist countries walked untrodden paths. Mankind's past experience could not suggest the answers to problems posed by the realities of life. Naturally, not everything went off without a hitch in this field. It will be recalled that the countries which formed the world socialist system had started off from largely different initial positions—both in levels of their internal development and in the external conditions of their existence. It was not always possible to draw timely conclusions from changes in the socialist world itself. Besides, the international situation left no time for reflection: new forms of relations had to be tested by trial and error. There were illusions which had to be overcome and errors which had to be paid for.

However, reviewing today's life in our countries we have good reason to say with satisfaction that we have learned a great deal, and that the community of socialist nations is a strong and healthy organism which plays an enormously beneficial role in the modern world. The mechanism of fraternal co-operation operates in the most diverse spheres of life in our countries and in different directions of our interaction in the cause of socialist construction. We discover by joint efforts ever more effective ways of harmonizing the common interests of the community with the interests of each of its member nations.

Of course, we cannot say yet that all our difficulties have been overcome, and we have attained an ideal. What satisfied us yesterday needs improvement today. The countries of our community are confronted with many serious tasks. These are the defence of our socialist achievements and values against the onslaught of imperialism, our joint struggle for lasting peace and a relaxation of tension, the continued perfection of political co-operation and, finally, lending added momentum to the process of economic integration.

Thus, there is a lot of work to be done. I wish to assure our friends that the Soviet Union for its part will do all in its power to ensure the consolidation and prosperity of the world socialist system.

The experience in the socialist solution of the nationalities problem is being thoroughly analysed in scores of countries which have thrown off the colonial yoke. Our successes in socialist construction, our victory over fascism, the flourishing of all nations and national minorities in the Soviet Union, have given a powerful impetus to the liberation struggle of the peoples.

The Soviet Union's active and determined struggle for the abolition of colonialism, its unfailing support for the cause of liberation and equality of nations, facilitate their advance towards freedom and progress. This is well known to the peoples of Asia and Africa, the Arab East and Latin America.

The young states which have freed themselves from colonial oppression are now going through what is not a simple period of national revival and social development. They are handicapped by backwardness inherited from their colonial past, internecine discord and conflicts. Countries which have not yet found their feet are threatened by numerous traps laid by the neo-colonialists. We are confident, however, that resolute resistance to imperialism, a well-planned strategy of economic and sociopolitical development, mutual respect for each other's interests and rights, will enable the peoples of these countries to overcome what is known as difficulties of growth. The Soviet people wish them great success in strengthening their independence, in their struggle for welfare and progress.

We regard with respect the nonaligned movement, whose policy of peace has a beneficial influence on international affairs. We resolutely and invariably take sides with those who have to fight today for the freedom and independence and the very existence of their peoples, who are forced to repel the onslaught of an aggressor or are threatened with aggression. This stand of ours is closely bound up with the struggle for lasting peace on earth that the Soviet Union is waging consistently and indefatigably.

During the last six decades the Soviet Union's position has radically changed, and its prestige and influence have grown immeasurably. Strong ties of peaceful co-operation link the Soviet Union with countries on all continents. Its voice commands general attention at international forums. The principles of peaceful coexistence, which are the basis for Soviet foreign policy, have won broad international recognition and have been incorporated into dozens of international documents, the Final Act of the All-European Conference at Helsinki in particular, and Soviet proposals have been adopted as the basis for the most important UN resolutions on the problems of promoting peace and security.

Every step in the direction of stronger peace, however, has taken and takes effort, demanding tense struggle against the imperialist "hawks". It has become especially bitter today when the most warlike groups in the West have markedly stepped up their activity. Their class hatred of socialism prevails over their sense of reality and often simply defies common sense.

The imperialists have not yet abandoned their plans of economic war against the socialist countries, of interfering in their internal affairs, hoping to undermine their social system, and seeking to achieve military superiority over the USSR and the entire socialist community of nations.

These plans, of course, are doomed to failure. Nobody will be able to reverse the trend of historical development. Attempts "to strangle" socialism proved to no avail even at the time when the Soviet Republic was still in its infancy and was the only socialist country in the world. That such attempts will come to nothing is all the more obvious today.

One cannot fail to see, however, that Washington's current policy has brought international tensions to an extremely high pitch.

The war preparations of the United States and the NATO alliance it leads have grown to an all-time high, assuming a scope without precedence in history. High-ranking officials in Washington are publicly discussing the possibility of waging "limited", "protracted" and other varieties of nuclear war. They are seeking to reassure people, to inure them to the idea of its acceptability. Indeed, one must be totally blind to the realities of our time to fail to realize that no matter how and where a nuclear conflict may break out it will inevitably get out of hand and grow into general catastrophe.

Our stand on this issue is clear: no nuclear war, either minor or major, limited or total, must be allowed. To stop the instigators of another war—no task is more important today. This is demanded by the vital interests of all nations. Therefore, the Soviet Union's unilateral commitment to refrain from first use of nuclear weapons was received with approval and hope throughout the world. If other nuclear powers follow our example, this will be a truly tangible contribution to the cause of preventing nuclear war.

It is alleged that the West cannot assume such a commitment because the Warsaw Treaty powers have superiority in conventional arms. First of all, this is not true, as is evidenced by facts and figures. Besides, as is known, we are in favour of limiting such armaments and of searching for reasonable mutually acceptable decisions on these problems as well. We are prepared to reach agreement to the effect that the two sides should refrain from first use of both nuclear and conventional armaments.

One of the main roads leading to a real lessening of the danger of nuclear war is, of course, the achievement of agreement between the Soviet Union and the United States on the limitation and reduction of strategic nuclear arms. We approach negotiations on this issue, being fully aware of our responsibility, and we are seeking a fair deal which will not be prejudicial to any side and at the same time will result in a reduction of their nuclear arsenals.

Unfortunately, we are witnessing a different approach from the American side for the time being. Paying lip-service to "radical reductions", it has in mind as a matter of fact mainly a reduction of the Soviet strategic potential. The United States would like to have a free hand left for itself to build up strategic armaments. It is absurd even to suppose that we shall agree to this. All this would, of course, satisfy the Pentagon, but can by no means be acceptable to the Soviet Union as indeed to all those who desire peace to be preserved and strengthened.

Take a look at the Soviet proposals for comparison. They proceed from the maintenance of parity. We are prepared to reduce our strategic arms by more than 25 per cent. The US armaments should be reduced correspondingly, so that the numbers of strategic arms delivery vehicles in possession of either state could be equal. We have also proposed a substantial reduction in the number of nuclear charges and a maximum limitation on improvement of nuclear weapons.

Our proposals apply to all types of strategic arms without exception, and envisage a reduction of their arsenals by many hundreds of units. They are meant to stop all possible channels for a further arms race in this field. But this would only be a beginning: agreement on the aforesaid basis would be the starting-point for an even greater mutual reduction of the numbers of such armaments, on which the two sides could agree, taking account of the general strategic situation.

While negotiations are in progress we propose what is suggested by common sense: to freeze the strategic arsenals of both sides. The US Administration is opposed to this step for a reason which is now clear to all: it has started out on a new significant nuclear arms build-up.

Washington's arguments attempting to justify this build-up obviously do not hold water. Allegations concerning a "lag" behind the USSR which the Americans have to catch up with are deliberate falsehoods, as has more than once been pointed out before. And arguments to the effect that new weapons systems, such as the "MX" missile, for instance, are needed to "help progress in disarmament talks" are simply ludicrous.

Programme of continued arms build-up will not force the Soviet Union to make unilateral concessions. We shall be forced to meet the challenge from the American side by deploying appropriate weapons systems of our own: respond to "MX" with a similar missile, and oppose the American long-range cruise missile with our own long-range cruise missile, which is already undergoing field tests.

These are not threats at all. We do not desire events to develop in this direction, and we are doing our level best to avoid it. It is necessary, however, that the US policy-makers and the public at large should clearly realize the actual state of affairs. If it is really believed in Washington that new weapons systems could be an American "trump-card" at negotiations, let them know that these will be fake "trump-cards". A policy motivated by an ambition to achieve military superiority over the Soviet Union is hopeless and only capable of aggravating the danger of war.

Now a few words about what is known as "confidence-building measures". We take a serious view of them.

With the great speed and power of modern weapons an atmosphere of mutual suspicion is highly dangerous. Even an absurd accident, miscalculation, or technical trouble may have tragic consequences. It is mandatory, therefore, to take one's finger off the trigger and set one's weapons to a safety-catch. Some steps are being taken in this direction, within the framework of the Helsinki accords in particular. The Soviet Union has proposed, as is known, measures that are more serious in character and wider in scope. Our proposals to this effect are on the agenda of the Soviet–American talks at Geneva on the limitation and reduction of nuclear arms.

We are also prepared to examine proposals in this field put forward by others, in particular the recent proposals of the US President. The measures he referred to alone, however, will not dispel the atmosphere of mutual suspicions, nor will they restore trust; something more is necessary: a normalization of the situation, renunciation of propaganda of hostility and hatred, and of nuclear war. And, of course, the high road towards trust and the prevention of nuclear war, including war that may break out by accident, is an end to the arms race, resumption of normal courteous relations between states, a return to *détente*.

We consider this important for all regions of our planet. But especially for Europe, where any spark may set off a worldwide conflagration.

Now this continent is exposed to another danger: the plans to deploy a few hundred American missiles in Western Europe. I must say frankly: this would make peace even more precarious.

We believe that the danger overhanging the European nations and the nations of the whole world for that matter can be averted. Peace in Europe can well be saved and strengthened, and without prejudice to the security of any side at that. It is precisely with this aim in view that we have been negotiating with the United States at Geneva for over a year a limitation and reduction of nuclear arms in the zone of Europe.

The Soviet Union is prepared to go very far. As is known, we have proposed an agreement on renunciation of all kinds of nuclear weapons, both medium-range and tactical ones, aimed at targets in Europe. This initiative, however, fell on deaf ears. Evidently, they are unwilling to accept it, but are careful not to reject it openly. I wish to emphasize again that this proposal of ours holds good.

We have proposed another option: the USSR and the NATO powers should reduce their medium-range armaments by more than two-thirds. So far the United States is opposed to it. For its part it has come forward with a proposal called a "zero option". It provides for the dismantling of all Soviet medium-range missiles not only in the European but also in the Asiatic part of the USSR, with NATO's nuclear missile arsenal in Europe being retained and even increased. Can it really be true that somebody seriously expects the Soviet Union to agree to this? It seems that Washington would like to thwart an agreement to be able to refer to the failure of negotiations and deploy American missiles on European soil one way or another.

The future will show if this is true or not. As far as we are concerned, we will continue our efforts to reach an agreement on a basis equitable to both sides. We are prepared, in particular, to come to an arrangement whereby the Soviet Union shall retain in Europe only as many missiles as Britain and France have, and not a single missile more. This means that the Soviet Union would dismantle hundreds of missiles, including a few dozen of the most advanced missiles known in the West as SS-20. As regards the Soviet–American issue of medium-range missiles, this would be a truly fair "zero option". Moreover, if the number of British and French missiles were subsequently reduced, the number of Soviet missiles would additionally be reduced by the same percentage.

Simultaneously, agreement should also be reached on a reduction to equal levels on both sides of the number of medium-range nuclear weapons-carrying aircraft available in the relevant region both to the USSR and to the NATO countries.

We appeal to our partners to agree to this clear and fair arrangement, to take advantage of this opportunity while it is still there. We wish, however, that nobody should delude himself; we will never allow our own security and the security of our allies to be put in jeopardy. One would also be wise to consider the disastrous effect the deployment of new American medium-range weapons in Europe would have on all further efforts to limit nuclear arms in general. In short, the answer rests with the United States.

In conclusion I wish to say this: we are in favour of broad and fruitful co-operation, free from dictation and interference in the internal affairs of others, between all nations on our planet to their mutual advantage and for the benefit of all mankind. The Soviet Union will do all in its power to secure a tranquil and peaceful future for the living and succeeding generations. This is the goal of our policy, and we are determined to pursue it.

* * *

Reviewing the path traversed by the Union of Soviet Socialist Republics over the last sixty years we can clearly see that all our achievements and victories are linked inseparably with the activities of the Leninist Party of communists. It is the Party that has been and remains the powerful creative and mobilizing force that ensures our continuous advance in all directions of social progress.

As regards its ideology, composition and structure, our Party is the living embodiment of the unity and cohesion of all Soviet nations, large and small. Aiming its policy at securing harmony between national and international interests, the Party creates the social conditions in which the flourishing and all-round development of each nation are a prerequisite for the advancement and prosperity of our entire fraternal union.

When we say "The people and the Party are united!" we acknowledge the indisputable fact that the aims and tasks pursued by the Party accurately express the aspirations and requirements of all Soviet citizens. By their practical work the multimillion Soviet people are translating the Party policy into reality. One of the most striking testimonies to this is the splendid record of achievement with which all our Republics are honouring the present jubilee.

Allow me to convey our profound gratitude to the millions of front-ranking production workers who have fulfilled or overfulfilled their socialist commitments assumed in honour of the 60th anniversary of the USSR.

Allow me to extend our warm congratulations on behalf of the Central Committee of the Communist Party of the Soviet Union, the Presidium of the Supreme Soviet and the Council of Ministers of the USSR to all Soviet citizens on the occasion of this red-letter day, the 60th birthday of our great Union.

Long live the friendship of nations building communism!

Long live proletarian, socialist internationalism!

Long live peace throughout the world!

May the Union of Soviet Socialist Republics flourish!

*Autonomous
7 Rep in
RSFSR*

We Will Defend Our Native Karelia!
Article in Smena (Young Generation) Magazine, Nos. 23-24, 1942

Some 150 years ago the Czar's viceregent sent the poet Derzhavin, who lived in Petrozavodsk and served as the Governor of Olonets Province, instructions to plant forests in Karelia. Derzhavin who was extremely familiar with this land of pristine forests read the letter in amazement and exclaimed: "Plant forests here? What nonsense!"

He chuckled, and scribbled upon the note in large and sprawling letters: "To plant new forests here is senseless, because it is a forest wilderness, untrodden by man."

Indeed, Karelia was a veritable fairy-tale woodland. It was known to the world only from the runes of the folk epic "Kalevala":

> Pohele is a land of cold,
> Of lakes and rivers fast asleep
> Under their coats of ice and snow,
> Of frosty air and sparkling sunshine,
> Of snow hares and hoary bears
> That roam its snow-covered hills.

Any European country would envy the natural wealth of Karelia. There are many rapid rivers here which could keep dozens of hydropower stations in operation. This precious energy, however, was wasted. In its primeval forests old trees stifled young ones: nobody had any interest in forestry. The low mountains of Karelia contained enormous deposits of granite, marble, diabase, gneiss, titanium and magnetite ores; all these riches waited for a frugal master to tap them.

The revolution awakened the dormant forces of nature and put them at the service of the people. In Soviet years Karelia has changed beyond recognition. Dozens of factories, plants and ore mines have sprung up; schools, hospitals and clubs have been opened in backwood villages. The Karelian people began a great life of construction, recalling their cheerless past only in their songs, as austere and simple as the land itself. The young Karelian republic was making rapid progress. It had a wonderful present and a radiant future.

THE WAR

June 22, 1941 was a day like all other days, but suddenly a war broke out, and everything changed.

The time of peace was over; the stormy clouds of war overcast our skies. The war was a grim reality.

We have learnt a lot during eighteen months of war; we have lost much, but we have also gained much. What matters most is that now we have fully realized what we have, and what the treacherous enemy is determined to seize from us. This realization is an inexhaustible source of patriotism in our young people.

In the early days of the war, girls from a neighbouring village came to a frontier post. They were smartly dressed, as if for a formal occasion.

Their request was short and simple: "We will fight by your side to defend the frontier. Give us rifles. You have trained us to shoot."

And they really fought bravely and staunchly, helping the frontier guards to repel the rabid onslaught of the enemy.

When a Komsomol skier battalion was being formed in the republic on the initiative of the YCL Central Committee we were literally thronged by volunteers. The screening procedure was very strict. Only those with the best staying qualities, sturdy and skilful skiers, were enlisted. Those who had been turned down protested, pleaded for another check-up, trying to prove in every way that their rightful place was in the firing lines. When the medical panel had rejected the Komsomol Vilnit who had rheumatic feet, he was in despair. He implored the panel to revise its decision, writing in his application that the could ski with ease, that his feet did not ache, that nothing was wrong with his heart, and that, finally, his father was in the army while his mother and sister were defending Leningrad, and hence he could not stay at home at this time of dramatic events.

More than 50 per cent of the Komsomols of Karelia have joined the fighting forces. They often left for the firing lines in full strength, as was the case, for instance, of the Komsomols of a hospital staff in the town of Belomorsk. Sometimes they left one by one, but eventually all of them found their way to the firing lines. That happened, for instance, on the May Day collective farm in the Medvezhiegorsky district. They left in groups of three, in pairs, or alone. Suddenly an indignant letter came from Vladimir Mosyagin, secretary of the YCL cell of the collective farm: he had been denied enlistment in the army. All the members of his cell had been enlisted as volunteers but himself.

Vladimir Mosyagin had applied for enlistment five times, all to no avail. Finally, he was offered the task of setting up a new YCL cell on his collective farm as a condition for his release from his duties and enlistment. When he finally joined the ranks, a close-knit YCL cell of eighteen boys and girls remained on the collective farm.

When the enemy advanced on their native areas Komsomols joined guerrilla units. Secretaries of town and district committees, members of the YCL Central Committee and rank-and-file members were to be found among guerrillas. Their friendship grew stronger, and they matured in battles.

The "Vperyod" (Forward) guerrilla unit was organized by I. I. Vakhrameyev, secretary of the YCL Central Committee. The life of this man, who died a hero's death, fighting for the freedom and honour of his country, is a splendid model of selfless dedication. Describing the courage of this fearless man in battle, young guerrillas proudly add at the end of their story: "He was a Central Committee secretary".

KOMSOMOL EXPLOITS: A CALL TO ACTION

Everyone in Karelia knows of the remarkable exploits of the Komsomol Peter Tikilainen, hero of the Soviet Union. His name has become a symbol of loyalty and utter dedication to his country. The story of his exploits is short. Junior sergeant Peter Tikilainen, with nine men under his command, was ordered to defend a position. They were heavily outnumbered by the enemy but staunchly stood their ground. The idea of retreat was hateful to them. They would rather die than let the enemy set foot on their native soil. At a critical moment of battle he looked his comrades in the eye: all of them showed a grim determination to fight to the last.

They fought like lions, because they were Komsomols. When they had run out of ammunition, and had no hand grenades left, they fought with daggers. Ten Komsomols held back an enemy force that outnumbered them many times over. This handful of courageous men were literally showered with shells and mines, but they would not budge an inch. The enemy finally beat a retreat, leaving on the battlefield 73 officers and men dead, five machine-guns, four tommy-guns and thirty-eight automatic rifles.

The Komsomol machine-gunner Konovalov showed remarkable presence of mind and staunchness. The enemy attacked him several times, but his machine-gun worked without a hitch and forced the Nazis to retreat. During these short moments Konovalov had a rest, and then again sprayed the advancing chains of enemy soldiers with bullets, hurling them back each time they came near.

Hit by a bullet, Konovalov passed out. When he came to, he saw the enemy attacking again. Ignoring his pain, he re-opened fire. Another bullet hit his hand. He raised the safety-catch with his teeth, pulled the trigger with his right hand, and the machine-gun blasted away until the enemy finally withdrew.

A platoon of frontier guards burst into the enemy defences. The squad commanded by the Komsomol Plyugin gave the attackers fire support from behind. All of a sudden an enemy machine-gun opened up from the other side supported by a few tommy-guns. The frontier guards hugged the ground. Plyugin instantly sized up the situation and took a bold decision: leading his squad, he swiftly bypassed the enemy positions and attacked them from the rear. The frontier guards killed the machine-gun crew with their bayonets, climbed into a trench and opened fire with the machine-gun captured from the enemy. The next moment they went over the top. Plyugin was the first to burst into the trenches of the second line of enemy defences, wiped out a fire nest, stabbed four soldiers with a bayonet and captured an officer alive.

There is a saying that fortresses surrender to the brave. To be brave, however, does not mean to risk one's life mindlessly. Only a skilful combination of courage, caution and presence of mind makes a good fighter. He that is provident and keeps his head under any circumstances invariably proves master of the situation. The Komsomol Kirjanaho is a courageous scout, but he thoroughly prepares for each of his raids.

Kirjanaho was given an important assignment: to infiltrate the enemy frontline defences.

He selected a few comrades and began to prepare for his raid along with a few sappers. They had to defuse a mine field and cut barbed wire entanglements to gain access to the enemy positions. They worked at night. The sappers crawled along on their bellies in front of him, detecting and defusing mines. They were followed by scouts.

They darkness was full of danger, and time and again enemy flares soared into the sky. The scouts had to work literally under the nose of the enemy. Finally the preparations were over. When night fell, Kirjanaho and six of his men were on their way.

They infiltrated the enemy front line uneventfully. All was quiet. The scouts crawled along towards the enemy dug-outs while Kirjanaho stood upright and went straight ahead without looking back. His comrades were watching him and waiting for a signal. At last he motioned to them to take their places in front of the dug-outs. At that moment an enemy sentry sprang up in front of Kirjanaho. However, he kept his presence of mind and said in Finnish that he was a tactical training officer.

The next moment the sentry was killed. It took a few seconds and caused no alarm. . . Then it was no problem to hurl hand-grenades into the dug-outs and wipe out their occupants. The raid had lasted about 20 minutes. The scouts wiped out 35 officers and men and took one prisoner.

KOMSOMOL TUESDAYS

The fact that the front line is near involves heavy responsibility. We are doing whatever we can to help our fighting men defeat the invaders.

In the spring the army requested mosquito nets. Komsomols began to make them. A special contest was announced. A girl called Anne Filippova of the Medvezhiegorsky district worked best of all. Together with Hurme Aino, she organized a team of girls who supplied 530 mosquito nets to the fighting forces.

When the army requested camouflage cloaks Komsomols also made these. When mine crates were needed, Komsomols were quick to help. When road repairs were necessary, the army appealed to Komsomols for aid. What else are Komsomols doing? They are mending skis, building bath-houses, doing laundry work and mending clothes for servicemen. . .

In the summer Komsomols undertook to make a few thousand rings for ski sticks for the army. At first this seemed an easy job. However, it was quite an effort to cope with it. Finished rings were brought to the YCL district committee offices and laid on the floor in large bunches like ring-buns on a string. From here the rings were delivered to factories. Komsomols of the Pudozhsky district proved the best workers. The district committee secretary Rita Ruokolainen organized this work efficiently, and it was completed on time.

Towards the winter Komsomols of the republic had pledged to mend old uniforms. There were no quotas, but each tried to do his level best. Shestikhina, Sokhina and Kharina, workers of the republic's Ministry of Finance, mended 50 under-helmets and 30 pairs of gloves each.

In the early days of the war the Komsomols of the White Sea timbering station took a decision to assemble after hours each Tuesday and work for the army. These "Tuesdays" quickly became a tradition.

The Komsomols are trying to give whatever help they can to the fighting forces. Here is one striking example. The whole population was evacuated from one of the front line villages. The chairman of the village Soviet alone remained to look after the crops. The rye fields promised a bumper harvest after a snowy winter. The chairman, however, did not feel at all happy: he knew that no manpower would be available to take in the harvest. Suddenly a Komsomol team arrived at the village from the district committee. The Komsomols settled in village huts, and soon merry curls of smoke rose from their chimneys. The chairman came to see them and asked, "What are you doing here?" One of the new arrivals answered: "We've come to gather the harvest. I'm the team leader, Fedor Larkin. I hope we'll get along well." The chairman felt relieved.

The harvest was gathered in and contributed to the Red Army funds.

At the Segezh paper mill, on the initiative of the Komsomol district committee, 32 Komsomol girls who had formerly done low-skilled work were trained as turners, fitters and milling-machine operators. They coped with their new jobs excellently from the start. The girl workers Shananina, Pashova and Kozyreva regularly fulfil their quotas by 300 per cent. The girls went through a crash programme of civil defence training, and are now being trained as communications ratings, machine-gunners, medical nurses and snipers.

The railwaymen are also working well in the hard front line conditions. The Komsomols among them are efficient and selfless workers. Many of them have been decorated with military medals. Among them are the electrician Lesonen, the deputy chief of the traction service Oleshko, the chief of the dispatcher shift Makkeleva, the engine-driver Kiryushkin, leader of the Komsomol shift of Matveyenko station. These people are not scared of enemy bombing raids. They do their duty calmly and confidently, ignoring the whining of bombs and mines.

A few words about the Komsomols of the Stalin collective farm. When the front line had come close to the farm, the Nazis began to bomb and strafe the village. Then, on the initiative of the Komsomol girl Degtyarenko, the village Soviet chairman, boys and girls began to dig dug-outs. They did their work competently, having learned this from the men of an army unit stationed nearby.

So the collective farmers settled in their new ground-level homes. They sow crops and gather the harvest. There are fifteen Komsomols on this collective farm. They maintain close relations with a neighbouring army unit. They help its men in every way: they sew camouflage cloaks, kit-bags, mosquito nets, mend skis, and wash clothes. Once a Nazi plane strafed collective farmers working in the field. Four Komsomols took their rifles and fired back. The Nazi vulture climbed towards the clouds and was soon out of sight.

THE WAR IN THE WOODS

It is hard to fight a war in Karelian woods with their treacherous quagmires, bottomless lakes and impenetrable forests. No obstacles, however, can stop the brave guerrillas. Their trails lie across thickets and swamps. Their eyes see everything, their ears hear every sound, and they fight the enemy with courage and skill.

The machine-gunner Sergei Zhiganov is only eighteen. He is a strapping fellow, appearing somewhat clumsy at first sight. In fighting, however, he is a different man, quick, agile and accurate.

In the last raid Zhiganov captured two portable wireless sets and a mortar. According to his story, one of the sets fell into his hands by accident. His party had encountered an enemy patrol. The two sides exchanged fire. Zhiganov soon ran out of ammunition while his second number was nowhere to be seen. There were only two cartridges left in the drum, but he remembered his commander's order: "Keep on firing!" Zhiganov rushed to look for his mate and noticed a group of enemy soldiers. There were six of them, and he was alone. What was he to do? Escape? This idea never crossed his mind.

Zhiganov bravely attacked the enemy. He ran forward, pushing branches aside and shouting: "Charge! We'll take them alive! Hurrah!"

When he burst into a forest glade, it was deserted. The enemy soldiers had fled, and he heard the crackle of broken twigs under foot. Then he caught sight of a portable wireless set they had abandoned.

For his courage and valour in fighting the Nazi invaders Sergei Zhiganov has been decorated with the Order of Lenin.

Nikolai Pimanov was sent with a message to another unit. He learned the message by heart and went off. There was a lake on his way. It was just covered with ice and was smooth and brilliant. Very soon he was noticed by the enemy who opened fire on him with a machine-gun and a mortar. He crawled on and on without stopping. Suddenly a veritable screen of fire rose in front of him. He pretended to be dead and lay still for a long time. When firing had ceased, he tore off the sides of his camouflage cloak which was frozen to the ground ice and made his way further. He crawled another 1,500 metres, then went 25 kilometres through a forest and delivered the message on time.

The guerrillas have taken the village of Vojenavolok. This is how the Komsomols are defending their native Karelia. Just as we were on the day when the flames of ware flared up on our frontiers, we are confident of victory. We will spare no effort, not even our lives, to bring the happy hour of victory nearer.

Love for the Native Land
Article in Komsomolskaya Pravda,
13 June 1943

1. THE COUNTRY, REGION, HOME

Before the war we did not do enough to foster in young people love of their native region, town or village. We often failed to satisfy the keen interest of boys and girls in local lore. A young fighting man in the firing lines defends his native region, his home, his family. Recollections of his native places are a boost to his morale. The better he knows and loves his native region, the stiffer his resistance to the invaders.

I recalled how at the height of the Battle of Stalingrad in August 1942 the YCL Central Committee of Karelia received a joint letter from the Karel Komsomols defending that great city. "Fighting for Stalingrad, we always see in our mind's eye the forests and lakes of our native Karelia", they wrote to their countrymen. Going into battle, young Karels carry with them memories of the shady birch groves of Karelia, of the wonderful songs sung by their grannies and mothers, of the quiet streets of their native town, of the familiar bench where they whispered their first words of love to their sweethearts. To this day we are not doing enough to make young people familiar with the natural wealth of this country's various regions and to inculcate in the younger generation curiosity, love of nature and an interest in local lore. Not infrequently we meet secondary school leavers who have only a vague idea of the natural riches of their native district.

At lessons in history and geography little information is given to schoolchildren about the region and district they live in. Young people must know the history of their native places, their wealth and splendid traditions.

Our Komsomol organizations are doing little to foster in young people love of their native region. Just listen to any report on the cur-

28

rent situation. What will the speaker tell the audience, when describing organizing work on the Soviet home front? He will speak, as a rule, of the country as a whole, but will hardly utter a word about his local district.

We must show young people the wealth and beauty of their native land.

Recently a number of Komsomol primary cells in our republic had meetings hearing reports on the history of Karelia, and the joint struggle of the Russian and Karelian peoples against foreign invaders. These meetings evoked enormous interest in the young audiences.

The Komsomols and other young people of the Kalevala district assembled under a famous pine tree where a century ago Elias Lenrot wrote down folk runes (tales) to put them together in the "Kalevala" epic. Komsomols of the White Sea district sponsored discussions of veteran seamen with young people. They invited the remarkable narrator of folk tales Svinyin, also a veteran seaman, to attend these meetings.

We are persuading youths and girls who have left their native villages to study at vocational schools or to work in town not to break off their ties with their fellow villagers. Letters from those who have found a job in town, joined the army or gone elsewhere are an effective means of educational work.

Love for one's native district grows when it is better developed culturally and provided with good amenities. To admire the natural scenery and beauty spots but feel oneself a stranger is too bad. It is quite another matter when young people themselves help improve the aspect of their town or village and provide it with good amenities.

In our republic dozens of new sports grounds have been laid out, flower beds arranged and hostels repaired. However, all we have done is just the beginning stage of a great and important work. This work must be widened and intensified.

2. MEN OF IRON SAIL ON SHIPS OF WOOD

Good folk traditions and customs can play a fairly useful role in cultivating a firm, strong-willed character in young people. Their roots are embedded in deep antiquity. Many of them live on among the people for centuries. They contain inexhaustible sources of creativity.

Everyone certainly remembers the famous Cossack horse riding contests and Tartar feasts known as "sabantui". Over the centuries the people's admiration for bravery, skill and courage has lived on and grown. With skilful organization of educational work we can and must take advantage of traditional folk contests, competitions in strength and agility to promote the physical training of young people.

Folk ski festivals have become a wonderful tradition in Karelia. Skiing is equally popular with men and women, young and old alike. People of all ages take part in ski races. Every family has its own distinctive style of training, its own recipe for making ski grease and other gimmicks. Those who intend to take part prepare for a contest long in advance. In some areas contests are not even announced, because everybody knows that a folk ski festival is to be held on a certain day every year.

Unfortunately, participation in these contests is perhaps the only attempt on record of our Komsomol organizations to take advantage of folk traditions and customs to educate young people in the right spirit. What enormous opportunities remain open in this field!

We know, for instance, of the age-old tradition of local seamen to take their sons on a sailing voyage. The son of a seaman — a fisherman or a sea game hunter — must succeed to his father's trade by all means. The hard conditions of work in the Arctic make a seaman's trade a formidable challenge. One must know all about the sea and its whims, and not be scared of work in a freezing wind, a snow blizzard or a rain storm. It is not for nothing that the seamen of the White Sea coast are described in folk legends as "men of iron sailing on ships of wood".

In the old days people got the knack of their difficult trade at a young age. Youngsters put to sea with their fathers as ship's boys to learn the secrets of seamanship. On the White Sea coast, in Sumsky Posad and other places, successive generations of excellent skippers were raised.

Unfortunately today this wonderful tradition is on the way to extinction. Young people are not to be seen among fishing ship crews. Sea game hunting is plagued by manpower shortages. This year seals drove enormous shoals of fish to the shores of the White Sea. The fish were so many that they could be caught with buckets. They were followed by seals driving shoals in front of them. The sea was black with swarming seals, but there was hardly anyone on the spot to hunt them.

The coastal areas of Karelia have always been famous for their master shipwrights. From time immemorial they built a variety of ships on which courageous local seamen sailed to the shores of Norway and even America. The art of shipbuilding was handed down from generation to generation. But what about now? Ships are being built mainly by venerable old men. Young shipwrights are very few. Therefore, the tradition of this craftsmanship, if we restored it, would be of enormous significance.

3. WHAT SONGS DO YOU SING?

To love one's native region or one's republic means, incidentally, to know and love folk songs, epic legends and folk dances.

Today, singing folk songs has passed out of vogue. We asked young people at a factory in the village of Segezh what folk songs they sang. We put the question to many of them. Only two, however, said they knew a song about the Cossack leader Ermak and the rebel leader Stepan Razin, and even that only partly.

The wonderful songs of the peoples of this country which praise the battle exploits of folk heroes, and the people's staunchness and courage in fighting foreign invaders, are sometimes absolutely unknown to young people.

Folk dances are almost forgotten. Here and there there are sceptics prone to think that to dance a Russian ring dance, a jig or a Karelian quadrille is beneath the dignity of a serious man. A tango, however, is quite popular. Is this not the reason why intolerable boredom reigns supreme at our evening parties?

Once an old woodcutter came to a club where young people had assembled for an evening party. He sat still for a long time, gazing at youths and girls dancing a foxtrot, shuffling their feet and pushing one another. He rose to his feet, came to the accordion player, winked at him mischievously and said: "Come on, boy, play a Russian jig! And with gusto, mind!"

The dancers formed a ring. The old man broke into a dance, followed by the youngsters. It was a merry sight. The old man, now played out, stood aside, muttering contentedly: "Now it's all right . . . When I first looked at you, I wondered if you were really youngsters . . ."

In a number of districts in the republic we sponsored seminars of organizers of songs and dances. Young people came to attend these unusual lessons from collective farms and timbering stations. Instead of a lecturer, however, we invited an accordion player with the manager of a local club. At first a few youngsters laughed, but then everybody felt pleased.

To make folk and Soviet songs popular we advised Komsomol functionaries to take gramophones to villages. At first they were at a loss: indeed, was it becoming for a district committee secretary to come to a youth meeting with a gramophone and a stack of records? Books, fresh newspapers and posters are a different matter. But a gramophone is certainly a strange thing to carry around . . .

Young villagers, however, enthusiastically welcomed this innovation. And Komsomol activists saw it was nothing to be ashamed of.

In the Loukhi district there are no plug-in radios in libraries and club rooms. Young people may want to listen to a song and to learn it by heart, but how can they possibly do so without a radio? Once girls heard the song: "Wait for me, Liz". But then it was broken off, and they had to invent the ending themselves.

On one occasion a district committee instructor came to a village and brought along a gramophone and records. Young people avidly listened to folk songs and wrote down the lyrics. Today they are singing these songs, which are taken up in one village after another.

In the White Sea district Komsomols, in collaboration with personnel of the community centre, are reviving a seamen's choir. Something is being done in this way in other districts as well. This, of course, is clearly not enough. We must revive traditional folk games, dances and festivals and restore them to their rightful place. We must inculcate in young people love of folk songs and traditional athletic games.

4. FATHERS AND SONS

We must help educate the younger generation in a spirit of respect and affection for their parents and old folk.

Members of Young Pioneer teams are told, if only a limited amount, about their duties in the family, whereas in our Komsomol organizations no such custom exists. A Young Pioneer is occasionally told at a meeting what he must do to help his Mum with her daily chores, while his grown-up Komsomol sister often does nothing about the house to ease the work of her parents.

A young man beginning to live on his own meets many formidable problems for the first time in his life. He must choose a career, find a job and make friends. Much depends here on advice from his parents and seniors made wise by experience. It oftens happens in life, however, that a youth or a girl, having attained the age of 16 or 17, stops to heed the advice of those to whom they owe everything.

Just talk to schoolchildren of a 9th or 10th form. All of them love their father and mother, of course, although most of them believe their parents "do not understand" what interests their children nowadays. For this reason many senior form pupils, Komsomols among them, feel contempt for their parents' advice. A girl, for instance, often thinks it absolutely unnecessary to take her boyfriend to her home to meet her Mum and Dad. When choosing his career an adolescent often thinks nothing of his mother's advice.

A Young Pioneer is told once in a while: "If you talk back to your parents, if you do not obey them, you are a bad Young Pioneer". Why not say to Komsomols: "If you write no letter to your mother for two or three months when you are away from home for study, or if you are ashamed to take your mother's arm in the street, you are a bad Komsomol".

Our vocational schools have recently trained a large body of youngsters willing to join industry's work force. Scores of thousands of adolescents and girls have started an independent life. Many of them work at places far away from their families. It is the duty of Komsomol cells to organize their work in such a way as to make every young worker always remember his parents, maintain close ties with them and help them with money. Komsomols must be a model in this matter.

ASW-B

We have recently sponsored Komsomol and youth meetings and parties and invited parents to speak there. In particular, parents of Komsomols and young workers addressed meetings of young workers in Segezh, Kem and Belomorsk. Letters from Red Army men to their parents were read out at Komsomol meetings in a number of organizations.

At a youth meeting in the town of Belomorsk the audience listened with bated breath to the mother of three Komsomols of whom two had died a hero's death fighting the Nazis. Comrade Leskova — that was her name — spoke of how hard it was for her to endure her tragedy.

My hatred of the Nazis, however, is more bitter than my grief, she said.

She did not weep, but everybody sensed her sorrow and the tears she could hardly hold back. Everybody admired this Soviet patriot, the mother of Komosomol fighters.

Indeed, most Soviet parents are like her. To love and respect them and to care for them is the sacred duty of any young Soviet citizen, and it is an important duty of Komsomol organizations to educate young people in a spirit of respect for the older generation.

These are a few of the questions which should be given high priority in educational work among young people. In this great and important matter the Komsomol expects effective aid from Soviet writers, theatrical workers and film makers.

We expect in the immediate future films and plays devoted to the combat traditions of the peoples of this country, praising our native land, folk customs, songs and dances. We expect books that will open our minds to the material and cultural wealth of this country's various districts.

All this will indisputably be of great service to the cause of educating Soviet youth.

Party Control in Production
Article in Pravda, 12 April 1951

Successful fulfilment of the tasks in communist construction demands continued enhancement of the standards of work of Party organizations. A skilful combination of political and economic work is the key to scoring new successes in all areas of economic and cultural development.

Correctly organized verification of performance is an important prerequisite for unswerving implementation of Party and government decisions, of fulfilment of state plans and assignments in industry. The effectiveness of Party control in production derives from the fact that it helps educate personnel in the spirit of strict observance of Party and state discipline.

Fulfilling the resolutions of the 18th Congress of the Party and the 18th All-Union Party Conference, the Party organizations have gained certain experience in exercising control over carrying out Party and government decisions. This experience indicates that where a correct combination of Party and economic work is secured, where Party organizations do not substitute for economic bodies but, on the contrary, enhance in every way their responsibility for the performance of state assignments, the tasks in production are implemented more successfully.

When exercising control over the economic activities of the management of enterprises, the Party organizations cannot confine themselves to formal verification of the state of affairs and the adoption of decisions based on materials obtained by verification. The main task is to involve broad sections of communists and all working people in the struggle to implement the programme of planned measures.

In this respect the experience of the work of the Party organizations of the Gumbaruchei timbering station in Karelia deserves our attention. It enables its Party organization to be familiar with the situation in production, so that it can expose and eliminate shortcomings in good time. It does not substitute for economic executives, or work for them, but operates in conjunction with them and helps them to implement the most important measures. The Party organization has ensured normal operation of the timbering station which copes with the state plan successfully.

Examples of skilful organization of Party control in production are numerous. It should be admitted, at the same time, that there are still many Party organizations in the republic which exercise inadequate control over the activities of the management of enterprises. This largely accounts for the fact that a number of enterprises of the timber and fishing industries have failed to fulfil their production plans.

Analyzing the activities of Party organizations in production, it should be noted that some of them exercise their rights granted them by the Party Rules far from completely. The methods of control over the economic activities of management are often lop-sided and hence fail to achieve the desired effect.

Not infrequently, control boils down to discussion of reports by economic executives at a Party meeting and a meeting of the Party bureau. Sometimes these reports are heard without a profound study of the subject. This results in the fact that resolutions often resemble one another. They contain few concrete instructions on how to eliminate as early as possible the shortcomings which are revealed, while an abundance of decisions deprives the Party organization of the possibility of securing effective control over their fulfilment.

Inability to concentrate on the key questions which have a decisive bearing on success in the operation of an enterprise is a serious shortcoming in the work of some Party organizations. Instead, they engage in fulfilling small matters of secondary importance, often assume functions outside their terms of reference, and substitute for economic executives.

Some economic executives regard the Party organization and the Party district committee as a "pusher" of his own interests. They do not hesitate to apply to a party committee with request for aid in obtaining additional quantities of raw materials for other resources. Party committees, for their part, often yield in the face of the economic executives' insistence, and support him even when his request is absolutely unfounded.

For instance, the Pryazhinsky Party district committee requested the Central Committee of the Communist Party of Karelia to assist the timbering station in procuring bricks, glass, nails and other building materials required for house repairs. Investigation revealed that bricks, glass, and heating equipment were already available at warehouses of the timbering station in requisite quantities.

By substituting for economic executives or extending protection to them, some Party committees, wittingly or unwittingly, cause grave damage to the cause of the Bolshevik education of cadres. Such practices generate the irresponsible attitude of some economic executives to their duties, give rise to sentiments of carelessness and complacency among them and stimulate them to perform their plan assignments without great exertion.

Correctly exercised, Party control is an effective means of organizing the masses to fulfil the tasks facing a given enterprise. Organizing work should be given high priority in the activities of Party organizations. It is not enough to adopt a decision and to plan measures to remove shortcomings. The main task is to mobilize the masses skilfully to carry out these measures. This requires daily organizing and political work within the masses.

Unfortunately, some Party organizations forget about this. Judging by the number of inspections carried out and decisions taken, the Segezhsky district Party committee, for instance, should be extolled as a model of attention to the operation of timbering stations. However, its decisions often look like instructions by the manager of a trust, something like a new edition of these instructions. The district committee forgets its duty to organize and educate people, forgets that its working methods should be different from those used by economic bodies. It fails to rely in its activities on the primary Party organizations of enterprises. With such a situation one cannot talk seriously of effective party control in production.

The strength of a Party organization derives from its close links with the masses. Party control in production can be effective only when, along with leading executives and communists, it is carried out with the participation of broad sections of working people, when the masses inspect the work of leading executives, identify their mistakes and help remove shortcomings in their work.

Experience has shown that where Party organizations ignore the increased political and labour activity of the masses, and have a negligent attitude to their criticisms and suggestions, shortcomings in the work of enterprises are not always brought to light and eliminated in good time.

This is exemplified by the experience of the Party organization of the Segezhsky paper mill. Its Party bureau failed to pay due attention to complaints from workers about serious cases of disorder in organizing registration and accounting, and of mismanagement, which were responsible for grave setbacks in work which had been in evidence for a long time. The Party bureau of the paper mill involved in the organization of control only a small circle of activists who were, in addition, dependent on the management and also failed to provide the requisite conditions for encouragement of criticism and self-criticism.

In certain instances primary Party organizations and district committees deal with production problems in a general way. However, genuine Bolshevik control over economic activity implies profound familiarity with the life of an enterprise, an ability to go into the details of a given matter. And here one cannot be content with general instructions. The decisions of a Party organization should be concrete and based on comprehensive knowledge of the matter and the situation. This by no means implies suppression of the initiative of economic executives in implementing Party decisions. A concrete solution helps both the economic executives and the Party organizations to implement the task pursued in the most effective way.

In exercising control over the economic activity of the management of enterprises, the Party organizations of the republic concentrate on efforts to introduce all that is innovative, advanced, and progressive. This can be seen, in particular, in the work of the Party organizations of many timber industry enterprises.

Up-to-date technology which the state generously supplies to timbering stations has required the application of new processes. At mechanized timbering stations a flowline method is used to increase overall output per worker 50-100 per cent. Alexei Gotchiev, a State Prize winner, has hundreds of followers who display skill and dexterity in work and contribute their energy and creativity to the cause of advancing the timber industry. The Komsomol tractor driver Ivan Kotov has initiated a movement for the economical and efficient use of machines and mechanisms. The Party organizations have broadly supported his initiative.

However, innovators in production still meet with quite a few difficulties and obstacles in their path. New technology and new and more productive methods of work are being introduced too slowly. One still encounters a conservative attitude on the part of some managers of timbering stations to suggestions from workers. Opposition to the broad application of mechanization has not yet been uprooted everywhere.

In exercising their control over the economic activities of the management of enterprises, primary Party organizations are in need of effective assistance from Party bodies. It should be admitted, however, that district and town committees of the Party still inadequately teach Party organizations a correct combination of Party, political and economic work. Until recently the Party's Central Committee of the republic itself took quite a few different decisions which stimulated Party organizations to unnecessary tutelage over economic executives.

The town and district committees of the Party fail to give sufficient encouragement to the initiative of primary organizations in utilizing latent internal reserves available to enterprises.

We are still making inadequate efforts to educate secretaries of Party organizations to be highly exacting in exercising control over the activities of the management of enterprises, in a spirit of intolerance of all manifestations of bureaucracy and procrastination. In certain instances, urgent problems of producton are pigeonholed for months by managers of enterprises and prompt solutions to problems are replaced by the compilation of plans of further measures, or by promising assurances by leading executives.

The Party organization of the republic is faced with great tasks. It is taking steps to improve the operation of enterprises, to raise the productivity of labour, to secure the most effective use of technology. Further progress in the work of industry largely depends on enhancing the standards of Party guidance. Measures are being taken to enhance in every way the responsibility of primary Party organizations for the performance results of enterprises. Correct combination of political and economic work, all-round encouragement of Bolshevik criticism and self-criticism are the major means of securing a new, still more powerful advance of socialist industry.

Leninism Illumines Our Path
Report at the anniversary meeting in Moscow commemorating Lenin's 94th birthday, 22 April 1964

Comrades!

As we are celebrating Lenin's 94th birthday today, we again cast our mind's eye to the image of the great man, whose ideas and deeds shook the old world to its foundations and illumined the path into the future before mankind.

Lenin's lifetime exploits are an inspiring example to all fighters for the working-class cause, for the triumph of communism. Lenin was a brilliant exponent of the aspirations and ideals, indomitable energy and dynamism of the communist movement of our great epoch. Lenin devoted his whole life as a fighter and thinker to a titanic task—the struggle for victory of the proletarian revolution, the building of a society without the exploitation of man by man and war, without poverty and ethnic oppression.

Lenin is immortal, because his ideas and deeds will live forever. He lives on in the accomplishments of socialism and communism, in the revolutionary struggle of the working people throughout the world.

Our successes are the most eloquent and convincing evidence of the vitality of Lenin's ideas. "We raise aloft our Marxist torch", Lenin wrote in his time about the Russian Bolsheviks, "and from every step of individual classes, from every political and economic event we draw practical evidence to show the truth of our doctrine."[1]

Leninism gives clear answers to questions concerning the most vital interests and aspirations of the peoples. The working people cherish Lenin's ideas, which show them the right way to follow in the struggle

---

[1] V. I. Lenin, *Collected Works*, vol. 13, pp. 163–164.

ASW–B*

for a better life. This is the main clue to the powerful influence of Leninism on mankind's historical destiny.

THE EVERLASTING DOCTRINE OF THE COMMUNISTS OF ALL COUNTRIES

The communist movement has grown into the most influential force of today because it is invariably guided by Marxist–Leninist theory. The great wealth of Lenin's ideas has always helped us, as it does today, to find the right solution to the urgent problems of our struggle. We derive our strength from our loyalty to Leninism.

At every new stage in mankind's development, at every turn of history, the theory of scientific communism is enriched and supplemented with new ideas and conclusions and advanced to a higher level. This is quite logical, since Marxism–Leninism is by nature a steadily developing creative doctrine. Only those who have failed to understand this truth can deny the present generation of revolutionaries a right to independent thinking, scaring with the bogey of revisionism all those who are trying to come up with innovative ideas in Marxist–Leninist theory.

Lenin never sided with those who regarded our great teaching as a collection of dogmas, as something like a mathematics textbook with readymade formulas or a pharmacy manual with a choice of prescriptions. He was a bold innovator in theory and practice, firmly convinced that Marxist theory must be constantly developed. "We by no means regard Marx's theory as something finished and inviolable; on the contrary, we are convinced that it has only laid the corner stones for a theory that socialists must advance further in all directions, if they want to keep pace with life", he writes.[1]

The need for a bold, creative solution to the cardinal problems involved in the struggle for socialism has never been so acute as in the postwar years. Our time is one of unprecedented revolutionary changes in social life, a gigantic acceleration of social progress, rapid development of productive forces, science and technology. There is no country, people, or sphere of human activity which have not

---

[1] V. I. Lenin, *Collected Works*, vol. 4, p. 184.

witnessed important changes during the last few decades. The struggle between two policy lines, two historical tendencies—the line of social progress, peace and construction, on the one hand, and the line of reaction, oppression and war, on the other—inexorably results in socialism winning from the old world one position after another on the historical scene. The prestige of capitalism, the capitalist way of development, is steadily declining. Seeking to preserve their rule, the imperialists are stockpiling weapons of mass destruction, resorting to intimidation and suppression of the masses, bribery and social demagogy. However, they are unable to check the onward march of history, to stop the peoples' advance along the path of progress, the path of socialism and communism.

In our epoch mankind has accumulated vast experience of revolutionary transformations, which had to be analysed. The realities of life raised some burning questions, which had to be answered.

Soviet society has entered a new stage of progress; this posed the most fundamental theoretical and practical questions as to how to advance socialism and to build communism, what methods to use to involve the masses in this great work, what part the Party and state are to play under the new conditions. It is to the credit of the CPSU and its Leninist Central Committee that they gave clear answers to them.

The formation of the world socialist system, the development of the socialist community of nations, called for working out the principles of relations among them, of organizing their all-round cooperation, and of charting the ways of building up the world socialist economy. The Marxist–Leninist parties undertook to solve these pressing problems by joint efforts and answered them not only in theory but primarily in practice, seeking to consolidate the friendly family of socialist nations.

The emergence of nuclear missile arsenals faced mankind with the danger of wholesale destruction, and this demanded that communists come up with a practical programme of struggle to avert another world war and learn to combine the struggle for peace even more closely with the struggle for victory of socialism.

Important changes took place in the economy and sociopolitical life in the capitalist countries; this required supplementing the arsenal of instruments of the class struggle with new methods, ways and means of struggle, working out new problems of the strategy and tactics of socialist revolution, new forms of involving the masses in the liberation movement. The communist parties of the capitalist countries mapped out a flexible and effective line of revolutionary struggle in the new situation.

Many innovations had to be introduced into Marxist–Leninist theory to bring it into line with the historic changes brought about in the world by the victorious national liberation revolutions in the vast continents of Asia, Africa, and Latin America. The realities of life faced the peoples of the newly-independent countries with the problem of choosing the ways of further struggle for complete independence and social progress. The Marxist–Leninists offered their own solution to these problems to meet the interests of the peoples.

The Marxist–Leninist parties carried out great work to sum up the latest phenomena of modern world development. Taking account of the new alignment of forces in the world arena, they outlined the ways of struggle against imperialism, war, and reaction, for peace, democracy, national independence, and socialism, and jointly mapped out the general line of the international communist movement. This work resulted in the Declaration of 1957, the Statement of 1960, and other remarkable documents of revolutionary Marxism–Leninism. As acknowledged by the fraternal parties, the conclusions and decisions of the Soviet Communist Party congresses are of historic significance for the entire communist and liberation movement.

Marxism–Leninism is inconceivable without these achievements of creative thought, which develop the ideas of Marx, Engels, and Lenin in close association with the present epoch and make them an effective instrument for remaking the modern world. Marxism–Leninism today includes not only the great heritage of the founders of communist doctrine but also the entire wealth of experience and theoretical activity of the Communist parties of the world, the experience of working-class struggle and the entire liberation movement.

This is a forceful expression of the international nature of the Marxist–Leninist teaching. It was not before the advent of Marxism–Leninism that a revolutionary theory was evolved, capable of uniting for joint action the peoples of different countries and different continents, living under widely diverse conditions. Our scientific theory alone indicates the path towards the summits of progress for all nations.

Leninism has never shut itself up within the confines of one country, but absorbed the international experience of the working class and the liberation movement of the peoples. In view of the wide variety of the specific conditions in which the peoples wage a struggle for their liberation Marxist–Leninist theory holds that there are no, nor can there be, hard-and-fast rules applicable to any time or any situation. Leninism indisputably requires revolutionary theory to be adapted to the specific historical and national distinction of the relevant country.

At the same time, all attempts to emasculate Leninism by depriving it of its revolutionary content, to ignore the experience of the international working-class movement, to substitute for the revolutionary working-class teaching various theories expressing narrow-minded national and sometimes even frankly nationalistic ambitions, run counter to Leninism, to the interests of socialism. Vindicating the theoretical heritage of Marx and Engels, Lenin set a classical example of struggle against great power chauvinism and other varieties of nationalism, which, on the plea of defence of national interests, actually undermine the people's strength in the face of their true enemies.

The realities of life frustrate at every step attempts to confine Leninism to narrow national limits or to interpret the advance of the peoples towards socialism from dogmatic, sectarian positions. The Marxist–Leninists have always been known for their broad views, their realistic outlook on life, their ability to combine a consistent struggle for communist ideals with active support for all progressive movements.

In our day the force of attraction of Lenin's ideas has grown immeasurably. This is due primarily to the historic achievements of socialism, the advantages of the new system which are increasingly visible in the practical field. The masses are realizing more and more clearly that socialism is the wave of the future. They see in it a dependable way of solving the problems facing society, and this is clear now not only to the working class but also to broad sections of other working people, the *petit bourgeoisie* of the Asian, African, and Latin American countries.

Many leaders of the national liberation movement reckon with this strong gravitation of the mass towards socialism and have come forward with slogans of struggle for socialist construction. Advancing these slogans, they take the road of far-reaching social reforms, whose implementation involves fairly great difficulties and many new problems. Small wonder, therefore, that they borrow more and more often from the experience of the socialist countries, from Lenin's ideas. This is a new trend in world development, one that is enthusiastically welcomed by all Marxist–Leninists. In the socialist aspirations of the masses we see the sign of the times.

The world communist movement has assumed unprecedented scope in our day. As our movement becomes more and more mature, we come to realize more clearly and thoroughly the profundity of Lenin's ideas, which are alien to both opportunistic amorphousness and sectarian narrow-mindedness. Our Party and the Marxist–Leninist parties of other countries may proudly say that they have proved their allegiance to Lenin's ideas not in word but in deed, and have raised aloft the banner of creative Leninism and proletarian internationalism. The CPSU is determined to bear this Leninist banner high in the future as well.

THE LENINIST CAUSE TRIUMPHS

Lenin has stated more than once that the most responsible and complicated task facing the working class is not destruction of the old order but construction. After the victory of the proletarian revolution the construction of a new socialist society becomes a practical matter for millions upon millions of people in the socialist countries. A true Leninist is not only a fighter against the old order but primarily the builder of a new world. The enthusiasm and genuine pleasure with which Lenin got down to practical work in construction immediately after the victory of the October Revolution is a matter of common knowledge. With his amazingly great powers of work and profound erudition in the most diverse fields of human endeavour Lenin masterminded all the initiatives of the young Soviet Republic. Whatever

matter he might handle, he did his duty with truly Bolshevik dedication, confidence in success, and businesslike efficiency alien to
dilettantism and visionary schemes. All his tireless activities and
exuberant creativity were dedicated to the sole purpose of service of
the working people. Communist humanism is the most salient trait of
Lenin and Leninism.

Speaking of personalities who made history, one is prone to
remember, in the first place, their public lives. Indeed, we speak of
Lenin as a revolutionary, a thinker, and a political leader. Lenin,
however, was not only an illustrious public figure. He was the "most
humane of humans", as the poet Mayakovsky said.

Lenin was a charismatic man, always friendly and cheerful, sincere
and kindhearted. All of these finest human traits were intrinsic to his
character. He was fond of people and hated whatever ruined their
lives. He was tough on enemies and traitors, but intolerant of vindic-
tiveness and cruelty. Lenin's high-principledness never had anything
in common with diehard bigotry. His broad outlook and ability for
self-criticism—these inalienable features of a creative mind—made
him an implacable enemy of narrow-minded dogmatism, arrogance
and self-conceit. "As simple as truth"—that was how Lenin was
viewed by revolutionary workers in Maxim Gorky's phrase. Gorky
reminisced about Lenin as follows: "I admired his vigorous love of
life and his bitter hatred of its injustices, and I was delighted by the
youthful ardour he put into whatever he did."[1]

This is how Lenin was seen by his associates. This is how he is
remembered and will live on in the memory of future generations.

For Lenin, socialism was not an abstract idea or an end in itself.
The purpose of socialism, as he saw it, was to "make the life of all
working people as easy as possible, providing them with the sources
of well-being".[2]

Highly-developed social production, creative work, genuine freedom and democracy, comprehensive culture, relations among individuals based on the principles of comradeship and brotherhood—
such are the working-class ideas of a society which is to be built as its

---

[1] Maxim Gorky, *Collected Works*, Moscow, 1974, vol. 20, p. 31.

[2] V. I. Lenin, *Collected Works*, vol. 36, p. 381.

supreme and ultimate destination. It is the ideal that Lenin expounded next to Marx and Engels.

Lenin vigorously opposed all attempts of the right-wing and left-wing opportunists to distort the ideals of socialism. He waged a relentless struggle against leftist elements and the Trotskyites, who reflected *petit bourgeois* ideology exaggerating the role of coercion, ignoring the positive, constructive tasks of the revolution, denying the people a right to aspire towards well-being and freedom, that is the main benefits for which the working people rise in rebellion. It was precisely because the Party, in keeping with Lenin's behests, concentrated on the practical tasks in socialist construction that the Soviet people have scored their historic successes of worldwide significance.

The Party has made an objective assessment of Stalin's role and contributions and is aware at the same time that in a number of important questions he committed violations of the Leninist principles of collective leadership and the norms of Party life. The 20th Party Congress not only denounced the personality cult but also restored the Leninist norms of life in the Party and state, created the requisite conditions for translating Lenin's ideals of socialism and communism into reality.

The Party has drawn up its new Programme, which is wholly based on the principle "everything in the name of man, for the benefit of man". The Party programme provision for the first-priority importance of building up the material and technological basis for communism organically embodies Lenin's idea of economic development and economic policy as crucial factors in the struggle for communism.

All practical activities of the Party and the Soviet people are wholly guided by this idea of Lenin's. We are proud to know that over the last decade *per capita* industrial output has grown 128 per cent in the Soviet Union, which compares favourably with 15 per cent in the United States.

Lenin's brilliant maxim "Communism is Soviet power plus country-wide electrification" is widely known. When he first declared it, Russia was eighteenth in the world's list of electric power producers. Today the Soviet Union is second and is swiftly moving up. In 1963 alone it commissioned more than 10 million kilowatts of new generating capacity. This is equivalent to almost seven GOELRO plans taken together.[1]

Life, however, is never at a standstill. In our day the scientific and technological revolution is bringing to the foreground ever new trends of scientific and technological progress. The Party believes that under present conditions the most effective means of boosting economic growth is the application of the latest scientific and technological achievements, the all-round development of the chemical industry in particular.

While displaying constant, truly Leninist, concern for advancing the people's well-being, the Party is paying keen attention to the development of agriculture as one of the most complex problems of the theory and practice of socialist construction. Over the last decade collective and state farm production has made considerable progress. Nevertheless, not all of the problems have yet been resolved. The Party and the people are well aware of that. At its plenary meetings the CPSU Central Committee has worked out a number of practical measures to advance the standards of crop farming and stock farming, to implement consistently the principle of material incentives, to improve the management of agriculture. Today the Party has formulated the crucial task of intensifying agricultural production and transferring crop farming and stock farming onto an industrial basis resting on the latest achievements in science and technology. All this will make it possible to raise agriculture to a much higher level.

Our age is rightly called the space age. We are lawfully proud of the fact that the Soviet people have been pioneers in this most modern field of science and technology. The Soviet space achievements epitomize all progress of socialist industry, science, technology, and culture. The Soviet people could blaze the trail into outer space because they firmly stand on the ground, because socialism creates excellent conditions for progress of productive forces and advanced science.

Lenin has taught us that the basic prerequisite for success in socialist construction is the broad and comprehensive development of

---

[1] GOELRO, the Russian acronym for the first Soviet nationwide electrification programe of 1921 (Translator).

socialist democracy, the involvement of the mass of the people in the management of production and all public affairs, encouragement of their initiative and creativity. Democracy is not only one of the main goals of socialism important in itself; without democracy it is impossible to develop productive forces successfully and build the material and technological basis for a new society.

The transformation of the state of proletarian dictatorship into a state of the whole people and of the working-class party into a party of the whole people is striking evidence of the development of socialist democracy.

Powerful and irresistible in its progress, this country is confidently implementing the great Lenin's behests. It is a busy scene of tireless work and creative endeavour, the steady emergence and assertion of a new life and of a new man, the man of communist society. All of the world's working people admire our progress, regarding it as their own cause.

Our successes are so evident that they are not denied, even by our adversaries. They are worried by the capitalist world losing its contest against socialism, and they regard this fact as a direct threat to themselves. A group of Columbia University experts in the USA in a recent study on the prospects of economic competition between the United States and the Soviet Union wrote with concern about the US lag in rates of economic growth. They said that the United States might adopt an old Russian tradition dating back to the democratic institutions of Novgorod. When this famous trading city was in danger, one of its citizens rang the tocsin. Then the city's whole population assembled in the central square to decide what was to be done. Now the tocsin is sounding the alarm for the United States.

This is the turn matters have taken today. In the face of the growing power of socialism the imperialists have to ring the alarm. They are scared of our growth, which is another proof that we are following the right, Leninist, way.

It is for almost two decades that the ideas of Leninism have been translated into reality not just in one country but in a group of countries, which have formed the world socialist system. The very fact that socialism has spread beyond the limits of one country to vast areas in Europe and Asia, and its emergence in the Western hemisphere, is a great triumph of Marxism–Leninism. Today the experience of socialist transformations includes not only the practices of the Soviet Union but also a large variety of ways and means of socialist construction in widely different countries.

As a true internationalist, Lenin eagerly desired the path of other nations to socialism to be easier than ours. He believed that the sacrifices made by Russia's proletariat, the difficulties it had to overcome in making the first breach in the chain of imperialist states, would make it easier for other peoples to embark on the path of building a new life.

It would be relevant to recall in this context Lenin's story about his discussion with a Polish communist, who said that the Polish revolutionaries would imaginatively use Soviet experience. "One of the finest comrades among the Polish communists" Lenin reminisced, "said in reply to my remark 'You will do differently': 'No. We will do the same but we will do it better than you did.' I had absolutely nothing to object to that argument. One must have a chance to fulfil this modest desire: to make Soviet power better than ours."[1]

The Soviet people have shouldered their heavy task as pioneers of socialism and built the world's first socialist society. And they feel happy, as Lenin would, to see the peoples of other countries borrowing from our experience cope with the tasks of building a new society at less expense, following the Soviet people's path with relatively easier effort. The Soviet communists highly appreciate the remarkable contributions being made by the peoples of the fraternal countries to the international experience of the struggle for socialism.

The Communist Party of the Soviet Union is consistently pursuing a policy of friendship with all the peoples of the world, a policy of brotherly alliance of the peoples which have taken the road towards socialism.

The Marxist–Leninists have never shut their eyes to the complexities involved in the emergence of socialism, which grows up not in a sterile test tube, figuratively speaking, but on a soil polluted by the domination of feudalism and capitalism for centuries. Our teachers harboured no illusions in this respect. Lenin writes that "the proletar-

---

[1] V. I. Lenin, *Collected Works*, vol. 38, p. 162.

iat will not be made infallible and guaranteed against mistakes and weaknesses merely by accomplishing a social revolution".[1]

Lenin saw a grave danger to the unity of socialist nations in the fact that the *petit bourgeoisie* taking part in socialist revolutions would invariably "introduce into the movement its prejudices, its reactionary phantasies, its weaknesses and mistakes". He predicted that socialism would "by no means immediately 'clean itself' of *petit bourgeois* slag".[2]

The realities of life have shown that the development of the world socialist system is really attended with certain difficulties involved in uprooting old traditions, the old mentality inherited from capitalism. It is also necessary to solve complicated problems involved in overcoming the economic backwardness of a number of countries which have taken the socialist road. All of these, however, are merely difficulties of growth, which can be effectively disposed of by joint efforts of the socialist countries.

It is impossible to abolish the historical law requiring all-round co-operation, organization and development of the brotherly alliance of the peoples which have taken the road of socialism. Mankind's advance towards socialism is a powerful mainstream, which can have only one bed—the unbreakable alliance of fraternal socialist nations.

TO FIGHT FOR UNITY IN THE LENINIST WAY

Lenin went down in the history of communism as the most consistent, dedicated and fervent fighter for cohesion of the revolutionary ranks of the proletariat, for unity of the world communist movement. He said more than once that unity would not come by itself, that it should be won and defended in a stubborn struggle against opportunists of every stripe, against *petit bourgeois* manifestations on the right and on the left.

"Every peculiar turn of history", Lenin writes, "causes certain changes in the form of *petit bourgeois* vacillations which are always in

---

[1] V. I. Lenin, *Collected Works*, vol. 30, p. 51.

[2] Ibid., pp. 54–55.

evidence by the side of the proletariat and always find their way to a varying extent into the midst of the proletariat.

"*Petit bourgeois* reformism, that is grovelling before the *bourgeoisie* camouflaged with sweet-worded democratic and 'social'-democratic phrases and helpless wishes and *petit bourgeois* revolutionarism—awe-inspiring, inflated, and arrogant in word and a rattle-box of fragmentation, dispersion, and mindlessness in deed—such are the two 'trends' of these vacillations."[1]

Lenin maintained that the methods of struggle for unity are determined by the prevailing conditions. The matter depends on what forces pose the grave danger to the unity of the world communism in a particular period and what situation takes shape as a result of their actions.

The last decade has been one of another peculiar turn of history, when forces criticizing and attacking the line of the Marxist–Leninist parties again stepped up their activities within the working-class movement.

Nevertheless, the Party is willing, as before, to search for ways of normalizing relations with the Communist Party of China on the principles of Marxism–Leninism, on the basis of the Declaration and Statement of the international meetings of the Communist and Workers' parties in Moscow in 1957 and 1969 and for ways of improving relations between the USSR and the People's Republic of China at government level.

There have been allegations to the effect that the CPSU is seeking to "expel" China from the socialist camp. This is nonsense, of course. We are firmly confident that eventually the Soviet and Chinese communists will join forces and struggle for socialism and peace in the same ranks.

The great Chinese revolutionary and democrat Sun Yat-sen in a message to the Soviet Union the day before his death, on 11 March 1925, wrote: "Dear comrades, members of the Central Executive Committee of the Union of Soviet Socialist Republics, I am dying from an incurable illness. My thoughts are now focused on you, on my Party, and on my country's future. . . .

---

[1] V. I. Lenin, *Collected Works*, vol. 44, p. 101.

"Dear comrades, saying my farewells to you, I wish to express my cherished hope that a dawn will come soon. The time will come when the Soviet Union will welcome a powerful and free China as its best friend and ally, when the two countries will march forward hand in hand and achieve victory in the great battle for freedom of the world's oppressed nations."[1]

These words expressed the Chinese people's innermost sentiments, their deep-rooted interest in friendship with the Soviet Union. There is not, nor can there be, any justification for those who, in defiance of the vital interests of People's China, are pursuing a policy undermining the mainstays of Sino-Soviet friendship, whose significance is realized, as before, by all progressive people in China.

We will continue to work for strengthening Sino-Soviet friendship on the Leninist principles of proletarian internationalism.

We are firmly convinced that the unity of the communist movement will be consolidated. Under present conditions, however, consolidation of this unity on the principles of Marxism–Leninism demands the most determined and consistent struggle of all communists, all who cherish the interests of our great cause against the dangerous policy and divisive activities of China's leaders.

This is demanded by the interests of the struggle against imperialism and colonialism, for peace, democracy, national liberation, and socialism.

Our Party, as in the past, will spare no efforts to unite all revolutionary anti-imperialist forces pursuing these objectives.

* * *

It has become a tradition in commemorating Lenin's birthday not only to pay a tribute of respect and affection to our great countryman, the acknowledged leader of the world's working people, but also to verify in accordance with Lenin's principles the correctness of our path and our policy. Our Party and the whole Soviet people can stand the test of responsibility to Lenin's sacred memories with clear conscience and an open heart. We are confidently following the path

---

[1] Sun Yat-sen, *Selected Works*, Moscow, 1964, pp. 556–557.

charted by Lenin towards the realization of mankind's greatest and noblest dream—communism.

We are confronted by formidable and complicated tasks demanding all our energy, initiative and daring creative quests. The Soviet people led by the Leninist Party will accomplish these tasks honourably.

The Party is gaining new successes in building a new society, strengthening the unity of the Marxist–Leninist parties, and scoring ever new achievements in implementing practically the general line of our movement, in the struggle against imperialism, for peace and socialism.

Long live the Communist Party of the Soviet Union raised by Lenin, the militant vanguard of the Soviet people building communism!

May the unity and cohesion of the international communist movement, all revolutionary forces of today, grow stronger!

Long live Leninism!

Proletarian Internationalism: the Fighting Banner of Communists

Excerpt from a report at the Berlin International Scientific Session in commemoration of the centenary of the First International, 26 September 1964

THE significance of some historic events extends far beyond the limits of their time and influences all world development. One such event, which had truly worldwide historic repercussions, was the founding of the First International—the International Workingmen's Association —the centenary of which is being celebrated by all progressive mankind today.

In those distant September days few people took notice of the modest meeting in St. Martin's Hall in London. Few realized at the time that the main citadel of capitalism was the mustering ground for a force that was destined to destroy to its foundations the world of capitalist exploitation and to build a new socialist society in which labour would reign supreme and peace and friendship of nations would be a guiding international principle.

"The First International", Lenin writes, "set the stage for proletarian, international struggle for socialism."[1] A century has passed since then. A broad and powerful movement has grown up on this foundation, for which the cornerstone was laid by Marx and Engels. This movement has become the most influential and massive force of today.

The constituent assembly of the First International was attended by a few hundred delegates from only six countries of Europe. Today

---

[1] V. I. Lenin, *Collected Works*, vol. 38, p. 303.

the world's ninety Communist and Workers' parties operating in all continents have a total membership of forty-three million.

Over the last 100 years Marxism has rallied under its banner hundreds of millions of working people.

Under this victorious banner more than one-third of mankind have freed themselves from exploitation and social oppression and are successfully building a new life.

Almost two thousand million people have shattered the fetters of colonial slavery and won independence.

Today when the world is witnessing the spectacular achievements of communism we again and again cast our mind's eye on the genius of Marx and Engels, the founders of our internationalist doctrine, whose exploits will live on in the centuries to come.

The communists are celebrating the centenary of the First International not only to pay tribute to the splendid record of the past. Our prime motive for such commemoration is to review again the vital problems of the world liberation movement and learn from the historic experience of revolutionary struggle the best ways of fulfilling the tasks of today.

PROLETARIAN INTERNATIONALISM AND THE COMMUNIST STRUGGLE FOR NATIONAL INTERESTS

Proletarian internationalism is not an abstract doctrine. It has been called into being by the realities of life, the most vital, immediate requirements of the class struggle as an inalienable part of the working class ideology.

The idea of proletarian internationalism expresses not only the communist views on relations between the working classes of all countries in the struggle against the capitalist system, but also the communist ideas of future society, of relations among different nations building socialism and communism. Marxism–Leninism is the doctrine of socialist revolution and building a new society in all countries of the world. Its founders naturally proceeded from the assumption that under communism relations among nations must be based on a totally new foundation: the principles upheld by the working class, the most progressive class in modern society.

The identical position and interests of the workers in all countries, their common ultimate goals, dictate the need for fraternal solidarity in opposition to their common class enemy—the international *bourgeoisie*. At the same time, the class struggle is waged in the concrete situation prevailing in a given country and hence inevitably takes national form and, as shown by experience, no proletarian party can ignore this fact, if it is willing to wield serious influence within the masses.

Proletarian internationalism is the fundamental principle of Marxist–Leninist ideology, which serves to unite the efforts of the national contingents of the working class and is a dependable guarantee against manifestations of national narrow-mindedness within the labour movement. International solidarity of the working class is an indispensable prerequisite for its victory. This is precisely the way Marx viewed this question in the "Constituent Manifesto" of the First International. "Past experience has shown", he writes, "that a scornful attitude to brotherhood which must exist between the workers of different countries and induce them to stand up staunchly for each other in their liberation struggle incurs a general defeat of their uncoordinated efforts."[1]

For the Marxist–Leninists, proletarian internationalism has always been and remains the guiding principle, the foundation of fraternal relations among the Communist parties and the socialist countries.

In our day proletarian internationalism has assumed a new dimension. First, the sphere of its action has markedly widened. Today proletarian internationalism is becoming the banner of revolutionary struggle not only of the working class but also of the multi-millioned mass of the working people, the oppressed nations of the whole world. It implies solidarity of all revolutionary, anti-imperialist forces, the world socialist community of nations, the working-class and democratic movement in the developed capitalist countries, the national liberation movement. This international solidarity embodies the Leninist slogan "Workers of the world and oppressed nations, unite!"

---

[1] Karl Marx and Friedrich Engels, *Works*, vol. 16, pp. 10–11.

Second, greater tasks are now confronting the communists and all forces loyal to the banner of internationalism. In the present situation proletarian internationalism implies united action in the struggle for consolidation and development of the socialist community of nations, for victory of proletarian revolution, for the national and social liberation of the oppressed peoples, for peace, democracy, and socialism throughout the world.

Unity of all revolutionary forces is a dictate of the times. It is indispensable for accomplishing the great tasks facing mankind in our day and the tasks confronting every national contingent of the working-class movement. Delivery of mankind from the danger of nuclear holocaust, complete liberation of nations from all forms of colonial dependence and their advance along the path of social progress, struggle for the triumph of socialism—all these tasks imperatively demand solidarity of the working class, unity of all working people and the oppressed nations.

One of the most salient characteristics of the present epoch is the fact that the transition to socialism is concurrent with the collapse of the colonial system, with the national liberation movement of the peoples making up two-thirds of humanity. This, of course, is not a chance coincidence. The revolutionary movement of the proletariat that has lent a powerful momentum to the struggle of the oppressed nations and the victories of the working class have laid the ground-work for success in this struggle.

It is indisputable that in our day the national factor has grown in both ideology and politics into an important force, which the communists cannot ignore. Our opponents have even started to allege that nationalism is destined to become a dam that will obstruct the further advance of communism.

These expectations of the anti-communists, however, are not bound to come true. An in-depth analysis of the social processes in our day leads one to conclude that the national factors operate by no means to the detriments of communism or in opposition to the ideas of international solidarity.

What processes dictate the need for consideration of the national factors in ideology and politics? These are primarily the dis-integration of colonialism, the emergence and development of scores of newly-independent states formerly oppressed by imperialism. These are, further, the upsurge of national sentiments in independent capitalist countries more advanced economically, whose sovereignty is threatened by large imperialist predators. These are, finally, the processes involved in the advancement and development of socialist nations, the consolidation of the independence and sovereignty of socialist countries.

All these are not only national but also social processes. They are generated by the struggle between social classes and social systems which determines the course of history, are interlocked with and influenced by this struggle and at the same time influence it themselves. The growth of the significance of the national elements in ideology and politics goes in the main along the same lines as the intensification of the social processes leading to the abolition of imperialism and the triumph of socialism, that is to the international-ist objectives pursued by the communists.

Naturally, these trends do not invariably coincide either in ideol-ogy or in politics. In certain cases they may even run counter to one another. Different classes have always attached different meanings to national tasks and national interests. The working class sees the supreme embodiment of national interests in abolishing capitalism in its country gaining the status of the nation's leading force, spearhead-ing the struggle to build a new society, in which the ideals of social and national liberation will triumph. The reactionary classes substituting their own selfish interests for common national interests seek to take the edge off the working people's class struggle and preserve the system of capitalist exploitation.

The struggle to make the ideology of the masses reflect the inter-ests of the working, patriotic majority of each nation against sub-stitution of nationalistic ambitions for national goals is associated with the actions of various social forces not only inside each country but also on a worldwide scale. Faced by a powerful upsurge of the national liberation movement today, the *bourgeoisie* is going out of its way to canalize the national movement in the direction of ethnic and racial strife, to divert it from its genuine task, that of national renascence, which is possibly only on a basis of social progress. The communists deem it their duty to struggle against any attempt to oppose national to social tasks, against any manifestation of racist, chauvinistic ideology.

The Marxist–Leninists have a totally different attitude to the national ideology expressing the people's legitimate aspirations towards liberation from all forms of ethnic oppression, primarily from colonialism and neocolonialism; this liberation improves the position of the working people in the countries concerned.

The unprecedented growth of the national liberation movement in the postwar period, the entry of scores of Asian, African and Latin American peoples on the path of independence, have naturally aroused a tremendous upsurge of national feeling, national pride, national self-awareness, a striving to consolidate national sovereignty, economic and political independence.

The Marxist–Leninists not only support the people's freedom struggle but also indicate the right way of securing final victory in the struggle for national independence: the way of social progress, of socialism. At the same time, the communists differentiate between the lawful aspirations of nations towards freedom, their efforts to strengthen their sovereignty and independence from the nationalism of reactionary forces in Asia, Africa, and Latin America.

The communists support whatever is progressive in the national liberation movement of the peoples of Asia, Africa, and Latin America. They are in favour of a strong alliance with this movement.

The Marxist–Leninists proceed from the premise that this alliance is of worldwide historic significance, since unity of all revolutionary forces today is not only indispensable for bringing to completion the tasks of national liberation, but is crucial to the destiny of the entire world revolutionary process.

The question of attitude to the national liberation movement is closely related to the multi-millioned allies of the working class in the struggle against international imperialism, for socialism.

Lenin regarded an alliance between the working class and the peasantry as the most crucial question of socialist revolution in Russia and world revolution in general. It was primarily because our Party successfully preserved and consolidated the proletariat's alliance with the peasantry that socialism has triumphed in our country.

In the present situation the working class is confronted on a worldwide scale by the problem of winning the sympathies of the peasantry as an ally in the struggle against imperialism. When the Soviet Union and other fraternal socialist countries, the communists of the world, render constant and all-round assistance to the revolutionary national liberation movement they are solving, in effect, the very same gigantic problem Lenin referred to in the twenties, since it is a matter of assistance to countries with a predominantly peasant population.

Today many areas of the world which have freed themselves from capitalism are, as it were, a giant social laboratory for evolving new forms of social life, for mapping out new ways of political and economic transformations. The struggle for national liberation is increasingly interlocked with the aspirations of the masses towards socialist ideals.

The different conditions of life, the distinctive historical path, traditions, and culture of a people find expression in a wide variety of ideological trends, a peculiar combination of national self-awareness with concepts of socialism. These concepts are in many ways discrepant with scientific communism. The communists, however, are by no means doctrinaires. They have no intention whatsoever to excommunicate other progressive parties and revolutionary forces from participation in the advance towards socialism.

The Marxist–Leninists do not seek to emphasize the difference between scientific socialism and the spontaneous gravitation of the masses toward socialism. While being aware of this difference, they bring to light and underscore the common interests which unite the socialist aspirations of the progressive workers and all democratic national forces, facilitating the latter's transition to the positions of proletarian, scientific socialism.

The growing part played by the national factor in the social life of the people has faced the international communist movement with the task of making a thorough analysis of its various manifestations, of advancing such slogans that would express the aspirations of the masses to strengthen their national independence and would stimulate their determination to advance along the road of social progress.

The Communist parties can successfully head the struggle of the peoples for victory of socialist revolution if they operate as a truly national force. This refers not only to the Communist parties in the

Asian, African, and Latin American countries, but also those in developed capitalist countries. In these countries the aggravation of social contradictions inevitably leads to isolation of the monopoly circles, which are opposed by joint actions of not only the workers but also other social strata, such as the peasantry, the petty and middle *bourgeoisie*, and the intelligentsia. The greater part of society in these countries is interested in restricting the power of the monopolies, in defence and widening of democratic freedoms, which are under attack from the monopolists, in the maintenance of peace. This holds out favourable opportunities for united action by the communists jointly with the socialists and other democratic parties and sets a broad social stage for a struggle for transformations extending beyond the framework of conventional reforms.

The entire course of historical development, particularly during the last few decades, indicates that in the capitalist countries the social tasks of the working class, by winning support from the mass of the people, increasingly acquire a common national character. At the same time, it is perfectly obvious to the communists that truly national tasks cannot be successfully fulfilled in isolation from the solution of international problems, that the national interests of every people cannot be separated from the interests of all progressive mankind.

The Marxist–Leninists believe that correct interpretation and application of the principle of proletarian internationalism makes it possible to meet the national requirements of any party and any section of the working people while preserving the unity of the communist movement and all revolutionary forces. This is precisely the kind of organic harmony required by the immediate tasks of the revolutionary movement.

The need for such harmony has been thrown into salient relief by the struggle for peace and peaceful coexistence of countries belonging to different social systems. Today, when enormous nuclear weapons arsenals have been built up and war would inevitably wipe out whole nations the preservation and strengthening of international peace has become the basic prerequisite for solving any national task. For a people to be able to resolve its national and social problems, it must above all display concern for preserving peace on earth, and this cannot be achieved otherwise than by adding its efforts to those of all other nations.

This holds true of another crucial task of the revolutionary movement, one of struggle against imperialism and colonialism. In spite of the bitter conflicts rending apart the imperialist camp, it comes out on the whole as a united force in the struggle against the revolutionary movement. Can one, indeed, seriously expect to defeat this reactionary force by scattered actions, without reliance on internationalist support from one's class comrades pursuing the same objectives? Obviously not. According to Marx, such separate actions are bound to end in failure. If the Marxists had not sacredly followed this behest of their teachers, there would not have been on earth today either a world socialist system or scores of young states which have freed themselves from colonial dependence, and imperialism would have held, as before, unchallenged sway over the international arena.

International unity of action is particularly vital to the struggle for socialism. The securing of favourable international conditions for the working class to come to power, defence of the independence of the socialist states against imperialist aggression, and the very development of new social relations are impossible without support from world socialism and the use of its experience.

If a working-class party in an effort to assert itself as a national force focused its attention exclusively on the fulfilment of national tasks and refused to take part in collective actions and actions of solidarity, it would wittingly or unwittingly oppose its perfectly just desire to act as a national force to its internationalist duty, to the common cause of the working class. It is extremely doubtful that in this way a working-class party can strengthen its ties with the masses and enhance its prestige in the country. Affiliation with the great world communist movement is the basic source of the prestige enjoyed by the Marxist–Leninist parties. A proletarian party cannot become an influential national force if it retreats into its shell, evades fundamental problems that can be solved only within the ranks of the international revolutionary movement, in common with the fraternal parties. He who attempted in one form or another to isolate himself from the communist movement, from socialism in being with all its achievements and difficulties, would of necessity dissociate himself from future triumphs of communism and betray his own future.

Concentration of efforts on a quest for new ways and means of securing an organic harmony between national and international interests is an exceptionally important task today.

Revolutionary practice and the experience of revolutionary struggle show that united action, and that solidarity of all democratic and progressive forces is the main political weapon of the working people, and that genuine internationalism is the decisive prerequisite for realizing the national aspirations of every people. This is the position that has always been consistently upheld by the Communist Party of the Soviet Union.

The Soviet communists believe that it is their internationalist duty to fulfil successfully the programme of communist construction and thereby to score new triumphs in the competition against socialism in all fields of life.

The CPSU deems it its internationalist duty to make its experience in political and economic work available to the Communist parties and young national states.

Along with the other fraternal parties, our Party takes whatever steps are necessary to strengthen the unity and cohesion of the socialist nations, to promote international friendship and co-operation, to advance the principles of socialist internationalism, the basis for relations between the socialist countries.

PROLETARIAN INTERNATIONALISM AND
THE WORLD SOCIALIST SYSTEM

Co-operation between nations which have opted for socialism has assumed special significance today. Following the growth of socialism beyond the limits of only one state, international relations between national contingents of the working class have turned today into inter-state relations, while political and ideological co-operation between the fraternal parties has been advanced to a higher stage and supplemented with economic co-operation between socialist countries. All this has served to strengthen the international ties between the fraternal parties and peoples which have taken the socialist road. At the same time, a number of new problems, which

ASW-C

have never yet been encountered by the revolutionary movement, have arisen in this field.

How can the national, state interests of each socialist country be harmonized with the interests of the entire community of socialist nations? How can the interests of individual socialist states be harmonized? How can the turbulent stream of enhanced national self-awareness associated with successes in socialist construction be directed along the path of socialist internationalism? These questions have been posed by the realities of life. The destiny of world socialism, mankind's future, largely depends on the right answers to them. The desire of the world's working people to see a model of truly new relations among nations in the socialist community lends added importance to the fulfilment of these tasks.

Reflecting on the ways of development of a socialist union of nations, Lenin wrote: "We want a voluntary union of nations that would tolerate no coercion by one nation against another, a union based on complete trust, on a clear awareness of their fraternal unity and absolutely voluntary consent. Such a union cannot be achieved immediately; it is necessary to work for it with great patience and caution so as not to wreck the matter, not to cause distrust, and so as to oust the mistrust left by centuries of oppression by the landlords and the capitalists, private property and enmity generated by its division and redivision."[1]

The socialist community of nations has existed for only two decades, but it can be safely said that over this short period many of the tasks Lenin referred to have been accomplished. The community of free nations has stood the test of time and demonstrated the advantages offered to nations by socialism, by all-round co-operation among sister nations.

The close-knit military and political alliance of socialist states has erected a barrier to imperialist encroachments on their independence. The countries which have taken the socialist path since the end of the Second World War have greatly increased their industrial output and made spectacular progress in all sectors of the national

---

[1] V. I. Lenin, *Collected Works*, vol. 40, p. 43.

economy, science and culture. Much has been done to work out various forms and methods of co-operation corresponding to the new type of international relations. This is exemplified by the Council for Mutual Economic Assistance (Comecon), which is carrying out great and fruitful work in organizing mutually beneficial co-operation between socialist countries and co-ordinating their efforts in the field of economic development.

However great the achievements in shaping new international relations, one cannot fail to see that only the initial stage has been passed, and now we are searching for ways to advance our co-operation to a new, still higher level.

It is common knowledge that in every country capitalist society has to go through a period of revolutionary transition into socialist society. This law of social development operates in a certain sense not only within the limits of individual countries but also in the sphere of relations between them. Socialist relations between states do not take shape overnight, but in a long and complex process in which the socialist countries get rid of the burden of relations inherited from capitalism and work out new standards of co-operation, *rapprochement* and relations conforming to the nature and principles of socialism.

The countries of the socialist system vary in levels of economic development and have different historical and cultural traditions. Today, when the problems of all-round economic and political co-operation have come to the forefront, these factors are assuming ever greater significance.

In the last twenty years the socialist countries have consolidated their economies, the sociopolitical foundation of the new system, and their statehood. Therefore, each socialist country has become more confident in its own strength, and their desire to play a growing part on the international scene is quite understandable. The enhanced national self-awareness of their peoples motivates the Communist parties' efforts to strengthen the national sovereignty, economic and political independence of their countries.

One may be confident that the policy of co-operation between sovereign socialist states pursued by the fraternal parties has laid a broad foundation for strengthening their genuine unity. This policy has yielded good results. However, they might have been much better if it had not been for the activities of China's leaders. The imperialists realize only too well that socialist countries separately are by no means what they are as a united force. Characteristically, in recent time the Western Ruling quarters, aware of the futility of their hopes for defeating socialism by force of arms, have been increasingly relying on economic and political methods in an effort to break up our community.

In this situation the CPSU and other Marxist–Leninist parties, loyal as they are to the principles of proletarian internationalism, deem it necessary to perfect and develop by daily efforts the fraternal relations between socialist countries. We are trying to prove not in word but in deed that historical truth is on the side of those who are upholding internationalist unity, who oppose national narrow-mindedness and selfishness, who are struggling to consolidate the community of socialist nations.

Our Party proceeds from the premise that socialist countries can achieve unity only if they strictly comply with the national interests of each socialist country. Lenin said in this context: "Our experience has firmly convinced us that only great attention to the interests of different nations removes the soil for conflicts, mutual distrust, and apprehensions of any intrigues, creates trust, particularly among the workers and peasants speaking different languages, without which peaceful relations between nations or any successful development of whatever is valuable in modern civilization is absolutely im-possible."[1] These precepts are the programme of work of the CPSU in the field of relations between socialist countries.

Experience has proved that in relations between socialist countries no policy can be pursued successfully if the complexity and at times a contradictory character of these relations are not taken into consideration. The task is evidently to do as much as possible to strengthen fraternal relations between sovereign socialist nations without attempting to go beyond existing historical conditions, with-out ignoring real processes and on the basis of consideration of the

---

[1] V. I. Lenin, *Collected Works*, vol. 45, p. 240.

interests of each country and the community as a whole.

The different levels of economic and political development, the different historical and cultural traditions, the different geographical position—all these *in toto* may lead in certain cases within the framework of our common line to differences of approach to specific problems and their solution. Such differences, of course, are undesirable and it would be better if they did not exist at all. Since they may arise, however, it is necessary to work out effective methods to overcome them. Our Party is convinced that in pursuing a correct, Marxist–Leninist policy balancing the national interests of each socialist country with those of the entire community and the communist and liberation movement different approaches to specific problems must not disturb our unity.

The vital national interests correctly interpreted, far from contradicting the common tasks of the entire socialist community of nations, can be secured more effectively when harmonized with the interests of other socialist countries and realized by their joint efforts. We are seeking unity based not on subordination of the interests of one country to those of another but on their common coals and vital, fundamental interests, within the framework of which each socialist country may have its own problems and its own interpretation of developments.

We respect the independence of every state and at the same time we are seeking to develop by joint efforts and in every way cooperation between socialist countries and to bring our peoples closer together steadily. The socialist countries are gaining experience of all-round co-operation, working out methods to overcome difficulties, and developing the principles of relations between states of the new social system.

These refer in the first place to the principles which socialism is consistently upholding on the international scene and which, naturally, must be strictly observed in relations between socialist states. These are equality, mutual respect for the sovereign rights and territorial integrity of each socialist country incompatible with interference in each other's internal affairs and with efforts of one country to impose its experience on other fraternal countries.

Along with these principles the principles stemming from the idea

of proletarian internationalism are assuming ever greater significance. This refers to the development and extension of economic and
political ties, brotherly co-operation of socialist countries in all fields
of social life on the basis of mutual advantage and respect for national
interests. This also implies co-ordination of the foreign policies of
socialist states, their joint actions on the international scene in the
interest of peace and peaceful coexistence. This, finally, means
integration of the efforts of socialist countries in the defence field,
their joint protection of the socialist gains of their peoples.

Among the principles on which the socialist community of nations
is based, great significance attaches to one of educating the peoples in
the spirit of proletarian internationalism and implementing internationalism in practice both in relations between socialist countries and
in questions of solidarity with the world revolutionary and liberation
movement.

All of us realize, of course, that the difficulty lies not in formulation of these principles, although here different approaches
and shades of opinion are evidently possible, but in preserving
and developing good relations, economic and political ties,
and strengthening the fraternal friendship among nations in spite of
possible differences of views.

This is insistently demanded by the objective interests of all
countries which have taken the socialist road. In our day the socialist
countries cannot advance their economies successfully and keep
abreast of the modern requirements of scientific and technological
progress without perfecting the international socialist division of
labour, just as all other forms of co-operation.

Consolidation of the unity of the socialist community of nations is
also facilitated by the internationalization of the way of life in the
socialist countries, by the broad exchange of experience in the most
diverse fields of economic, cultural, and party work, and in developing socialist democracy. Predicting the inevitability of certain one-
sidedness and incompleteness in concepts of socialism generated by
the experience of any one country, Lenin wrote in his time that ". . .
only through a number of attempts each of which, taken separately,
will be one-sided, will suffer from certain discrepancy, that complete
socialism will be built by the revolutionary co-operation of the work-

ers of all countries".[1] Such complete socialism taking shape before the eyes of our generation is made precisely by summing up the experience of the socialist countries.

There is only one way of disposing of the "one-sidedness" and "discrepancy" pointed out by Lenin. This is the study of the experience of others, a thorough analysis of all socialist practices in other socialist countries. The CPSU willingly takes advantage of whatever is best in the experience of building a new society in the fraternal countries. At the same time, the Soviet people are delighted, as Lenin himself would be delighted, whenever the peoples of other socialist countries, learning from our positive experience, as well as from the difficulties and setbacks we have suffered, accomplish the tasks of building a new society at lesser costs and traverse with relative ease the path the Soviet people followed for the first time in mankind's history.

The CPSU is firmly convinced that whatever difficulties may be encountered in the development of the world socialist system they will be overcome. The principles of proletarian internationalism will triumph. Our Party is doing its best, as it has always done, for this time to come as soon as possible.

PROLETARIAN INTERNATIONALISM AND THE STRUGGLE FOR STRENGTHENING THE UNITY OF THE INTERNATIONAL COMMUNIST MOVEMENT

The history of the international communist movement is a history of struggle for the triumph of proletarian internationalism, for unity and cohesion of the communists of all countries. It will be no exaggeration to say that the successes of revolutionary forces depended on how much they were united at the relevant stage of historical development. This has to be recalled today in view of the actions of China's leaders.

The vast majority of the Communist parties reaffirmed their

---

[1] V. I. Lenin, *Collected Works*, vol. 36, p. 306.

allegiance to the Declaration of 1957 and the statement of 1960, their determination to struggle for implementing the decisions of the Moscow conferences worked out by collective efforts. Many of the fraternal parties justly emphasize that in the present situation it is not enough simply to desire unity, because this desire by itself cannot remove the difficulties that have arisen. It is necessary to fight for unity and cohesion. To fight stubbornly and consistently, just as the great Lenin did. To fight for unity and cohesion means to mobilize revolutionary forces against our class enemies, to expose splitters opposed to the unity of our ranks.

Along with other Marxist–Leninist parties the CPSU regards it as its internationalist duty to prevent such developments that could weaken the unity and power of the communist movement and thus weaken all forces opposed to imperialism.

Seeking to overcome the difficulties created by the CPC leaders, our Party has more than once come forward with constructive initiatives. It is guided by Lenin's instructions to the effect that "the differences inside political parties and between political parties are usually settled not only by a polemic on questions of principle but also by the development of political life itself; it may even be more correct to say: not so much by the first as by the second".[1] The principled line of the CPSU is as follows: along with defence of the collectively charted line of the international communist movement to carry out concrete actions to direct the development of political events into the necessary channel, to show in practice by facts the correctness of our common course aimed at frustrating the aggressive ambitions of imperialism.

The successful fulfilment of the programme of communist construction in the Soviet Union, the development of its economy and culture, the restoration and further development of the Leninist principles of socialist democracy—all these are practical steps proving the historic correctness of the line mapped out by the 20th and 22nd Congresses of the CPSU.

The certain relaxation of international tensions, the treaty on termination of nuclear weapons tests in the three media, and the

---

[1] V. I. Lenin, *Collected Works*, vol. 11, p. 133.

agreement on non-deployment of nuclear weapons in outer space, the Soviet Union's assistance to young, developing states—all these are internationalism in action.

Scattered efforts of Communist parties and socialist countries cannot produce anything like the effect of the joint efforts of the fraternal countries and parties. Here one is confronted in its full dimensions by the problem of practical forms of co-ordinating the actions of the Marxist–Leninist parties in the struggle for peace, national liberation and socialism in the present concrete situation.

Experience has shown that joint actions of the fraternal parties require flexible forms and a sensitive reaction to changes in the international situation. These forms must secure unity of action on the cardinal issues and guarantee the independence and equality of all Communist parties. The realities of daily life indicate that organizational conservation in practice is no less harmful than dogmatism in theory. Nobody will evidently call in question the fact that the greater maturity of the Communist parties, their independence and equality must become the solid foundation for strengthening proletarian internationalism, for working out new effective forms of international co-operation of communists.

Genuine unity and solidarity do not contradict or rule out a wide variety of approaches and assessments, differences in views and tactics. It is indisputable, however, that the more attention we give to the infinite variety of local conditions and the concrete situation, the greater the need to secure that with all this variety and differences the general principles of Marxist–Leninist theory are upheld and developed, that in our actions we never lose sight of the prospects of our common struggle for the triumph of communism.

As far back as the seventies of the last century Marx and Engels wrote that the programme of the International was "limited to charting the main lines of the proletarian movement, whereas their theoretical elaboration is carried out under the influence of the requirements of practical struggle and as a result of an exchange of opinions within sections, in their organs, and at their congresses, where all shades of socialist convictions are allowed without discrimination."[1]

---

[1] K. Marx and F. Engels, *Works*, vol. 18, p. 31.

ASW-C*

It is precisely a "practical struggle" and a live "exchange of opinions" along the common "main lines" of the working-class movement that provide the solid foundation for strong working-class solidarity, for securing harmony between national and international tasks, for finding such forms of joint struggle that best meet the interests of the international brotherhood of communists.

Recognition of the general, cardinal principles of Marxism–Leninism, a live friendly and fruitful exchange of experience and opinions on burning problems of communist theory and practice, united action in the struggle against international imperialism, for the common goals—such are the concrete manifestations of proletarian solidarity, the international unity of communists in the present epoch.

The CPSU, just as other fraternal parties, believes that in our day the most practicable forms of pooling the efforts of the Communist parties, of reaching unanimity of views, are contacts, exchange of experience, bilateral or multilateral meetings devoted to individual problems and, finally, broad international conferences to study the general problems of the communist movement and the conclusions deriving therefrom.

In particular, the experience of the communist forums of 1957 and 1960 has proved highly valuable. It has been demonstrated in practice that under present conditions an international conference is the most fruitful form of joint creative work of the world's communists, an effective way of consolidating the fraternal parties and strengthening their unity.

The next conference of Communist and Workers' parties is also confronted by great and complex tasks. It is called upon to review the results of world development over the last few years, to assess new processes taking place in both the capitalist and socialist worlds, to map out ways of strengthening the unity of the communist movement, and to outline the common tasks facing all Marxist–Leninist parties.

Seeking to discredit the very idea of the conference, China's leaders allege that its purpose is to "excommunicate" the CPC from the international communist movement, to "expel" the PRC from the socialist camp. Such allegations misrepresent the true aims and intentions of the fraternal parties. Despite its strong disagreement with the present policy of China's leadership, the CPSU will continue to pursue its line towards unity. In this matter our Party is guided by the supreme interests of cohesion of all the main revolutionary forces of today: the socialist countries, the working class and the national liberation movements. We are convinced that if the CPC leadership displayed goodwill and a desire to reckon with the views of other parties, the exchange of opinions and the debate that would take place at the conference could help towards overcoming the existing differences on the principles of Marxism–Leninism. However, even if CPC representatives do not attend the conference, it will contribute substantially to the cohesion of the fraternal parties on the basis of Marxism–Leninism, the principles of proletarian internationalism.[1]

* * *

Marx, Engels, and Lenin regarded proletarian internationalism as the fundamental principle of building the future brotherhood and association of all nations. They linked the final solution of the nationalities problem with the triumph of communism on a world-wide scale. This is our objective, and the path we are following lies in this direction.

This path, however, is not a geometrically straight line; it is difficult and tortuous, it includes temporary retreats and passes through periods of difficulties in relations between individual socialist countries. Such is precisely the period we are living through now, when the indisputable success of world socialism and the entire world communist movement are concurrent with certain difficulties.

Our Party is confident that the communist movement will successfully overcome all these difficulties and achieve the unity of its ranks on the principles of Marxism–Leninism. This assurance is based on a sober analysis of the situation, of the concrete factors operating in spite of the aforesaid difficulties.

---

[1] The international conference of Communist and Workers' parties was held in Moscow in 1969 (Ed.).

The need for unity of the communist movement stems not from wishful thinking or good intentions, but from the objective interests of the working class of all countries and its Marxist–Leninist vanguard, from the vital interests of the peoples of the socialist countries, all progressive forces of today. Sooner or later these real, cardinal interests of the peoples will prevail over the subjective factors associated with wrong ideas of reality.

However much the imperialists may gloat over the present differences within the communist movement, whatever dismal predictions they may make about further developments, they will not succeed in stemming the great advance of the peoples towards socialism.

In our day a test of each Communist party for strength and maturity is a test for internationalism, an ability to maintain the right balance in fulfilling national and international tasks. ". . . Let us recall", Marx said, "the fundamental principle of the International: solidarity. We shall achieve the great goal we are aspiring to, if we firmly implant this vital principle among all workers in all countries.[1]"

Our Party and other fraternal Communist and Workers' parties are doing their utmost to uphold and develop this vital principle, to strengthen the unity of the world communist forces.

---

[1] Karl Marx and Friedrich Engels, *Works*, vol. 18, p. 155.

Some Problems of the Development and Consolidation of the World Socialist System

Excerpt from a speech at a meeting with members of the faculty and students of Moscow University named after Mikhail V. Lomonosov, 2 November 1966

Comrades!

Party activists, communists, and all Soviet citizens display a keen interest in the problems of the development of the world socialist system. This is a logical interest. Indeed, it is a question of the decisive force of world development, the main component of the revolutionary movement, the situation of which has a great bearing on the course of modern history.

The development of world socialism as a system of sovereign, equal, states linked by the community of their systems and the unity of their goals gives rise to a number of great and complicated problems in the fields of both practical policy and theoretical research. In this context I would like to recall Friedrich Engels's statement to the effect that "socialism since it became a science demands that it should be treated as a science, that is to be studied".[1] This statement is all the more valid in the present epoch when socialism is not only a scientific theory but also a reality, and not within the framework of one country but on an international scale.

A scientific approach to the study of the world socialist system as a socio-economic formation unknown in the past dictates the need to go further and deeper, to reveal the various processes encountered by the socialist countries without limiting oneself to an acknowledgement of

---

[1] Karl Marx, Friedrich Engels. *Works,* vol. 18, p. 499.

77

what has been achieved and a description of successes and victories. This requires a serious comprehensive analysis of the problems arising in the course of socialist construction in countries with different conditions, traditions and levels of development. There is also need for an analysis of problems arising in the course of the formation of international relations of a fundamentally new type which is taking shape within the socialist community of nations.

Today, when rich and varied experience has been accumulated, the CPSU and other fraternal parties are well equipped for the solution of these problems.

The world socialist system has existed for two decades. This is a sufficient period on which to draw some general conclusions. As you know, such conclusions are made in resolutions of the CPSU and other fraternal parties of the socialist countries, and in documents of conferences of the international communist movement.

The main conclusion is that the socialist countries have not only fully proved their viability but have also demonstrated their advantages and superiority over the system of capitalism, and have become the decisive factor in the development of human society.

It has now been proved historically that socialism can be built in all countries regardless of the differences in their concrete historical conditions and the levels of their development. The socialist revolution has been accomplished in such economically advanced countries as Czechoslovakia and the GDR, and in such countries as Vietnam and Mongolia which were in effect at the pre-capitalist stage of development.

Historical experience has confirmed that socialism has secured for all these countries the most effective way of progress in all fields — in the economy, in socio-political relations, and in culture. The achievements of the socialist countries in all spheres of social life signify the triumph of Marxism-Leninism and its great vitality.

The year 1965 was, for many socialist countries, the period of completing the five-year plans for national economic development. The economy of the socialist community of nations has been outstandingly strengthened over this period. In the period 1961-1965, the overall industrial output in the socialist countries increased 42 per cent, whereas the respective figure for the countries of the capitalist world was 33 per cent.

Today the socialist world is in possession of an enormous productive potential. In 1965, for instance, the socialist countries produced 137 million tons of steel or about 30 per cent of the world total; 1,200 million tons of coal, that is 50 per cent of the world total; 770,000 million kilowatt-hours of electricity, that is 20 per cent of the world total.

Great progress has been made in the cultural development of the peoples of the socialist countries. Today the socialist countries are ahead of advanced capitalist states in relation to the student body in schools and institutions of higher learning, the annual graduation of specialists, the network of scientific institutions and many other indicators of a similar kind.

All this proves conclusively that by abolishing the antagonism between the social character of production and private appropriation of its results, and by removing social and ethnic oppression, socialism opens up the broadest horizons for the development of productive forces for meeting the material and cultural requirements of the working people, and for their conscious historical creativity. This is the source of the strength and invincibility of socialism.

The past two decades have also demonstrated the advantages of socialism in the field of inter-state relations, where it encountered the difficult heritage of the past such as national alienation, territorial problems, the problems of national minorities and other difficulties. Despite all these, relations between the countries of the socialist community have been steadily developing for the last twenty years along the lines of growing consolidation of friendship and cooperation, and effective forms of solving international problems have been evolved. Of fundamentally great significance is the historic fact that relations of a new type have been affirmed and are developing — relations that stem from the very essence of the socialist system which has triumphed in the fraternal countries, the community of their vital interests in the struggle for the final triumph of communism. The socialist character of these relations makes it possible to combine harmoniously the strengthening of the sovereignty and independence of the socialist countries with the advantages of mutual assistance and comradely support. These relations are a practical expression of socialist internationalism.

The entry of socialism into the international arena as a system of state has brought about a change in the general situation on the world scene, and the ever more manifest superiority of the socialist forces over imperialism. We can see that along with the consolidation of world socialism the international situation more and more drastically changes in favour of the peoples struggling for independence, democracy and social progress. By rendering a great favourable influence on international relations throughout the world, socialism has helped consolidate democratic norms within them, and restricted the sphere of operation of the norms established by imperialism. The influence of socialism has put on a realistic footing the principle in international relations of settlement of conflicts not by force of arms but through negotiations on the basis of the standards of international law, the principle of the sovereignty of nations, the equality of states, and the right of nations to self-determination.

The two decades of the existence of the world socialist system have widened and multiplied the force of attraction of socialist ideas for all people. By their example, the fraternal socialist countries revolutionize the minds of the working people in the capitalist countries, inspire the fighters of the national liberation movement, and enormously facilitate their struggle for national and social liberation. The changes taking place in the so-called developing countries, that is in the states which have won their independence and liberated themselves from the colonial yoke, are especially significant. Over these years countries which have taken a stand in favour of socialist orientation have made quite considerable progress.

The increase in the force of attraction of socialist ideas has been quite important in the developed capitalist states as well. Indeed, the situation there greatly differs from that in the developing countries. The fraternal communist parties and the working class in these countries have to deal with a most experienced and powerful enemy. In these countries too the ruling classes are compelled to reckon with the socialist system as a real factor influencing the course of world development. The fact that the working class in the capitalist countries has wrested significant concessions from the bourgeoisie, both in the field of economic affairs and in the field of social legislation, has been largely due to the successes of the socialist community, the force of its example and its revolutionizing influence.

The fact that world socialism has proved its viability and its powerful force is acknowledged today not only by friends of socialism. It is also recognized in their own way by our class enemies, and not only in sociological theories but in political doctrines, and even in the tactics of the struggle against socialism.

How did imperialism receive the birth of the world socialist system? At first it had in its arsenals the doctrines of so-called "liberation" and "rolling back". For all their differences these doctrines have one thing in common — orientation on a frontal attack against socialism, and on the restoration of capitalism by force of arms, even if it came to another world war.

Imperialism today hates the socialist system no less than it hated it 15 or 20 years ago. However, it has had to admit that its hopes for turning back the course of history by force of arms have been dashed. Of course, the imperialists have not yet fully desisted from their attempts to test the strength of socialism by force of arms. One example of this is the war in Vietnam which is a victim of open US aggression.

It is also obvious that imperialism has more and more often to use a different tactic of struggle against socialism — a tactic of deep bypass manoeuvres which proceed from a tacit recognition of the fact that the new system has taken firm root in the socialist countries and can no longer be overthrown by military force. In its struggle against socialism, imperialism today increasingly reposes hopes in the notorious "evolution" of the socialist countries, in some internal changes in socialism that would satisfy the champions of capitalism, and which they are attempting to induce by means of various political, economic and ideological methods.

It is necessary, of course, to realize the dangers of these tactics, which must be exposed and opposed by our own skilful tactics. One cannot fail to see behind this change in the tactics of the imperialists the steadily growing influence of world socialism, the influence of its successes and its consolidation; nor can one fail to see that the transition to these new tactics means the acceptance by imperialism — in its own peculiar way, of course — of our challenge of peaceful competition. It is natural that in this situation the consolidation of socialism, the successful solution of the problems involved in building a new society, and the strengthening of the socialist community of nations are assuming growing significance. The contest between the two world systems must be decided not by missiles or atomic bombs, but by the laws of history and by the extent of our skill in learning them. Needless to say, we should not forget about missiles either. In view of the aggressive intentions and actions of imperialism, the Party's Central Committee and the Soviet government are taking whatever measures are necessary to strengthen our splendid Armed Forces so that their standard would conform to the demands of the international situation.

Reviewing their record of successes, their achievements and victories, the countries of the socialist community must be aware of the fact that the formation of this community is not an easy and simple matter.

Many difficulties in the path of progress in this direction are associated with the objective complexity of the very process of building a new society. The road towards socialism, Lenin pointed out, "will never be straight, it will be incredibly difficult".[1] Revolutionary transformation is implemented not only in individual elements but in all aspects of social life; the heritage of the past is overcome and the new man with the communist world outlook is raised. These breathtaking tasks are being implemented by the fraternal communist and workers' parties with the concrete national distinctions of each country in view.

The construction of a new society and the formation of relations of a new type are taking place in a situation where imperialism is going out of its way to interfere with the process of the emergence and development of the world socialist system, and is seeking to bring pressure to bear on the socialist countries to cause dissension between them.

All these complexities and difficulties, however, cannot abrogate the laws of the development of social progress, the general laws of socialist revolution and socialist construction.

Many difficulties in the construction of the world socialist system stem from the following two objective trends in its development: the

---

[1] V. I. Lenin. *Collected Works,* vol. 36, p. 47.

trend towards the integration of nations and states and the trend towards the flourishing of every nation, the growth of its national economy, the advancement of its national culture, and the consolidation of the sovereignty of the socialist countries.

We remember Lenin's statement to the effect that the path towards the integration of nations and national cultures lies across their flourishing and developing national culture. It is known that Lenin had primarily in mind nations within one state. Our experience, like the experience of other multinational socialist states, indicates that this process is not easy even within the confines of one country. All the more complex are the problems involved in relations between the peoples of sovereign states.

One must draw a clear-cut boundary line between phenomena which have points of contact but are different in their significance; between nationalism, on the one hand, and national sentiments and interests on the other. Experience has demonstrated that no working-class party in power can afford to ignore the national feelings and interests of its people. This is particularly relevant to those socialist countries which experienced ethnic oppression in one form or another in the past and where, naturally, national feelings are especially sensitive.

In many of these countries the revolutionary movement, from its very inception, had not only a social but also a national liberation orientation. Therefore, the revolution fulfilled two tasks simultaneously — the tasks of social and national liberation.

I would like to emphasise that an exacerbated national feeling is not only the product of past epochs. It is also connected with the processes occurring today. The flourishing of the national economy and culture, the strengthening of the sovereignty and independence of the fraternal countries, the growth of their prestige on the international scene, naturally entail growth of the national pride of socialist nations. This is a perfectly legitimate process. National sentiments act in such cases as an important ideological and political motive force and help the peoples to achieve success in their struggle to consolidate their independence and build a new society.

It is clear, however, that the very same soil which nourishes feelings of national identity and patriotism may, under certain circumstances, grow such monstrosities as nationalism which subordinates all other interests to the interests of the nation, narrowly and wrongly interpreted, and leads to its isolation and opposition to other nations. The historical experience of world socialism indicates that under certain circumstances nationalism may find its way into a party, and subordinate to itself its ideology and policy to a varying extent.

The fraternal parties indicate that nationalism is a real danger. It should be fought consistently, stubbornly and skilfully. It is indisputable that in this struggle our positions are quite firm, since in the socialist system the principal tendency is one of consolidation, convergence and integration of the socialist countries. This tendency expresses the most vital economic and political interests of their people. The future unquestionably belongs to this tendency, which fights its way along in the course of a difficult struggle whose progress largely depends on the correct, truly internationalist policy of the Marxist-Leninist party.

Another conclusion from the experience of the past two decades is the fact that over these years, and particularly over the most recent period, our concepts of the laws governing the construction of socialism have greatly deepened and widened. The Declaration of the Moscow Conference of 1957 formulated certain principles referring to the general laws of socialist construction. The Statement of the Conference of Representatives of Communist and Workers' Parties of 1960 points out that these general laws will be applied in reckoning with the historical distinctions of each country, and the interests of the socialist system as a whole. The theoretical and practical problems involved are the object of keen attention on the part of the Communist and Workers' parties.

This refers in the first place to the problems of the economy, and economic progress in the socialist countries. The economic reforms being implemented in most socialist countries of Europe graphically illustrate the acuteness and urgency of the problems involved in perfecting the methods of economic work, and of the management of the economy.

Taking a retrospective look at our record of achievements, we can say that the methods of economic work which were established in this country at one time and in other countries at a later date have proved their value in full. However, with the progressive change in conditions, the socialist countries turned into highly developed countries with a widely ramified economy, so that it was increasingly mandatory to link the development of the economy with the revolution in science and technology, and to improve the methods of economic management to bring them into line with these new conditions.

I will not touch on the decisions of the September 1965 plenary meeting of the CPSU Central Committee in this country, since this is a special subject. As far as the fraternal countries are concerned, I can say that the limited experience already available over the period of implementing economic reforms indicates that they are of major significance for advancing the national economy and help to fulfil the rich potentials inherent in the socialist economic system.

The new forms and methods in the economic management sphere also apply to agriculture. In this area the situation in most socialist countries is not simple. Agricultural production does not always catch up with the population's and industry's growing demands. Remaining, as before, major exporters of important items of agricultural produce, the socialist countries are compelled at the same time to import large quantities of grain and other foodstuffs. It should be noted that the measures being undertaken by the fraternal parties to advance agriculture are similar in the main with the measures defined by the March 1965 plenary meeting of the CPSU Central Committee and are being implemented in this country with great success.

Evolving new forms and methods of managing the national economy is a great contribution by the fraternal parties, illustrating their maturity, and their creative Marxist-Leninist approach to fulfilling complicated tasks advanced by the realities of life.

The 20-year-old experience of the world socialist system permits us to understand more clearly the laws of the political development of socialism, and the tasks of perfecting its political mechanism in particular.

There is no need to explain the importance of this problem. The destiny of socialism is directly and immediately dependent on the methods and direction of work in exercising the Party's leading role, the functioning of the machinery of state, and the real extent of involvement of the mass of the people in the management of the affairs of state and society. Over the last 20 years the Communist and Workers' parties have considerably increased their membership and grown stronger ideologically and politically. They constitute the vanguard of society and lead the working people in their struggle to fulfil the tasks in socialist construction.

One of the fundamental principles of the political organization of socialism is the principle of democratic centralism. In theory, everything seems clear: centralism should be combined with democracy and democracy with centralism. In practice, however, the matter is much more complicated.

Historical experience has shown that where theory and practice are united, where the centralism of political leadership is skilfully combined with the broad development of democracy and the activity and initiative of the masses, the process of development proceeds successfully.

Unfortunately, however, we occasionally witness a different picture. We have learned from our historical experience, in particular, that rigid centralisation (which is objectively indispensable under certain conditions) inevitably leads, when it is hypertrophied, to unwarranted curtailment of socialist democracy and the emergence of negative phenomena.

No less dangerous is the other extreme: underestimation of the Party's leading role in the field of economic work, in forming the communist consciousness of the masses.

Speaking generally, the results of the last two decades of our progress can be summed up in this bold conclusion: despite the difficulties and complexities inevitable in such an enormous cause, we have a full right to be proud of the successes of the socialist community and of the role it plays in the world arena today. As a result of the development and consolidation of the world socialist system realistic opportunities have been provided for solving the key problems of today in a new way, in the interest of peace, democracy and socialism.

The Statement of the Conference of Representatives of Communist and Workers' Parties of 1960 reads in part: "The main content, the main direction and the main distinctions of the historical development of human society in the modern epoch are determined by the world

socialist system, the forces struggling against imperialism, for remaking society along socialist lines''.[1]

At the same time, we cannot fail to see that many intricate problems
are still awaiting their settlement. To resolve them correctly means to
secure further accelerated development of world socialism.

The report of the CPSU Central Committee delivered at the 23rd
Party Congress by the CC CPSU General Secretary Leonid Brezhnev
stated that our relations with the communist and workers' parties of
the countries of the socialist community, with our fraternal countries,
have been enriched and have become closer and more cordial. Both in
the economic and political sphere, as well as in other areas, we have
continued as we do today, to strengthen all-round relations with our
friends; we give one another mutual support, help one another to deal
with complex political problems at home and abroad. As you know, a
great role in this field is played by official and unofficial contacts
between Party and government leaders which have become
traditional, especially during the last two years since the October 1964
plenary meeting of the CPSU Central Committee.

Now for the developments in Vietnam. The problem of Vietnam is a
cause of concern to the entire progressive humanity. The heroic
Vietnamese people are giving a condign rebuff to imperialist
aggression. In their just struggle they rely upon the all-round
assistance of the Soviet Union and other fraternal socialist countries.

As far as relations with China are concerned, the Soviet press, as
you know, keeps the Soviet public fairly fully informed of
developments in that country. Soviet information, as well as material
from other fraternal parties on the Chinese problem which is regularly
published in our press, enables one to gain a general picture of the
situation in the PRC. Therefore, I shall dwell only on a few recent
events.

You know that on October 27 of this year Peking announced tests
of a missile tipped with a nuclear warhead. We regard this as another
illustration of the fact that the leadership of China, ignoring the severe
economic situation in their country, and the enormous privations and

---

[1] *Programme Documents of the Struggle for Peace, Democracy and Socialism.*
Moscow, 1964, p. 40.

difficulties experienced by the working people of the PRC, stop at nothing to manufacture nuclear weapons.

There is another aspect of this problem which merits attention. There has been a great commotion over the tests both in China itself and in the West. The bourgeois press has also raised a provocative clamour about the fact that many Soviet cities and industrial complexes are now threatened with nuclear attack. Someone is clearly attempting to put this situation to advantage.

Within China itself, its nuclear tests are being presented as a great sensation. Numerous meetings and demonstrations are organised throughout the country where new oaths of allegiance to Chairman Mao are taken, and appeals are being voiced for "great raids" against the enemies of "Mao's ideas", for persecution of all representatives of "old culture, old ideology, old customs and old mores". The Hsinhua (New China) news agency reports from Peking with delight: "The whole city is in jubilation" — which is, it should be presumed, "atomic jubilation".

You know that the situation in China has been greatly exacerbated as a result of the "cultural revolution". However, the masterminds of the "cultural revolution" regard this as inadequate. Datsibao wall posters are calling for the setting up of an "international organization of Hungweiping (revolutionary guards)" which would propagate "Mao's ideas". It is called upon to fulfil the tasks in establishing a "united anti-imperialist, anti-revisionist front", setting up broad ties with "revolutionary youth" and disseminating "Mao Tse-tung's ideas" throughout the world and educating cadres for a "world-wide revolution".

One cannot fail to see that the "cultural revolution" is a reflection of new tendencies in the home policy of the PRC. Plans are being made in fact to exterminate, with the aid of Hungweipings, all persons who are opposed to the present leadership of China and to Mao Tse-tung personally. A smokescreen for this has been invented — the struggle against the "bourgeois degeneration" of statesmen and party executives.

I would like to say in this context that apart from the goals pursued by the organizers of the "cultural revolution" which are quite apparent — to deal a blow at the Marxist-Leninist, internationalist forces in the PRC, to suppress the growing discontent with Mao Tse-tung's policy, to cover up the debacles in foreign and home policies suffered by China as a result of the adventurist line of its leadership in the last few years, and to establish their unchallenged rule — there is another highly important aspect of the matter which is relevant not only to China but also to all Communist parties and, primarily, other socialist countries. Thus, the so-called "cultural revolution" lays the groundwork not only for Peking's future policy at home but also for a foreign policy which is dangerous to the cause of peace and socialism.

What is taking place in China today has not appeared overnight. These events have a pre-history of many years, connected with the distinctive conditions in which the Communist Party of China emerged and developed. They are associated with the specific conditions in which the Chinese revolution developed. Finally, the fact that many leaders of the Communist Party of China and Mao Tse-tung himself have always been weakly linked with the international working class movement and accepted Marxism-Leninism with reservations. This has been more than once mentioned before.

I must say here that we have not enough material to give an exhaustive answer to the question of the character of the CPC and the essence of present-day Chinese society: also, the developments taking place there have not yet come to a close. However, one can now say that the most striking distinction of Chinese society is the clear-cut contradiction and struggle between the Marxist-Leninist, internationalist forces and the petty bourgeois, nationalistic forces, between socialist and anti-socialist tendencies. On the one hand, there is public ownership of the means of production in town and country, a sincere aspiration of the masses towards socialism, and the existence within the CPC of forces opposed to Mao Tse-tung's adventurist line. The fact that many communists adhere to such a stand is shown, in particular, by the wide scope of the current purges. Finally, it is evidenced by the fact of the existence of the world socialist system, which objectively influences the situation in China. All these factors objectively provide the possibility for China's further progress along the road towards socialism.

On the other hand, we are witnessing distinct symptoms of petty bourgeois anarchy increasingly invading the CPC, symptoms of a nationalist degeneration of the Maoist clique who have usurped power. Relying on the army and taking advantage of the extreme backwardness and a certain conservatism of Chinese society, the CPC leaders are clearly bent on replacing the principles of scientific socialism with Maoist ideology called upon to substantiate theoretically and to sanctify complete suppression of socialist democracy and the establishment of unchallenged supremacy by the ruling Maoist clique for the purpose of implementing its nationalistic, great-power, hegemonistic ambitions.

The development and exacerbation of these contradictions have been clearly in evidence during the last decade. From this point of view the "cultural revolution" is one of the principal stages in the harsh internal struggle between socialist and anti-socialist, petty bourgeois, tendencies. The 11th plenary meeting of the CPC Central Committee has shown that the latter have taken the upper hand. Can one say, however, that the nationalistic leadership have already nullified all the gains of the Chinese revolution and radically changed the entire system of social relations in China? No, of course not; although we must clearly see that the policy pursued by the present leaders of the PRC and the CPC is a real threat to the achievements of socialism, a threat which affects today — and this should be emphasized — not only individual "components" of the socialist social organism but its essence and nature as a whole.

What course will developments take in the future? If the Maoist clique succeeds in its efforts to fortify the present political line for a long time, if it continues its retreat from the principles of Marxism-Leninism and scientific socialism, we may perhaps become witnesses to a historical regression in the development of Chinese society. I believe, however, that such a prospect is by no means inevitable. Evidently there exist healthy forces in China.

In our policy we must take account of all opportunities, possibilities and variants and be prepared for any turn of events.

What are the fundamental principles of our policy in relation to China at the present stage?

On the one hand, in the situation prevailing we cannot but oppose the anti-socialist policy pursued by the Maoist clique leadership. Its policy is causing harm to the entire communist movement, and to world socialism as a whole. What is more, it confronts us with grave problems both in the context of our defence of our national interests and in the context of national defence.

On the other hand, we must simultaneously struggle for the Communist Party of China, for People's China, for that country adhering to the positions of socialism, for socialism to grow stronger and win victory there, for normalising relations with China. This is a cause of enormous significance for both our countries, and for the interests of world socialism and the communist movement.

It is emphasised in the documents of the 23rd CPSU Congress that continued development of cooperation with the socialist countries and consolidation of the world socialist system are one of the main directions of the foreign policy pursued by the Party and the Soviet state. This policy is being unswervingly carried into effect. The CPSU is doing everything in its power in order that the world socialist system may gain in strength and score new triumphs.

In developing its cooperation with the fraternal countries our Party has always attached, as it does today, exceptional significance to further improvement of its forms and methods.

In his report at the 23rd Congress of the CPSU the General Secretary of the CPSU Central Committee Leonid Brezhnev pointed out that "in the process of their development the countries of the socialist system constantly meet with new problems which are generated by the realities of life with all their complexities and variety. Needless to say, there is not nor can there be ready-made solutions to all these problems. Therefore, the development of the world socialist system constantly requires a creative approach to problems on the time-tested basis of Marxism-Leninism and requires an exchange of experience and opinion."[1]

In this connection I would like to dwell on two closely interconnected tasks which are being fulfilled by our Party jointly with the fraternal parties of the socialist countries.

The first is the task of further improving the system of mutual relations between the socialist countries.

The second task is to consolidate the material foundation for the cohesion of the socialist countries in the form of a well-adjusted

---

[1] L. I. Brezhnev. *Following Lenin's Course,* Moscow, 1973, vol. 1, p. 269.

mechanism of bilateral and multilateral economic ties and cooperation, convergence and integration of their national economies.

I shall first of all touch on the continued perfection of the system of mutual relations between socialist countries. I want to make a reservation at once that this presentation of the question does not mean that we are now building them from scratch. No, much has already been done in this area. It may even be claimed that the foundation for this system has already been laid. At the same time, we must clearly realize that this is a long-lasting process which is still far from completion.

What are the initial premises we are guided by here?

In short, the system of relations within the world socialist community must secure practical unity of action and coordination of policy in the solution of the cardinal problems of today and at the same time leave definite leeway for a policy aimed at protecting the specific interests of each country. All countries, including the Soviet Union, have an interest in establishing such a system.

There is another important premise for our policy in the socialist community. It is being implemented in the sphere of relations between sovereign states. We often say quite correctly that we are linked by the bonds of friendship and brotherhood. We emphasise at the same time that it is a question of sovereign states and sovereign parties which are responsible primarily to their own peoples. It is precisely from these positions that the CPSU develops its relations with the fraternal parties of the socialist countries.

Relying on these initial premises, one can more clearly understand the basic, central ideas of the activities of our Party and state which are aimed at perfecting the system of relations within the socialist community of nations.

In developing our relations with the socialist countries we proceed from the principle that our policy must take account of certain distinctions between them, the specific features of their positions on specified problems, the specific features of their policies and other factors.

Another important idea of our Party's policy within the socialist community is that relations between socialist countries must be based on a strictly legal contractual foundation. The system of treaty relations is by no means becoming extinct; it is not a survival of the past; on the contrary, other socialist countries just as much as ourselves are greatly interested in its consolidation.

Over the last two years, great work has been carried out in strengthening the state foundation of our relations with the fraternal countries. The activities of the Warsaw Treaty Organization have been appreciably galvanized. Our country has renewed a series of state treaties, such as those with Mongolia and Poland. We are determined to go ahead in this direction.

The CPSU and other fraternal parties regard perfection of the mechanism of coordination of policy of the socialist countries as an important practical task. Such a mechanism, if it is well adjusted and operates effectively, allows defence of the common interests of socialism in the world arena with greater success.

Over the last two years especially great work has been carried out in this direction. All of you know that permanent business meetings and contacts, often unofficial ones, have been affirmed as a norm in our relations. Such work is very important and yields good practical results. It can be safely said that this is one of the methods which have led to the consolidation of our relations and to deeper mutual understanding between us.

Inter-party ties between the CPSU and other Marxist-Leninist parties have been developed considerably and a broad exchange of practical experience is under way. Along with bilateral meetings, multilateral metings have come to be used on a broader scale, particularly within the framework of the Warsaw Treaty.

A highly important element in the Party's policy of developing and consolidating the world socialist system is working out methods and norms which make it possible to settle differences without extending beyond the limits of normal relations between fraternal parties and countries.

In the initial period of the formation of the world socialist system little experience was available in this field to us and to our friends. Today such experience does exist and the right conclusions are drawn from it. Whenever difficulties are encountered we find it easier to define ways of eliminating them. In the field of relations between socialist countries special tact, attention, patient work and comradely discussions are indispensable. In isolated cases it is necessary to bide one's time, which helps resolve some problems better than an open polemic would.

The second task of our policy within the socialist community is, as pointed out above, to consolidate the economic foundation for its cohesion and for integrating the economies of the socialist countries. We all know that economic factors are of enormous significance in all international relations. They cannot but influence relations within the world socialist system as well. In consolidating our economic ties with the socialist countries we are seeking to perfect the system of relations so that it will give not only purely economic benefits but also reinforce materially the policy of internationalism, and the sentiments of proletarian solidarity.

The significance of this cause is truly enormous. Today successful and rapid development of any country is inconceivable without broad international ties, without the division of labour and specialization of production. Such is the requirement dictated by the development of productive forces at the present stage. Each one of the fraternal socialist countries is not in a position to build up an all-embracing economy, or to develop all sectors, especially in a situation of rapid scientific and technological progress which requires specialization and great capital investments in new sectors which make production profitable only with mass-scale manufacture of products. It is clear that autarchy is unthinkable here.

Thus, the future of the entire world socialist system largely depends in the final analysis on the further perfection of the system of economic ties and cooperation securing a normal life and broad prospects of development for all socialist countries. This refers to a system of mutually beneficial relations which would satisfy each of the socialist countries and help build communism.

On the whole, our economic relations with the fraternal socialist countries are beneficial both to our partners and to our own country.

The way of enhancing the effectiveness of our economic ties is primarily a deepening of the division of labour, perfection of specialization and cooperation in production.

We are now doing much work to accomplish these tasks and have a record of success in this field.

Of course, to deepen the international division of labour is not a simple matter. It is complicated by certain difficulties, both of an objective character associated with the complexity of this process and subjective factors associated with overcoming autarchic tendencies which still make themselves felt in isolated cases.

I would like to say in this context that although our state policy is alien to autarchic tendencies, such sentiments occasionally become manifest among individual executives. Of course, we can prove and have already proved to the whole world that our country is in a position to manufacture any machine and any product. Is it necessary, however? This is an economic and political problem and by solving it practically we must always be guided by economic interests as well as by political considerations connected with our relations with the fraternal countries.

The consolidation and development of the world socialist system is a matter of enormous importance. Further successes of the world revolutionary process will depend to a considerable extent on how matters will be handled within the socialist community of nations.

At the 23rd CPSU Congress General Secretary Brezhnev stated: "The Central Committee of the CPSU has put forward as one of the main directions of the foreign policy of the Party and the Soviet state in the future as well the development and consolidation of ideological, political, and organizational ties with the communist parties of all socialist countries on the principles of Marxism-Leninism, the development and consolidation of the political, economic and other ties of the USSR with the socialist states, all-round assistance and promotion of the cohesion of the socialist community, the strengthening of its power and influence. The CPSU will do its utmost to make the world socialist system ever stronger and score new triumphs."[1]

All of you know what great significance the Party attaches to the education of Soviet citizens in the spirit of socialist internationalism. All of you are also aware of the fact that this task cannot be fulfilled with appeals alone and that education by concrete, visible deeds is far more effective.

---

[1] L. I. Brezhnev. *Following Lenin's Course,* Vol. 1, p. 273.

In view of the character of this audience I would like to say in conclusion a few words about what the CPSU Central Committee is entitled to expect from our research workers.

First of all, a profound and objective analysis of the processes taking place within the world socialist system. There is much work in store here. This is important and responsible work whose results must constitute the scientific foundation for planning the political line of the Party.

It is no less important to intensify in all directions the study and assimilation of positive experience accumulated by our friends. I wish to emphasize that in this case I have in mind not only an exchange of scientific and technological achievements but also what may be called "social experience", that is the forms and methods of organizing social life.

At one time the only "supplier" of such experience was our country and our party. Now the situation has changed. Today we can ourselves find much of interest and use in the practices of the fraternal socialist countries. The task is to make such quests more active.

Consolidation of the socialist community of nations is an important cause to which all of us can and must make an effective contribution. This is our common cause and the Central Committee is confident that this is precisely the way it is interpreted by our Party, all communists, and all Soviet citizens.

Soviet State Security Service:
Fifty Years

**Report at the anniversary meeting in the
Kremlin Palace of Congresses
20 December 1967**

Comrades,

All of us have been deeply moved by the message of greetings to the state security service from the Central Committee of the CPSU, the Presidium of the USSR Supreme Soviet and the USSR Council of Ministers. A large group of state security servicemen have been decorated by the government in acknowledgement of its high appreciation of their work. Allow me to express on behalf of the state security servicemen our heartfelt thanks to the Communist Party and the Soviet Government for their trust and high assessment of our work and to assure them that the Soviet security men will spare no efforts to fulfil their duty to this great country.

In the annals of world history the year 1967 will always have a distinctive place as the year of the fiftieth anniversary of the October Revolution, which ushered in a new, communist era for mankind.

The celebration of the fiftieth anniversary of the October Revolution, which became a striking demonstration of the indissoluble unity of the Soviet people, has proved again that the cause of the October Revolution, of the Communist Party, has become a matter of vital concern to all Soviet people; that the Soviet Union, relying on its vast experience of struggle and construction, is confidently looking to the future.

The celebration of this anniversary, which also became a review of the triumphs of the new social system, has shown again that the ideas of Marxism-Leninism, of the October Revolution, remain as in the past the mainspring of social progress throughout the world, that their victorious march over the planet is irresistible.

ASW-D

The current year opens a veritable galaxy of red-letter days, each of which is a milestone in the history of the Soviet state. Following the fiftieth anniversary of the Soviet militia and the Soviet judiciary system, the state security service is marking its fiftieth anniversary today, and in two months from now we shall be honouring the heroic Soviet Army.

All these splendid dates in the history of the Soviet state are closely interconnected and have a profound meaning. From the early days of its existence Soviet government established institutions called upon to safeguard and preserve the gains of the world's first victorious revolution of workers and peasants.

"A revolution is worth anything only if it can defend itself", Lenin said.[1] The half-a-century history of the Soviet state has fully borne out the truth of this statement. All this time the Soviet people were not only building a new, socialist world, but they had to display great vigilance, heroism and self-sacrifice to defend their state against attacks from their internal and foreign enemies. Soviet government was established by the working class, all the working people of this country in a struggle against the old order. This government was consolidated and developed and won remarkable victories largely because the Leninist Party had taught the masses to defend and protect their achievements.

The Soviet people have traversed a heroic path. The state security service has always been by their side on this path. It takes its origin from Cheka, which was the acronym of the All-Russia Extraordinary Commission for Struggle Against Counterrevolution and Sabotage, instituted on Lenin's initiative on December 20, 1917. The Party and people entrusted Cheka to stand guard over the gains of the October Revolution. That was the beginning of the fighting record of Cheka, which became a veritable sword and shield of the October Revolution. Since then the state security service has been tirelessly at work to fulfil its difficult and honourable duties.

The Bolsheviks came to power because they had experience in the class struggle and were equipped with the most advanced and the only correct theory of social development — Marxism-Leninism. Of course, no theory, even the most profound one, could give the answer

---

[1] V. I. Lenin. *Collected Works,* vol. 37, p. 122.

to all the problems arising in the course of the country's revolutionary remaking. It was necessary to experiment, to search for new ways, and in certain cases to remake what had already been done, and to return again and again to problems that seemed to have been finally resolved. One thing, however, was clear to the Bolsheviks: without strong political power the working class would be unable to perform its historic mission of worldwide significance: to build socialism. This power, which Marx called the dictatorship of the proletariat, and which was established in this country by the victorious socialist revolution, was to become and really became the main lever the working class and all working people of Soviet Russia possessed in the bitter fighting against the old world and to build a new, socialist world.

Lenin repeatedly emphasized that the main task facing the dictatorship of the proletariat was one of construction. To build up socialist industry and socialist agriculture, to carry out a cultural revolution, to remake on socialist principles the entire system of social relations — such were the key directions of the gigantic drive for socialism that was launched in the vast expanses of this country. This drive, however, was fiercely opposed by our class enemies, armed counter-revolutionaries and foreign interventionists.

Our socialist revolution required at the time such an institution of the dictatorship of the proletariat that could lay bare counterrevolutionary conspiracies and suppress any intrigues of counterrevolution by a "reprisal, relentless, prompt, immediate and based on the sympathy of the workers and peasants", as Lenin put it.[1] Cheka was called upon to perform precisely these functions.

It was set up to defend the revolution against the enemies and to suppress the resistance of the exploiter classes which opposed the people. Its activities were in complete accord with the whole democratic spirit of Soviet government and were totally subordinated to the interests of the working people, and to the tasks of the struggle for socialism.

Lenin clearly defined the fundamental principles of Cheka's work: utter dedication to the revolutionary cause, close links with the people, unshakeable loyalty to the Party and Soviet government, staunchness in the struggle against the class enemies, and lofty pro-

---

[1] V. I. Lenin. *Collected Works,* vol. 44, p. 327.

letarian humanism. These democratic principles have always been and remain the basis for the activities of the Soviet state security service.

Since the Party's Central Committee attached special significance to safeguarding the achievements of the October Revolution, it staffed Cheka with Veteran Party cadres. Its first Chairman was Felix Dzerzhinsky, a prominent Party leader and a loyal Leninist with a gruelling record of underground work, imprisonment and hard labour, a man infinitely dedicated to revolution and intransigent to its enemies. Such remarkable Party veterans as V. R. Menzhinsky, M. S. Uritsky, J. C. Peters, M. S. Kedrov, I. K. Ksenofontov, V. A. Avanesov, M. J. Lacis, I. S. Unschlicht, S. G. Uralov, J. J. Buikis and many others who made up the Bolshevik core of the state security service worked in Cheka at different times.

The enemies of the revolution responded to the establishment of Cheka with malicious lies and slander. They had quickly learned that the revolutionary sword of justice in the hands of the Party struck accurately and inexorably. In their combat against the experienced secret services of the imperialist powers and the White Guards' underground the men of Cheka were the victors and lived up to the trust of the Party and people.

In 1918 Cheka rounded up the counterrevolutionary organization led by the well-known Socialist-Revolutionary terrorist Boris Savinkov, who was linked with the British and French intelligence services. In the same year Cheka exposed and dealt with the conspiracy headed by R. H. B. Lockhart, the British Consul General in Moscow, who had attempted to bribe the Kremlin guards and engineer a counter-revolutionary coup d'etat. A year later Cheka wiped out the so-called "National Centre" in Moscow, which was associated with the counter-revolutionary forces under General Denikin, and then the "Tactical Centre" of espionage in Petrograd. The long succession of defeats of the counter-revolution and its foreign patrons in their war against Soviet government and its punitive arm extends from the abortive Lockhart conspiracy, in which the French and American envoys were also implicated, to the total rout of various White Guard organizations.

A splendid cohort of security servicemen inspired by the ideals of the October Revolution have matured and steeled themselves in the

struggle against the enemies of Soviet power. These men were the pro-
totype of the image of the Cheka serviceman admired by the people —
a dedicated revolutionary of sterling integrity and great courage, intransigent to the enemies, inflexible in matters of duty, humane and
ready for self-sacrifice for the people's cause to which his whole life is
devoted.

State security servicemen deem it their sacred duty to live up to this
unstained and noble image in all their activities.

The transition from the Civil War to peace time required a radical
reorganization of the work of all Party and government bodies. The
state security service was also to redirect its efforts to meet the exigen-
cies of the new situation. Security servicemen and special-purpose
troops were still fighting armed gangs of criminals, the counterrevolutionary bands in Tambov region, the kulak[1] revolts in Siberia, the
"basmach" bands in Central Asia. The work in exposing and tracking
down spies of imperialist powers also needed a good deal of attention.

At the same time, the agencies of Cheka, later superseded by
OGPU,[2] took a direct part in the efforts to solve a number of acute
economic and social problems. They actively joined in the struggle
against famine and economic dislocation, the bottlenecks in the
transport services, helped to fight typhus epidemics and to procure
foodstuffs and fuel.

The campaign to ease the plight of homeless waifs throughout the
country is an unforgettable page in the history of Cheka-OGPU. That
was a task of unprecedented difficulty and enormous significance for
the country. The Soviet Republic had inherited from the war a large
army of homeless and hungry orphans, many with a record of
antisocial behaviour.

The extraordinary commissions as agencies of the dictatorship of
the proletariat, a Cheka circular said, are called upon to "give Soviet
government whatever assistance they can in its efforts to protect and
provide for the children . . . Concern for the children is the most effective means of wiping out counterrevolution."

Servicemen of Cheka saved thousands upon thousands of children

---

[1] Kulak (Russ.) A wealthy peasant employing farm hands (Translator).

[2] OGPU. The Russian acronym for the Integrated State Political Administration
(Translator).

from death by starvation. On its initiative hundreds of children's homes, orphanages and work communes were set up throughout the country, where former homeless waifs were surrounded with care and attention and raised as fully-fledged Soviet citizens.

As we recall today these and many other episodes from the history of Cheka, we go back in thought to the humanistic sources in the work of Soviet state security agencies. Today the situation is different, and the tasks facing us are, naturally, different, too. However, the active and purposeful communist humanism, the awareness on the part of every state security serviceman of his duty to protect Soviet citizens, their peaceful work, their safety and tranquility, have been and remain the solid foundation of all activities of the state security service.

As the foundations for socialism in this country were gradually consolidated, the requisite conditions developed for changing the character of the activities of the state security service. Concurrent with the abolition of the hostile classes the emphasis was shifted more and more from suppression of the resistance of the class enemies at home to the struggle against enemies operating from abroad. In the prewar period, the state security service had no task more important than that of dealing with the intrigues of the intelligence services and other subversive activities of Nazi Germany and militarist Japan. The state security service deserves much of the credit for their failure to disorganize the Soviet people.

During the Second World War the state security service was geared to the Soviet war effort. The Soviet frontier guards took the first blows from the invaders and fought them to the last ditch, inscribing quite a few heroic pages and exploits of self-sacrifice in the war record. Aided by the Soviet High Command and the political agencies of the Soviet Army, Navy and Air Force, the military counter-intelligence effectively neutralized enemy spies, saboteurs and terrorists and guarded the operational plans of the Soviet High Command against the enemy.

Soviet intelligence agents fearlessly worked deep in the enemy rear. The courage and presence of mind of the celebrated Soviet intelligence men, Heroes of the Soviet Union N. I. Kuznetsov, I. D. Kudri, V. I. Molodtsov, V. A. Lyagin, S. I. Solntsev, F. F. Ozmitel and many other secret service officers who operated in the midst of the enemy have become legendary. The deep raids behind the enemy lines of the guerrilla units under the command of Heroes of the Soviet Union D. N. Medvedev, K. P. Orlovsky, M. S. Prudnikov and I. A. Prokopyuk, who were also officers of the state security service, will never be forgotten.

Performing their sacred duty to this country quite a few state security servicemen laid down their lives in fighting its enemies. Their names will live forever in the people's memory.

The state security service has traversed a long and difficult path. It has made a valuable contribution to the cause of defence of the achievements of the Revolution, to socialist construction. Today we speak with lawful pride of the splendid deeds of the men committed by the Party and people to guard the security of the Soviet State.

Taking a look at the history of the Soviet state security service, we can see clearly that success in their activities was associated primarily with their strict abidance by Leninist principles. Only on this foundation and under the leadership of the Party is it possible to fulfil effectively the tasks of safeguarding the interests of the socialist state.

Nor do we have a right to forget the time when the political adventurers who had wormed their way into key positions in the state security service attempted to lead it astray from Party control, to isolate it from the people, and committed acts of lawlessness, which caused grave harm to the interests of the State, the Soviet people, and the security service itself.

Over the last few years the Party has taken vigorous steps to strengthen socialist legality. Perversions in the work of the state security service have also been corrected, daily Party and government control have been established over its activities, and dependable political and legal guarantees of socialist law and order have been laid down.

Thus, the Party has unambiguously shown that a return to any violations of socialist legality is out of the question. The state security service is guarding and will continue to guard the interests of the Soviet State, of all Soviet citizens.

The Party outlines the tasks in maintaining security at the present stage with an eye to both the international and internal conditions of the development of the Soviet state.

In the last few years substantial changes have taken place in Soviet society. Having healed its war wounds, this country has moved far ahead in all fields of economic, social and cultural life. The spectacular progress made in building a developed socialist society and in transition to communism has augmented the power of the Soviet state and consolidated its democratic foundations.

The time when this country was encircled by hostile capitalist states has long passed. The emergence of the world socialist system, the growth of its power and influence, the successes of the international working-class and national liberation movements, have radically changed the alignment of forces in the world arena in favour of socialism and progress.

As a result of all these historic achievements capitalism has completely lost whatever social basis it used to have in this country, and on the world scene the imperialist forces have weakened and lost their former positions of domination.

The danger to the security of the Soviet Union and other socialist countries, however, has not ceased.

The realities of life indicate that as long as imperialism exists with its economic and military might there is a real danger to the peoples of this country and other socialist countries, to all progressive forces, to world peace. This is evidenced in particular by the U.S. imperialists' dirty war against the heroic Vietnamese people, the active support by the imperialists of Israel's aggression against Arab countries, the constant interference of the United States in the internal affairs of Latin American, Asian and African countries.

The Party and the Soviet Government steadfastly pursue a policy of peaceful co-existence of states belonging to different social systems. The Soviet people are aware, however, that this policy will be all the more effective as this country's security is guaranteed more firmly, as its borders are more securely closed to agents of imperialism as its rebuff to its enemies is stiffer and more vigorous.

In his report on the occasion of the 50th anniversary of the Great October Socialist Revolution, Leonid Brezhnev formulated the main objective of Soviet foreign policy as follows: "To defend the gains of the October Revolution, to frustrate the imperialist intrigues against the homeland of socialism, to ensure the requisite external conditions for building a communist society . . ."[1]

Under present conditions the imperialists can hardly expect to defeat socialism by a frontal attack. Leaders of the imperialist powers are trying to learn a lesson from their setbacks, to adapt to the new situation in the world, and are resorting to whatever sophisticated and treacherous methods they can use to implement their policy.

In the period when the struggle in the world arena has assumed a strikingly manifest class nature and has become more complicated, the scale and limits of the espionage and subversive activities of the imperialists are changing. The intelligence service headquarters of some Western powers, primarily the United States, have much influence on the foreign policy of their governments. They are assigned an important role in carrying out active operations and subversion. Today this activity of intelligence services is targeted not only against the armed forces, the defence and other industries of the socialist and other peace-loving countries. The imperialists are conducting their subversive operations on a widening scale in the most diverse spheres of social life.

The imperialists do not scruple to use the most heinous ways and means in their secret struggle against the peoples. They engineer and encourage reactionary coups, military takeovers and provocations, circulate misinformation and slander. They use their intelligence agencies not only for espionage, sabotage and acts of terrorism but also for attaining their political objectives. The secret services are instructed to do whatever they can to weaken the power of the socialist countries, to undermine their unity and their solidarity with the working class and national liberation movements. The Soviet state security service, jointly with the relevant agencies in the fraternal socialist countries, is giving a condign rebuff to these hostile operations.

The imperialists make no bones about the fact that the operations of their intelligence services are directed mainly against the Soviet Union, the bulwark of socialist, national liberation and peace forces throughout the world. The secret services of the Western powers spare no efforts to gain information about the Soviet Union's military and economic potential, its armed forces, its home situation, and its latest

---

[1] L. I. Brezhnev. *Following Lenin's Course. Speeches and articles,* vol. 2, p. 120.

scientific and technological achievements. At the same time, they are actively involved in organizing ideological subversion to undermine the Soviet people's ideological and political unity. The imperialist secret services thoroughly co-ordinate their operations with those of their gigantic propaganda machine, which is also used to misinform and mislead the public, to try and undermine trust in the socialist state and the operation of its agencies.

It should be pointed out that the imperialists are increasingly using to their own advantage the chauvinistic, divisive policy pursued by Mao Tse-tung's clique that has launched an indiscriminate campaign of slander against our Party and the Soviet people, against the communist movement as a whole.

Our Party and the Soviet Government organize a determined and timely rebuff to the subversive activities of the imperialists in all directions. Wherever the specific conditions of struggle require it, the state security service also plays a part in this work. It deals effectively with the complicated problems of exposing and thwarting the aggressive designs of imperialist powers and the hostile operations of their secret services.

The state security service has recently tracked down and apprehended a number of agents of imperialist intelligence services and emissaries of anti-Soviet organizations operating abroad, cut off many criminal channels of communication between foreign agents and intelligence centres, and frustrated many acts of subversion and sabotage. The relevant items published in the Soviet press shed some light on this aspect of the activities of the state security service. Each of its operations in this field requires skill and dedication on the part of Soviet counterintelligence personnel.

Our frontier guard troops are faced with highly responsible tasks. Today, of course, the situation along the Soviet borders is different from what it was in the past. Over long stretches of the border our neighbours are socialist and other friendly countries. However, there are still sections where great vigilance is necessary. Our adversaries have not yet given up their attempts to smuggle their spies into this country, to provoke conflicts and commit acts of subversion. The fact that most border incidents do not develop into something bigger than attempted violations is due to the strenuous and persistent work, courage and high vigilance of Soviet frontier guards. They cope with their difficult duties well.

Consistent implementation of the Leninist principles, undeviating abidance by the directives and instructions of the Communist Party, strict observance of the laws of our socialist state, and permanent and close ties with the masses firmly guarantee success in the work of the state security service and its correct approach to its duties.

Regarding Cheka as a political agency, as a formidable weapon in the hands of the proletariat and all working people, Lenin called for efficient and intelligent use of this weapon in accordance with the situation prevailing and the concrete tasks of the revolution. He warned against complacency and carelessness in the struggle against counterrevolution and against abuse of coercive methods, against mistakes, however slight, likely to harm honest citizens.

The complete and final triumph of socialism in this country, the abolition of the exploiter classes, the consolidation of the ideological and political unity of the Soviet people, have left nothing of what might have been the social basis for organized anti-Soviet activity on the part of some classes or sections of the population. However, it would be folly to shut one's eyes to individual offences against the state, hostile anti-Soviet behaviour and actions which are committed often under the influence of hostile foreign ideology.

Imperialist propagandists take advantage of such facts to denigrate socialism and the Soviet system. All their efforts, however, are to no avail. Any unbiased observer will easily see that Soviet society is united and monolithic. The Soviet people have been following the Leninist Party for half-a-century along the path of socialism and communism they have chosen for good and all, and have achieved spectacular successes in this progress.

As for individuals who fall now and then into the trap of the CIA and other subversive centres, such turncoats by no means express the sentiments of the Soviet people. Of course, even in the period of formation of new, communist relations, one may find a few types who for personal reasons or under the influence of hostile propaganda from abroad turn into useful tools of foreign secret services.

We know, however, that none of such individuals has been or will ever be able to get any serious support. In the end all these victims of "soul hunters" from the CIA and other imperialist intelligence services are exposed with the aid of Soviet citizens, who deem it their sacred duty to safeguard the security of the Soviet state.

This is only natural. Indeed, this country is a socialist state of the whole people. The defence and maintenance of its security is a matter of concern to all Soviet citizens.

This is also what determines the profoundly democratic nature of the activities of the state security service. It has not, nor can it have any other aims but defence of the gains of the October Revolution, the achievements of the Soviet people. State security servicemen know that by suppressing any encroachment on the interests of the Soviet State, they act in the interest of the whole people.

In the conditions of the socialist state of the whole people, the state security service is linked with the working people by especially strong ties. It is only our enemies who have good reason to fear and hate Soviet security men, that depict the Soviet security service as a kind of "secret police". In fact, this service has been set up by Soviet society itself for self-defence against the intrigues of imperialist secret services and the operation of hostile elements. It performs its work on the principles of socialist democracy, under constant control on the part of the people, the Party and government.

In keeping with the finest traditions of Cheka the state security service is conducting important work to prevent criminal offences, and to persuade and reeducate those who commit politically harmful actions. This work helps to eliminate the causes likely to generate criminal offences against the State.

The efforts made by the Party and the Soviet State to prevent cases of infringement of the lawful rights of working people, disregard for their needs, and excessive red tape, as well as the education of citizens in the spirit of socialist patriotism and honest fulfilment of their civic duties help remove the soil for antisocial behaviour. This is also facilitated by improvement of the working people's living standards, the continued development of socialist democracy, and the growing cultural level and awareness of the masses in this country.

Our Party has always regarded the activities of the state security service as an important area of political struggle. Daily guidance by the Communist Party and its Leninist Central Committee is the main and indispensable prerequisite for a correct political line in all activities of the state security service. In its work at the present stage it follows the guidelines set by the 23rd Congress and plenary meetings of the Central Committee of the CPSU.

Menzhinsky[1] said in his time: "For all the infinite enthusiasm of Cheka personnel . . . it would never have been possible to build up the state security service known in the history of the first proletarian revolution, if Dzerzhinsky, with all his qualities as a communist organizer, had not been a dedicated Party executive, law-abiding and modest, to whom a Party directive was the supreme law."

This statement about the man who was and remains a model to all servicemen called upon to safeguard the security of the Soviet state holds as true today as ever. The Party assigns to work in the state security service politically mature and well-trained cadres dedicated to the communist cause. The Party educates security personnel in the spirit of high responsibility to the people, close ties with the masses, revolutionary vigilance, courage, staunchness and heroism.

The Soviet state security service, which is the flesh and blood of the Soviet people, is aware of its lofty duty and responsibility for the cause entrusted to it by the Party and government. In war time and in peace time, at the time when Soviet government was taking its first steps and today when the Soviet Union has become a mighty power, the state security service has been invariably at work to contribute to the cause of defence of the Soviet people's vital interests. Celebrating the 50th anniversary of the Soviet state security service, its personnel, who are infinitely devoted to the Communist Party, this great country and its people, are determined to pursue steadfastly the general line of the Soviet Communist Party, and to do their level best to promote the great cause of the struggle for communism.

Allow me to assure our Party, its Leninist Central Committee, the Soviet government, all Soviet citizens on behalf of all Soviet state security servicemen that they will continue to stand guard firmly over the achievements of the October Revolution, the gains of socialism in this country.

Long live our Soviet homeland!

Long live the glorious Communist Party of the Soviet Union!

Long live the great Soviet people!

---

[1] Vyacheslav R. Menzhinsky. Head of the Soviet state security service from 1926 to 1934 (Translator).

The Friendship of Soviet Nations—the Inexhaustible Source of Our Victories

Report at a joint solemn meeting of the Central Committee of the Communist Party of Estonia and the Supreme Soviet of the Estonian SSR on the occasion of the decoration of the Republic with the Order of Friendship of Peoples and of the City of Tallinn with the Order of Lenin, 27 December 1973

Dear comrades!

Today the Estonian Soviet Socialist Republic is to be presented with the Order of Friendship of Peoples, and the City of Tallinn with the Order of Lenin.

On behalf of the Central Committee of the Communist Party of the Soviet Union, the Presidium of the USSR Supreme Soviet, and the Soviet government I cordially congratulate you on these high awards. They are a token of recognition of the great contributions of the Republic and its capital to communist construction, to developing friendship and fraternal co-operation among Soviet nations, to strengthening the Soviet state. At the same time, this is a recognition of the contribution to the common cause for the benefit of this socialist country made by each of you, every working man and woman of Soviet Estonia.

Estonia is one of the Soviet Union's young republics. The Soviet people remember, however, that the socialist revolution began here on 7 November 1917 just as in Petrograd.

From the very first steps of the revolution our peoples were con-

fronted by the most complicated social and national tasks. The whole
world was waiting to see how the Bolsheviks would behave after the
conquest of power, whether they would be able to harmonize the
right of nations to self-determination they had proclaimed with the
slogan of unity of workers of the world.

For centuries the best minds of mankind had searched for ways
towards a happy life of the nations, towards just and equal relations
among them. It was only the communists, however, that indicated the
right way. They brought together the revolutionary struggle to build a
new society with the struggle of the oppressed peoples for their
national liberation.

Apologists of the *bourgeoisie* proclaimed upon the house-tops that
the Bolsheviks were unable to resolve the nationalities problem. At
the same time they referred to the fact that the Leninist Party frankly
spoke of the subordination of the nationalities problem to the general
social tasks of the revolution. This presentation of the question,
however, by no means signified an under-estimation of the nationalities problem. The Soviet Union's historical experience has graphically confirmed the correctness of Lenin's ideas. It is only in the
context of fulfilling the class tasks of the socialist revolution that the
most correct and complete solution to the complicated nationalities
problem can be found. As Marx and Engels had predicted, the
victory of socialism has done away with hostility between nations
along with the abolition of the antagonisms between classes inside
nations.

The enemies of the Soviet state expected that the centrifugal forces
of nationalism would prevail over the ideas of internationalism. Contrary to their expectations, however, a qualitatively new socialist
statehood emerged from the ruins of the former tsarist empire. The
revolutionary ideas helped millions of workers and peasants to realize
that unity of their forces was the guarantee that their dreams of social
justice and national equality would come true.

In their message of January 1918 the Estonian communists said:
"Not secession from Russia but the closest and fraternal union with
the working people of Russia—such is . . . our slogan.

"The workers' revolution has united us with Russia's working
people. . . .

"The working people in town and country must not forget, not for a moment, that they are members of the international family of workers."[1]

The working people of Estonia were loyal to this impassioned appeal through all the hard years of revolutionary struggle.

The imperialist world opposed the victory of the revolution in Russia with bayonets, not in a figurative but in the literal sense of the word. Military intervention, blockade, blackmail—everything was put into action so as to tighten the noose on the neck of the socialist revolution. International imperialism in collusion with the domestic counter-revolution strangled Soviet government in Estonia at that time. It was incorporated into the capitalist system. But what were the consequences of that for Estonia and its working people?

The two decades of bourgeois government in Estonia were an ugly period of the domination of political reaction, the suffering of the working people, the country's conversion into an agrarian and raw materials appendage of the capitalist market. Under the government of the *bourgeoisie* and rich landowners, Estonia shared the fate of the small countries "politically, formally independent", in Lenin's phrase, "but in fact entangled in the spiderweb of financial and diplomatic dependence".[2]

The imperialist powers attempted to use Estonia and other Baltic countries for the so-called *cordon sanitaire* against the Soviet Union.

The Estonian people, however, had their say. They resolutely declared what path they were determined to follow. Soviet Estonia voluntarily joined the friendly family of Soviet republics. That secured for the Estonian people defence of their national interests and the successful solution of their vital sociopolitical problems. The accession of the young Baltic republics to the Soviet Union augmented in its turn the strength and potentialities of the Soviet people.

The friendship of Soviet nations forcefully expressed itself in the years of the Second World War. The plans of the enemies to drive a

---

[1] *The Great October Socialist Revolution in Estonia. Collected documents and materials*, Tallinn, 1958, pp. 397, 398.

[2] V. I. Lenin, *Collected Works*, vol. 27, p. 383.

wedge between socialist nations, to disunite them, burst like a soap bubble. Nazi Germany was routed. All the peoples of the USSR contributed to victory. Twenty-one thousand Estonians were decorated by the government for their heroism and valour in the war against the Nazi invaders. The high title of Hero of the Soviet Union was conferred on thirteen Estonians. The Soviet people sacredly revere the memory of servicemen who laid down their lives for victory in the war.

The Soviet people have lived in peace for more than three decades. Their constructive work has lent still greater strength to the internationalist ties between all nations and national minorities of the Soviet Union, which we rightly call the Leninist friendship of nations.

From all their life experience the Soviet nations have drawn the conclusion that their cohesion in the fraternal union of socialist republics secures favourable conditions for their development in all fields of political, economic and cultural life. It is only under socialism, in the friendly family of Soviet nations, that the true potentialities of the Estonian working people have been brought into play. Suffice it to say that today the Republic's industrial output is 34 times that of 1940.

It is for good reason that we turn primarily to the economy to describe the results of our progress. Indeed, the economy is the material basis for Soviet society's successful advance towards communism.

The achievements of every republic are at the same time the common property of the Soviet people. It is with legitimate pride that we review the results of the work carried out in the third year of the five-year plan. The current year is distinctive for us. It has become the decisive year in our struggle to fulfil the five-year plan as a whole.

As you know, the recent plenary meeting of the CPSU Central Committee held in December 1973 discussed in comprehensive detail the results of Soviet economic development and plans of further progress in this field. At the meeting Leonid Brezhnev thoroughly analysed the Party's activities, the Soviet people's constructive efforts in the current five-year plan period. He put forward fundamental ideas concerning the ways and means of economic development, the fulfilment of the assignments of the five-year plan, the continued advancement of the economy, the material and cultural standards of life of this country's working people.

You know that last year was a very difficult one for our economy. The Party outlined timely and effective measures to improve economic management. It took vigorous steps to find an effective solution to the problems plaguing the economy, to overcome shortcomings. These measures helped preserve the high economic growth rates. For the Party, local government and economic bodies this year has been a gruelling test. And now we have full reason to claim that we have passed this test with flying colours. Such is the main political result of the Party's work.

The selfless efforts of the people, the political and organizing activities of the Party have made it possible not only to attain the plan targets but also to surpass them. For instance, industrial production developed at a higher rate than planned. It has grown 7.3 per cent as against 5.8 per cent envisaged in the plan. Over 7000 million roubles' worth of produce has been turned out over and above the plan.

You know, however, that for society it is important not only to produce a certain quantity of goods but also to do it at minimum costs. This is why in the current five-year plan special attention is given to advancing the efficiency of social production, to stepping up the rates of scientific and technological progress. Significantly, the increase in the productivity of labour accounts for four-fifths of the entire increment in industrial output.

Soviet farmers have achieved outstanding success this year. They have gathered a bumper grain and cotton harvest. There has been an increase in the output of other products as well. What has made these record results possible? Perhaps only favourable weather conditions? No, these successes cannot be attributed to good weather alone. Incidentally, in many areas of the country the weather by no means helped us. The main thing is that now the measures taken by the Party to reinforce the material and technological basis for agriculture, to improve its organization are yielding a steadily growing effect.

Economic development is not an end in itself. Our Party invariably regards industrial and agricultural growth as the basis for improving the life of the Soviet people. It can be stated with full reason that on this plane the assignments of the five-year plan are being fulfilled consistently and purposefully. The earnings of one in every three factory and office workers have increased. *Per capita* real income has grown roughly by 13.5 per cent. More than 11 million people have improved their housing conditions during the current year alone.

The working people of Estonia have also made their contribution to fulfilling the assignments of the five-year plan. The face of your Republic's economy is its modern power industry, chemical industry, precision machine-building, and electronics. The establishment of the most up-to-date industries has been made possible by large investments made by the state. Today the Republic produces every ten days more industrial goods than it manufactured in 1940. In 1973 the workers of industry assumed high socialist pledges to fulfil their plans ahead of schedule. Yesterday they completed their assignments for the total volume of industrial product sales and for the production of key items. No praise is too high for your selfless work.

Estonian crop farmers and stock breeders have considerably increased marketable surpluses. Although today manpower employed in the Republic's agriculture is equivalent to only one third of that in 1940, the output of farm produce is greater by 50 per cent.

For centuries Estonian peasants had cursed stones and swamps which interfered with agriculture. They had struggled against them with pick and shovel throughout their lives. Today the Soviet state has put at the disposal of Estonian working people modern machinery which has enabled successful reclamation of large tracts of land.

The crews of the Republic's fleet of fishing trawlers have also come up with a good record this year.

By their work the Soviet people have gained the necessary foothold for successful fulfilment of their tasks in the remaining two years of the five-year plan. There is no need to cite concrete targets from the national economic plan for 1974 adopted by the recent session of the USSR Supreme Soviet. You know them well. Thinking of these figures and comparing them with the rate of our development in the past one feels profound satisfaction and pride: within only one year the Soviet people can cope with gigantic tasks that would have taken years to fulfil formerly.

We have already put in a great deal of work but much still remains to be done. At the home stretch it is necessary to exert all our strength and potentials. This is why the Party appeals for all-round development of the creativity and initiative of the masses for dissemination of progressive experience and for a struggle against lingering shortcomings. Indeed, in the final analysis, success will depend on the performance results of every labour collective, every Soviet citizen.

The Party's appeal for an all-out effort to fulfil and over-fulfil the assignments of the fourth year of the five-year plan has evoked enthusiastic response among the working people in town and country. A socialist emulation drive has been launched throughout the country, and the numbers of communist shock workers are growing. This movement of millions of people embodies such remarkable features as fraternal co-operation and mutual assistance characteristic of the Soviet way of life. These features are inherent not only in individual labour collectives. They exemplify the entire system of mutual relations between the Union Republics, the entire process of communist construction. The Soviet Union takes pride in the labour exploits of its workers and collective farmers, in the spectacular achievements of scientists, engineers and technicians of all Soviet republics. And small wonder. Each of them contributes by his work to the achievement of common national tasks, to strengthening the economic foundation of the union and brotherhood of Soviet nations.

We have no other sources but labour for advancing the welfare of the people. This is why shock work for the benefit of Soviet society is so highly valued in this country. This is why those who perform labour exploits are entitled to honours and respect. The Soviet people know well the names of many Estonian men and women who have come forward as initiators of the socialist emulation drive. Among them are Heroes of Socialist Labour Alfred Waldov, a markers' team leader at the Tallinn engineering plant; Aksel Pertel, a team leader at the "Estonslanets" shale-mining complex; Ruppert Kaik, an instructor engine driver at the Tallinn locomotive yard; Zinaida Agafonova, a weaver at the "Baltiiskaya Manufaktura" textile factory; Friedrich Tamm, captain of a fishing trawler; Oscar Kjais, a tractor driver; Tomas Sooaluste, a state farm director, to mention but a few.

We also owe our profound thanks to workers of the public

education and public health services, scientists and engineers, members of the literary and artistic community of the Republic. Their work benefits all Soviet nations. Such remarkable masters of Estonian art as Georg Ots and Tiit Kuuzik enjoy nationwide renown. The Soviet readership admires the works of Juhan Smuul, Augustus Jacobson, Egon Rannet, and many other Estonian authors.

The process of consolidation of national cultures in which they draw ever closer together by no means leads to their levelling to monotony, as various western bourgeois "Sovietologists" are vainly trying to prove. Soviet socialist culture develops as a multi-national culture and at the same time it is profoundly internationalist in its basic essence. It absorbs the progressive features and traditions from the folk art of each of the fraternal nations, the finest fruits of their creativity.

I realize, of course, that today's festive event is not the best occasion for a discussion of shortcomings. However, we communists are loyal to Lenin's behest: to be intolerant of self-complacency and to remember about unresolved problems during holidays as well. Another reason why this subject should be touched upon is that some of the negative symptoms which are in evidence in the Republic's economy are causing surprise, to put it mildly.

Over the period of eleven months in 1973 twenty-six enterprises have failed to cope with their assignments for labour productivity growth. Much working time is still being wasted at a number of enterprises. This is hard to explain, since Estonians have always been known as hard-working people remarkable for their organization, discipline and persistence.

Nor can one reconcile oneself to the fact that the plan for commissioning basic productive facilities had been fulfilled by only 63 per cent towards December. Or let us take housing construction. Our goal is to provide good housing conditions for every family. How does it happen that in your republic one third of the work under the annual plan for commissioning new housing is handled during the last month of the year? Indeed, this gives rise to last-minute rush work and naturally adversely affects the standards of construction.

As you see, the Party, local government, trade union and YCL organizations have much to work upon. The chances to bring into full play the gigantic creative forces inherent in Soviet socialist society largely depend on their skill and persistence in implementing ideological education and organizing work.

There is no doubt that the working people of Estonia will attain the targets of the five-year plan. You have raised remarkable people, veritable makers of a new life. The Estonian communists have gained vast experience in guiding political, economic and cultural development. They have on their record the battles of the October Revolution, the grim years of the underground, the heroic fight against the Nazis for the freedom and independence of our Motherland. Service of the great ideas of communism, the vital interests of the people has invariably been and is their lofty goal.

The Soviet people are looking ahead with confidence. Our communist optimism rests on the great vital force of Marxism–Leninism, on the creativity of the masses. The guarantee of our success is in the fact that the advance towards communism is spearheaded by the battle-hardened Leninist Party equipped with knowledge of the laws of social development. Under its leadership the Soviet Union's working people have built developed socialist society and are now making steady progress along the path towards communism. The Soviet people proudly call our Party their honour, conscience and wisdom. In all our accomplishments the Soviet people see the guiding activities of the Leninist Central Committee, its Politbureau, the indefatigable work of the General Secretary of the CPSU Central Committee, Leonid Brezhnev.

Our achievements, the experience of socialist and communist construction in the USSR have become the internationalist property of the entire world socialist system, the entire international communist movement. Lenin said in his time: "No force in the world, however much evil, misfortune and sufferings it may yet bring to millions and hundreds of millions of people will take back the main achievements of our revolution, because they are no longer 'our own' but world-historic achievements".[1]

The fulfilment of economic and cultural development plans is inseparably linked with the consistent struggle waged by the Soviet

---

[1] V. I. Lenin, *Collected Works*, vol. 45, pp. 136–137.

Union to implement the foreign policy charted by the 24th CPSU Congress. This refers to the efforts to strengthen peace and avert the threat of world thermonuclear war. This also involves the efforts to provide the most favourable conditions for communist construction in this country, for developing the struggle for socialism and progress throughout the world.

It was but recently that the world froze from the chills and blizzards of the Cold War. It cast its gloomy shadow on all corners of the world. The strategy of a peace offensive by our Party and country and the entire socialist community of nations has brought about a marked improvement in the political climate, yielded real, tangible fruit.

What is the main trend in the development of present-day international relations as we see it? It is above all the current visible turn from military confrontation to a relaxation of tensions, to greater security and peaceful co-operation. This turn has been made possible by a change in the alignment of forces in favour of socialism. This change is the direct result of the growth and consolidation of the power of the Soviet Union, the other countries of the socialist community, all revolutionary forces of today.

Never before has Soviet foreign policy been so effective or produced so significant results over such a short period of time. As you know, Leonid Brezhnev's visit to socialist countries, to the United States, the German Federal Republic and France have greatly contributed to achieving these results. The recent Soviet–Indian top-level talks and the documents signed in the process are also a practical realization of the aims and tasks formulated in the Peace Programme adopted by the 24th CPSU Congress. These visits and all foreign policy activities of our Party have had the result that the international situation today is taking shape largely under the impact of the Soviet Union's peace initiatives.

The Soviet Union acts on the international scene in close co-operation with the fraternal socialist countries. Our Party sees its prime internationalist duty in strengthening in every way the positions of world socialism, the unity of the socialist states, friendship and all-round co-operation with them. Relations between the fraternal countries in the political, economic and cultural fields are steadily widening and become more diversified. The practical implementation of the programme of socialist economic integration has got under way. The combat alliance embodied in the Warsaw Treaty Organization is also growing stronger.

We are satisfied to know that the aggression in Vietnam has been ended. Favourable changes have taken place in Soviet relations with the Western countries. At the Conference on Security and Co-operation in Europe concrete work is under way to draw up measures to secure lasting peace in the continent. In other words, problems on which no progress could practically be achieved earlier are being resolved today.

The entire course of international developments is furnishing conclusive evidence that the Party has worked out a correct foreign policy line, the only right line under present conditions.

While acknowledging the existence of favourable trends in international affairs, we by no means shut our eyes to the dangerous actions of aggressive imperialist circles. The enemies of *détente*, who cannot think otherwise than in terms of military confrontation, are active in the capitalist states to this day. Reactionary forces, who are advocating a continued arms race in defiance of the aspirations of the peoples, still wield considerable influence in the West. As Leonid Brezhnev has pointed out, "all these protagonists of the Cold War have a common platform, which is opposition to steps in the direction of peace and greater international co-operation. We must maintain vigilance in relation to their intrigues."[1]

The timeliness of this warning has been confirmed by the recent events in the Middle East. As you know, the Middle East conflict has been in evidence for a quarter of a century now. It is being kept up by the stubborn refusal of the Israeli extremists supported by imperialist forces to abandon their aggressive ambitions and recognize the lawful rights of the Arab peoples. The activities of the Tel Aviv "hawks", just as the most rabid Zionist circles outside Israel, meet with increasing denunciation and opposition all over the world. The Soviet Union's position on this issue is clear. It is one of consistent support

---

[1] L. I. Brezhnev, *Following Lenin's Course. Speeches and articles*, Moscow, 1974, vol. 4, p. 249.

for the Arab peoples in their just struggle against Israeli aggression. The Soviet Union comes out for the withdrawal of Israeli forces from the Arab lands occupied in 1967 and for securing the lawful rights of the states and peoples of this region, including the Arab people of Palestine. Only on this basis can a just and lasting peace settlement be achieved in the Middle East.

The situation developing in Indochina also merits attention. It is aggravated primarily by the sabotage of the Paris agreements by reactionary, aggressive forces. They have recently stepped up their attempts to change in their favour the balance of forces in South Vietnam. In this situation the patriotic forces are giving a rebuff to the armed provocations of the Saigon administration.

The tragic events in Chile are another illustration of the subversive operations of the enemies of peace and democracy. The military junta, using fascist methods, is flagrantly trampling on the elementary human rights and perpetrating bloody massacres of Chilean patriots. The Soviet people wrathfully condemn these crimes of reaction and express their solidarity with the struggle of Chile's democratic forces.

Needless to say, the process of relaxation of international tensions does not imply a cessation of the class struggle in the international arena. Imperialism is adapting to the new situation in the world and trying to exploit it in its class interests. It is attempting to intensify its "ideological infiltration" of the socialist countries, the Soviet Union in particular. In these plans not the least role is assigned to the emigrant nationalistic rabble. The aims of such actions are to induce manifestations of nationalism, to achieve an "erosion" of socialist society. Under the hypocritical slogan of "defence of human rights" some circles in the West are seeking to gain a right to interference in our domestic affairs, to conducting subversive activities in the socialist countries. We must tell such politicians outright: "It won't work!" We are in favour of an exchange of cultural values. We have much to share with others, much to show them. However, we resolutely oppose and will oppose in the future any attempt to use such exchanges in contravention of our laws and traditions.

We have to acknowledge with regret that the current activities of China's leadership in the world arena are linking up even more closely with the efforts of imperialist reaction. The Chinese leaders have taken a stand against *détente* and are clamouring for "colossal upheavals in the world". Contrary to truth they are talking about the alleged "Soviet threat" and fomenting great-power nationalistic psychosis in China. The Soviet people reject this crude slander on their country. The USSR has never threatened and is not threatening China, nor does it make any claims to her territory. While upholding resolutely the integrity of the principles of Marxism–Leninism, the interests of our socialist country, the CPSU and the Soviet government invariably come out for normalizing relations with the PRC, for restoring good-neighbourliness and friendship between the Soviet and Chinese peoples.

Today we have full reason to say that neither the military industrial complexes of the West nor the intrigues of the Maoists determine the trends of international development. The main trail of history is being blazed by the forces of peace, progress and socialism. The peace offensive of the Soviet Union and other socialist countries is developing successfully. The effectiveness of Soviet foreign policy stems from its faithful expression of the objective laws of world development. This policy meets the vital interests of the Soviet people and the working people in all countries. In the struggle against imperialism for lasting peace and security we come out jointly with the fraternal Communist and Workers' parties, with all fighters for freedom and social progress.

The World Congress of Peace Forces held in Moscow recently was a striking illustration of the broad recognition of and support for the Soviet foreign policy line. This wide and prestigious forum, which was attended by representatives of political parties of various orientations, trade union, women's, youth and other public organizations, demonstrated the growing activity of all peace forces.

The Soviet Union has scored great successes in achieving its internal and international tasks. Entering the new year 1974 we proudly review the record of our achievements. It is indisputable that the peoples of this socialist country, led by the Communist Party and its Leninist Central Committee, will make new spectacular progress in communist construction.

Allow me to announce the decree of the Presidium of the USSR

Supreme Soviet on the decoration of the Estonian SSR.

I congratulate you once again on your high awards and wish you new successes in your work for the benefit of the entire Soviet people.

Long live the Estonian Soviet Socialist Republic!

May the unbreakable friendship of Soviet nations grow stronger!

Long live the Communist Party of the Soviet Union!

The Indissoluble Unity of the Party and People

Speech at a meeting with the Novomoskovsky District constituency on the occasion of nomination for election to the Supreme Soviet of the Russian Federation, 9 June 1975

Dear comrades!

I express my heartfelt thanks to this audience and to the entire electorate of the Novomoskovsky District for my nomination for election to the Supreme Soviet of the Russian Federation. I regard this as a high honour and an expression of trust on your part. Full credit for this trust is due to the Communist Party, of which I am proud to be a member. It is indisputable that by nominating communists to serve as their deputies Soviet citizens express their unanimous support for the home and foreign policy of the great party of Lenin.

It is for the third time that you have chosen me to represent your district in the supreme legislature of the Russian Federation. Your trust, of course, involves a high responsibility on my part. It is eight years since I was first elected as your deputy. Over the period I have set up effective business ties with the Novomoskovsk city Party and Executive Committees, and with many labour collectives of your district. As a deputy I have worked to the best of my ability to help fulfil the tasks in developing production and improving living conditions in the city and district. This work, perhaps, was not fully successful at all times and in every field, but I have invariably tried to be useful to my constituency, and I am determined to work in the same way in the future as well.

Every next election to the legislative bodies of this country is an

124

event of great social significance for the Soviet people. Indeed, it is a matter of shaping the organs of government that will carry into effect the will of this country's working people, express their interests and aspirations.

The present elections are to take place in a remarkable year, in which the fulfilment of the Ninth Five-Year Plan is to be completed and preparations for the 25th Party Congress are assuming ever wider scope. The socialist emulation drive in honour of the Congress is developing throughout the country. This is a highly significant fact, because the socialist emulation drive and its results are a materialization of the Soviet people's great moral and political uplift and their devotion to the communist cause.

The organization and process of elections are a graphic illustration of the development of socialist democracy. In the course of the election campaign the results of the fulfilment of the election programme are reviewed, and new tasks are outlined in all fields of socialist construction. Elections contribute to further strengthening of the unity of the communists and the unaffiliated masses, to still greater solidarity of all working people with the Communist Party of the Soviet Union.

At the same time, elections again show clearly that all power in this country belongs to the people. Recently the Central Electoral Commission announced official data concerning candidates nominated in the current election campaign. Among the registered candidates for election to the Supreme Soviet of the Russian Federation 35 per cent are workers and more than 15 per cent are collective farmers. These figures reflect the Party line of broad and active involvement of working people in the administration of state.

Such broad representation of the working people in the supreme body of government is not to be found in any capitalist country, even among those which boast of their traditional democracy. Take, for instance, the US Congress. Bankers, businessmen and lawyers of large corporations constitute the absolute majority of its members. There is not a single worker in Congress, and the so-called "average Americans" are represented by just a few members.

Such is the picture of the ruling body of a country which lays claim to being the criterion of the Western way of life and likes to lecture other states on matters of democratic development.

The enemies of socialism who are worried by the growth of Soviet prestige in the world are trying to sow doubts about the genuine democracy of the Soviet system. Shamelessly distorting facts, they talk about some "violations" of human rights in the USSR, oppose to our system the principles of so-called "pure" democracy, seek out and exaggerate individual shortcomings in Soviet reality.

Of course we have certain shortcomings. They are bound to exist in the construction of a new society in such a vast country as ours. In the early years of Soviet government Lenin said: "Soviet power is not a magic talisman. It does not heal immediately from survivals of the past, from illiteracy, from lack of culture, from the aftermath of the savage war, from the legacy of predatory capitalism. However, it makes possible a transition to socialism. It makes possible the advancement of those who were oppressed and enables them to take into their own hands more and more all administration of state, all management of the economy, all management of production."[1]

Soviet government could not do away at one stroke with all shortcomings and difficulties inherited from the past. However, it immediately gave the masses what mattered most. It enabled them to become actively and directly involved in the management of all affairs of state and society. The working people, the entire multinational Soviet people, manage the affairs of state through their organizations, primarily through the Soviets of Working People's Deputies.

The communists have never concealed the fact that socialist democracy has a class character. It is democracy for millions upon millions of working people. Any soviet citizen whose interests are in harmony with the interests of society feels the full scope of our democratic freedoms. The matter is different if there is no such harmony, as is the case with a few individuals. Here we have to say frankly: priority must be attached to the interests of all society, all working people. We believe this is a fair principle.

Socialist democracy implies not only rights and freedoms. It also

---

[1] V. I. Lenin, *Collected Works*, vol. 38, p. 239.

implies the duties of every citizen to all society and strict discipline. Taking part in government of the people, in the administration of state, the working people themselves are vitally interested in maintaining law and order, in strict observance of the principles and norms of socialist community life, which are established at their own will in Soviet laws, in the ethical and moral standards. The wider the scope of democracy, the people's participation in the management of national affairs, the higher the responsibility of each member of society for the common cause, for strengthening labour and state discipline.

Speaking of socialist democracy and its cardinal difference from bourgeois democracy, it is necessary to emphasize another characteristic aspect of this question. Soviet government not only proclaimed the democratic rights of Soviet citizens but also guaranteed their practical realization. In addition to political rights, there are guarantees of socio-economic rights, such as the right to work, rest and leisure, to education and material security in old age.

Indeed, how can one claim that the civil rights of the masses are respected in the capitalist countries where people live in constant fear of losing their jobs and hence their earnings? According to official statistics, the rate of unemployment has surpassed 8 million in the United States, 1,200,000 in Italy, is almost just as high in Japan, is greater than 1 million in the FRG and about 1 million in Great Britain.

When analyzing the main trend in present-day bourgeois criticism of Soviet democracy, one is bound to draw the conclusion that although this criticism is camouflaged with "concern" for freedom, democracy, and human rights, it is directed in fact against the socialist essence of Soviet society. We communists are not surprised by this fact. Such criticism only confirms that all ideological conceptions of imperialism, on problems of democracy in particular, pursue the object of defence of the interests of the *bourgeoisie*. These interests were antagonistic to the interests of the working people in the past, and they are just as antagonistic today.

For socialism the development of democracy is a vital need, the main line of the Party in all its work to strengthen the Soviet state and perfect the political organization of Soviet society. The measures implemented in this field over the last few years pursued precisely these goals.

We Soviet citizens are accustomed to the fact that our five-year plans are a dependable criterion of our progress. The nine soviet five-year plans, however, are not simply nine identical stages in the development of the Soviet Union. Each of them has its distinctive features, its own image, so to say. The current five-year plan is distinguished by the enormous scale of work in progress, a comprehensive approach to the solution of national economic tasks, the successful attainment of the targets outlined by the 24th CPSU Congress.

One can clearly see today how the quantitative growth of the economic power of the Soviet state transforms into qualitative advancement in the sense that it enables us to solve new large problems, drawing large economic areas into their orbit. Take, for instance, the development of the energy and raw materials resources of Siberia and the Far East. Of course, we had been aware of the advantages of such development before. We had long been planning to gain access to these resources, but some plans were frustrated by the war, while others could not be implemented for lack of practical possibilities. Today the situation is different. The level of Soviet economic advancement makes it possible to carry on development work on a truly gigantic scale.

The short acronym "BAM" (Baikal-Amur Main Line) has become known all over the world. It has entered the world's languages, just as the Russian words "kolkhoz" and "sputnik" became part of other languages in the past.

It would seem there is nothing extraordinary about the construction of a long railway line. It should not be forgotten, however, that the Baikal-Amur Main Line is a powerful lever by which the image of a vast forestland will be totally changed. Man will get access to coal, ores, timber and other wealth that could not be reached through roadless terrain. Large tracts of unused land will be cultivated. In short, BAM will provide a solution to major economic and social problems.

It is hard to overestimate the significance of the comprehensive programme of developing the Non-Black Earth Belt of the Russian

Federation. The Soviet people have rightly described the work started in this zone as another virgin land development programme. Indeed, it is a question of fundamental transformation of this vast region of Central Russia inhabited by almost a quarter of this country's total population and of providing the basis for high rates of growth of agricultural production.

The implementation of the plans outlined will contribute substantially to the growth of Soviet economic potential and the solution of current and long-term tasks.

The whole country is involved in the work to renovate and advance the areas of the Non-Black Earth Belt. The implementation of this programme requires primarily the mobilization of all internal resources, the efforts of all those working in this zone, including the working people of the Tula region and your district. The Tula workmen have long been famous in this country and in the world for their skill, persistence at work and excellent workmanship. They will indisputably manifest these remarkable qualities still more forcefully in the solution of the major economic and social problems outlined in the programme of developing the Non-Black Earth Belt.

In the period of the earlier five-year plans the Soviet Union moved to first place in the world for the output of many important industrial and agricultural products. In the last four years of the current five-year plan new targets have been attained. Last year this country produced more coal, crude oil, steel and some other industrial items than any other state and became the world's largest manufacturer of mineral fertilizers. This is not simply a quantitative but also a qualitative indicator.

As you know, mineral fertilizers are a special product. Their production illustrates not only the country's industrial power but also the real possibilities for the development of agriculture. In the difficult year 1919 Lenin signed a decree, which stated in particular: "All fertilizers are to be assimilated to grain in respect of transportation and are to be delivered to their destination urgently as top-priority goods".[1]

---

[1] *Decrees of Soviet Government*, Moscow, 1971, vol. 5, p. 170.

ASW–E

From the time of the early five-year plans, the Party took steps to develop the production of mineral fertilizers. It was only in the last decade, however, that we became capable of undertaking this work on a qualitatively new level. A fundamental role was played in this field by the March 1965 plenary meeting of the CPSU Central Committee, which drew up on scientific lines a programme of comprehensive development and advancement of agriculture. The plenary meeting outlined the task of wide-scale chemicalization, without which stable high yields are inconceivable today.

At the end of the last five-year plan this country still lagged far behind the United States in production of mineral fertilizers. Incidentally, we started competition in this field from different initial levels. In Imperial Russia the production of mineral fertilizers was equivalent to only 3 per cent of the US output. The same proportion was in evidence in relation to Britain and France. Today the Soviet Union's output of these important products is larger than that of the United States and of all Common Market countries combined. This is a spectacular success, to which the personnel of the Novomoskovsky Chemical Complex have made a major contribution.

The commissioning at this Complex of two ammonia production facilities means that the labour collective of the Complex has fulfilled the task set by the 24th CPSU Congress excellently. The new facilities extend far beyond the framework of routine increase in capacity. They have integrated the latest achievements of the scientific and technological revolution with the much advanced skills and enormous labour enthusiasm of the workers, specialists and office personnel. The new installations are almost twice the capacity of all this country's ammonia plants in 1948. The fact that they enable an increase in labour productivity many times over is especially significant.

Miners and building workers, workers in transportation services and agriculture, are also contributing effectively to fulfilling the assignments of the current five-year plan. It is a pleasure to know that the working people not only of the Novomoskovsky District but of the Tula region as a whole have provided good prerequisites for its completion ahead of schedule.

Speaking of this country's economy as a whole, it should be

pointed out that the increment in industrial output over the first five months of the current year has amounted to 7.6 per cent. This is a higher rate of growth than planned (6.7 per cent). We have ample reason to say that the country has now advanced to such levels as will enable it to complete successfully the assignments of the current five-year plan.

In the Soviet state economic development is subordinated to the achievement of the main task set by the Party—one of advancing steadily the material and cultural standards of life of the people.

Advancement of the people's standards of living is a many-sided task as regards its significance and content. Our approach to it is not a mechanical increase in the production of colour TV sets, refrigerators and cars, although we are developing the manufacture of these goods in every way. The well-being of the people implies not only an increase in the quantity of material benefits for the consumer but also man's intellectual advancement, the development of his creativity, his moral perfection, the promotion of public health and environmental protection.

Over the last four years of the current five-year plan *per capita* real incomes have grown 19 per cent. The average monthly earnings of factory and office workers have been raised considerably. Over the five-year plan period 80 million factory and office workers will have their pay raised, and 40 million persons will be granted increases in pensions, allowances or stipends. Adding to this the growth in the incomes of collective farmers, it will be easy to see that practically almost every Soviet family now feels an improvement in the material conditions of life. The state maintains stable prices of basic consumer goods and foodstuffs, which is particularly visible in the background of the current run-away inflation in the capitalist world.

The main political result of the last four and a half years of the five-year plan is that dynamic economic progress has been assured, a new long step has been taken in the fulfilment of key social tasks, in the further development of Soviet society.

Reviewing the results of the work performed, the Party not only acknowledges the progress achieved, but also gives attention to shortcomings and unresolved problems. This high-principled, truly Leninist approach to work is characteristic of the activity of the plenary meetings of the CPSU Central Committee and the Party as a whole.

The Party pays close attention to the ideological sphere of life in Soviet society. The 24th CPSU Congress emphasized that the moulding of the new man is one of the main tasks in communist construction.

No figures can fully express the results of the Party's ideological work, its activities in the political education of the masses. The entire Soviet people, however, feel the results of this work.

The Soviet people's communist convictions and their new, communist attitude to work have grown stronger. The moral atmosphere in Soviet society is conducive to a respectful and solicitous attention to man, to an exacting attitude to oneself and to others, to trust combined with a keen sense of responsibility, genuine comradeship and mutual assistance.

This is why in our day one is especially intolerant of such phenomena alien to the Soviet way of life as bureaucracy and money-grubbing, stealing of public property and breaches of labour discipline, drunkenness and rudeness. We say that these evils are survivals of the past. This is really so, because the moulding of the new man is a far longer and difficult process than reconstruction of the economy. What is more, we are not alone in the world, nor are we separated from other states. Bourgeois ideologists are trying to influence unstable individuals in this country, advertizing morals and life styles alien to socialism.

In recent time the countries of the socialist community have witnessed more and more often such actions of imperialist forces that may be qualified as ideological subversion. The Soviet people dealt with such subversion before. This is one of the perfidious methods used by the capitalist world in its struggle against socialism. Throughout the history of the establishment and development of the socialist state the enemies of Soviet power resorted to subversion to undermine its economic and defence potential. These methods have failed to bring about the results expected by the imperialists and check the Soviet people's spectacular progress in socialist construction.

Today the enemies of *détente* are placing special emphasis on ideological subversion. As is known, an acute struggle is developing in this field between socialism and capitalism. "However, we will work for this historically inevitable struggle to take a course which is not fraught with the menace of war, dangerous conflicts, an unrestrained arms race", Leonid Brezhnev has said.[1]

The imperialists resort in the ideological field to various ways and means of subversion so as to distort through deception and falsification the Soviet Union's foreign policy of peace and provoke some anti-social, anti-socialist manifestations inside this country.

The enemies of socialism realize that today it would be a hopeless venture to offer the Soviet people the idea of restoration of the capitalist system. Therefore, they dress themselves in the garb of advocates of "democratic" socialism seeking its "improvement". The true objectives of such "solicitude" are easy to see. They boil down to undermining Soviet power from the inside and liquidating the gains of socialism.

The Soviet people are clearly aware of these goals. This is why the Soviet public gives such determined and unanimous rebuff to whatever attempts are made in this direction. The unbreakable sociopolitical and ideological unity and the vigilance of the Soviet people surely guarantee that present acts of ideological subversion are doomed to the same total failure as was suffered by the earlier subversive operations against the Soviet state.

The Party's activities and the Soviet people's constructive efforts to fulfil the breathtaking plans of economic, social and cultural development, are inseparably linked with the struggle for implementing the Peace Programme advanced in Leonid Brezhnev's report to the 24th CPSU Congress.

The past few years have marked a turning-point in affirming the principles of peaceful coexistence in the practice of international relations. A turn has been made from the Cold War which lasted for over a quarter-century to a relaxation of tensions, to normalizing and developing relations between states with different social systems.

We rightly attribute these favourable changes to the increased impact produced on all international affairs by Soviet policy and reunited actions of the countries of the socialist community. The growth of the power and prestige of the fraternal socialist nations

---

[1] L. I. Brezhnev, *Following Lenin's Course. Speeches and articles*, vol. 4, p. 81.

have become a decisive factor in securing a relaxation of international tensions.

The foreign policy line charted by the Soviet Communist Party is aimed at providing favourable conditions for the Soviet people's constructive efforts, for the consolidation of world socialism, for strengthening the forces struggling for their national liberation and social progress.

We say openly that *détente* agrees with the interests of socialism. In view of this it is sometimes claimed in the West that the Soviet Union derives some unilateral advantages from *détente*. This absurd conclusion, of course, does not hold water. Indeed, the peoples of other countries of Europe, Asia, Africa and America have no less interest in the prevention of war and nuclear holocaust of human life. He who wants peace is also in favour of *détente*. All nations equally need peace, *détente*, and greater mutual trust.

As is known, the all-European conference has entered a decisive phase. The very fact that 35 nations belonging to opposite systems and military political alliances are jointly working out measures to guarantee security and develop co-operation among European nations is of enormous political significance. It is clear that such a conference could not have been convened in conditions of confrontation. Only in a situation of international relations changed in the direction of *détente* has it been finally possible to hold this conference.

Do the Soviet Union and other socialist countries alone need security and good-neighbourly relations in Europe? Are they less necessary to other countries swept by two destructive and bloody world wars in the present century? It is clear to every sober-minded person that the consolidation of peace in Europe benefits all states regardless of their social systems.

In the situation of *détente* new opportunities have appeared in the field of international economic relations.

Over the last few years the Soviet Union and other socialist countries have concluded economic agreements and large contracts with capitalist countries. Such ties are indisputably beneficial to this country, because they ease the fulfilment of some important economic tasks. As is known, however, trade and economic relations in general are a mutually beneficial affair. It is only natural, therefore, that the business community in many Western countries soberly assesses the current situation and displays initiative in setting up contacts with the Soviet Union.

The Soviet people know the price of peace only too well. Twenty million Soviet men and women laid down their lives in the last war. Revering the memory of those who died in defence of this country and defeated fascism, concerned for mankind's destiny, the Soviet Union has addressed the peoples, parliaments and governments of all countries with an appeal for ending the dangerous Cold War policy for all time and directing their efforts to securing a strong and lasting peace on earth.

For their part the CPSU and the Soviet state are doing their best for the process of *détente* to gain ground steadily and become irreversible. General Secretary Leonid Brezhnev has stated in this context: "As a result of the Party's consistent and stubborn policy of peace, of the growth of the power and influence of world socialist forces the danger of another world war has been pushed back. We will do whatever is necessary to have this danger eventually removed in general."[1]

This is indeed a lofty and noble goal. It is being pursued by the Soviet Union and other socialist countries at the all-European conference, at the Vienna talks, and at the top-level bilateral talks and meetings with Western leaders.

We realize of course that *détente* is opposed by certain forces who have a vested interest in the continued arms race and have not desisted from their attempts to put pressure on the Soviet Union and force it to make concessions.

It has to be admitted that China's leaders are active opponents of *détente*. Our principal line in relation to China was clearly formulated in the resolutions of the 24th CPSU Congress and remains in force at present.

The CPSU has repeatedly pointed out that *détente* cannot develop under its own momentum. It is necessary to struggle for it actively. As Leonid Brezhnev has said, "there can be no pause or respite in

---

[1] L. I. Brezhnev, *Following Lenin's Course. Speeches and articles,* vol. 5, p. 293.

this struggle",[1] because *détente* is an uninterrupted process demanding steady advancement and practical implementation of the agreements reached. This approach to the process of *détente* meets with increasing understanding in the world. This is why our constructive proposals and practical steps in this direction are approved of and supported by the world public, by all those who are committed to peace.

The April 1975 plenary meeting of the CPSU Central Committee took a decision to convene the 25th Party Congress. This will be an event of nationwide significance in the life of the Soviet people, for whom resolutions of Party congresses invariably open up new prospects and horizons.

Fifty-eight years ago, at the First All-Russia Congress of Soviets in June 1917, there occurred an episode which went down in history. When one of the leaders of the opportunist parties declared that in Russia there was no political party capable of taking all power into its own hands, Lenin exclaimed from the audience: "Yes! Such a party does exist. It is the Bolshevik Party!"[2] Within a few months, in October 1917, the Bolsheviks led the working people in a victorious assault on the old world.

The Great October Socialist Revolution established the Communist Party in power. Since then it has invariably been at the helm of this socialist state. This fact in itself is of enormous significance in the political history of our century. Indeed, taking a look at bourgeois parties, one can see numerous examples of how some of them disintegrated as soon as they published their programmes, while others, although they remained on the political scene, now and then experienced deep shocks, coming to power or going into opposition.

The CPSU enjoys infinite trust of the people, who have assigned to it the leading role in the life of the country. What is the reason for this great trust in the Communist Party? It is the fact that our Party, just as the other fraternal Communist and Workers' parties, expresses in its programme and practical work the vital interests of the working people, the objective requirements of social development. The Party

---

[1] L. I. Brezhnev, *Following Lenin's Course. Speeches and articles,* vol. 5, p.292.

[2] V. I. Lenin, *Collected Works,* vol. 32, p. 267.

is capable of expressing authentically the interests and requirements of the people because it is equipped with an instrument for scientific cognition and transformation of the world—the Marxist–Leninist theory which, in conformity with the course of history, it develops creatively, enriches and translates into reality.

The Party has proved in practice that it is successfully performing its role as the leader and organizer of all activities of the Soviet people. It demonstrated this in the period of the early five-year plans, when the foundation of socialism was being laid, in the Great Patriotic War in which the Soviet people routed Nazi Germany, and in the years of postwar recovery, when we had to rebuild what had been destroyed by the flames of war.

All these events have now become part of history. However, they are alive in our hearts, in the constructive efforts of today. These events are clearly remembered by the Soviet people because they actively participated in these events, struggling under the leadership of the Party for the triumph of the great communist ideals. This struggle was the crucible in which was forged the indissoluble unity of the Party and people which makes the most characteristic feature of Soviet life.

In developed socialist society the role of the CPSU as the leading and organizing force of this society is steadily growing. The scope of our constructive activity is widening, and the rate of social progress is accelerating. The Soviet people are firmly convinced that for all their complexity and wide scope the tasks facing them will indisputably be accomplished. They will be accomplished because we have both objective and subjective factors working in this direction. They will be accomplished because, as Lenin said, we have a party under whose leadership we can cope with tasks of any complexity.

*   *   *

The Soviet people unanimously support the home and foreign policy of the Party and enthusiastically approve of the activities of the Party's Central Committee and its Politburcau headed by General Secretary Leonid Brezhnev. These sentiments find expression in that the Soviet people name Leonid Brezhnev with great pride and affection as their first candidate for election to the Supreme Soviet.

Today, as in the past, the Party has come forward with a clear programme for the coming elections. This is a programme of further economic and cultural development, of advancing the Soviet people's well-being, of perfecting socialist democracy, of strengthening the forces of socialism, progress and peace. By casting their votes for candidates of the Communist and non-Party bloc the Soviet people will again demonstrate their common determination to struggle for the triumph of the great communist cause.

I express once again my heartfelt gratitude to the working people of the Novomoskovsk electoral district who have nominated me for election to the Supreme Soviet of the Russian Federation, the electoral agents and all comrades who have spoken at this meeting. I assure you that I will do all in my power to live up to your trust.

I wish you new great success in your work for the benefit of this socialist country.

Leninism: the Science and Art of Revolution

Report at a ceremonial meeting in Moscow dedicated to the 106th anniversary of Lenin's birth, 22 April 1976

Comrades!

Today it is 106 years since the birth of Vladimir Lenin, a genius of revolution and a great thinker, the founder of the Soviet Communist Party and of the world's first workers' and peasants' state. We are celebrating this red-letter day soon after the 25th Congress of the CPSU, in a situation of a new nationwide upsurge of enthusiasm and further growth of the political and labour activity of the Soviet people.

The victorious proletarian revolution, which ushered in a new era in world history in the twentieth century, was carried out under the leadership of Lenin, who continued the great cause of Marx and Engels. The world community of socialist nations which has taken shape in the twentieth century also draws inspiration from Lenin's ideas. The irresistible movement towards freedom and justice, towards socialism and the summits of social progress, is gaining momentum and wider scope under the banner of Lenin, of Marxism–Leninism.

Time has no power over Leninism. This doctrine correctly interprets the objective laws of history, relying on all the achievements of progressive social thought of the past and constantly absorbing innovative ideas coming up with the march of time. Leninism is an endless process of creative thinking, analysis and summing up of social change, of constant self-renovation of revolutionary theory under the impact of revolutionary practice.

"All of Lenin's life", Leonid Brezhnev has said, "was incessant

139

creative effort—in theory, in politics, in organizing the class struggle of the proletariat, in building up the Party and the State. These qualities of creative genius he also fostered in the great Party which continues honourably to carry aloft Lenin's banner, the banner of communism."[1]

The Communist Party of the Soviet Union regards loyalty to Leninism as an immutable law of its theoretical and practical activities. This is why for the Party a strictly scientific approach, a consistent revolutionary outlook, a penetrating analysis of social phenomena, and selfless service of the interests of the people are inseparable components of a coherent whole. This is why the Party links the creative development of theory with the practical work of the masses, the vital tasks in communist construction in the USSR, the progress of world socialism, the international communist and working-class movement as a whole.

For the CPSU and the proletarian revolutionaries of the whole world, Leninism has always been and is a dependable guide to success, the science and art of revolutionary creativity opening new horizons before mankind.

THE 25th CONGRESS OF THE CPSU: A HISTORIC MILESTONE ON THE PATH TOWARDS COMMUNISM

Every year on this red-letter day we review our progress in reverence for our fond memories of Lenin. Today we are reviewing the spectacular achievements and inspiring prospects profoundly and vividly revealed by the 25th Congress of the Soviet Communist Party.

The Congress was a milestone on the road of Soviet society's advance towards communism. Its documents fully reflect the distinctive character of the current historical stage of Soviet society's development, of the tasks and problems it is faced with by the realities of life.

The Congress has shown that the possibilities of this country have

---

[1] L. I. Brezhnev, *Following Lenin's Course*, Moscow, 1970, vol. 2, p. 562.

increased enormously. The unity and cohesion of Soviet society are as strong as ever before. The unity of all classes and social groups, all nations and national minorities, all generations of the Soviet people is truly unbreakable. The Soviet Union today has a vast economic potential, which has doubled during the last ten years alone. This impressive rate of economic growth has become a matter of course. Never before have we had such a large force of highly skilled personnel as we have today. Soviet science has developed into a direct productive force, a powerful booster of social progress. Along with other fraternal socialist countries the Soviet Union exerts an ever stronger and deeper influence on the course of world developments, on the system of international relations in general.

Relying on this solid foundation, the Party has started implementing plans which are bound to bring new successes in communist construction, further to strengthen peace and the positions of socialism on the international scene.

In the field of home policy, primarily in economics, this refers to the continued advancement of the working people's standards of living, the development of industry and the programme of advancing agriculture, increasing production of consumer goods, combining organically the revolution in science and technology with the advantages of socialism, and enhancing drastically the efficiency of social production as a whole.

In the foreign policy field we are determined further to consolidate the socialist community of nations, to develop our co-operation with the countries which have freed themselves from the colonial yoke, to lend added momentum to the current turn from international tensions and the Cold War towards international relations based on the immutable principles of peaceful coexistence of states belonging to different social systems.

The 25th Congress has once again demonstrated that Lenin's teaching and cause have dedicated followers. The spirit of Leninism and Leninist logic permeate the report delivered at the Congress by Leonid Brezhnev, General Secretary of the CPSU Central Committee. The Party has emphasized the historic significance of the Soviet record of achievements, acknowledged its admiration and respect for the dedicated constructive effort of the Soviet people, and advanced to the foreground the problems still unresolved, the tasks which have yet to be accomplished. The strategic line of the CPSU mapped out in the Central Committee's report and supported unanimously by the Congress is a model of creativity in Leninist style displayed by the Central Committee and its Politbureau in handling the fundamental problems of home and foreign policy.

We all recall the warm feelings and great appreciation expressed by Congress delegates speaking of Leonid Brezhnev's outstanding contributions to planning and implementing Party policy. In the final analysis the political skill of a communist leader of the Leninist stamp consists in his ability to perceive and understand the demands of the time, to sense and translate what the working people desire into reality. And what they desire is to live better, to live and work in peace. His profound understanding of these seemingly very simple yet in fact the most vital problems calling for the most responsible and complex political decisions is the basis for the single-mindedness and consistency which are so characteristic of Leonid Brezhnev, of all his activities. The attachment of first priority to the problems of public welfare, which involves organically a thoroughly considered formulation of the immediate tasks in Soviet economic development, the Peace Programme, which has won renown throughout the world are all associated with the name of the General Secretary of the CPSU Central Committee, whose tireless activity has gained nation-wide recognition and support.

The Soviet people have appreciated the resolutions of the 25th CPSU Congress as a breathtaking programme of further advance to the ultimate goal which Lenin described as one of ensuring "full prosperity and free all-round development of all members of society".[1] Among the wide variety of large and small tasks claiming daily attention, the supreme forum of Soviet communists has placed emphasis on advancing the efficiency and quality of all our work. These tasks of crucial significance at the present stage of Soviet society's progress have been outlined in profound detail by Leonid Brezhnev and discussed in the report of Alexei Kosygin and the speeches of other delegates to the Congress.

---

[1] V. I. Lenin, *Collected Works*, vol. 6, p. 232.

The Congress described advancement of the efficiency and quality of work as a many-sided and comprehensive problem, which largely determines the dynamics of economic growth, the rates of further improvement of the people's living standards, of continued perfection of social relations and the political system of society.

Of course, the Party has invariably displayed concern for the efficiency and quality of work at all the stages of socialist construction. Otherwise growth of labour productivity and present socioeconomic progress would have been impossible. Formerly, however, priority had to be attached to quantitative growth more than to other aspects of work. Today we view the relationship of quantity and quality from the height of what has been achieved, in the light of our new possibilities and new requirements.

Today we are capable of accomplishing many truly gigantic projects which have long been on our minds but which were not feasible. Each of them whether it is the programme for developing the non-chernozem (non-black soil) belt of the Russian Federation, the West Siberian, the Karatau-Dzhambul, or the South Tajik complexes, the Kursk Magnetic Anomaly area, or the Baikal-Amur Railway—is a major contribution to Soviet economic progress. They mean millions of tons more grain, crude oil, metal, and other important products. Furthermore, they mean new towns, roads, schools and hospitals, theatres and stadiums. All this implies not just an increment in economic potential but also the transformation of vast areas, complete sectors of the economy, far-reaching qualitative changes in the country's productive forces.

Organizing the working people to accomplish the fundamental tasks of the Tenth Five-Year Plan, the Party is advancing the standards of economic management to the level of new requirements in keeping with its Leninist principles. The rates of our growth and our progress in general now largely depend on improvement of management in the broad sense of the word, that is, on enhancing the standards of planning work, the efficiency of organizing efforts, a more skilful use of economic incentives and levers. Soviet co-operation with foreign nations and, of course, the deepening of socialist economic integration are assuming a new dimension.

All of us realize that implementing the Congress decisions will not be a simple and easy matter. There is a lot of difficult work to be done. The Party regards further development of the labour activity and initiative of Soviet citizens as an indispensable prerequisite for implementing the plans outlined. The working people's solicitous concern for improving the economic performance results in their labour collectives and in the country as a whole, their civic awareness and activity are most widely and fully expressed in the nationwide socialist emulation drive, in the movement for a communist attitude to work. Enhancement of the productivity and discipline of labour, efforts to improve product quality, to speed up the practical application of the achievements of scientific and technological progress, to save time, labour, and materials are the main fields of the creativity of the masses.

The Soviet people's enthusiastic work has secured first successes in implementing the Tenth Five-Year Plan. The plan of industrial output in the first quarter of this year was fulfilled by 102 per cent. Good progress is being made in spring fieldwork on the farms.

The nationwide communist Subbotnik[1] was a striking demonstration of the Soviet people's initiative and patriotism. The working people taking part in it did a great deal of important and useful work. The significance of Subbotnik, however, is not confined to this alone. It was an expression of the people's profound respect and never-fading affection for Lenin, their allegiance to their splendid traditions and of the fact of historic significance that socialism has truly become the vital cause of all Soviet citizens.

Lenin regarded the Party's unity with the people as the source of its strength. The Soviet people know well that the CPSU is doing its utmost for the benefit of man, in the name of man. This slogan is inscribed on our banner and recorded in our Party Programme. Its consistent implementation is the meaning of the activity of the Party and all communists. This is what Lenin taught us to do, and we are acting in accordance with his behests.

---

[1] *Subbotnik* (from Russ. *subbota*)—Saturday work for free (Translator).

SOVIET SOCIETY AND
SOCIALIST DEMOCRACY

In outlining immediate and long-term targets of economic and sociopolitical development, the Party proceeds from the fact that a developed socialist society has been built in this country and is steadily developing into communist society. The distinctive features of this stage of progress were vividly reflected in the deliberations of the 25th Party Congress. Its resolutions integrate a description of new factors of social progress with a new vision of key problems, the immediate practical tasks and long-term programme goals. These resolutions illumine the theoretical background of Party policy in a long historical perspective, one, as Lenin put it, of "effective communist construction, of creating new economic relations, a new society".[1]

Developed socialism is the supreme achievement of social progress today. In the early days of Soviet government Lenin spoke of transforming economically backward, ruined and illiterate Russia into a highly developed, industrialized socialist state, a land of complete literacy and high standards of culture. It was merely a dream at that time. Lenin's dreams, which were far ahead of his time, however, were never divorced from reality. And today the world sees Lenin's dreams come true in the main features of developed socialism, in the impressive picture of its accomplishments presented by the 25th Party Congress.

All that has been gained and created by the Soviet people is inseparably connected with the activities of the Leninist Party. As Soviet society ascends the stages of social progress, as the scope of its constructive work steadily widens, and the scale of the task it has to handle at home and abroad becomes larger and larger, the Party has a growing role to play as the leading and guiding force of society, as the political vanguard of the working class, all working people, the nation as a whole.

Soviet society is making steady progress, which is a process involving along with the economy and culture the development of

---

[1] V. I. Lenin, *Collected Works*, vol. 39, p. 13.

social relations and the political sphere. The Party has set in this context the task of further advancing Soviet socialist statehood, the style and methods of work in all fields of social activity.

The Soviet Union is a state of the whole people. This means that it abides by the will of the whole people and that all activities of the bodies of government serving, as they do, the interests of the people are carried out with their daily support and direct participation. The development of the political system, the political institutions of society—processes which are directed by the Party—organically combine the consolidation of socialist statehood with the promotion of socialist democracy.

In all its efforts to accomplish this task the Party will continue to rely on the time-tested Leninist principles.

Lenin has taught us that a socialist revolution and socialist transformations can be implemented successfully only under the leadership of the working class. In his view this idea, the worldwide historical mission of the proletariat as the maker of socialist society, is the core of Marxist doctrine.

It was natural, therefore, that the titanic efforts of Lenin himself as the theoretician and practical leader of the proletarian revolution were focused on developing this fundamental idea of Marxism creatively and on translating it into reality. This implies detailed elaboration of the practical ways and means, forms and methods of leadership to be used by the working class and its party in the revolutionary struggle and in implementing socialist transformations to secure a transition from capitalism to socialism.

Whatever form political guidance of society by the working class may take it invariably expresses the fundamental interests of the working majority and rests upon a broad social basis, far-flung class alliances, involving in the process of socialist transformations all progressive, viable and honest forces of society. It was not fortuitous that Lenin considered self-isolation from the people, sectarianism, just as dangerous to the socialist cause as reformism, unprincipled concessions to the class enemy.

Lenin has taught us that victory of socialism, its development and success in building a communist society are inconceivable without broad government of the people, without developing democracy. The working class embraced the ideas of democracy as its own ideas as far back as the times when it had to fight for its rights under the iron heel of capitalism. The proletariat, Lenin writes, is fighting for democracy "in the van of the struggle . . . and heads the struggle".[1]

As far as Soviet society is concerned, it will be recalled that already in the period of proletarian dictatorship it made a gigantic leap forward in developing democracy, using the power of government as an efficient instrument for social transformations carried out by the working people to promote their own vital interests. The steady process of widening and advancing of democracy goes hand in hand with the consolidation and development of socialism, the evolution of a state of the whole people from the state of proletarian dictatorship.

Lenin has stated that democracy has always had and continues to have a class nature. There is no democracy in general, only bourgeois or socialist democracy. The working class and the communists naturally attach great significance to those democratic rights and freedoms that can be won at the cost of a stubborn struggle under the rule of capitalism. This, however, does not change the class nature of bourgeois democracy, nor does this disprove the fact that socialism alone can ensure genuine government by the people.

Socialism has done away with the exploitation of man by man and social injustice for all time. Another of this country's great achievements is the complete abolition of ethnic oppression. We were the first to enforce the political equality of women in practice. It is an epoch-making accomplishment of socialism that all citizens are

---

[1] Socialism is democratic by nature, since it cannot exist and develop without involving the multi-million mass of the working people in creative political activities, in the management of the affairs of society and state. This has been fully borne out by this country's experience.

This conclusion is in no way contradicted by the fact that at a certain stage of the struggle for socialism in this country the leading role of the working class was exercised as a dictatorship of the proletariat. This scientific concept was viciously attacked, distorted and vulgarized with the sole aim of depicting the dictatorship of the proletariat as the opposite of democracy. In fact, Lenin opposed the dictatorship of the proletariat not to democracy but to the dictatorship of the *bourgeoisie*, which is inherent in the rule of capital. In Lenin's interpretation, in real life this dictatorship, that is the political power of the *bourgeoisie* based on the system of coercion it has established, exists even in states with the best-developed institutions of bourgeois democracy.

guaranteed access to education and culture, which were the privilege of the propertied minority for centuries. The Soviet Union was the world's first country to guarantee vital social rights along with political rights to all members of society. It is socialism that in practice involves working people in the management of government and public affairs, which is done through the Party and the Soviets, the trade unions, the public organizations, the press and nationwide discussion of the most important laws and decisions, through the entire socialist way of life.

All of these are spectacular achievements of Soviet society, as well as enormous success in developing socialist democracy. What has already been done in this field has long put socialism far ahead of the most democratic capitalist states.

The Party and the Soviet state, however, do not intend to rest on their laurels. In the political as well as the economic field the new frontiers of progress attained by Soviet society afford a still clearer view of the tasks facing it and of its new possibilities.

It is quite natural, therefore, that problems of developing democracy in this country are raised, worked out and consistently resolved precisely by the Communist Party. The reason for that is that the Party concentrates and meets in its political decisions the vital interests and needs of all classes and social groups, all nations and national minorities, all generations of Soviet society, but that is not the only reason. The Leninist Communist Party itself is a profoundly democratic body affiliating more than 15 million front-ranking members of the working class, collective farmers and members of the intelligentsia. The strenuous efforts of the Party to reinforce the Leninist principles of Party life, to communicate the spirit of these rules to the entire multi-millioned communist membership have naturally created within Party organizations an atmosphere of comradeship and creativity, and, at the same time, of exactness and high-principledness.

Several important directions of work being moved to the foreground in this country's political development were emphasized at the 25th Party Congress.

One of them is, as before, the effort to bring into full play all the potentials of socialist government by the people inherent in the working people's mass organizations, primarily in the Soviets of

Working People's Deputies, which make up the political foundation
of the Union of Soviet Socialist Republics. Further progress towards
communism also requires the trade unions, the Young Communist
League, the creative unions of intellectuals, and other public associations to play a greater part in political, economic, and cultural affairs.

The Party has outlined important tasks to be fulfilled in the continued efforts to strengthen the rule of law. Soviet laws express the
will of the working class and all working people. It is important that
they should be observed scrupulously. They are equally binding on all
Soviet citizens regardless of their official position or the nature of the
work they do. Strong socialist legality guarantees the rights and
interests of Soviet citizens, as well as the interests of society as a
whole.

Quite naturally, Soviet laws do not recognize anybody's "right" to
harm society, to infringe on the public order, to disturb the normal
life, work, and leisure of honest citizens. Universal respect for the
law, the inevitability of sanctions against offenders, cultivation in
Soviet citizens of intolerance of any antisocial behaviour are important aspects of socialist community life.

The development and improvement of the socialist way of life
demand more vigorous opposition to anything that contradicts the
Leninist principles of attitude towards work and towards individuals.
This refers primarily to the struggle against bureaucratic routine,
which Lenin stigmatized as the worst enemy of the new society, and
to protection of Soviet citizens against callousness and incivility, red
tape and arrogance on the part of certain officials. The Party is
intolerant of any such attitudes, which are alien to a society building
communism.

The 25th Party Congress reaffirmed the principle that criticism and
self-criticism are an inalienable feature of Soviet life. They are a
powerful and highly efficient instrument of socialist democracy. The
Party believes that a businesslike, public and well-meant critical
discussion of the state of affairs in any area, as well as a self-critical
analysis of the shortcomings in evidence, must be part and parcel of
the work style of each organization and each labour collective.

It is our aim to get every citizen to understand and feel that the
management of public affairs and the very progress of society depend

on him personally, on his work performance and political activity. Socialist democracy grants all citizens broad rights and freedoms and requires them to display a high level of awareness and self-discipline, social responsibility and civic activity. The higher the level of political awareness, the less need there is for any restrictions. Hence the ever-growing importance of all aspects of educational work.

The 25th Party Congress has outlined great and varied tasks in further developing and perfecting the political system of Soviet society. In its consistent and sustained efforts to fulfil these tasks, to strengthen the state, and to advance socialist democracy the Party attaches top priority to the interests of the Soviet people, the interests of communist construction. "Whatever contradicts these interests we reject, and nobody will convince us that this is the wrong approach. We are firm in the knowledge of what direction we take in advancing our political system. We are convinced that we have chosen the right course", Leonid Brezhnev has said.[1]

The Soviet Union has advanced a long way in the political as well as the economic and social fields. Our Party is strong enough and confident of its rightness to review this road objectively, without embellishing anything. It was a hard road indeed. We had to build socialism under incredibly difficult conditions and under constant attack from our enemies. The Party and the Soviet people were blazing the trail across unknown terrain with no experience, their own or anybody else's, to rely upon. They had to learn many practical lessons, not only from their successes but also from their mistakes and failures. The Party frankly admits that, boldly exposes shortcomings and corrects them, and takes whatever measures are necessary to prevent any digression from the Leninist rules. For all the complications encountered on that road, however, nothing can detract from the worldwide significance of the historic triumphs achieved by the world's first socialist country and the Party founded by the great Lenin. This accounts for the lasting value of the experience in socialist construction which has been gained by the Soviet Union and is being thoroughly studied throughout the world.

---

[1] L. I. Brezhnev, *Following Lenin's Course. Speeches and articles*, Moscow, 1976, vol. 5, p. 546.

Our experience is there for all to see. The Soviet communists do not push it on anybody, but they are naturally glad to see it being used creatively by our friends and fraternal parties in their own work, contributing to the common treasure of worldwide experience in revolutionary struggle and enriching it with new tactics and new solutions to economic, social, and political problems. The Soviet communists well remember this phrase of Lenin's: 'All nations will arrive at socialism—this is inevitable, but all will do so in not exactly the same way, each will contribute something of its own to some form of democracy, to some variety of the dictatorship of the proletariat, to the varying rate of socialist transformations in the different aspects of social life."[1]

Developments have shown the truth and profundity of Lenin's idea. Developments have shown at the same time that for all the variety of prevailing conditions, for all the differences in the forms of transition to socialism, there are basic laws governing this historic process laws that can neither be abolished nor evaded. One of these is that socialist transformations require the working class and its allies to establish government capable of defending the gains of the revolution. This government should be capable of effectively performing its constructive functions, of releasing the mighty creative forces of the people, and of mobilizing the most active support of the mass of the people. This is the universal, international significance of the Leninist teaching on the socialist state and socialist democracy first translated into social practice by this country's working people under the guidance of the working class and its vanguard, the great Party of Lenin.

PEACEFUL COEXISTENCE AND THE BATTLE OF IDEAS

The 25th Party Congress has demonstrated anew the Party's unswerving loyalty to Lenin's ideas. All Soviet foreign policy—from Lenin's Decree on Peace to the Programme of continued efforts for peace and international co-operation, for the freedom and independence of

---

[1] V. I. Lenin, *Collected Works*, vol. 30, p. 123.

nations adopted by the 25th Party Congress—is pervaded with Lenin's ideas and aimed at implementing them in real life.

". . . From the very beginning of the October Revolution," Lenin has said, "foreign policy and international relations have been the main questions facing us . . . ."[1]

The triumph of the October Revolution placed this problem on an absolutely new plane as a problem of the principles and conditions on which relations between the first ever socialist state and the capitalist world would be founded. This problem was especially acute in view of the fact that in the years when the Soviet Republic was, as Lenin put it, in "international isolation" it was a life and death question for the revolution, for the new society it had bred.

The principles of socialist foreign policy were worked out in an extremely difficult international situation, which was complicated by a bitter controversy within the Party itself. Lenin's genius and iron will, the wisdom and maturity of the Party he had fostered, were required to work out and consistently pursue the only correct policy—a policy of peaceful coexistence, or, as it was then termed, a policy of "peaceful cohabitation" of the two different systems of ownership, the two opposite economic, social, and political systems.

At that time, of course, there was no question of banishing war from international life. The great realist Lenin understood that the imperialist powers would not leave Russia alone and that the peace won in the hard struggle could only be a deferment of war, no more than a peaceful respite.

This country had that respite. We gained two decades of peace time. That helped us to win a war which was the most terrible and bloodiest of all wars mankind had ever known.

The rout of the Axis powers and the far-reaching social and political changes in the world that followed brought about a radical change in this country's position on the international scene and led to the emergence of the world socialist system.

Today the Soviet Union is advancing along the road of socialist and communist construction hand in hand with quite a few fraternal

---

[1] V. I. Lenin, *Collected Works*, vol. 37, p. 153.

countries. We are united with them by our common goals and interests, ideals and policies. The socialist community of nations is exerting an increasingly profound influence on the course of world developments, on the hearts and minds of millions of people.

Unshakeable guarantees that no aggressor or coalition of aggressors will be able to defeat socialism have already been established and grow stronger year after year. Nevertheless, the question of the foundations on which relations should be built between the socialist and capitalist worlds has not lost its significance and gravity, because it is a question of war and peace. As it was reaffirmed at the 25th Party Congress, this remains the most crucial question of our day.

Though this is by no means a new question, it is put and is being solved in a new way today. This is due to the new factors that emerge in international relations as the power and influence of world socialism grow, as the working-class movement continues to mount, and the national liberation movement wins new victories. This is also due to the development of new weapons of enormous destructive power, which make the consequences of war truly catastrophic. This creates realistic prerequisites, on the one hand, and inevitable necessity on the other, for reducing and eventually removing the danger of another world war and, if I may say so, of expanding the limits of peaceful coexistence. The goal the Party is pursuing now is not to gain a peaceful respite but to establish a just and lasting peace on earth.

The last few years have seen a radical turn from the Cold War to peaceful coexistence of states belonging to different social systems. This success has been gained in a sharp struggle, through intensive and complex work. As the Party had expected, the road towards the consolidation of peace was not an easy one. However, we advanced and will advance along this road indefatigably, never losing sight of our goal. This was re-emphasized by Leonid Brezhnev at the 25th Party Congress.

As is known, the policy of peaceful coexistence implies negotiating agreements, a quest for mutually acceptable, at times compromise, solutions, and organizing mutually beneficial co-operations with capitalist states. This was the case in Lenin's lifetime and is also the case today.

At the same time, our policy is a class policy as regards both its principles and its aims.

It is a class policy because it stems from the vital interests of socialism, the interests of socialist and communist construction. The new society needs peace, since it is easier to build a new society with a relaxation of tensions and a reduction in the arms burden.

Soviet foreign policy is a class policy also because the Party, while pursuing persistently a consistent and sincere policy of peace, firmly adheres to the principles of proletarian internationalism and solidarity with the peoples' struggle for freedom and social progress. There is no contradiction here. In the conditions of *détente* we do not expect the monopoly *bourgeoisie* and the governments complying with its will to side with the revolutionary struggle of the proletariat or the national liberation struggle of the oppressed peoples. The Soviet Union is not making such demands on the West. For its part, the Soviet Union reasonably expects not to be faced with demands for renouncing its solidarity with the fighters against exploitation and colonial oppression.

The Soviet Union has no intention to interfere in the affairs of other countries or to "export" revolution. Revolution, as Lenin has said, is bred by society's own development. It "cannot be made to order, or by agreement" in a foreign country.[1] Every people itself shapes its own destiny. However, if it takes the path of struggle, and is forced to fight the colonialists and repel attacks from foreign invaders and hired assassins, it may rely on our solidarity.

Our policy is a class policy also because it stems from a realistic awareness of the deep-seated divisions between states belonging to opposite social systems, which make their competition and a struggle of ideas inevitable. We are strongly convinced, however, that this must not undermine lasting peace and good relations that the Soviet Union offers to other countries.

This country is seeking to make the competition between states with differing social systems truly peaceful, free from military rivalry and constructive rather than destructive in nature. Such a

---

[1] V. I. Lenin, *Collected Works*, vol. 36, p. 457.

competition would open up broad prospects for mutually beneficial co-operation as well.

As far as the ideological struggle is concerned, the communists believe that no one can "abolish" it, just as no one can "abolish" the class struggle in general. Ideas reflect the interests of the social classes, their aims and ideals, their concepts of the ways of social development. As long as these ideas and concepts are in conflict the ideological struggle is inevitable.

The principles of peaceful coexistence, however, imply abstention from interference in each other's internal affairs under the guise of a struggle between ideas. In this area, however, a rather strange situation may be observed.

The very same circles and leaders of the capitalist world who accuse communists of hampering *détente* by vindicating the struggle of ideas themselves by no means renounce their ideological struggle against socialism. In this respect we constantly witness campaigns of lies and slander, attempts to conduct propaganda by methods which were in great favour during the Cold War and which must certainly be abandoned now in the period of *détente*.

It goes without saying that a relaxation of tensions implies a widening of cultural ties, of contact between individuals, and information exchange. This country has signed quite a few agreements in these fields and is determined to abide by them scrupulously. One should remember, however, the content and purpose of these agreements. These were steps designed to strengthen mutual trust and mutual understanding, to help consolidate peace and develop mutually beneficial co-operation.

We did not agree, however, on facilitating actions designed to harm socialism. The plans of reactionary circles connected with them are absolutely alien to the relevant sections of the Final Act signed at Helsinki.

Speaking of peaceful coexistence and the ideological struggle, it is also important to keep in mind the following. *Détente* itself is still the subject of bitter ideological controversy. Perhaps no other issue is arousing so much discussion and heated debates now.

Disputes about *détente* have become part of the internal struggle which has flared up in many Western countries. The enemies of *détente* are becoming more vociferous. In the heat of argument one may often hear statements harking back in content and even in phraseology to the Cold War. The world listened to such effusions for a quarter-century. They proved only one thing: the Cold War policy, the policy "from positions of strength" is senseless and dangerous. It is a threat to all, a threat to peace. It is dangerous and pointless for the West itself.

In the nuclear era there is no reasonable alternative to peaceful coexistence. It is beyond doubt that whatever turn may be taken by developments in the near future, the interests of the peoples and the objective trends in the development of international relations will call for the maintenance and promotion of *détente* and for enforcing the principles of peaceful coexistence.

The objective nature of these processes, however, does not relieve governments and political leaders of their responsibility. A hold-up in the progress of *détente*, let alone its backsliding, may cost dearly, leading not only to a senseless waste of material resources but also to dangerous exacerbations in the international situation.

The struggle for peace, peaceful coexistence and *détente* has grown into the broadest and most massive democratic movement on earth. This lends a new dimension to the responsibility of the communists, who are in the vanguard of all democratic progressive movements. Following the splendid traditions of proletarian internationalism, the communists oppose the multinational bloc of the enemies of peace and social progress by their united front, their solidarity, and their ability to rally the mass of the people. Today there is perhaps no better way of paying tribute to the memory of Lenin than being equal to these requirements and tasks and working tirelessly to implement them.

We live in a glorious and unique epoch when the most radiant dreams, the most daring plans of the working people, are coming true and materializing. This lends a special historic meaning to the struggle and constructive activities of the working class placed by history in the vanguard of social progress, to the struggle and activities of the Marxist–Leninist parties. Hence the lasting significance of Lenin's heritage of profound ideas and his immortal art of revolutionary creativity.

Celebrating Lenin's birthday each year, we draw new strength, as it were, from the life-giving source of Leninism. We learn from Lenin the science and art of finding creative solutions to problems raised by life.

The Party and country have started implementing the majestic tasks outlined by the 25th Party Congress. The Congress decisions embody Lenin's ideas developed creatively. Working to translate them into reality we are confidently advancing along the path charted by Lenin.

Long live the Soviet people following the Leninist path of communist construction!

Long live the Communist Party of the Soviet Union, the Party of Leninists!

Long live Marxism–Leninism, the international teaching of the working people of the whole world!

Faith in Communism as the Source of Inspiration for the Builders of a New World
Speech at a solemn meeting in Moscow commemorating the centenary of F. E. Dzerzhinsky's birth, 9 September 1977

Comrades!

Today we are celebrating the centenary of the birth of Felix E. Dzerzhinsky, an outstanding Communist Party leader and Soviet statesman, an associate of the great Lenin, one of the most illustrious members of the splendid cohort of Bolshevik Leninists.

Lenin and the Leninist generation of Bolsheviks were advanced to the political arena by the entire course of social development, and they themselves actively influenced the course of history. Their faith in the correctness of Marxist doctrine, their infinite devotion to the Party and working-class cause, their preparedness for self-sacrifice, their inflexible will and great humaneness, made up the image of these fighters steeled in the crucible of revolutionary struggle.

Rallied around Lenin and united by their common faith in his ideas, the Bolshevik Leninists constituted that stable core of leaders maintaining continuity, without which, to use Lenin's phrase, no revolutionary *movement* can be durable.[1]

". . . Only people who were truly brave and high-principled, only those who were not scared of either selfless, hard work or police persecution, those who placed the working people's happiness above everything else, only those people were capable of the exploit per-

---

[1] V. I. Lenin *Collected Works*, Vol. 6, p. 124.

formed by the first Leninist generation of communists of this country."[1]

AN ARDENT COMMUNIST REVOLUTIONARY

Everyone who reads about Dzerzhinsky's life and work admires the life of struggle full of incredible hardships and mortal danger he had to live along with all those who led Russia's proletariat in the battle against the tsarist autocracy and oppression by the exploiter classes.

His Party comrades and associates in the revolutionary struggle called Dzerzhinsky "the knight of revolution", "a proletarian Jacobin", "the iron Felix". He called himself by a much more modest name—a soldier of the revolution. As a soldier loyal to his duty and oath of allegiance, Dzerzhinsky defended the Party cause and struggle for a happy life of the working people as long as he lived. His communist convictions made him a staunch fighter, a professional revolutionary, and was the inexhaustible source of his energy and revolutionary ardour. He traversed the path from membership of the Social Democratic Party of Poland and Lithuania to membership of the Central Committee of the Bolshevik Party, one of the organizers and leaders of the Great October Socialist Revolution and socialist construction.

As a youth of seventeen years of age Dzerzhinsky pledged to "fight against evil to the last breath". He remained loyal to this pledge always and everywhere. Imprisoned in the Warsaw citadel by tsarist authorities, Dzerzhinsky wrote in a letter from his cell: "One should have an intrinsic awareness of the necessity to meet one's death for the sake of life, to go to jail for the sake of freedom and have the will-power to live through the hell of life with open eyes, looking for beauty, truth and happiness in this life."[2]

At the time of the October Revolution Dzerzhinsky was forty years old. He had worked for revolution for nearly half of his life. He had a record of eleven years of jail, exile and hard labour. He had escaped

---

[1] L. I. Brezhnev, *Following Lenin's Course. Speeches and articles*, vol. 4, p. 203.

[2] F. E. Dzerzhinsky, *Selected Works*, Moscow, 1967, p. 533.

from exile three times. After every escape he continued his revolutionary work underground.

Dzerzhinsky was a model of a genuine internationalist who was fully aware of the significance of the class struggle. A son of the Polish people oppressed by tsarism and an ardent Polish patriot, he was able to rise above the narrow nationalistic interests professed by the *bourgeoisie* and to realize that a true solution to the nationalities problem could be found only in alliance with the workers and peasants of Russia, in the struggle for the social liberation of the working people of the whole country.

Russia at the time was being torn apart by bitter antagonisms. A proletarian revolution was imminent. For that revolution to be accomplished, however, titanic efforts were required to educate and organize the masses.

In the country chained by tsarism, where all that was progressive was ruthlessly suppressed, where the ominous figure of a gendarme symbolized autocratic rule and lawlessness, where thousands of freedom fighters languished in prisons, victory in a revolution critically depended on the existence of a Marxist–Leninist party cemented by iron discipline, common will and actions, full of revolutionary determination and irreconcilable to opportunism of any kind.

". . . Give us an organization of revolutionaries, and we will transform Russia!" Lenin wrote.[1] Lenin founded such an organization. Lenin and the Leninist revolutionaries following him, Dzerzhinsky among them, headed the political movement which came to be known as Bolshevism in the history of the Russian and international working-class movement. Lenin and the Bolsheviks, Leninism and Bolshevism, are names and concepts which are linked inseparably in our minds.

The October Revolution was successful primarily because the working people were led by the Bolshevik Party, whose strategy and tactics were based on a scientific understanding of the laws of social development, a party deeply rooted in the midst of the people and capable of channelling the revolutionary enthusiasm of the masses towards the achievement of their common goals.

---

[1] V. I. Lenin, *Collected Works*, vol. 6, p. 127.

Such a party, however, was necessary not only for overthrowing the old system. It became quite indispensable when the Soviet Republic embarked on a programme of construction demanding great persistence and staunchness.

It was necessary to inspire millions of workers and peasants with faith in the righteous cause of communism and the triumph of its ideals, to stir the masses by concrete plans they could easily understand and lead them to that unprecedented exploit without which it was unthinkable to revive the backward, devastated and famished Russia. "We will build a new world of our own!" In these words of the proletarian anthem, the Bolsheviks proclaimed their faith. And the working people adopted this faith as their own convictions.

The communists devoted all their thoughts and actions to realizing their impassioned desire to advance the working man to the level of a conscious maker of history, to make his life better. "Our communist spirit", Dzerzhinsky said, "is our unity, the common aspirations and will of the proletariat from which we draw inspiration and strength to remove all obstacles in our way."[1]

In the process of building a new society the Party creatively develops revolutionary theory and practice and enriches Marxist–Leninist doctrine, thoroughly preserving its revolutionary principles and the spirit of Bolshevism. Its loyalty to Lenin's behests is embodied in the Party's imaginative approach to any problem in the political, economic, ideological and cultural fields.

Equipped with Marxist–Leninist theory, the Soviet Congress creatively summed up the experience in building developed socialist society in the USSR, the valuable practical record of the fraternal socialist countries, outlined new targets for our advance towards communism, and comprehensively substantiated the practical ways of achieving the tasks facing Soviet society.

Needless to say, these constructive tasks for their character and scope are hard to compare with those the Party was faced with in the early years of Soviet government. Our present economic strategy, social policy and foreign policy reflect the specific features of the present stage of historical development, the requirements of mature

---

[1] F. E. Dzerzhinsky, *Selected Works*, Moscow, 1977, vol. 1, p. 266.

socialist society. We have for their practical realization such enormous potentials that Lenin and his associates could only predict and dream of in their time. However, the early years of Soviet government and our times have in common what makes an inalienable feature of all our life, what is characteristic of communists in general—implicit faith in the ideals of communism. This has always been and remains the main source of the Soviet people's inexhaustible energy, of the Party's creativity and of all our achievements.

Dzerzhinsky's whole life exemplified such faith in the communist cause.

THE INTERESTS OF THE PEOPLE—THE SUPREME PRINCIPLE OF INTERNATIONALISM

Speaking of Felix Dzerzhinsky, it is necessary to recall his part is establishing revolutionary law and order and in defending the gains of the October Revolution.

Lenin said in his time "a revolution is worth anything only if it is capable of defending itself . . .".[1]

Lenin maintained that the dislodged exploiter classes cannot be abolished immediately after the conquest of power by the proletariat. He predicted that they would put up stiff resistance to the revolution, and that under certain conditions the class struggle may assume an *extremely bitter character*.[2]

The revolution in Russia bore out Lenin's prevision. Open armed rebellions and secret acts of subversion, terrorism and black-market operations, gangsterism and sabotage—all these were used by the former rich landowners and capitalists with direct support from imperialist forces in a desperate attempt to regain their positions of wealth and power.

Resolute measures were necessary to repel the onslaught of the counter-revolution. One of such retaliatory measures was the establishment of the All-Russia Extraordinary Commission for Struggle Against Counter-Revolution and Sabotage. Its first Chairman was

---

[1] V. I. Lenin, *Collected Works*, vol. 37, p. 122.

[2] V. I. Lenin, *Collected Works*, vol. 39, p. 280.

Felix Dzerzhinsky, who enjoyed the absolute trust of the Party and Lenin.

In keeping with Lenin's instructions, Dzerzhinsky laid the groundwork for the splendid traditions of the state security service. Under his immediate direction this service inscribed quite a few heroic pages in the record of struggle against the enemies of Soviet government.

Dzerzhinsky educated state security men in the spirit of utter devotion to the Party cause and this socialist country. As his associate Menzhinsky wrote, "he was able to merge the work of his Commission into the working-class cause so well that during all those years, in days of victories and in days of hardship, the mass of the workers regarded this work as their own cause and the Commission itself as their own organ of dictatorship, the dictatorship of the proletariat."[1]

The class enemies of the Soviet Republic circulated malicious lies about it and the activities of the Commission. Their attempts to depict the revolutionary reforms that were in progress and defence against sabotage and violent resistance as indiscriminate destruction and a reign of terror were deliberate and flagrant untruths. Such inventions and slander were intended to influence the mentality of the petty bourgeois, to mislead the public abroad and discredit the socialist system.

The revolution, indeed, involved destruction. It was destroying, however, only the old world of exploitation and oppression, because without that it was impossible to build a new, socialist world. The Soviet government confiscated landed estates, factories and banks from the landed aristocracy and the capitalists and made them the property of the people. The dislodged classes supported by world capital did whatever they could to frustrate that radical abolition of the system of exploitation of man by man. To thwart their counter-revolutionary plans the Soviet Republic had to resort to revolutionary coercion. That was the only practicable way of defending the revolution in the prevailing situation.

Lenin wrote in this context: "It is indisputable that without revolutionary coercion the proletariat could not have won its victory, but it is just as obvious that revolutionary coercion was a necessary and

---

[1] Felix E. Dzerzhinsky, *Reminiscences, articles, stories by his contemporaries*, p. 94.

legitimate method of revolution only at certain stages of its development, only under definite and specific conditions, whereas organization of the proletarian masses, organization of the working people was and remains a far more profound and permanent aspect of this revolution, a pre-condition for its victories."[1]

As Lenin repeatedly emphasized.

Construction was and remains the main function among all the fundamental functions of the Soviet state. The most conclusive evidence of that is the first decrees of the Soviet government on the land and on peace, its consistent policy of developing the economy and culture, of promoting the unity and brotherhood of all nations and national minorities of this country.

When the Soviet Republic had started its work of economic recovery and reconstruction, the Party entrusted Dzerzhinsky with the solution of formidable economic problems, leaving him in charge of the state security service. He was appointed People's Commissar for Transport Communications and organized the restoration of the war-ravaged network of transport services. Then he was charged with chairmanship of the Supreme National Economic Council and came forward as an active fighter for implementing the Leninist policy of socialist industrialization of the country. He actively contributed to the efforts to build up the iron-and-steel and other industries, to strengthen the country's defence capability, and worked selflessly to convert the USSR into a mighty industrial power. Whatever field the Party assigned him to work in, he invariably displayed his ability to organize people, to infect them with his enthusiasm, and to develop in them a keen sense of responsibility to the country and people.

Emphasizing this responsibility, Dzerzhinsky wrote as follows: ". . . just as in the days of the October Revolution when the victory of the workers and peasants was secured by their active efforts, self-sacrifice and class consciousness, now on the production front, with the workers in power and the *bourgeoisie* and its ownership of factories and plants abolished, only active and conscious efforts by the mass of the workers can secure our victory."[2]

---

[1] V. I. Lenin, *Collected Works*, vol. 38, p. 74.

[2] F. E. Dzerzhinsky, *Selected Works*, Moscow, 1977, vol. 2, p. 22.

Those who knew Dzerzhinsky personally, his associates in the revolutionary struggle, his colleagues at work, admired his exceptional integrity of character, his constant concentration on the efforts to cope with the most urgent and difficult tasks. For all his enormous prestige in the Party and among the people, he was an extremely modest man, unusually exacting to himself and attentive to others, intolerant of affectation and bombastic phraseology. "In this revolutionary", Clara Zetkin wrote, "everything was genuine and honest: his love and his hatred, his inspiration and his anger, his words and his deeds."[1]

Dzerzhinsky was known for his remarkable personality traits of a true Bolshevik Leninist: closeness to the people, kind-heartedness and humaneness. These qualities became especially obvious in his efforts to help homeless children.

In the early years of Soviet government child homelessness was a formidable and painful problem. The long years of the imperialist First World War and the Civil War had left in their wake more than five million child waifs. Despite the heavy burden of his regular duties and the difficulty of the situation prevailing, Dzerzhinsky, on instructions from the Party, extended the protection of the state security service to the care of homeless children. Millions of children were thus saved and became builders of a new society. This is another vivid evidence of the humanism of Soviet power.

Lenin and the Party paid great attention to making the laws of the new state, to the establishment and development of socialist law and order. This work was of exceptional sociopolitical significance. Fully aware of this fact, Dzerzhinsky struggled indefatigably for progress in this field.

The enemies of the Soviet Republic alleged that the dictatorship of the proletariat was incompatible with legality and the rule of law. That was a lie. In fact, immediately after its advent the new system began making its own laws, extending and developing all democratic achievements of the proletariat. From a tool for suppression of the working people, legislation was converted into a form of expression

---

[1] Felix E. Dzerzhinsky, *Reminiscences, articles, stories by his contemporaries,* pp. 41–42.

of the will of the workers and peasants. Soviet laws guaranteed the rights and freedoms of the working man, served to establish and maintain new and equitable law and order, and safeguarded society against the activities of hostile forces.

Socialist legality, just as Soviet government in general, was established in fierce battles against its class enemies. It had to be defended, often by force of arms, against saboteurs, anarchists, kulaks (rich peasants), bandits, and other counter-revolutionary elements. This struggle was waged by Red Army men and state security personnel, the workers' and peasants' militia, special-purpose units and armed workers' detachments.

From the early days of the October Revolution the Party pursued a policy of compliance with the Leninist principle of socialist legality in all elements of the machinery of state. This referred equally to the activities of the state security service. Its establishment was an extraordinary measure, dictated by the need to protect the security of the young Soviet Republic. Even in a situation of bitter class war, however, this service operated in strict conformity with revolutionary laws. Dzerzhinsky said in an address to state security servicemen: ". . . You are obliged to follow the path charted by the Party and Soviet government, the path of revolutionary legality, abiding by government decrees and strictly observing their fulfilment." He invariably demanded in most emphatic terms strict compliance with revolutionary legality in all activitities of the state security agencies and the militia, and took immediate action against the slightest abuse of authority.

Soviet laws express the main directions of Party policy and serve as a dependable instrument for state guidance of society. Their distinctive feature is genuine democracy and lofty humanism.

It is known that certain years were clouded by illegal repressions, violations of the principles of socialist democracy, the Leninist norms of Party and state activities. These violations were associated with the personality cult and contradicted the essence of the Soviet system, the character of the political system of socialist society. However, they could not halt the progress of socialism. The Party resolutely denounced and eradicated such violations and established secure guarantees of observance of socialist legality.

Soviet laws are perfected along with the consolidation and development of Soviet society. At the same time, they preserve continuity in what matters most—in the principles laid down by Lenin.

A remarkable example of that is the new Soviet Constitution, an outstanding political document of the times. It is a logical expression of all development of the Soviet state, and at the same time it offers a broad perspective of its further progress. The significance of the new Constitution was profoundly revealed in Leonid Brezhnev's report at the CPSU Central Committee's plenary meeting in May 1977.

The nationwide discussion of the draft Constitution conclusively proves that the Soviet people regard the new fundamental law as an embodiment and expression of their will and vital interests. They legitimately associate the democratic nature of the new Constitution with the consistent Leninist policy of the CPSU Central Committee, with the name of Leonid Brezhnev, who has won enormous prestige in the Party and among the people by devoting all his talent and strength to his tireless work for the benefit of the Soviet people, for the triumph of the great cause of communism, for peace throughout the world.

The enemies of socialism for obvious reasons are going out of their way to lessen the impression produced on the world public by the Soviet draft Constitution. Imperialist propaganda is trying to conceal the true meaning of the Soviet fundamental law and maliciously distorting it. This refers particularly to those provisions which formulate our understanding of the relationships between the state and the individual, between the rights and duties of citizens. In the West one may hear allegations to the effect that the rights and freedoms of Soviet citizens are sufficiently wide in themselves, but they are reduced to naught by making their enjoyment and application dependent on the interests of the state and society.

Soviet citizens see no contradiction in such dependence. They proceed from the premise that the individual enjoys genuine freedom if his activity is in line with the general trend of social progress.

By liberating man from all forms of social and national oppression socialism creates fundamentally new relations between the state and the individual, linking the interests of society and its members in organic harmony. This integration is deeper and more complete in the phrase of mature socialism.

Soviet laws grant broad political freedoms to every citizen in accordance with the democratic nature of socialist society. At the same time, they guard the Soviet system against attempts by certain individuals to exploit these freedoms to the detriment of society and the rights of other citizens. This is both democratic and fair, since what serves to strengthen the new society agrees with the vital interests of every honest Soviet citizen.

Naturally, we do not think that the mechanism of socialist democracy has reached the upper limit of development and perfection. It is one of the merits of the draft of the new Constitution that while widening the guarantees of the rights of Soviet citizens it clearly indicates the main lines of perfection of Soviet democracy. Such perfection will go hand in hand with the further development of social relations, the enhancement of the political consciousness of members of Soviet society, their socialist moral and ethical standards.

The nature of socialist society implies an expansion of rights and freedoms as a process organically linked with an enhancement of the responsibility of each of its members to society, the fulfilment of civil duties. Indeed, whenever a member of Soviet society neglects his duties or ignores the standards of social behaviour, he causes harm thereby to himself and to other persons, not to speak of the interests of society.

The great humanist Maxim Gorky wrote in his time: "Yes, I am against freedom, beginning from the line where freedom turns into dissoluteness. . . . This conversion begins where man, losing an awareness of his real social and cultural value, gives free rein to his hidden ancient individualism of a Philistine and shouts: 'I am so charming, so original, so inimitable, yet I am not allowed to live at my own sweet will.' It is not so bad when he only shouts, because when he begins to act at will, he becomes either a counter-revolutionary, or a hooligan. . . ." This statement of Gorky's has fully retained its relevance to date.

For the vast majority of Soviet citizens the fulfilment of their civil duties, respect for the law and abidance by its standards have become an inner want, a matter of habit, a rule of conduct. However, we cannot shut our eyes to facts of an underdeveloped sense of social duty which are still encountered in Soviet society.

Embezzlers of socialist property, hoarders, hooligans, money-grubbers, and persons evading socially useful work are still to be found in Soviet society. Therefore, while displaying utmost concern for intensive educational work, for legal enlightenment of citizens in particular, attaching prime significance to persuasion, the Soviet state at the same time resorts to coercive measures against individuals committing antisocial acts.

In the last few years the Party and government have taken a series of steps to improve the work of administrative bodies and to reinforce them with highly-qualified personnel. Today's tasks ensuing from the new Constitution of the USSR make still higher demands on the competence and efficiency of personnel of the courts of law, procurator's offices, the state security service, the militia, all those whose duty is to maintain socialist law and order.

All these bodies are now functioning under new historical conditions. Their basic function, however, remains unchanged. It is the function of safeguarding vigilantly the gains of the Great October Socialist Revolution, the security of the Soviet state, the Soviet social order.

The traditions laid down by Dzerzhinsky, the traditions of the state security service dating from Lenin's time, serve to this day as an authentic criterion for assessing the qualifications of every member of the state security service and the militia. To be superior to one's adversary intellectually and morally is the only possible way to identify and defeat him. Continuous self-advancement is indispensable to this end.

Communist convictions and high professional competence, moral integrity and loyalty to duty, constant vigilance and responsiveness, tactfulness and faith in people, general culture and a keen sense of civic responsibility—such are the qualities that make up the image of a Soviet security serviceman as seen by Dzerzhinsky and as seen by the people today. These qualities are cultivated by the Party, by the YCL, by all realities of socialist life.

The personnel of the state security service and the internal affairs agencies are fully aware of their responsibility for the area of work entrusted to them. They realize the fact that there are still quite a few shortcomings in their work which require elimination. They understand the need for further advancing the standards of all their activities, as is demanded by the Party's Central Committee.

The Soviet agencies guarding the security of the state and maintaining law and order derive their strength from constant guidance and unremitting control by the Communist Party.

They derive their strength from subordination of all their activities to the interests of the people and the Soviet state, from their reliance on their permanent and organic ties with the people, enjoying full trust and support of the masses.

THE IDEOLOGICAL AND POLITICAL UNITY OF SOVIET SOCIETY AND A REBUFF TO THE INTRIGUES OF THE ENEMIES OF SOCIALISM

Today, when this whole country is preparing to celebrate the 60th Anniversary of the Great October Socialist Revolution, and when we are casting our mind's eye down the path we have traversed, we can see that all enormous constructive work of the Soviet people was carried out in a situation of unending struggle against the forces which stood in the way of this country's socialist progress, interfered by various means with our efforts to build a new life and attempted to strangle the Soviet Union.

We have experienced and lived through foreign military intervention, economic blockade, counter-revolutionary conspiracies, fascist aggression, atomic blackmail.

The realities of life have shown the indestructibility of the Soviet system, the unflagging determination of the Soviet people to defend the gains of the October Revolution.

The enemies of socialism, however, are still unwilling to desist from their attempts to undermine the new system or at least to hinder its development if it is impossible to overthrow it by force of arms. They are waging a struggle against socialism in the political and economic fields, as well as in that specific field where intelligence services are operating, where espionage and subversion, including ideological subversion, are used.

The imperialist special services are shamelessly distorting the aims and the very essence of the policy of the CPSU and the Soviet state, denigrating Soviet reality and implementing in the ideological field other operations which are intended, in effect, to undermine the Soviet system and have been rightly called ideological subversion. They are seeking to erode and weaken the communist convictions of Soviet citizens, to implant in their minds views and morals alien to socialism and eventually to try and engineer political and social changes in Soviet society to the advantage of imperialism.

All this is, unfortunately, an inalienable part of the realities of the harsh world we are living in. Therefore, today too we must display high vigilance and take whatever measures are necessary to neutralize the subversive intrigues of the enemies of socialism. The Party regards this as the duty of not only the state security agencies but also all government and public organizations, all communists, all citizens of this country.

We have full reason to consider the unity of Soviet society our greatest achievement. History has never known a social system like ours, one that could unite in a friendly family all classes and social groups of society, all nations and national minorities of the country. However, it is precisely because the ideological and political unity of Soviet society has become a major source of its strength that the enemies of socialism are directing their most vehement attacks against this unity.

This is, in particular, the reason for the vociferous campaign of Western propaganda over the issue of "human rights" and the so-called "dissidents". It should be said that the very term "dissident" is a shrewd propaganda trick designed to mislead the public. This word is applied, as is known, to one who disagrees with the majority. Bourgeois propaganda has given currency to this term in an effort to prove that the Soviet system is intolerant of independent thought among Soviet citizens and persecutes anyone who "thinks differently" from what is allegedly prescribed by official policy. Such allegations have nothing in common with the truth.

In one of his recent statements Leonid Brezhnev clearly presented the Party stand on this question. "In our society nobody is forbidden to 'think differently' from the majority, to assess critically this or that aspect of social life. We regard comrades who come forward with justified criticism, trying to help matters, as conscientious critics and are thankful to them. Those who criticize by mistake we regard as deluded individuals."[1]

It would be educative for bourgeois ideologists to read Article 49 in the draft of the new Soviet Constitution. It clearly formulates the right of Soviet citizens to criticism and to making proposals for consideration by various bodies. Moreover, it expressly forbids persecution for criticism in this country.

The matter is different when a few individuals who have divorced themselves from Soviet society engage in anti-Soviet activity, violate the law, supply the West with slanderous information, circulate false rumours, and attempt to provoke various antisocial incidents. These renegades have not and cannot have any support within the country. This is precisely why they do not dare to come out openly at a factory, on a collective farm or in an office. They would have to take to their heels from there, figuratively speaking. The existence of the so-called "dissidents" has been made possible exclusively by the fact that the enemies of socialism have geared the Western press, diplomatic, as well as intelligence and other special services to work in this field. It is no longer a secret to anyone that "dissidence" has become a profession of its own kind, which is generously rewarded with foreign currency and other sops that differ but little, in effect, from what the imperialist special services pay to their agents.

Some Western figures invite us to explain what is in their view an "embarrassing" question: why are there "dissidents" in the USSR after sixty years of Soviet government?

This question is "embarrassing" only at first glance. Indeed, it would be unrealistic to imagine that among the Soviet population of over 250 million there are no individuals thinking differently from the vast majority on some specific issues.

We know from statements by Marx and Engels and from real life that the moulding of the new man requires much time and effort, even more than is taken by deep-going socioeconomic transformations. Moreover, the moulding of the new man in the socialist countries is a process taking place not in a vacuum but in conditions

---

[1] L. I. Brezhnev, *Following Lenin's Course. Speeches and articles*, Moscow, 1978, vol. 6, p. 336.

of a stiffening ideological and political struggle in the international arena. Comparing the sixty-year record of the new life with the thousand-year-old tradition of private ownership psychology and morals, one need not be surprised to discover occasionally in Soviet society individuals who are at odds with the collectivist principles of socialism. Such individuals, however, are dwindling in number, and we have every reason to regard this fact as our great success.

When every fundamental decision on home and foreign policy is submitted to a nationwide discussion, as is the case with the draft of the new Constitution now, when Party policy is embraced by the Soviet people as their own vital cause, when practically 100 per cent of the electorate vote for this policy, is it not conclusive evidence of the ideological and political unity of Soviet society?

This does not mean, however, that developed socialist society is guaranteed against the appearance of individuals whose actions are incompatible with either moral or legal norms of Soviet society. The reasons for this are various: political or ideological delusions, religious fanaticism, nationalistic obsessions, resentment caused by personal offence or failures interpreted as the result of underestimation of one's merits and abilities by society, and even mental imbalance to be found in some individuals. All of such cases do occur in our society. The construction of a new society, a new communist civilization is a complex and difficult process. And it cannot be otherwise.

As I have said, in Soviet society deluded individuals are helped through persuasion to correct their mistakes. Different measures are required when some of the so-called "dissidents" commit acts infringing Soviet laws. There is a handful of such persons in this country, just as, unfortunately, there are thieves, bribe-takers, profiteers, and other criminals. All of them cause harm to Soviet society and have to be penalized in accordance with the law.

All talk about humanism in such instances is irrelevant. We consider it humane to stop in good time the activity of those who are interfering with the normal life and work of Soviet citizens.

By the way, the number of citizens convicted for their anti-Soviet activity in this country is now smaller than at any time in the history of Soviet government. They are literally a paltry handful. This is the logical result of the political and socioeconomic processes of further consolidation of the unity of Soviet society.

Such is the true state of affairs as far as the so-called "dissidents" are concerned. It is as far removed from the scenes painted by bourgeois propaganda as heaven from earth.

The ideological struggle between the socialist and capitalist world has been going on since the early days of the October Revolution. This struggle is generated by the objective laws of social development, by the very existence and struggle of social classes, by the existence of states belonging to different social systems. Relations between these states may change, but the struggle of ideas remains an inevitable accompaniment to their coexistence.

The forms and methods of ideological struggle, however, are liable to vary with changes in relations between socialist and capitalist countries. The ideological struggle was an inalienable and important part of these relations in the period of the Cold War as well. At that time, a specific type of propaganda—"psychological warfare"—was launched through the efforts of the imperialist governments, and a special mechanism was established to conduct this propaganda. Its sole aim was to excite hatred of the socialist countries and to interfere in their internal affairs. Over the last few years a turn has been achieved at the cost of strenuous efforts from the Cold War to a relaxation of international tensions. New relations meeting the interest of nations in preserving peace and developing mutually beneficial co-operation are beginning to take shape between states belonging to different social systems, although this process runs a meandering course and is not always as smooth as it should be. Of course, in this situation too there is no cessation of the ideological struggle, that is the historic dispute over the merits of either social system and ways leading mankind to the summits of social progress. Such a struggle will inevitably continue in the future as well. Nevertheless, our Party believes that clearing the field of ideological struggle from the debris left in the aftermath of the Cold War is an important prerequisite for normalizing the international situation.

This has to be reiterated because the ultrareactionary quarters of the Western powers are stubbornly clinging to the discreditable methods of "psychological warfare". Far from curtailing, they are stepping up and refining the activities of the agencies specially set up to conduct it, such as Radio Liberty and Radio Free Europe, émigré organizations hostile to socialism, and other subversive centres. Moreover, it is demanded that we should not cause obstruction to the activities of these organizations.

Why do we oppose such activities? Of course, we have nothing to fear from bourgeois propaganda, even in its most vicious forms. The Party has implicit faith in the ideological staunchness of the Soviet people and is confident that nobody will ever succeed in undermining their unbreakable unity. The reason is different. Constant attempts to interfere in our internal affairs and slanderous propaganda campaigns cannot be interpreted by the Soviet people as anything but evidence of hostile intentions running counter to the principles of *détente*, to the spirit of the Helsinki accords.

This is precisely the reason why these activities are meeting and will meet in the future determined opposition on the Soviet side.

Increasing mutual understanding and trust today is a major prerequisite for success in the efforts to strengthen peace, to limit the arms, to achieve disarmament and normalize the international situation. If the ruling quarters of the United States and other Western powers are prepared, as they claim, to contribute to these efforts, the attempts to fan the atmosphere of hostility should be stopped. This is as clear as day and should be understood in the West, the sooner the better.

Over the six decades since the October Revolution the Soviet people led by the Communist Party have carried out sweeping transformations in all fields of social life and given an example of the practical solutions of fundamental problems advanced to the forefront by the entire course of human history. Today the Soviet people closely rallied behind the Party and its Leninist Central Committee headed by Leonid Brezhnev are confidently advancing towards communism and straining with great political and labour enthusiasm to fulfil the historic decisions of the 25th CPSU Congress, to attain the great and complex but inspiring targets of the Tenth Five-Year Plan.

At work and in battle, in all our life, we draw inspiration from Lenin's immortal ideas. We learn to struggle with selfless dedication for the implementation of these great ideas from the Bolshevik

Leninists. Felix Dzerzhinsky was one of them. For us they have always been and remain a model of dedication to communism and revolutionary ardour. They are always with us in the struggle for the triumph of communism. The finest monument to them is the Soviet people's historic accomplishments of worldwide significance.

Long live the Soviet people building communism!

Long live the Communist Party of the Soviet Union leading the Soviet people along the path charted by Lenin!

A High Award for Labour and for Courage in Battle

Speech at the presentation of the Order of the Red Banner of Labour to the City of Petrozavodsk, 5 August 1978

Dear comrades!

The city of Petrozavodsk is to be presented today with the Order of the Red Banner of Labour.

On behalf of the Central Committee of the Soviet Communist Party, the Presidium of the USSR Supreme Soviet, and the Soviet government, on behalf of General Secretary Leonid Brezhnev, I cordially congratulate you on this high award.

The decoration of Petrozavodsk is a recognition of its important role and place in the history of this country, its splendid revolutionary and war record, its significant contribution to the strengthening and further development of the economic and defence potential of the Soviet state. It is also an expression of high appreciation of the labour efforts of communists, workers, collective farmers and members of the intelligentsia, all working people of Soviet Karelia in implementing the assignments of the Tenth Five-Year Plan, the historic decisions of the 25th Party Congress.

Every city makes its own inimitable contribution to the common treasure store of material and cultural wealth of the country. But there are cities, large and small, which have been chosen by history to play a special role in the formation and development of the Russian state and this socialist country. The good fame of these cities does not fade, but lives on and grows with time. A distinctive place among such cities belongs to Petrozavodsk, which has celebrated its bicentenary.

Here under the decree of Tsar Peter I Tula casters and armourers

177

organized what was at the time large-scale production of iron, firearms and cannon for defence of the frontiers of the Russian state. The city which sprang up around the Peter works became the main industrial and administrative centre of the Olonetsk territory and played an important part in the economic and cultural development of Northern Russia.

Situated a short distance away from the new Russian capital St. Petersburg, Petrozavodsk and the entire Olonetsk territory could not but be influenced by progressive Russian thought, the progressive culture and revolutionary sentiments of the Russian proletariat.

The great Russian poet Derzhavin and the artists Shishkin and Polenov visited and lived in Petrozavodsk at different times.

Here in Karelia, Mikhail Kalinin and other Bolshevik Leninists carried out revolutionary work and inspired the working people with the determination to rise for an assault on the old world, with faith in their righteous cause. A backward and oppressed province of Russia, Karelia was drawn into the powerful mainstream of revolutionary struggle. As far back as 1906 a Social Democratic group adhering to the Bolshevik platform was set up in Petrozavodsk.

Under the leadership of the Bolsheviks, the working people of Karelia expelled from the Olonetsk provincial Soviet the Mensheviks and Socialist Revolutionaries who were unwilling to recognize Soviet government and who were insisting on Karelia's secession from revolutionary Russia. In January 1918 the Soviet government won the final victory in Petrozavodsk and set the stage for building a new life on Karelian soil.

The new Soviet government had to cope with formidable problems in overcoming economic and cultural backwardness and the ethnic problems inherited from the old system.

The overthrow of the exploiter system, as had been foreseen by the Marxist–Leninists, brought into play the working people's creativity on a scale unknown before and determined the development of new, socialist statehood which united them in a friendly family of free and equal nations. This was vividly demonstrated by the working class, the toiling peasants of Karelia.

In response to the attempts of the imperialists to tear Karelia away from Soviet Russia by open armed intervention and by organizing counter-revolutionary actions, the working people of Karelia declared their firm determination to stay with the Soviet Republic, "to defend the workers' and peasants' government to the last drop of blood".[1]

The desire of the Karelian people to build a new life in alliance with the Russian and other peoples of the Soviet Republic met with full understanding and support on the part of the Soviet government. The situation taking shape in the territory, the ways and means of solving the most complicated socioeconomic problems, the methods for the most effective solution of the ethnic problems, were the object of close attention and constant concern of Lenin and the government of the young Soviet Republic. Lenin said that he believed in the radiant future of the freedom-loving Karelian people.

By a decree of the All-Russia Central Executive Committee the Karelian Labour Commune was proclaimed on 9 June, 1920. This act reflected a quest for a practical solution to the question of autonomy for nations and national minorities rallying around Soviet Russia. This set the stage for the development of the national statehood of Karelia.

The ideas of international unity were expressed in the resolutions of the 1st All-Karelia Congress, which decreed that the Karelian Labour Commune "must remain in indissoluble union with Soviet Russia and develop its economy and culture in close co-operation with the worker and peasant masses of Russia. . . . Only a close union with Soviet Russia will safeguard Karelia against encroachments by the capitalists".[2]

Today we can see in the achievements of the working people of Karelia, just as the other peoples of this country, a brilliant practical expression of Lenin's idea of achieving the actual equality of nations as an indispensable prerequisite for securing and strengthening their international fraternal unity.

"In our country", Leonid Brezhnev has said, "there has emerged and strengthened a great brotherhood of working people united irrespective of their nationality by their common class interests and

---

[1] *Essays on the History of Karelia*, Petrozavodsk, 1964, vol. 2, p. 135.

[2] *Together with Lenin. Reminiscences, Documents*, Petrozavodsk, 1970, p. 318.

aims, there have emerged relations without precedent in history which we rightly call the Leninist friendship of nations. This friendship is our priceless possession, one of the most significant achievements of socialism which are cherished by every Soviet citizen. We Soviet people will always cherish this friendship as the apple of our eye."[1]

At the stage of developed socialism, nations reach new summits of progress and draw still closer together and the economy and culture of all Soviet nations and national minorities develop comprehensively. The Party consistently implements the principles of internationalism in the field of inter-ethnic relations and strengthens the friendship of nations as one of the fundamental achievements of socialism. Irreconcilable struggle against all manifestations and survivals of nationalism and chauvinism, against the trends of nationalistic narrow-mindedness and exclusiveness, idealization of the past and the glossing over of social antagonisms in the history of nations, against the customs and mores interfering with communist construction is an immutable principle of the Party's nationalities policy.

The fraternal friendship of nations, the unbreakable unity of Soviet society, became still stronger in the crucible of the Great Patriotic War and honourably withstood this test.

Heroic Soviet soldiers and partisans—Karels and Russians, members of other nations of this socialist country—shed their blood on Karelian soil. Tens of thousands of Karelian men and women were decorated by the government for their courage and heroism and twenty-eight of them were awarded the title of Hero of the Soviet Union. Eight of these heroes are natives of Petrozavodsk.

Petrozavodsk fought in the war and healed its war wounds together with the whole country. The city lay in ruins and it seemed impossible to rebuild it in a short time. The will and persistence of the Soviet people, however, gave it a new lease of life. The new, beautiful capital of Karelia rose from its ashes literally before our eyes.

What has been accomplished by the working people of the Republic, of Petrozavodsk first and foremost, particularly during the past few years, has completely changed the face of our land.

---

[1] L. I. Brezhnev, *Following Lenin's Course. Speeches and articles*, vol. 4, p. 50.

Soviet Karelia today is as before a beautiful land of forests and lakes, but it is also an industrial region with scores of new large modern factories and plants. Along with the development of such traditional industries as the fishing and timber industries, rapid progress is being made by new industries—general engineering, power and non-ferrous metallurgy supplying the needs of many areas of the country. Products of the Petrozavodsk Engineering Complex are well known outside the Republic. The Onega Works accounts for over one-half of the output of timber-hauling tractors manufactured in the Russian Federation. Newsprint produced at Kondopozh is used to print the Party's central organ—the newspaper *Pravda*.

The forty million roubles' worth of products over and above plan manufactured and marketed by Karelia's industrial enterprises over the last two and a half years of the current five-year plan is evidence of the increased scope of industrial production and the tense, enthusiastic work of the Republic's working class. Standing behind this figure are tens of millions of kilowatt-hours of electric power, hundreds of tractors and machine-tools, timber and pulp wood, fish and other products.

More than a quarter of Karelia's industrial output is produced in Petrozavodsk. Over the last two years of the current five-year plan the city's industrial output has increased almost 13 per cent. In the first half of the current year it has grown 7 per cent from the corresponding period of last year.

Today the people of Petrozavodsk are adding to the fame of those who struggled for the establishment of Soviet government here, who fought the invaders, and took part in rebuilding the city. Widely known beyond the boundaries of the Republic are the names of Heroes of the Soviet Union: Pavel Chekhonin, a turner of the Onega Tractor Works; Klavdia Petushkova, a brick-layers' team leader; Ilya Ovchinnikov, a building work team leader; Ivan Huttunen, a worker of a house-building complex; Evgeny Bekrenev, a worker of the "Petrozavodskmash" engineering complex; Evgeny Larchenko, a smith at the locomotive yard; Lidia Kopat, a worker of the mica factory, who has already fulfilled her assignments for four years of the current five-year plan. Many other workers follow their example in their work performance.

No praise is too high for the splendid work of personnel of the public education and health services, scientists and cultural workers, and workers of the consumer-oriented services. The art of E. S. Tomberg, People's Artist of the USSR, the writer A. N. Timonen, State Prize Winner of the Russian Federation, the composer G. N. Sinisalo, People's Artist of the USSR, is part and parcel of Soviet national culture.

The Order of the Red Banner of Labour is to be presented to Petrozavodsk at a time when this country has passed the equator, if I may say so, of the Tenth Five-Year Plan. The main political result of the past half of the five-year plan period is the successful implementation of the tasks outlined by the 25th Party Congress. A new important step has been taken in the solution of major social problems, in the further development and perfection of socialist democracy. The dynamic and steady development of the country's entire national economy has been ensured.

The immeasurably increased economic potential of this country can be illustrated by the following figures. Over the last two and a half years output has been greater than that during all prewar five-year plans: in electric power 9.5 times, oil 4.6 times, steel 2.6 times, mineral fertilizers 10 times. Such is the tremendous growth in Soviet production today.

Satisfaction of the people's material and cultural needs has always been and remains a matter of prime importance to the Party. Therefore, we are particularly proud of the spectacular record of fulfilment of the social tasks. In the first half of this year the average monthly earnings of factory and office workers were equal to almost 160 roubles as compared with 146 roubles in 1975. In Karelia this figure is even higher: 188 roubles. Over the period almost 5 million apartments have been built in the country, which has made it possible to improve the housing conditions of 25 million persons. There has been an increase in payments and benefits available from social consumption funds; they amounted to an enormous sum—50,000 million roubles—in the last half-year alone.

We do not conceal the fact that not all problems have yet been solved. We still experience shortcomings in supplies, shortages of high-quality goods and housing. Every honest working man and woman knows, however, that these difficulties tend to decrease year after year, that the Soviet state follows the line of fulfilling complex tasks which can and must be accomplished with the most active support and participation of all Soviet citizens wherever they may work.

The 24th and 25th Party Congresses advanced to the foreground the task of intensifying social production and of enhancing the efficiency and quality of all work. This is an objective requirement, a law issuing from the realities of life. Today it is necessary to fulfil plans not at any cost but with minimum inputs of manpower and materials. The essence of the policy of advancing efficiency lies in an ability to use skilfully, in a truly rational way, the enormously increased potentialities and advantages of the Soviet economy, the rich experience accumulated over the six decades of Soviet government, the competence and skills of our excellent specialists, the achievements of the scientific and technological revolution.

The July 1978 plenary meeting of the Party's Central Committee closely examined the problems involved in the continued advancement of agriculture. Leonid Brezhnev analysed in comprehensive and profound detail the Party's activities in developing agriculture at the present stage. In his report he formulated the principles and practical measures outlining the main ways of converting agriculture into a highly-developed sector of the national economy, of securing its further progress in accordance with the Leninist agrarian policy.

Experience has proved the correctness of the line charted by the March 1965 plenary meeting of the CPSU Central Committee. The Party's agrarian policy is being translated into reality by the efforts and will of the Soviet people. The material and technological facilities of agriculture have been reinforced considerably. Much has also been done to develop those branches of industry which supply agriculture with machines, equipment and mineral fertilizers. The implementation of the comprehensive programme of advancing agriculture is already yielding tangible results. Over the last seven years the average annual gross output of farm products has grown almost 50 per cent from the corresponding period before the March plenary meeting of the CPSU Central Committee. For instance, grain production has increased by 61.5 million tons and production of raw cotton by

3 million tons. Positive shifts are also in evidence in the development of stock breeding.

The plenary meeting reaffirmed the necessity to continue the line of intensifying agricultural production on the basis of its all-round mechanization and electrification, chemicalization and land reclamation. At the same time, the meeting pointed out the need to increase output per unit of manpower inputs and investments.

It is clear that determination of the concrete ways and means of further advancing agriculture extends far beyond the limits of this sector of the economy. The decisions of the Central Committee's plenary meeting are of general significance for the entire national economy.

The implementation of the measures outlined for the continued advancement of agriculture, just as the fulfilment of the assignments of the five-year plan as a whole, is determined in the final analysis by the work performance of each working man and woman, every labour collective in town and country. This, of course, is a matter of prime concern to Party organizations, to every communist.

In this country the communist has been and remains invariably the leading figure in town and country. As Leonid Brezhnev has said, the communist has never had, nor has he now, any special benefits or privileges except for one privilege and one duty—to lead the way in an attack in wartime and to give more strength and energy than others for the common cause in peacetime, to struggle and work better than others for the triumph of the great ideas of Marxism–Leninism. Today, as in the past, the communists are leading the way, setting splendid examples of selfless work, intolerance of manifestations of negligence and mismanagement, breaches of labour discipline and offenders against socialist morals. It is the duty of every communist to stand up vigorously for his convictions, to encourage people, to inspire them with confidence and determination, to lead them in all situations.

The constructive efforts of Karelia's working people are guided by the Republic's Party organization, a time-tested and battle-hardened contingent of the Leninist Party. At all stages of the formation and development of Soviet Karelia its party organization stirred its people to action in peacetime and in wartime, and led them along the right path charted by the Party's Central Committee.

There is no doubt that today too the communists of Karelia will be in the vanguard of the production front of this country. Karelia's working people will indisputably achieve still better results in all areas of communist construction.

The Soviet people are confronted by great and inspiring tasks. They have gained a secure foothold for attaining successfully the targets set by the 25th Party Congress. The Party pursues a time-tested economic and social policy on scientific principles in keeping with the great Marxist–Leninist theory. We have inflexible faith in our righteous cause and the wise leadership of the Soviet Communist Party.

The seventies, particularly their first half, were marked by important changes in world politics, the growth of the positive processes which have come to be known as *détente*. Relations between states belonging to different social systems have been developed with growing reliance on the principles of peaceful coexistence, which have provided the basis for developing mutually beneficial political, economic, and cultural ties. The danger of nuclear missile war has been lessened. The accords and principles recorded in the Final Act of the Helsinki conference signed at summit level three years ago are intended to promote *détente*, to safeguard the security of nations and ensure lasting peace on earth.

It would seem that the road lying ahead is clear. This is a road of patient and constructive settlement of conflicts and differences, new steps to slow down the arms race, to widen and deepen relations between countries belonging to different social systems, between all states of the world. To make *détente* irreversible is the task set before mankind by history. This has been clearly and consistently stated by Leonid Brezhnev, the leader of the Soviet Communist Party and a loyal Leninist. The Soviet Union and all nations of the socialist community have got down to work with great energy and determination to accomplish this task.

The advantages of *détente* for the peoples of all countries have been clear in the past and today. For all that, Washington's policy has of late been departing more and more appreciably from the stance of political realism, laying emphasis on the exclusive right of the United States to lecture everybody and tending towards moves unfriendly to the Soviet Union and even attempts to put pressure on it.

I have no comment on the extreme, to put it mildly, naivety of those who believe that a language of lecturing and threats may be used to talk to the Soviet Union. The record of international relations since the victory of the October Revolution has proved the absolute futility of attempts to this end. All the more hopeless are such attempts today when our strength has grown immeasurably, when a new life is being built along with the Soviet Union by the fraternal socialist countries, when the scope of anti-imperialist struggle is growing in Asian, African and Latin American countries, when the movement for democracy and social progress is mounting in the capitalist countries. If anybody stands to lose from the ill-conceived actions of the Washington administration, this will certainly be the American side, the American business community in particular.

But let us discuss this question on a different, broader plane. Why is the US administration inclined to retreat under pressure from the enemies of *détente*? Why is the wing gravitating towards the times and practices of the Cold War growing stronger within the American ruling quarters?

The point is that by all indications American imperialism has difficulties in revising its policy to adapt it to the new realities of international life. These realities are as follows.

A relaxation of international tensions is inevitably accompanied by a change in the character of the entire system of international relations. The principles of peaceful coexistence, equality and justice are beginning to play an ever greater part in these relations, which leaves less and less room for a policy of imperialist dictation, pressure and various kinds of "power play". An easing of world tensions stimulates the process of favourable social change, increases the influence of the working class and all working people on the policy of bourgeois governments. At the same time, *détente* has a favourable impact not only on the general atmosphere of world politics but also on the political climate within the capitalist countries.

In other words, *détente* on the one hand gives free scope to the operation of progressive tendencies, and on the other hand compels the ruling circles of the capitalist world to adapt to these tendencies, to introduce corresponding amendments into their foreign and home policy.

Needless to say, different sections of the *bourgeoisie* react differently to these objective dictates of the times.

Some of them, who hold realistic views, are aware of the fact that with the present alignment of forces in the world arena there is no sensible alternative to *détente* and therefore capitalists must adapt to the new situation, that is to recognize the need for peaceful coexistence with the socialist countries and even for co-operation with them, to revise the character of relations with the developing countries, to display greater flexibility on the fronts of social struggle.

Others, known as "hawks", who represent the interests of the military industrial complex, are resisting *détente* for all they are worth. They are calling on the West to take up whatever stick is heavier and wield it until the world lapses into a dangerous East–West confrontation and returns into the trenches of the Cold War.

Finally, there is another section, whose members realize in general outline the disastrous consequences of a global thermonuclear war. They are even prepared to reach limited agreements reducing the level of international tensions. However, they are scared of the change *détente* brings in its wake in international and internal affairs. Hence the instability, vacillations in policy, the growing discrepancy between word and deed, the efforts to play up to the right wing and concessions to the frankly militaristic, ultra-reactionary forces.

Of course, in our day it is not so easy to proclaim for all to hear a renunciation of the policy of *détente*, to call for a retreat to the positions of the Cold War. The enemies of *détente* have to use cunning and to dissemble, to mislead public opinion. This is precisely the reason for reviving the myth of the "Soviet menace" and other vociferous propaganda campaigns.

All this has naturally adversely affected the state of Soviet–American relations and caused relapses of international tensions. This is inseparably linked with the arms race stepped up by imperialism, with increased imperialist interference in the life of foreign nations, with persistent attempts to play the notorious "China card" against the Soviet Union.

The CPSU Central Committee and the Soviet government are closely watching the development of the situation and the manoeuvres of the enemies of *détente*. We take account of vacillations in

Washington's policy. At the same time, our own strategic line remains unchanged. The Soviet Union, Leonid Brezhnev has said, regards as its central aim in international affairs "Prevention of mankind's slipping to war, defence and consolidation of peace, universal, just and durable peace. This is our steadfast policy. It does not depend on any current expediency. It is legislatively laid down in the Soviet Constitution. We translate this policy into reality by all means at our disposal."[1]

The struggle for *détente* today is a struggle against the arms race, for peace, for restructuring the system of international relations on truly democratic principles. For the Soviet Union *détente* is a line of principle emanating from the very socioeconomic nature of the Soviet state, a continuation of the policy of peace proclaimed by the October Revolution and bequeathed to us by Lenin.

The foreign policy of the Party and the Soviet state is aimed at securing the most favourable conditions for successful implementation of the breathtaking tasks in communist construction, for maintaining international security and peace on earth.

The Soviet Union invariably comes out in the international arena side by side with other countries of the socialist community. Leonid Brezhnev's recent meetings in the Crimea with leaders of the fraternal parties of the socialist countries have demonstrated again that we have common aims, a common jointly planned strategy, that we realistically appraise the world situation with all its complexities, its pluses and minuses.

The difficulties being encountered by *détente* are to a certain extent inevitable. The world we live in is too heterogeneous. The contradictions dividing the two world systems are too deep-seated. The inertia of the past, the momentum of the Cold War, suspicion and mistrust are too great. We are convinced, however, that the states, social forces and political movements coming out for a relaxation of international tensions will win and secure a strong and lasting peace for all nations.

This is precisely why we display a maximum of restraint and come

---

[1] L. I. Brezhnev, *Following Lenin's Course. Speeches, messages, articles, reminiscences,* Moscow, 1979, vol. 7, p. 322.

forward with reasonable constructive initiatives. The Soviet Union is prepared to come to an agreement based on the principle of equal security at negotiations on a variety of issues, primarily on strategic arms limitation and at the Vienna talks.

We can see that the chills coming from Washington in certain cases unfortunately affect some West European capitals. We hope, however, that their political wisdom will enable our partners to overcome their time-serving vacillations and zigzags. The Soviet Union's European policy remains unchanged. It has repeatedly stated that a normalization of the political climate in Europe is one of the most crucial peaceful achievements of the last decade, that this achievement must be constantly supported, strengthened and widened. This is particularly important now when the enemies of *détente* are again exacerbating the international situation. Our stand is clear. Europe must become a continent of peace and good-neighbourly co-operation.

Here in Karelia I cannot but emphasize the full significance of the long record of good-neighbourly, truly equitable and mutually beneficial co-operation between the Soviet Union and Finland. Soviet-Finnish relations today are an integral and stable system of co-operation on a basis of equality in various political, economic and cultural fields. This is in fact an example of *détente* embodied in daily contacts, *détente* which makes peace stronger and human life better and safer. This is in the final analysis the highly humane purpose of socialist foreign policy, the foreign policy efforts of the Party and the Soviet government.

The international positions of this country are strong and stable. Aware of its material and spiritual strength, confident of its rightness, loyal to its internationalist duty, the Soviet Union has always been and remains a consistent champion of the cause of peace, the freedom and independence of nations.

I warmly congratulate you again and wish you and all working people of Karelia good health, a happy life, new great success in your efforts to implement the Party's decisions, in your work for the benefit of the entire Soviet people.

Long live the Soviet people building communism under the leadership of the Leninist Party!

Ideological Subversion —
the Poisoned Weapon of Imperialism
Excerpt from a speech at a conference at the Committee for State Security of the USSR, February 1979

Comrades!

In the great, complex and many-sided process of communist construction exceptional importance attaches to our Party's ideological work in the communist education of the working people. To build communism means not only to provide the requisite material and technological basis for communism but also to mould the new man worthy of his epoch. It is to educate the new man in the spirit of the most progressive and humane moral principles, in the spirit of noble ideas, loyalty to which has been sacredly preserved in this country since the time of the Great October Socialist Revolution.

Marx and Engels pointed out that "people developing their material production and their material association change along with this reality of theirs, their thinking and products of their thinking".[1] In the process of building up socialist relations of production, in the process of building up gigantic productive forces available to this country today, the thinking and spiritual image of Soviet citizens changed. As a result of the objective changes in the sphere of economic relations, the Party's active and purposeful ideological and political work, and its offensive against bourgeois ideology, the unchallenged supremacy of the Marxist-Leninist world outlook has been established in our society. Such remarkable qualities of Soviet citizens as ideological dedication, political activity, the spirit of collectivism and comradeship, a sense of responsibility to society and an awareness of the significance of their

---

[1] Karl Marx and Friedrich Engels. *Works,* vol. 3, p. 25

work for the common cause of the people, intransigence in relation to whatever contradicts the socialist norms and morals and interferes with the building of communism, manifest themselves with increasing clarity.

The guidelines for the ideological education and ideological work of the Party in general at the present stage are set in the resolutions of the 25th CPSU Congress. These resolutions are a militant programme of action for Party organizations, for all communists, all Soviet citizens. Carrying out its ideological work the Party emphasises that under present conditions, in a situation of relaxation of international tensions, the ideological confrontation between the two opposite systems, far from abating, on the contrary becomes stiffer.

In his report at the 25th Congress of the CPSU General Secretary Brezhnev emphasised that "in the struggle between the two world outlooks there is no room for neutralism and compromise. What is needed here is high political vigilance, active, prompt and conclusive propaganda work, a timely rebuff to ideological subversion".[1] This instruction fully determines the political importance of the work of the state security agencies in the struggle against ideological subversion used by the special services of imperialist powers to undermine the social system in our country.

What do we have in mind when we speak of ideological subversion of imperialism directed against socialism? What are its characteristic features, what is its interrelationship with the ideological struggle? A correct answer to these questions makes it possible to plan and use the most effective and expedient ways and means of opposing it.

Ideological subversion is undertaken in the area covering political, philosophical, legal, ethical, aesthetic, religious and other views and ideas, that is, the sphere of ideology where a battle of ideas is in progress. Therefore, ideological subversion has many characteristic features instrinsic to the ideological struggle. But it is not the conventional ideological struggle which is the objective result of the real existence of the two opposite systems. Ideological subversion is primarily a form of the subversive activities of imperialism against socialism. Its purpose is to weaken and unhinge the socialist system. It

---

[1] L. I. Brezhnev. *Following Lenin's Course*, vol. 5. p. 533

is conducted by special means and often amounts to direct interference in the internal affairs of socialist countries which contravenes the generally recognized standards of international law and socialist laws. The fact that it is being conducted in the field of ideology does not change its subversive, illegal character. This is what determines in the first place the sternness and intransigence of our struggle against ideological subversion in whatever form.

Lenin pointed out in his time that, unable to stem the spread and oppose the influence of Marxian theory, the enemies of socialism resort to the most treacherous methods in the struggle for the minds of men. "When the ideological influence of the bourgeoisie on the workers declines, is undermined, and weakens", he pointed out, "the bourgeoisie always and everywhere resorted and will resort to the most blatant lies and slander".[1] As can be seen from the above, Lenin not only exposes the causes inducing our opponents to resort to means of subversion in the ideological field but also directly points to the most essential methods of ideological subversion — lies and slander.

Ideological subversion is wholly and completely based on lies, fabrication and crude distortion of facts. It is also distinguished by the fact that in our day it is carried out not by a conventional propaganda staff but by specially organized services. These special services take advantage of course, of the machinery of bourgeois propaganda, use all the mass media, but place their main stakes on special subversive facilities.

Ideological subversion has been used by opponents of socialism since the early days of the October Revolution. It was used at all stages of the struggle of world capitalism against this country, against the forces of world socialism.

Today, however, we have come face to face with its unprecedented escalation and stiffening, and the fact that imperialism reposes great hopes in this subversion.

Why is this so? At one time the capitalists attempted to defeat socialism by force of arms. As is known, this proved to no avail. They could not defeat us in war. Today a direct military conflict with the socialist world will not give imperialism any chance of victory. They

---

[1] V. I. Lenin. *Collected Works*, vol. 25, p. 352

have no chance to win such a war, because our defence capability has grown immeasurably, because the alignment of forces in the world arena has changed in favour of socialism, and because of the character of nuclear missile war in general.

Nor can imperialism arrest our socio-economic development by means of economic sanctions as it attempted to do in the past. It has no chance in this field because the Soviet Union today is in possession of enormous productive forces, a highly developed economy, and a great scientific and cultural potential, and because the power of the countries of the socialist community has increased tremendously.

In this new changed situation the imperialist circles are seeking to achieve their former goals by means of under-mining socialism from within, using various weapons including ideological subversion. This subversion has become one of the most important weapons of struggle against the Soviet system in the hands of these gentlemen and their mercenaries.

The Soviet people are rightly proud of the fact that one of the greatest achievements of socialism is the socio-political and ideological unity of Soviet society. "In the years of socialist construction in our country", General Secretary Brezhnev has said, "a new historical community of men — the Soviet people — has come into being. In their joint work and struggle for socialism, in battles in defence of socialism, new harmonious relations have emerged between classes and social groups, nations and national minorities — relations of friendship and cooperation. The Soviet citizens are united by their common Marxist-Leninist ideology, the lofty aims of the construction of communist society".[1]

The socio-political and ideological unity of the Soviet people is generated by the very nature of socialism. This unity is organically inherent in the socialist system which has done away with the system of exploitation of man by man and affirmed social and ethnic equality. For its part this unity lends special strength and viability to Soviet society and the socialist system. This is one of the most important manifestations of the dialectics of our social development.

Imperialism is also aware of these dialectics. This is precisely why it

---

[1] L. I. Brezhnev. *Following Lenin's Course.* Moscow, 1973, vol. 3, p. 279

intends to undermine the unity of our society, its cohesion with the Leninist Party by means of ideological work in general and ideological subversion in particular.

This subversion is aimed at influencing the views and sentiments of citizens, their world outlook and, through their consciousness, their political and moral conduct.

Ideological subversion is used by opponents of socialism to try and retard the process of the enhancement of the communist awareness of the working people which is linked inseparably with the general socio-economic progress of Soviet society and for its part exerts an influence upon it.

The imperialist special services resort to ideological subversion to alienate Soviet citizens from the principles of our ideology, that is, from Marxism-Leninism; to alienate them against the moral and ethical norms of social community life. Here, in the sphere of struggle for the minds of men, imperialism does not rely exclusively on the means of conventional ideological struggle, on bourgeois ideas which have long been exposed as antipopular and reactionary. It brings into play the poisoned weapon of ideological saboteurs — misinformation and slander, falsification and lies.

In this way it seeks to incite citizens against socialism or at least brainwash them ideologically, to generate sentiments of selfishness, mistrust, uncertainty, to sow the seeds of political indifference, to cloud and poison their consciousness with nationalistic prejudices, to undermine their communist convictions. Indeed, it is precisely the morally impotent, politically spineless individual, susceptible to various sensations and rumours, that becomes the first victim of ideological subversion.

Our class adversaries take this into account. They operate adapting themselves to the concrete conditions prevailing and to the mentality of the individual. For instance, in the early period of Soviet government the enemies attempted to influence the masses by intimidating them with fabrications about "garrison socialism", a "ban on personal property" and even about "socialization", "proclaiming wives common property". These were crude tactics designed mainly for individuals with a low level of political awareness. Needless to say, today such primitive fabrications would not be believed by anybody in the Soviet Union. Times have changed. Today imperialism is operating by more delicate means. It seeks to adapt itself to the processes of further perfection and development of all aspects of our social life and socialist democracy. In this context imperialists cry from the house tops about the "flaws" of the socialist system, the "suppression" of human rights and freedoms in our country, about the need to "improve socialism". And all these arguments are presented, of course, in the bourgeois spirit. Particularly active in this field are warlike zionist organizations, acting as a tool of the most reactionary imperialist circles.

The imperialist special services are trying to infiltrate all ideological spheres and take advantage for their ulterior motives of both acute political problems and problems not at first glance connected directly with politics and related to the mores, tastes and habits of individuals. They are trying to "work" and attack socialism from the front and from the flank, employing various means, ranging from those which look outwardly harmless to those which are frankly hostile.

We are waging a determined fight against the subversive actions of imperialism. This, however, by no means implies, as some persons in the West are trying to depict, that the Soviet state is opposed to broad association with other countries in the most diverse branches of science and culture. In our day no society can develop successfully without an exchange of advanced achievements of world civilization. The Soviet Union is in favour of developing scientific and cultural exchange with other countries. However, we are opposed to cultural exchanges being used for subversive purposes which have nothing in common with a genuine exchange of cultural values.

We are sometimes faced with the question: "How can individual anti-social behaviour or negative actions by a handful of outcasts pose any danger to Soviet society? Can they really unhinge the foundations of socialism?"

Of course, not, if we regard each case of such actions or politically harmful behavior in isolation. However, viewing them *in toto* and taking into account their links with the content and aims of ideological subversion by imperialism, such actions are not harmless at all. Indeed, our adversaries expect to mislead gullible individuals by means of gradual erosion of their faith in communist ideals, to push them further and further along an alien and dangerous road and sometimes to entangle them in a spider's web of espionage work, taking advantage of such monstrous survivals of private-owner mentality as hoarding, greed, and so on. Through "erosion" of the consciousness of individuals they are trying to undermine the political institutions of socialism, our entire social system. We cannot afford to ignore such actions.

In implementing its ideological subversion imperialism pursues another goal. It is trying to discredit real socialism in the world arena, to weaken its revolutionizing influence and thereby take the heat out of the class battles in the capitalist countries, to split the communist ranks, the working class and all working people, to paralyze their will to struggle against their exploiters. This is why the fight against ideological subversion is not only our internal affair but an internationalist cause as well.

In the struggle against ideological subversion there are two aspects — external and internal. Its masterminds remain abroad, but their subversive operations are directed into the depth of this country and against Soviet citizens.

As is known, in the Soviet Union there are no social class foundations generating anti-Soviet activity. This does not mean, however, that individuals whose views and behaviour contradict our morality and our laws cannot exist under socialism. Such views and behaviour can be generated by various causes. They may be due to inadequate ideological dedication and political delusions, to religious fanaticism and nationalistic survivals, to family difficulties and moral degeneration and sometimes simply an unwillingness to work. It is precisely such individuals that are in the focus of ideological subversion on the part of our adversaries.

Of course, not every one of them would go to the length of committing a crime against the state under the influence of the enemy. Experience has proved, however, that everyone who has taken a path hostile to socialism has a history of moral degradation and departure from the standards of social morality.

Safeguarding the interests of Soviet society, the state security agencies aim their strikes against the actions of the masterminds of ideological subversion — against the special services and subversive centres of imperialist powers. The struggle against them has a determined and relentless character.

Taking a look at the second, internal aspect of this question, it should be clearly remembered that here we have to deal with Soviet citizens. This fact makes it incumbent upon us to be particularly considerate and cautious.

The state security men are called upon to fight for every Soviet citizen whenever he has made a slip and strayed from the path, so as to help him return to the right track again. This is one of the major aspects of the activity of the state security agencies. It is of great political significance, ensues from the humane essence of our system, and meets the requirements of the Party's ideological work. With their specific means, in their specific area of work, the state security men are fighting against everything that is alien to our ideology and morality, and making their contribution to the great cause of moulding the new man. They safeguard Soviet citizens against the subversive operations of imperialist special services. So when one sees that his work yields fruit one cannot but experience a feeling of not only professional but also Party, civic, satisfaction as a Party member and citizen. We must pursue this line in our work still more actively, energetically and purposefully in the future as well.'

The entire record of struggle against ideological subversion by imperialism illustrates the futility of its attempts to undermine the socialist social system, the ideological convictions of Soviet citizens. Under the leadership of the Leninist Party the Soviet people have repelled all attacks of their enemies, successfully accomplished the constructive tasks of the revolution and built a mature socialist society for the first time in mankind's history. These achievements have been recorded in the new Constitution of the USSR. It gives a powerful impetus to acceleration of our advance towards communism, towards the continued consolidation of the socio-political and ideological unity of Soviet society.

Our Party regards the education of all working people in the spirit of strong ideological dedication and loyalty to communism as one of the main directions in its ideological work. The 25th CPSU Congress called attention to the task of moral education, to the need for every communist and every Soviet citizen to assume an active stand in life, to develop a conscious attitude to his public duty, lofty sentiments of

Soviet patriotism and proletarian internationalism. The Party is conducting this work on the solid foundation of Marxism-Leninism. The Soviet citizens derive from it their confidence in the righteous Party cause, their unshakeable faith in the triumph of our great cause.

Our class enemies are compelled to admit the strength and unity of Soviet society, the cohesion of the Soviet people with the Communist Party. Small wonder, therefore, that they admit with regret in the imperialist camp that various political provocations have no chance of success within Soviet society.

Can we claim, however, that the acuity and significance of the struggle against ideological subversion have now diminished? No, we cannot. This is primarily due to the exacerbation of the ideological struggle between the two opposite systems on the world scene, the sharp escalation of ideological subversion by imperialism, and the attempts of its special services to influence individual Soviet citizens and prod them to a path of anti-social behaviour.

In this situation we are obliged to enhance our political vigilance and to increase the effectiveness of our measures to thwart ideological subversion.

It can be seen from the aforesaid that the work of the state security agencies to neutralize ideological subversion by imperialism is first and foremost political work. The state security men must always remember that they are the political fighters of our Party in the most crucial areas of the class struggle. The main and indispensable condition for a correct political line to be pursued in all activities of the state security agencies is their daily guidance by the Communist Party and its Leninist Central Committee.

The specific conditions of the work of the state security agencies make especially stringent demands on those who have been assigned by the Party to work and struggle in this area. Among all these demands pride of place is held by the qualities of communists — ideologically dedicated, politically mature and vigorous fighters for the Party line. They are obliged to be high-principled, selfless and loyal to the Party.

Every one working in this area must be constantly aware of his great political responsibility, of the profoundly humane Party goals of the cause he serves. This is a cause worthy of a life-long struggle, of complete dedication and enthusiasm.

Under the Banner of Lenin, Under Party Leadership

Speech at a meeting with the Stupino District constituency on the occasion of nomination for election to the Supreme Soviet of the Russian Federation, 22 February 1979

Dear comrades!

It is for the third time that you have nominated me for election to the supreme body of government of this country—the USSR Supreme Soviet. Allow me to express my heartfelt thanks and deep gratitude to you and the entire constituency of the Stupino district for the profound trust bestowed upon me.

I realize that your trust in me is primarily an expression of your confidence in the Communist Party of the Soviet Union, your approval and support for its policy motivated by the vital interests of the Soviet people and designed to secure for them a life of peace and prosperity.

The trust of the electorate implies high commitments on the part of the deputy. I have worked to the best of my ability to cope with my duties as an elected representative of the people. This refers to the area of work I am responsible for. This also refers to my participation in the activities of the USSR Supreme Soviet. Finally, this refers to the fulfilment of your mandate. I understand that not everything has been done as we would like it to be done, that not all problems have been resolved. Your mandate, however, is being fulfilled on the whole. It is your right to give an assessment of my work as your deputy.

The elections to the USSR Supreme Soviet and the current election campaign are a great and important political event in the life of this country. In accordance with tradition, the election campaign is accompanied by a nationwide discussion of the results of the efforts we have made, a serious debate on the pressing tasks in economic and cultural development. This is socialist democracy in action, which implies practical participation of each and all in the discussion and management of the affairs of state, production and society.

Soviet democracy, the entire Soviet social and state system, take their origin from the Great October Socialist Revolution. It is for over six decades that the Soviet people led by the Party has been steadily advancing along the path opened by that revolution.

"To follow the path of the October Revolution", Leonid Brezhnev has said, "means to strengthen the economy of this country, to enhance the productivity of labour, to advance the living standards and culture of the people.

"To follow the path of the October Revolution means to develop socialist democracy, to strengthen the friendship of Soviet nations, to educate the people persistently in the spirit of the lofty principles of communism, to cherish the unity of the Party and the people as the apple of one's eye."[1]

Discussing the burning problems of today we go back in thought to our sources and realize with crystal clarity that our achievements, all our life are a continuation of the ideas of the October Revolution, a development of the enormous revolutionary potential it called into being, which lives on in the decisions of the Party, in all our constructive activities.

Reviewing the path we have traversed since the October Revolution we realize again the correctness of the simple but brilliant idea of Lenin's that socialism is created by the masses. "All that we have achieved", Lenin said, "shows that we rely on the most miraculous power in the world—the power of the workers and peasants."[2] Indeed, all that we have achieved, all that we possess and can be proud of, has been created by the working people of the Soviet Union. It is precisely the Soviet working people and their ideological

---

[1] L. I. Brezhnev, *Following Lenin's Course. Speeches and articles,* vol. 2, p. 145.

[2] V. I. Lenin, *Collected Works,* vol. 44, p. 234.

and political vanguard—the Communist Party—that have always been and remain the motive force of social transformations, the force which has assumed government of society and state. This is the deep-rooted unshakeable foundation of socialist democracy, which makes the working man the central figure in the entire political and social system of socialism.

The current elections are to take place at a significant time. Taking a look at what matters most to the Soviet people today it can be safely said that the decisions of the 25th CPSU Congress in the field of home and foreign policy are being successfully translated into reality. We have entered the fourth year of the five-year plan, that is we have reached the frontiers of progress which will determine the results of the fulfilment of the plan as a whole.

Much of what was planned has already been done. The economy has been advanced to a higher level of development by the selfless efforts of the Soviet people. Hundreds of large modern industrial projects have been built and commissioned. Among them are such giants as the KAMAZ motorworks and the "Atommash" nuclear engineering complex, the Armenian, Leningrad and Chernobylskaya atomic power plants, the Ust-Ilim and Toktogul hydropower stations, the Orenburg gas complex, the Lebedinsky ore-dressing complex, to mention but a few.

At the time of the last elections the BAM railway project had just got off the ground, and today more than 1500 kilometres of steel tracks have been laid. As the Party indicated, the construction of this line will solve not only transportation problems but will also inspire a new life into a vast undeveloped area with a variety of natural resources.

In the Seventh Five-year plan period 1 per cent of the increment in industrial output was equivalent in monetary terms to 1600 million roubles, whereas today its real value has grown to 5000 million roubles. This truly gigantic figure has behind it the tense, inspired work of those who design new factories and plants, those who build them, those who man machine-tools and those who make them ever more efficient, those who organize production and those who directly produce material values. This figures expresses the great scope of our plans and decisions, which embody the will and experience of the masses and in which every working man and woman clearly sees a reflection of their interests and aspirations, the result of their participation in the management of production and all public affairs.

Agriculture is also making steady headway. As you know, a record grain harvest was gathered last year. The annual average grain production in the last three years was 36.6 million tons larger than in the previous five-year plan period. There has been a growth in production of cotton, sugar beets, vegetables, and livestock farm products. This success is the direct result of the efforts made by the working people in town and country to reinforce the material and technological facilities of agriculture. It is also graphic evidence of the correctness of the Party's agrarian policy reaffirmed by the July 1978 plenary meeting of the CPSU Central Committee.

As your deputy I am very pleased to know that the working people of the Stupino, Kashira, Serebryano-Prudsky and Domodedovo districts are contributing effectively to the common labour efforts of the Soviet people. You have quite a few remarkable masters of their trade, who smelt metal and produce electric power, fly aircraft and build machines, grow grain and vegetable crops, obtain large increments in meat and milk production. It is necessary to have more and more such front-ranking workers. It is necessary to work without lags on the part of certain individuals to prevent concealment of facts of negligence and mismanagement with good overall performance. This is a dictate of the times and a demand of the Party.

In short, never before has this country been in possession of such an enormous economic, scientific and cultural potential, such broad possibilities for advancement. It is necessary to take advantage of them in a rational way, with utmost efficiency. Hence the key task set in the Tenth Five-Year Plan: to raise the efficiency and quality of all our work.

How is this task being implemented? It is being attacked by every working man and woman, every labour collective, who persistently mobilize latent reserves, more strictly observe production discipline and the regime of economy, work with great energy and initiative. Growing demands are made on the standards of management of the national economy. The CPSU Central Committee is demanding improvement of all planning work, more active and skilful use of economic incentives so as to link together more closely the interests of society, labour collectives, and each of their members.

The Party has always regarded and regards economic development as the only possible way of supplying the growing material and cultural needs of the people. As Lenin taught us, the ultimate goal of socialism is to secure "complete well-being and free all-round development of all members of society".[1] Our Party is unswervingly following this line.

The assignments for increasing the incomes of the population set for the first three years of the five-year plan have been fulfilled. Over the years since the last elections the wages and salaries of factory and office workers and remuneration for the work of collective farmers have been increased. Over the same period the housing conditions of 54 million persons have been improved. This figure is comparable to the population of a large country.

Citing these facts I wish to emphasize that the growth of the people's well-being is directly dependent on the quality of our work, the labour efforts of each and all. We live well, if we work well. And if we want to live better, we must work still better, we must stimulate those who lag behind to catch up, and we must be intolerant of shortcomings.

Praising our successes, therefore, the Party at the same time discusses the existing difficulties in a frank and straightforward manner, and indicates the concrete ways and means of overcoming them. Such a high-principled discussion took place at the November 1978 plenary meeting of the Party's Central Committee. As you know, it placed strong emphasis on the need to put an end to dispersion of capital investments, to the growth of uncompleted construction projects, to breaches of planning discipline, to losses in agriculture.

"The Soviet people can understand difficulties caused by bad weather", Leonid Brezhnev said at the plenary meeting, "but they cannot and will not accept facts of mismanagement, irresponsibility and negligence as a justification for the existing difficulties. This is why we have full reason to say today that the problem of losses of

---

[1] V. I. Lenin, *Collected Works*, vol. 6, p. 232.

grain, vegetables, fruit, and cotton has not only economic implications. It also has important political implications. . . .''[1]

This statement, which is pervaded with concern for the needs of the
Soviet people, must become a guide to action for all Party, local
government and economic bodies.

The CPSU Central Committee and the Soviet government constantly keep in the focus of attention everything that is related to the
people's conditions of life and to meeting their demands.

Of course, each of such problems must be approached realistically.
We are building an enormous amount of housing. Nevertheless, a
housing shortage is still to be felt. It would be unreasonable to
promise to meet all needs and requests immediately. However, we
are consistently and stubbornly advancing and will advance towards
this goal.

Keen attention is paid to measures called upon to put an end to
shortfalls in supplies of some kinds of foodstuffs, especially meat, to
the population. The Party has drawn up a programme for resolving
this programme. Its successful implementation will make it possible
to improve the supply of the population substantially. The same is
true of the continued development of industrial consumer goods
production. In short, whatever is necessary and possible is being done
to further improve the life of the people.

I wish to emphasize that there is only one way to resolve all these
problems: a general increase in the efficiency of social production. In
other words, it is necessary to produce as many high-quality goods as
possible and to utilize what has been produced as best we can, in the
most rational way. This is truly a task for the whole people. The
better and the more effectively all of us will work, the sooner this task
will be accomplished.

Soviet people rightly say that the new Constitution of the USSR is
a crucially important political and legal document which reflects our
achievements and the prospects of communist construction in this
country. Not much time has elapsed since the adoption of the
Constitution. However, it is already clearly obvious that it is exerting

---

[1] L. I. Brezhnev, *Following Lenin's Course. Speeches, messages, articles, reminiscences*, vol. 7, p. 533.

a highly favourable influence on all aspects of social life and has become an organic part of the current practice of communist construction. The whole Soviet people took part in formulating the fundamental law of their state. And now that the Constitution has come into force the Soviet people are actively translating its provisions into reality.

Further development and perfection of socialist democracy is one of the main directions of the activities of the Party and state. This has been laid down in the resolutions of the 24th and 25th Party Congresses and is recorded in the Constitution. There has been a corresponding growth in the role and significance of the Soviets, which Lenin described as a "form of democracy which has no match in any other country'.[1] Public organizations and labour collectives are ever more actively involved in the management of all affairs of state.

The constitutional rights and freedoms of Soviet citizens have become wider and more effective. Simultaneously the guarantees of these rights and freedoms and the democratic principles of relations between the individual and the state have been reinforced.

Exercising their rights Soviet citizens perform their duties as well. The more profound the awareness of all Soviet citizens of the inter-relationship between their rights and duties and the more responsible their approach to the fulfilment of their civic duties, the more meaningful and effective is socialist government of the people which was established by the October Revolution and which has absorbed the experience of mass political creativity of over sixty years.

The socialist way of life and socialist morals have taken a firm root in this country. This is not to say, however, that we have created an ideal world inhabited by ideal people. Unfortunately, we still encounter such phenomena alien to socialism as deliberate breaches of labour discipline, drunkenness, hooliganism, bribery, embezzlement of socialist property and other anti-social acts interfering with the normal life and work of Soviet citizens.

The Communist Party and the Soviet state are doing much to eradicate crime and to prevent offences against the law. The struggle against criminal offences and anti-social behaviour, however, is a task

---

[1] V. I. Lenin, *Collected Works*, vol. 35, p. 238.

not only for government agencies but for the whole society, a civic duty of all honest Soviet citizens, all labour collectives. The more actively this duty is performed, the earlier we shall uproot this evil.

You know what area of work I have been put in charge of by the Party and the government. Allow me to say in this context a few words about the state security agencies.

The main prerequisite for a correct political line in all activities of the state security service, for success in their work, is daily guidance by the Communist Party. Speaking at the 25th CPSU Congress, Leonid Brezhnev said: "The state security agencies carry on all their work, which takes place under the Party's guidance and unflagging control, in the light of the interests of the people and the state, with the support of broad masses of working people, and with strict observance of constitutional rules and socialist legality. That is the main source of their strength, and the main earnest of the successful exercise of their functions."[1]

The central task of the state security service is to neutralize the subversive operations of reactionary imperialist forces against this country. Agents of Western intelligence services, emissaries of foreign anti-Soviet organizations are attempting to ferret out our secrets, take part in organizing acts of ideological subversion, seek to "brainwash" and corrupt some unstable, weak-willed individuals. Therefore, as the CPSU Central Committee indicates, constant vigilance on the part of all Soviet citizens remains an important and pressing demand of the day.

Inside the Soviet Union there is no social basis for anti-Soviet activity. Nevertheless it would be wrong to ignore still existing facts of criminal offences against the state, anti-Soviet acts and misdemeanours committed under the influence of hostile forces from abroad.

There are also renegades of various kinds who maliciously slander Soviet reality and sometimes directly collaborate with imperialist secret services. Some figures in the West call the activities of such renegades "defence of human rights". The Soviet people, however, have never granted and will never grant anybody a right to harm

---

[1] L. I. Brezhnev, *Following Lenin's Course. Speeches and articles*, vol. 5, p. 543.

socialism, for the triumph of which they have laid down so many lives and exerted so much effort. To safeguard society against such criminal activities is both fair and democratic. This fully accords with the rights and freedoms of Soviet citizens, the interests of society and state.

Needless to say, this does not meet the interests of the enemies of socialism. One can occasionally hear in the West hypocritical lamentations over the alleged infringements of democracy in this country and cries that the KGB is making life impossible for some "human rights champions". In fact they are worried not so much by the fact that Soviet state security agencies, acting in strict compliance with Soviet laws, stop the criminal activities of these renegades as by the latter's resolute denunciation on the part of the whole Soviet people. This is why sad voices about the hopelessness of their activities in the USSR are heard more and more often in the West.

Soviet society is monolithic and united. The Soviet people, who are dedicated to the lofty ideals of the October Revolution, to the communist cause, will not allow anybody to interfere in their internal affairs, to slander their achievements, to harm Soviet society.

A special chapter in the new Constitution of the USSR legislatively formulates the Leninist principles of Soviet peace policy. These principles came into being in the unforgettable days of the October Revolution. We take pride in the fact that the October Revolution, the Communist Party, the Soviet State, as Lenin wrote, "raised aloft the banner of peace, the banner of socialism before the whole world".[1] Our Party has been loyal to this banner for over sixty years.

The Party's foreign policy programme expresses the vital interests of the Soviet people, who know what war brings in its wake only too well and therefore are wholly dedicated to peace. The noble and humane aim of Soviet foreign policy is to preserve peace, to prevent another war from being unleashed.

We come out in defence of peace jointly with our allies, other socialist countries, all progressive forces of mankind. Our policy of peace is opposed by a policy aimed at frustrating *détente* and counter-

---

[1] V. I. Lenin, *Collected Works*, vol. 37, p. 54.

ing the principles of peaceful coexistence. The danger of this policy should not be underestimated.

Under present conditions we are obliged to attach high priority to consolidating the might and defence capability of the Soviet Union. As long as the forces which threaten the peaceful work of the Soviet people and our allies are actively operating, strong and dependable defence is vitally necessary. Our defence might holds in check the most aggressive reactionary circles, compels imperialism to recognize parity in the military field, and has a sobering effect on those who have not yet abandoned for good their attempts to stop the progress of socialism by force of arms.

At the same time, our Party proceeds from the premise that peace and international security cannot be strengthened by military rivalry. The arms race undermines trust between states, poisons the international atmosphere, increases the risk of crisis situations growing into military conflicts. This is why the CPSU and the Soviet state attach paramount significance to a limitation of arms, followed by their reduction, to a peaceful settlement of disputes and conflicts, to promoting *détente*, to developing mutually beneficial international co-operation. We are firmly convinced that there is no sensible alternative to this policy.

The struggle for the triumph of peace policy is not a simple matter. *Détente* has quite a few enemies, who have become appreciably more active of late. Scaring the public with the imaginary "Soviet menace" they are stepping up the arms race. Interfering in the internal affairs of foreign nations, they aggravate the general international climate. They are trying to depict *détente* as a kind of an agreement on freezing and conservation of outdated social relations and reactionary political regimes. If peoples break such relations and topple such regimes, they raise a hue and cry about the notorious "hand of Moscow", about KGB agents who allegedly organize social upheavals all over the world.

We shall not search now for those who stand behind such allegations. In some cases they are deliberate lies. In others they are the result of naivety or delusions. No, it is not "the hand of Moscow" but the bony hand of hunger, not "the intrigues of communists" but privations, oppression and suffering, that compel people to take up arms, drive them into the streets, and make radical changes inevitable. This has happened in Angola, Afghanistan and Kampuchea. This is now taking place in Iran. Nothing, absolutely nothing can stop the irresistible forces of history which eventually work their way contrary to Pinochets, Pol Pots, Smiths and the like, contrary to the attempts of reactionary forces to retard social progress.

It would be extremely unreasonable and dangerous to jeopardize *détente* and the cause of peace each time internal political changes occur in some country, which are objectionable to politicians and ideologists of the West.

We are satisfied to acknowledge that the tendency towards a relaxation of tension which emerged in the seventies is coming out with increasing clarity as the main tendency in international affairs. This is evidenced, in particular, by the situation in Europe, by the strong shoots of new relations on the continent which sprang in the period of preparation and holding of the Conference on Security and Co-operation in Europe. It is indisputable that the restructuring of relations between European states could proceed more quickly, could produce a greater political and economic effect, if it were not held back by the attempts of aggressive circles in the West to bury *détente*, to whip up the arms race, to return the world to the times of the Cold War.

However, the attempts to arrest positive changes, to resume the Cold War have failed. And we hope that the spirit of realism, a sober attitude to the pressing problems of Europe will be preserved in European capitals. As far as the Soviet Union is concerned, it will struggle with even greater persistence jointly with other socialist countries for converting Europe into a continent of peace and co-operation among nations based on equality.

You know that in the last few years relations between the Soviet Union and the United States have been developing very irregularly. Vacillations and zigzags in Washington's policy have more than once resulted in declines and exacerbations and interfered with progress in matters of prime significance. Since the autumn of last year certain changes for the better seem to have appeared in this field. Progress in preparing a new agreement on the limitation of strategic offensive arms has been stepped up.

The Soviet government attaches great significance to improving Soviet–American relations as one of the key directions of its policy aimed at preventing nuclear war and achieving a general normalization of the international situation. Therefore, we are doing whatever is possible and necessary to resolve the major issues which have a bearing on the development of relations between the USSR and the USA.

Among the factors aggravating the international situation is China's armed attack on Vietnam. Imperialist politicians hope to use China as a tool for opposition to the Soviet Union and other socialist countries. This calculation, however, may easily turn into miscalculation.

As you see, there are quite a few complicated problems and situations in the world today. However, the complexity and at times the contradictory character of events in the world arena do not change our approach to foreign policy. The Soviet people can see ever more clearly the correctness of the policy pursued by our Party, the importance of a further consistent and determined struggle for a relaxation of international tensions, for a limitation of arms, for disarmament and the development of international co-operation.

All successes and accomplishments of the Soviet people are inseparably linked with the activities of the Leninist Party. The record of experience proves conclusively that as the scope of the Soviet Union's socioeconomic and cultural development grows, as ever new tasks in communist construction are accomplished, the Communist Party—the guiding and mobilizing force of Soviet society—has a growing part to play.

In all its theoretical and practical work the Party is invariably guided by the Marxist–Leninist doctrine. Lenin's ideas are alive today, and they will live on in the centuries to come, because they authentically reflect the objective course of history, the laws of social development and the class interests of the masses. Fidelity to Leninism, the creative development of Lenin's heritage is the dependable guarantee of new majestic accomplishments, of the triumph of communism.

The quiet and businesslike political atmosphere pervaded with communist high-principledness which has formed in the Party and country is of enormous significance for the fulfilment of all our plans. This atmosphere is the result of the purposeful activities of the Central Committee, its Politbureau and the General Secretary of the CPSU Central Committee, President of the Presidium of the USSR Soviet, Leonid Brezhev. Many good and warm words have been said about him at today's meeting. These words are an expression of the truly nationwide recognition of his wisdom as a statesman, his political foresight and his great humaneness. The communists, all working people of this country, rightly regard Leonid Brezhnev as a political leader of the Leninist stamp, who is inseparably linked with the people, who has devoted all his life to the people, and who is doing his utmost to advance the well-being of the people and to guarantee the security of our motherland.

The Communist Party of the Soviet Union is contesting the elec-tions with a comprehensive programme of economic and cultural development, of raising the living standards of the people. It is set out in the message of the Central Committee to the electorate. The aim of this programme is to make this socialist country still more beautiful and stronger, to make the life of the Soviet people still better and fuller, to make peace on earth still stronger and more dependable. The Soviet people are well aware of that. They give their unreserved support to the Party and respond to its appeals with practical deeds. This is the most dependable guarantee that all our plans will be fulfilled, that this country will score new successes in its great onward march towards communism.

Allow me to express once again my heartfelt gratitude to the labour collectives which have nominated me for election to the USSR Supreme Soviet, the electoral agents and all comrades who have spoken at this meeting. I promise to do my best to live up to your honourable trust.

I wish you a happy life and new successes in your work for the benefit of our Soviet Motherland.

The Unity of the People: A Great Force

Speech at a meeting with the electorate of the Prioksky district for election to the Supreme Soviet of the Russian Federation in the City of Gorky, 11 February 1980

Dear Comrades!

Allow me to thank you and all voters of the Prioksky electoral district for the trust you accord me by nominating me as your candidate for election to the Supreme Soviet of the Russian Federation.

I regard this trust primarily as an expression of your trust in our Party. Speakers here have said many good words about the Communist Party of the Soviet Union and its Central Committee which has now been headed by the loyal Leninist Leonid Brezhnev for over fifteen years. The working people of this country associate with his name the Party's correct political line, to the planning and implementation of which General Secretary Brezhnev is contributing all his enormous experience and competence, all his strength and energy. Service to the vital interests of the Soviet people, securing favourable conditions for their fruitful work and happy life, for lasting peace on earth and the triumph of the great ideals of communism are invariably in the forefront of his multifarious activity.

I convey to all residents of Gorky cordial greetings and wishes for new labour achievements from General Secretary Brezhnev, who has repeatedly visited your city and has a constant interest in the life and work of the working people of the city of Gorky.

The people of Gorky take a lawful pride in the past and present of their city. Today, making a round of the plant named after V. I. Ulyanov, we have as it were reviewed the facts of the heroic struggle of those unforgettable days when here in Nizhny Novgorod the young

212

working class of Russia stood up for a resolute battle against capitalism at the dawn of the 20th century. Hundreds and thousands of fighters for the revolutionary cause assembled for proletarian May Day meetings, and built barricades side by side with the working class heroes Pyotr Zalomov and Dmitry Pavlov. The protest actions of Nizhny Novgorod's proletarians showed, in Lenin's phrase, growing determination to struggle "for the freedom of the whole people, for the freedom of steady advance of labour towards a radiant socialist future".[1]

By the efforts of the people and at the will of the party the radiant future for which the Leninist Bolsheviks fought has become a reality and the way of life of all Soviet citizens.

People of my generation remember well the old wooden Myza with its semi-artisan workshops. Today new residential neighbourhoods have sprung up there. Products of the plant named after V. I. Lenin, the plant named after V. I. Ulyanov and other enterprises of the Prioksky district are supplied to all parts of this country and far beyond its borders.

Impressive changes are to be seen today in the image of the entire city on the Volga. The first giant Soviet motorworks, the legendary Krasnoe Sormovo shipyards, the aircraft and other factories have made your city famous and are making their contribution to the industrial power of this country.

One of the fundamental achievements of the Soviet society is the fact that a new, socialist working class has been raised, has taken shape and continues to develop in this country. Marx dreamed of a time when the working class would convert from a class in itself into a class for itself, into the main motive force of social progress. This time has arrived. The social and political role of the working class, its moral image and its psychology have radically changed. Under the impact of the scientific and technological revolution the structure of the working class is changing, social groups which have attributes of the working class and the intelligentsia have come into being and are growing.

Most of the workers today are people born in the Soviet period. Young people with good professional training hold a growing place

---

[1] V. I. Lenin. *Collected Works,* vol. 7, p. 65.

among them. Today the Soviet working class incorporates members of all nationalities living in this country, including those which formerly were denied access to advanced types of work and production. A person with a secondary education is becoming a typical member of the working class and is known for his competence in the most sophisticated modern types of technology and processes.

The main achievement, however, is the radical change in the social role played by the working class. From an exploited class forced to wage a bitter struggle to preserve its elementary right to work and its very existence, the working class has become the master of production, the backbone of all social structure.

In the conditions of a developed socialist society the working class is the leading class, the first among equals, a model to all other social groups of society. The Soviet worker is a frugal, skilful and efficient master in production, the central figure in the entire system of popular government. He is an active participant in economic and social planning, and in the discussion and adoption of decisions within his own work collective and on a nation-wide scale. The working class of the Soviet Union is a model of ideological dedication, socialist morality, patriotism and proletarian internationalism. The concept of a worker's honour has become the flesh and bone of all Soviet working people. Our whole society derives from the wealth of moral strength and convictions of the working class, powerful stimuli to a struggle for the construction of communism.

The current election campaign has its characteristic features, its own remarkable traits. The Tenth Five-Year Plan is nearing completion. The majestic scope of our accomplishments are ever more visible. New horizons for further development of Soviet society, for the national economy of this country, can be seen with increasing clarity.

As is known, the possibilities and potentialities of the national economy are largely determined by the expansions and renewal of main productive facilities. During the last four years of the current five-year plan they have been renewed by 30 per cent in industry and by 41 per cent in agriculture. Behind these figures are thousands of new and modernized enterprises, more advanced machine-tools and equipment and, in the final analysis, new opportunities for continued economic progress.

The material basis for agriculture has been reinforced. This allows us to overcome at lesser costs the consequences of unfavourable weather conditions. Over the last four years the annual average grain production has been 27 million tons greater than it was in the last five years. This is an important achievement. The same holds true of other sectors of agricultural production although on the whole it still falls short of our demand, which has an adverse effect on food supplies to the population. This is precisely why the Party is focusing the attention of all organizations on measures to increase further the output of agricultural produce.

We invariably regard the results of our economic development from the viewpoint of the extent to which the working people's material and cultural requirements are satisfied. This is fully understandable. Indeed, the aim of Soviet economic development is precisely ever greater satisfaction of these requirements. Enhancement of the standards of life is the task which the Party has invariably advanced as the main task in economic work.

Today we have every reason to claim that the tasks outlined by the 25th Party Congress in raising the wages and salaries of factory and office workers and of the incomes of collective farmers are being fulfilled. Real per capita incomes have increased 13 per cent. Housing construction continues to develop at a high rate. During the last year (1979) alone almost 10 million people moved into new well-appointed flats.

As your candidate I am particularly pleased with the fact that the working people of the City of Gorky have attained new frontiers in economic and cultural development. It is gratifying that thousands of front-ranking workers of the Prioksky district have fulfilled their personal five-year assignments. The task is to ensure that the initiative of the front-rankers become available to all, so that there can be no laggards. This is one of the fundamental prerequisites for success in the performance of our plans.

Reviewing the record of our economic development over the last four years, we can see that we could have achieved still better results. Of course, certain objective difficulties have had an adverse effect on our performance. The main thing, as was pointed out at the November 1979 plenary meeting of the CPSU Central Committee, is that the emphasis in work on efficiency and quality has not been placed everywhere with due consistency.

In his speech at that plenary meeting, General Secretary Brezhnev made a profound analysis of the problems of strategy for the long-term prospects for this country's economic development, and discussed in detail the problems of current management and pressing tasks in individual sectors of the economy. The attention of all communists, all work collectives, Party and economic executives must now be focused on unused latent possibilities, and on the need to mobilize internal latent reserves, to secure further enhancement of the efficiency of production and the quality of work. A comprehensive and critical assessment of the record of work, strictness and meticulousness in relation to leading executives guilty of omissions in the organization of work is a model of the Leninist style of leadership.

Our plans for the future are based on a solid economic foundation. We are already accustomed to the truly gigantic scale of our accomplishments and regard them as a matter of course. The enemies of socialism cannot fail to see them either. Although they certainly see them, they are unwilling to recognize the socialist nature of the Soviet Union's successes.

Time and again a clamour is raised in the capitalist world about an "economic miracle" now in Japan, now in the FRG, now in Brazil. Well, we have absolutely no intention of denying the economic achievements of these countries, although we have our own idea of their character, associated in the final analysis with the intensified exploitation of the working class. If rapid economic development is to be called a miracle at all, one cannot fail to see it in the rapid progress of the Soviet economy.

Some persons in the West are disgruntled when we, in comparing the results of the economic contest between the two systems, point out the different initial levels from which it was started. It is a fact, however, that to attain the present level of economic development we have had to overcome formidable difficulties associated with our country's backwardness in the past, with the economic blockade imposed by the capitalist world, and the need to divert funds from civilian work to defence in view of the threat of war from imperialism. Despite all these handicaps, our country today is an advanced and mighty power which is in possession of all that is necessary to defend firmly the achievements of the October Revolution.

The viability of our economy is inherent in the very essence of the socialist economic system. This is precisely what the opponents of socialism are unwilling and afraid to recognize. When the Soviet people were just embarking on the construction of the socialist economic system, they predicted its rapid collapse. They did not only confine themselves to predicting our doom but they went out of their way to push us to the brink of such a collapse. However, all their efforts proved to no avail. The socialist system took firm root and has proved its advantages over the capitalist system.

Critics of our economic system can be occasionally heard today too. They have to satisfy themselves mainly with speculation about our difficulties and outstanding problems. What can one say about this? Indeed, we do have difficulties and outstanding problems. However, they are not associated with the character of our economic system, but primarily with the fact that we have not yet learned to bring into full play the enormous advantages offered by the socialist mode of production. This is precisely why we openly discuss such problems and difficulties, in order to overcome them more speedily.

The whole world can see that our country is developing steadily and dynamically. This is strikingly visible against the background of the economic cataclysms and slump experienced by capitalist countries. "The two methods of economic management — the socialist and the capitalist"[1] — Lenin referred to yield two different results. In 1979 Soviet industrial production was 70 per cent greater than in 1970, whereas the respective figure for the United States and other advanced capitalist countries was 40 per cent.

On the whole the member countries of COMECON have developed their industrial production at a rate 50 per cent faster than the Common Market countries.

In the middle of the last decade the capitalist world was hit by the worst economic crisis in the last half century and its sequels are to be felt to this day. These are above all low economic development rates, chronic mass unemployment, and increasing fuel and raw materials shortages. Inflation has reached an all-time high. The currency chaos

---

[1] V. I. Lenin. *Collected Works*, vol. 42, p. 77.

continues unabated. The traditional methods of state monopoly regulation have proved helpless in the face of these phenomena. Summit meetings of leaders of the main capitalist powers have also proved ineffective. The main burden of the consequences of the crisis has to be shouldered by the working people. The number of jobless in developed capitalist countries in 1979 was double the figure for 1970 and ran to over 13 million. It is the result of bourgeois human rights and freedoms that today one in every seventeen working people in the United States and Britain is looking for a job.

Over the seventies consumer prices have doubled in the United States, Western Europe and Japan. At the same time inflation affected most of all the prices of staple goods and services crucial to the level and way of life of the working population. For instance, over this period bread prices soared 40 per cent in the United States and Britain, 80 per cent in the FRG, 130 per cent in Japan and France, and more than 200 per cent in Italy. The rent in these countries grew 100 to 200 per cent. In the United States only one day of staying in hospital costs the patient 200 to 250 dollars.

The picture in the Soviet Union is quite different. Stable low prices of staple foods have been preserved for many years, which also holds true of industrial goods and city transport fares, low rent, free medical services and free education.

Of course, much still has to be done. We are making good progress and we are fully determined to advance at the same rate. However, to make progress, to provide still better conditions for life, means primarily to work better. This is why the Party constantly orients the Soviet people towards achieving higher work performance results and on further improvement of the economic mechanism. It is a question, in the final analysis, of obtaining greater returns on investments and labour inputs in all areas of economic work.

As is pointed out by the CPSU Central Committee, work to enhance Party, state and labour discipline plays an important part in accelerating this country's economic and social development. This stems from the very character of socialist society, from the specific features of work under socialism.

The question of enhancing labour discipline is not new. Under present conditions, however, in developed socialist society this old problem has assumed a new dimension. Indeed, the more developed the production apparatus, the denser and more complex the network of relations between enterprises, the higher the requirements made on the coordination and organization of work. In this situation any violation of labour discipline, failure to fulfil a plan, or bungling of work adversely affect the general rates of production and its end results.

In the years of Soviet government the discipline of the whip and the stick, hunger and the danger of unemployment which prevailed in Imperial Russia has been replaced, to use Lenin's phrase, by an absolutely different, free and conscious discipline of the working people themselves.[1]

A person who has a frugal and conscientious attitude to the affairs of his work collective is keenly sensitive to all affairs within the state, and is fully aware that the significance of his own work in the common labour efforts of the people is precisely what determines the new socialist concept of labour discipline.

It should be frankly admitted, as we all know, that side by side with front-ranking workers with an excellent record in socialist emulation one can see persons who neglect their duties, who are shirkers or drunkards. We still encounter cases of theft, eyewashing and red tape, attempts to deceive the state, to work as little as possible and to gain as much as possible.

The reason, of course, is not some intrinsically private owner "nature" of man, as is claimed by bourgeois ideologists. In fact, the moulding of the new man is a complex and long-lasting process which takes place in a situation of hard ideological struggle between the two systems. This process is retarded by the viability and tenacity of the survivals of the past. To educate a new citizen — a builder of socialism — means not only to give him the knowledge for and habits of highly productive work, but also to inculcate in his mind an awareness of the importance and usefulness of his work in the interest of society and for his own benefit.

It is necessary for everyone to realize that whatever area of work he may be employed in his personal labour contribution is important for our common success and hence for improving the life of all Soviet citizens. That is why a violation of discipline affects the interests of

---

[1] See V. I. Lenin. *Collected Works*, vol. 39, pp. 13-14.

the whole society. That is why concern for enhancing labour discipline is our common cause. Therefore, every honest man and woman, every work collective, and society as a whole are entitled to bring to account any negligent worker whatever post he may hold and, if necessary, to punish him appropriately.

Speaking of the international situation, it has to be pointed out that it has markedly worsened in recent time.

We often hear from the West voices about a "crisis" and almost a "collapse" of detente. The public wonders how the world situation continues to develop and what direction this development will take, whether the positive record achieved in relations between states with different social systems in the seventies will be discarded and lost to mankind for good.

It should be frankly stated that concern about the future, about the destinies of detente and peace, is well motivated.

The cause of the exacerbation of the international situation is well known. It is Washington's irresponsible and dangerous policy. By all indications, the first fiddle there is now being played by the arch ultra-reactionary forces linked with the military-industrial complex, forces who are bent on restoring the old days when the imperialist powers were in a position to impose an order of their own liking on other countries and peoples.

The sources of such "political nostalgia" can be traced to the fact that definite circles in the United States were unable to accept with sober minds the social and political change in the world and understand its objective essence.

The world is really in a turmoil. Pro-imperialist dictatorial regimes are crumbling and opposition to the neo-colonialist policy is stiffening. More and more countries which were dependent on capitalist states until recently are opting for a socialist orientation. Such is the objective course of history.

Some people beyond the ocean believe that all this is happening because the United States has not been careful enough to look after its interests and hence has suffered losses. Hence the desire to remedy and galvanize its foreign policy and thereby retard the process of socio-political change. Hence the appeals for a forced arms build-up relying on which one could guarantee one's special rights to the natural wealth belonging to other states, to bring pressure to bear on the Soviet Union and other socialist countries, to force them to give up their support for anti-imperialist movements. At the same time Washington is evidently not averse to putting pressure on its own allies, drawing them into dangerous adventures and shifting onto their shoulders part of the burden of the arms race which is felt more and more acutely within the United States itself.

Of course, it is realized in Washington that it would be extremely unprofitable to disclose the genuine motives and aims of this policy. Therefore the most shameless lies about a Soviet "military menace" are circulated to mislead the public. Such fabrications are being spread with especial zeal in connection with the developments in Afghanistan. What is more, these developments are described as the main reason for the worsening of Soviet-American relations and the international situation in general. Such allegations are absolutely absurd. The true causes of the present revision of Washington's policy should be sought not in developments in Afghanistan or in the Soviet Union's actions. These causes are the fear of the US ruling quarters of the wave of social change and their desire to turn the world back by force of arms to the "halcyon days" of imperialist domination.

As far as the developments in Afghanistan are concerned any unbiased person can easily understand them.

Eighteen months ago a revolution in Afghanistan opened the way towards broad and sweeping socio-economic reforms. This greatly disgruntled some circles in the United States where any successes of the national liberation movement and social progress are interpreted as prejudicial to the "vital interests" of the United States. So Washington resorted to the mechanism of interference in foreign internal affairs tested in Chile and earlier still in Guatemala, South Korea, and South Vietnam.

Malicious slander of the new popular government, direct incitement for actions against it, bribery and planting of secret agents, the formation of bandit gangs of feudals who have escaped the people's wrath — all these have been put to work. In this shameful affair Washington's authorities have found accomplices among Peking's leaders, who see in the events in Afghanistan an opportunity to prod the world towards the dangerous brink of war, and the possibility of implementing their far-reaching hegemonist ambitions inherited from Mao.

In a situation where the Afghan revolution has met with crude interference from the outside (which cannot be described more aptly than military intervention), when a dangerous seat of tension emerged on the southern borders of the USSR, where a long hand worked from beyond the ocean, our country responded to the Afghan government's repeated requests for aid and sent to Afghanistan a limited troop contingent to help the people's government to repel aggression. This step, which was by no means simple for us to decide upon, was made in full compliance with the Soviet-Afghan treaty, and with the letter and spirit of the UN Charter. It was a lofty act of loyalty to the principle of proletarian internationalism indispensable for defence of the interests of this country.

As General Secretary Brezhnev pointed out in a Pravda interview, the Soviet military contingent will be withdrawn from Afghan territory as soon as the reasons which induced the Afghan leaders to request our aid are no longer valid.[1] It should be said that the shameless fuss about the counter-revolutionary rabble assembled in Pakistan territory and carrying out from there bandit raids on Afghani towns and villages is by no means evidence of any desire on the part of its masterminds to seek a normalization of the situation in Afghanistan. One cannot hear any statement from Washington and Peking concerning an end to the broad intervention in the internal affairs of Afghanistan. On the contrary, this intervention is assuming ever wider scope. It brings to light the ulterior motives of its organizers and their true attitude to the situation which has emerged in connection with the events in that country.

Today it is particularly important to analyze and understand the true meaning of the aggravation of the international situation associated with US policy. Real danger lies in the fact that, in trying to capitalize on the events in Afghanistan, Washington in effect brings about a situation which undermines detente, and undermines the agreements already reached. There is much food for thought here for those who are now hastily expressing their solidarity with the war cries from Washington.

---

[1] See L. I. Brezhnev. *Following Lenin's Course.* Moscow, 1981, vol. 8, p. 247.

The Soviet Union has a responsible approach to international affairs and its role in world politics. We will not give in to provocations from beyond the ocean. As in the past, we are in favour of detente. To us detente means primarily the overcoming of the mistrust and hostility of the cold war period, and a settlement of differences and disputes not by force or threat of force but by peaceful means at the negotiating table.

Detente, which reflects objective, far-reaching changes in the world arena, has taken deep root and means too much for the destiny of mankind to allow any forces to gamble on it motivated by considerations of hostility to socialism or internal political struggle.

The Soviet Union declares that it is in favour of continued negotiations and reaching agreement on all key problems of present-day international relations. These negotiations can be conducted only on the basis of compliance with the principle of parity and equal security. Let nobody be deluded about the fact that attempts to achieve unilateral advantages and to put pressure to bear upon us are absolutely hopeless. "As far as the Soviet Union is concerned," General Secretary Brezhnev has pointed out, "we have no intention of surrendering any part of the good record scored on the international scene in the seventies. What is more, we deem it necessary to go further ahead. This refers both to holding back the arms race and stamping out seats of conflict in Southeast Asia, in the Middle East, and to converting the Indian Ocean into a zone of peace as is proposed by the coastal states. Any road leading to lasting peace is acceptable and desirable to us."[1]

All our successes in communist construction, in the struggle against the aggressive designs of imperialism, for peace and social progress, are inseparably associated with the guiding activities of the Leninist Party.

The Party effectively fulfilled and is fulfilling its role as the leader of the labouring masses thanks to its unshakeable loyalty to the teachings and cause of its great founder and leader, Vladimir Lenin. The Soviet people are preparing to celebrate the 110th anniversary of his birth in a festive atmosphere.

The Party has come to the elections with a platform which expresses

[1] L. I. Brezhnev. *Following Lenin's Course,* vol. 8, pp. 260-261.

the vital interests of the working people. It is a platform of further developing the Soviet economy and improving the living standards of the Soviet people. It is a platform of securing of dependable guarantees of the security interests of this country. It is a platform of the struggle for peace and international cooperation. This is precisely why all the provisions of this platform express the thoughts and aspirations of the Soviet citizens, who enthusiastically approve and unanimously support the general line of the CPSU, and its home and foreign policies.

In conclusion, I would like to express once again my deep gratitude to you and through you to all work collectives which have nominated me for election to the Supreme Soviet of the Russian Federation, and I assure you that I will do my utmost to live up to this great trust.

I wish all working people of the Prioksky electoral district and all residents of the City of Gorky new successes in their work and new creative accomplishments.

Thank you.

At Workers' Parade on Red Square

Meeting with General Secretary of the Central Committee of the Socialist Unity
Party of Germany and President of the Council of State of the GDR,
Erich Honecker

Conversation with the editor of *Der Spiegel*

Meeting with the Soviet cosmonaut pilots A. P. Berezov and V. V. Lebedev

Leninism: the Mainspring of the Revolutionary Energy and Creativity of the Masses

Report at a ceremonial meeting in Moscow commemorating the 112th anniversary of Lenin's birth, 22 April 1982

Comrades!

The great Lenin, a revolutionary and thinker, his ideas and his work brought about a decisive change in mankind's destiny. The October Revolution of 1917, which was led by Lenin, burst, as it were, the uniform fabric of historical time. At one pole there has emerged and is making rapid progress a world of liberated labour oriented on the future. At the other pole there has survived a world of exploitation and coercion rooted in the past. The coexistence and confrontation of these two worlds is the most fundamental and deep-seated phenomenon in the social and political development of human society in the twentieth century.

The dynamics of this change have radically altered the social image of our planet. Our Motherland—the Union of Soviet Socialist Republics—has grown into an impregnable fortress of socialism. The socialist community of nations is developing and growing stronger. The once powerful colonial empires have sunk into oblivion. In place of them there have emerged liberated states many of which are socialist-oriented. The situation in the main citadels of capitalism remains unstable economically, socially, and politically. The reforms by which the *bourgeoisie* retreating under pressure from the working-class and communist movement attempted to stabilize the situation have failed to produce the expected effect. The ideas of socialism and freedom have struck a deep root on all continents and are supported by powerful mass movements.

All these changes bringing nearer the triumph of a new, communist civilization are inseparably associated with the name, work, and ideological legacy of Lenin. Leninism has been, is and will be the irresistible weapon of the world proletariat, all those who are struggling against the old world and building a new world.

Lenin's teaching, like Marxism–Leninism as a whole, is a science. And just like any science it is intolerant of dogma. Leninism is the theory of revolutionary renovation of the world. Relying on a system of fundamental principles repeatedly tested in practice, on materialistic dialectics, this teaching lives on and develops, reflecting all new processes and phenomena, new turns of history.

The secret of the eternal youth of Leninism lies in the fact that Lenin's teaching, its principles and ideals are close and understandable to the multimillion masses, that every new generation of people find in it clear answers to problems exciting them. It illuminates mankind's path into the future, brings peace and progress to the nations of the world.

In this lies the inexhaustible vitality of Leninism. In this lies the strength of our Party, which preserves and constantly enriches Lenin's priceless heritage.

Commemorating the 112th anniversary of Lenin's birth we pay a tribute of gratitude and respect to the founder of our Party and state. On this day we again and again collate our plans and our policy with Lenin's guidelines. And we have full reason to say that the Communist Party of the Soviet Union is loyal to Lenin's great cause, to Marxism–Leninism. The Soviet people closely rallied around the Party and its Central Committee headed by the outstanding Leninist Leonid Brezhnev are confidently advancing along the path of communist construction.

LIVING, CREATIVE SOCIALISM IS THE WORK OF THE MASSES THEMSELVES (V. I. LENIN)

Lenin pointed out in his time that with every new step of history, with every large change in the sociopolitical situation and practical tasks, different aspects of Marxism as a living theory come to the foreground. This fully applies to Leninism as well. Today we devote close attention to Lenin's ideas of the people's decisive role in revolutionary remaking of the world, his idea of socialism as the result of conscious creativity of the masses.

Inseparable ties with the masses were Lenin's inherent quality. "Wherever Lenin might be brought by fate, wherever he might be and whatever he might be doing, he was linked with the people by thousands of threads. Meetings and discussions with workers and peasants, soldiers, scientists and cultural figures were an organic necessity for him. That was a political leader's need to compare his conclusions with the experience of the masses, to verify his broad generalizations by what seemed particular cases, by the personal destinies of those who make revolution and build socialism", Leonid Brezhnev has said.

Enormous attention to the experience of the masses, faith in their inexhaustible creative potential, an ability to translate their aspirations and interests into clear political slogans and programmes of action run through all the history of Leninism.

Let us go back in thought to the legendary time when soviet government was taking its first steps under Lenin's guidance. To say that it was a hard time is to say very little. By conventional criteria, from the standpoint of "common sense", the tasks Lenin and his followers had set themselves seemed absolutely impossible. Nevertheless, they had won total victory.

That victory was often called a "miracle" at the time. That was not true, of course. And Lenin with his sober, realistic cast of mind realized that better than anybody. Russia had had a corrupt and decrepit feudal-capitalistic system of government weakened by war. The world was torn apart by bitter antagonisms which interfered with the consolidation of the foreign enemies of the Soviet Republic. The Bolshevik Party founded by Lenin was a close-knit political vanguard of Russia's proletariat steeled in class battles. That vanguard was linked by unbreakable ties with the working class and the peasantry and enjoyed full support from the masses. Russia's working people had placed their faith in the Party and Lenin and risen in revolt. The revolution had triumphed.

Thus at the very beginning of the socialist era there formed the unity of the Party and people, which became a powerful constructive force of the new society. This unity has an objective nature, since the aims, the programme of the Leninist Party authentically express the working people's interests. At the same time, this unity is the result of the deliberate, purposeful efforts of the communists, who are convinced that only the people themselves can create a truly democratic social system.

Lenin repeatedly emphasized this idea. "Socialism", he said, "cannot be decreed from on high. Its spirit is alien to formal-bureaucratic automatism; living, creative socialism is the work of the masses themselves." This is why our Party regards it as a matter of first priority to display constant concern for enhancing the political awareness and culture of the working people. The better we cope with this task, the more rapid and fuller the mainstream of the historical creativity of the masses.

All the development of Soviet society, its past and present, eloquently demonstrate what wonders the working man's unchained initiative can work. It has concentrated centuries of progress in a few decades. The results of this progress are visible to the whole world today. This is our Soviet government by the people and for the people. This is our socialist economy built by free labour and serving the welfare of each and all. This is the great unity of all nations and national minorities in the Union of Soviet Socialist Republics, whose 60th anniversary we are preparing to celebrate. This is the triumph of socialist ideology in our society.

The main sphere of the Soviet people's activities is the economy. This is why it is precisely in this sphere that the conscious creativity of the masses, their initiative and resourcefulness, their desire and ability to work conscientiously are so important. Indeed, the performance of all our plans and programmes expressed on the scale of a concrete production collective and working place immediately reveals its dependence on the responsibility, activity and occupational skills of every working man and woman.

Our standards of life today and tomorrow are determined, in the final analysis, by the degree of efficiency of the Tyumen oil-field workers, the tunnel builders and track-layers employed on the BAM railway project, the builders of the powerful hearts of atomic power plants at the "Atommash" nuclear power engineering complex, the farmers who are now carefully placing in spring soil seeds of wheat and cotton to raise this year's harvest, the teachers of our children and the doctors who care for our health. Soviet citizens work in a variety of areas and under different, at times quite arduous, conditions. All of them, however, have one thing in common: their dedication to the common cause of constructive work.

The nationwide effort to implement the decisions of the 26th CPSU Congress, the assignments of the Eleventh Five-Year Plan, the widespread socialist emulation drive for improving work efficiency and product quality, for making the economy truly economical—these are concrete, visible evidence that the tasks of the Party are a matter of vital concern to all Soviet citizens.

Time has already counted off a quarter of the current five-year plan. This is a fairly long period. Much has already been done. Growth of industrial output has been secured. Labour efficiency has risen. As the Congress resolved, consumer goods production has been increasing at a faster rate. The social measures planned have been implemented consistently.

As masters of their land the Soviet people have an exacting attitude to all areas of work, aware that they can solve the existing problems, relying on their own resources. This refers primarily to overcoming the lag of agriculture, expanding production and improving the quality of foodstuffs and industrial consumer goods, and developing the consumer services. These tasks are being tackled and will certainly be fulfilled.

Needless to say, the historical creativity of the masses is not confined to the economy alone. It manifests itself in all fields of social life. This graphically illustrates the most fundamental property of our system: its inherent democracy. Soviet citizens learn from their own experience about the organic relationship between success in socialist construction and development of democracy. It is quite logical that developed socialist society has become a society of constantly developing democracy.

Our revolution, Lenin said, has drawn millions upon millions of people through Soviet government into active participation in the development of the state. The Soviets are a form of political organization which has opened up unsurpassed opportunities for collecting, accumulating, and turning to common advantage the creativity and initiative of the masses, for analyzing a wide range of opinions and suggestions in solving any problem. This is a guarantee of adopting such decisions that meet precisely and completely the interests of all classes and social groups, nations and national minorities, all generations of Soviet society.

As is known, the question of participation of the masses in the management of the affairs of state, the principles of socialist democracy, are the subject of acute ideological and political controversy in the world arena. Of late, for instance, the thesis of "pluralism" as an inalienable attribute of democracy has been intensively circulated. But how is one to understand this thesis?

Speaking of the existence in society of different, divergent viewpoints and interests, there is no society without such phenomena. This is equally true of capitalism and socialism. There is one essential distinction however. Under capitalism the difference of interests assumes the character of a class antagonism. On the political plane this antagonism finds expression in the existence of different parties with opposite class orientations. The existence of and struggle between such parties is, indeed, an attribute of democracy but this is formal, bourgeois democracy which by no means guarantees genuine freedom for the labouring masses.

Since in socialist society there is no private ownership of means of production, no exploiter classes, the discrepancy between the interests of different social groups does not reach the degree of antagonism. In the new society there is no soil for the formation of political parties hostile to socialism. As far as consideration, comparison and harmonizing of different interests are concerned, different mechanisms can work here, depending on historical traditions and concrete circumstances.

In the Soviet Union and in other socialist countries with one-party political systems, consideration of the interests of different social groups and harmonizing them with the common interests of the whole people are effected within the framework of one party, through bodies of government elected by the whole people, through the trade unions and the entire widely ramified system of public organizations. In those socialist countries where a few parties exist each of them has its own social support with its own specific interests. It is a matter of fundamental importance, however, that all of them adhere to socialist positions.

This is precisely what disgruntles the Western champions of "pluralism". They desire an organized opposition to socialism to be established, if only artificially, in the Soviet Union and other socialist countries. It is clear that this desire is entertained by enemies of our system. The Soviet people, however, will never agree to that, and they are capable of guarding themselves against all kinds of renegades and against their foreign patrons. In short, we communists are for developing democracy in the interest of socialism, not to the detriment of socialism.

We can see socialist democracy in action every day in the ever wider involvement of the masses in the management of the affairs of society and state, in the harmony between the fundamental interests of society and the individual, in the sensitive, objective and attentive consideration of Soviet citizens' aspirations and interests which are basically identical but highly individual at the same time. The Party's demand for attention to be given to every individual is an expression of its concern for human individuality so that it may not be obliterated and the voice and opinion of each may be heard and heeded.

The labour efforts, social and political activity of the masses, the attention to the needs, requests and opinions of Soviet citizens largely determine the moral and political atmosphere in any collective and in society in general. It is also determined, of course, by how the Party, government and economic bodies work at all levels without exception. As is known, at one time there were problems, not simple ones, associated with a departure from the Leninist norms here. Our Party under the guidance of its Central Committee has overcome the negative consequences of that. We have done this work and learned the necessary lessons from the difficult record of historical experience.

The political situation which has now taken shape in Soviet society, the entire atmosphere of the life and work of Soviet citizens are healthful in keeping with the norms and principles of developed socialism. This does not mean, however, that we have no shortcomings and problems, phenomena that must be fought consistently and resolutely.

Soviet citizens are justly indignant at facts of embezzlement, bribery, red tape, a disrespectful attitude to people and other antisocial acts. It does not matter much whether they have been inherited from the past or brought from abroad and spongeing on certain shortcomings in our development. Once these phenomena exist, they are a hindrance to us, and it is the duty of every communist, every citizen, to fight them. The Soviet people fully support measures taken by the Party to uproot these phenomena.

It is not easy to go along an untrodden path. Much here is impossible to predict or anticipate. As the Party is teaching us, to be able to go forward confidently it is important to combine courage and flexibility in solving objectively pressing problems with a precise, strictly scientific assessment of the existing record of achievement, without underestimating or exaggerating our resources and possibilities.

"We Marxists", Lenin said, "must strain for all we are worth to study scientifically the facts making the basis for our policy."

It is precisely this approach that enables our Party and people to implement the tasks facing Soviet society in the last two decades of the 20th century. Viewed as a whole, these tasks boil down to what may be called perfection of developed socialism. The Soviet Union is at the beginning of this long historical stage, which will in turn have its own periods and phases of growth. It need not be proved that progress from phase to phase is a complex process inevitably involving efforts to overcome contractions and difficulties, which are a matter of course in any development. Some efforts will be more successful than others. In some areas we shall be able to make faster progress than in others. Such is the real course of social progress. It cannot be straightened out with a ruler.

At its 26th Congress the CPSU outlined a comprehensive programme of the country's economic and social development at the present stage. The efforts of the Party and people are concentrated on implementing the Congress decisions, on translating them into concrete actions. This is the pivot of all our work, to use Lenin's phrase. Success in this work is inseparably linked with the ever more intensive expression of the intellectual and moral powers of the working people, the finest qualities of our people, the growth of the lively interest of the masses in the affairs and concerns of their Motherland, their creativity and initiative.

All this once again became manifest in their enthusiastic work at the Leninist communist Subbotnik. Over 155 million people, that is, practically all who could afford it took part in Subbotnik. Each of them sensed again the greatness of Lenin's idea of free labour which makes the working man genuine master of his country.

This feeling of active involvement in shaping one's own life and society is the mainspring of the great energy which no other system but socialism possesses or can possess. By developing consistently and skilfully directing this energy we will accomplish any tasks and lend still greater momentum to the great cause of communist construction. This is a cause, as Lenin put it, which "attracts all of us, which all of us desire, which we must advance, and to which we will devote all our efforts and all our lives".

The active involvement of the masses in the conscious making of history is a striking feature of the present epoch.

Within a brief historical period the socialist community of nations has grown into a global factor of modern political development. The combining of the ideological, political, economic, scientific and technological potentials of the fraternal nations augments the power of socialism in being, allows it to develop dynamically, to counter effectively the aggressive policy of imperialism and hegemonism, and to influence actively the course of world developments.

Socialism, however, is not built under laboratory conditions. It forms in a situation of class confrontation between the two systems, of hard pressure from imperialism, and in the process of overcoming its internal difficulties. All this affects the rates of our progress. However, this socialism, though not an ideal one but really existing on earth, proves ever more conclusively that the future belongs to socialism.

The socialist world is a constantly renovated creation of many nations. It is expressed in a variety of ways of revolution, methods

ASW-H*

and rates of socioeconomic transformations, ways of implementing pressing tasks in various spheres of social life, a diversity of forms of the political and social organization of society.

Socialism is alien by nature to visionary schemes and stereotypes. Every Communist party in power contributes to the cause of socialist construction, proceeding from the realities of the situation prevailing, national distinctions and traditions.

The variety of forms of socialism is predetermined by real life but its essence is invariable. The socialist system in any country is brought into being by implementing the fundamental principles of communism correctly modified, as Lenin taught us, in details to adapt them to national and national state distinctions.

In this context I will touch on the question of "models" of socialism so much in vogue today. It has been argued that the difficulties encountered by some socialist countries stem from the alleged imposition of the Soviet "model" upon them. It is a strange conclusion. Suffice it to take an unbiased look at reality to understand the complete absurdity of such allegations. In every socialist state one can see vivid manifestations of original national, historical, cultural and other distinctions.

That socialist construction in any country must correspond to its historical, political and cultural traditions is indisputable. The subject for a debate appears when talk about various "models" leads to an increasingly vague and nebulous idea of the very essence of socialism, its cardinal distinctions from capitalism. And, of course, strong objections are voiced to efforts to denigrate the experience of the peoples which have taken the socialist path, to what is in fact a rejection of the general laws of socialist construction.

The CPSU has repeatedly stated its stand on this issue. We believe that the best form for each country is the one which has been adopted by its people and agrees with their interests and traditions. However, the fundamental principles of the socialist social system, its class nature and its essence are the same for all countries and peoples.

The worldwide growth of interest in socialism is a significant feature of the times. The ideas of socialism are gaining ground in developed capitalist countries. They are also forcing their way in countries which have freed themselves from colonial oppression. This is the logical result of what is at times a spontaneous involvement of the masses in the anti-imperialist struggle, in efforts to overcome backwardness, poverty, and dependence. The variety of conditions in which the struggle for social progress is waged, the diverse composition and nature of the political forces waging this struggle give rise to a wide spectrum of different ideological trends and views.

We communists are convinced that the practice of the class struggle and social transformations, the general advancement of material and spiritual culture, the experience and influence of the nations of the socialist community will set the stage for ever wider propagation of the ideas of scientific communism.

Different ways lead to socialism. However, once this path is taken it is important not to stray and to arrive precisely at socialism rather than stop half-way or remain within the capitalist system. To achieve their goal the working people need their own political party. This should not be an ordinary party but a party of the fundamentally new, Leninist type.

Only a party of this type is in a position to translate the interests and aspirations of the masses into the language of conscious political struggle, to infuse the masses with its faith and determination, to mobilize their energy and direct it into the mainstream of struggle. Such a party alone can achieve a recognition of its vanguard role by the masses and lead them to socialism through any trials, however severe.

THE BEST EXPRESSION OF DEMOCRACY IS ITS STAND ON THE FUNDAMENTAL ISSUE OF WAR AND PEACE (V. I. LENIN)

The problems of world politics, particularly the problems of war and peace, occupy an exceptionally important place in the theory and practice of Leninism. Lenin clearly realized that the destiny of Russian revolution, the entire liberation struggle of the peoples largely depended on a correct solution to these problems.

It was Lenin who laid down the fundamental principles of foreign policy to be pursued by the proletariat in power. The founder of our Party invariably made a distinction between just and unjust wars. His views on the problems of war and peace constitute a coherent theory. Its essence is a consistent and uncompromising affirmation of the idea of organic connection between peace and socialism. This connection stems from the fact that the new society has no need for war, since war contradicts all its interests and ideals, all aspirations of the working people. Today when the problem of war and peace has become a life and death question for whole nations, for human civilization in general, these ideas of Lenin's have assumed unprecedented urgency.

All our experience since the October Revolution proves that peace cannot be solicited from the imperialists. We remember Lenin's behest that a revolution must be capable of defending itself. Following this behest our Party and the Soviet people have formed their valiant armed forces and built up an indestructible defence capability.

At the same time the Soviet Union has never proceeded from the premise that lasting peace can be secured exclusively by military power and by a policy based upon it. Such a policy would lead not to peace but to an arms race, to confrontation and eventually to war. This is precisely why our Party and the Soviet state so consistently uphold the principles of peaceful coexistence, so steadfastly pursue their policy of peace and international cooperation.

"The best expression of democracy is its stand on the fundamental issue of war and peace", Lenin said. The profoundly democratic character of Soviet foreign policy consists exactly in expression of the fundamental vital interests of the mass of the people, who have no need for war.

An exhaustive history of our epoch will perhaps be written some time. It can be safely said that inscribed in gold letters in that history will be the indisputable fact that if it had not been for the Soviet Union's firm policy of peace our planet would not only have been a much more dangerous place for man to live in but it might well have been overtaken by a fatal disaster. If we have avoided this disaster, if we have lived in peace time for almost forty years, if we are confident of our future, this is very largely due to the Soviet Union's foreign policy in the past and today, its efforts to avert the danger of nuclear catastrophe, its struggle for life, for mankind's survival and prosperity.

The Soviet people, all progressive forces on earth highly appreciate Leonid Brezhnev's multifarious activities for the benefit of peace. His indefatigable work and selfless efforts devoted to this noble cause have won the General Secretary of our Party's Central Committee broad recognition and gratitude of all the people. Every great cause gives birth to its own heroes and champions. In our day such a great cause is the struggle for peace. Leonid Brezhnev, who himself fought in the war as long as it lasted and went through the hardships of postwar recovery, is waging this struggle with determination, wisdom and consistency, sparing no efforts to preserve peace.

Pursuing its fundamentally new, Leninist policy of peaceful coexistence, the young socialist state was also to search for new ways of implementing this policy. The advent of new, socialist diplomacy was called upon, in Lenin's conception, to demolish the wall by which the exploiter classes had always barred the labouring masses from foreign policy, to convert the masses from an object of foreign policy into a force actively influencing international affairs in their own interest.

The very advent of socialist foreign policy helped bring vital international problems out of the quiet of imperial offices into the streets despised by the *bourgeoisie* and made them accessible to the workers and all working people. That was a fundamental class-oriented change in accordance with the Party principles. It enabled the masses for the first time to influence policy actively, helped the antiwar movements to win broad public support.

In our epoch when mankind is exposed to the most terrible danger—the danger of nuclear war—such movements have become a serious political factor, whose role, by all indications, will grow.

Frightened by the upsurge of antiwar movements, the imperialist *bourgeoisie* resorts on a widening scale to the weapon of lies, to refined deception. Just take a look at what Washington is doing now. One hysterical propaganda campaign is followed by another. The public is brainwashed now with fabrications about a "Soviet military menace", now with shameless lies about America's strategic "lag". It is intimidated with stories about "international terrorism" or told fables about the events in Poland, in Central America, in South and South East Asia. There is logic, albeit perverted, in this propaganda:

indeed, to advertise weapons of mass destruction and to prod the world to war the imperialists have to deceive the masses.

The Soviet people are convinced that another world war can be prevented. This requires active efforts by all peace forces, all governments, political parties and leaders who are concerned for the future of nations and of mankind as a whole. Our Party and the Soviet government are doing their best for Soviet policy to serve effectively the cause of peace, to enlighten the masses, to expose the intrigues of the apologists of the arms race and aggression. It serves these aims not only in word but also in deed, by all its peace initiatives.

This is assuming crucial importance today. In fact, faced with an unprecedented rise of the mass anti-war movement, the apologists of the Cold War are stepping up not only their propaganda efforts but also their political manoeuvres. Attempts are being made to take advantage of diplomatic talks, including talks on arms limitation and disarmament, to mislead the public. One gains the impression that consent to enter into such talks sometimes pursues the sole aim of creating illusions so as to lull the vigilance of the public and carry on the arms race.

Indeed, is it not the line pursued by the West at the Vienna talks on arms and troop reductions in Central Europe? The Soviet Union and other socialist countries have more than once attempted to lead them out of their stalemate. Each time, however, our Western partners came up with new arguments to obstruct an agreement.

It seems that US negotiators had the same scheme in mind when they came to the talks on the limitation of medium-range nuclear weapons in Europe. All the more so that there is a time limit here: if an agreement is delayed by another year or a year and a half, it may be possible to begin implementing in practice NATO's decision to deploy a few hundred new American missiles in Europe.

As is known, Washington has recently promised again that the United States will soon be prepared to enter into negotiations on strategic arms limitation and reduction. Well, we need not be persuaded to reciprocate. The Soviet Union has long been ready for such negotiations. We proceed from the assurance that this crucial problem can be settled, if negotiations are conducted in a constructive spirit on the basis of the principles of parity and equal security.

In a *Pravda* interview the other day concerning a possible Soviet–American summit meeting Leonid Brezhnev reaffirmed the Soviet Union's willingness to have a constructive dialogue with the United States.

The Communist Party has always been aware of the fact that the path towards lasting peace is an arduous, thorny path. One cannot expect walkovers here, and every step of progress takes great efforts. Since we realize this quite clearly, we have never been dizzy with success. And we do not lose heart, when we come up against difficulties.

Leonid Brezhnev compared the present situation to a forking road, emphasizing thereby the critical importance of the choice facing mankind. Either it will step on the road leading away from war and to peace or it will take the road of a further arms race and confrontation.

We have long made our choice. We are determined not to stray off the path of peace and co-operation charted by Lenin. For us this is a matter of vital interests of the people and country. For us this is a question of principle.

It seemed that not only the Soviet Union but also the main powers of the capitalist world had made this choice and passed this road fork in the early seventies, guided by the full record of experience in the earlier decades. This experience clearly shows that there is no sensible alternative to peaceful coexistence, that the Cold War and the arms race have no prospects, while a "shooting war" will bring victory to no one.

Some governments, just as individuals, however, are prone to forget the experience and lessons of history. This is now evident in the case with all the US administration, which is trying to push all the development of international relations to a path of danger. It is clear that the United States will achieve no success on this path. However, one cannot ignore the fact that this policy is aggravating the situation as a whole and increasing the danger of war. The only response to this policy must be greater vigilance and an even more stubborn struggle to preserve peace. It is precisely these tasks that are being implemented by Soviet foreign policy.

In response to the attempts of the aggressive imperialist forces to achieve military superiority over the Soviet Union we will maintain our defence capability at a sufficient level so as to guarantee dependably, as Leonid Brezhnev has stated, the security of this country and the entire socialist community of nations.

We counter the attempts to poison the atmosphere and step up tensions with new peace initiatives. In his speech at the 17th Congress of Trade Unions in Tashkent Leonid Brezhnev put forward a wide range of constructive proposals. These new initiatives face, in effect, every country, its government and public with the same question: which road to follow? The road of peace and *détente* or the road of fomenting tensions, the arms race and war? Nobody can evade an answer to this question.

We are not alone in our historic struggle against the danger of nuclear catastrophe. The cause of peace has on its side the socialist community of nations, the fraternal Communist parties, the international working-class movement, the peoples of the nonaligned countries. Peace is being defended by the mass of the people on all continents, in all countries, including Western Europe, Japan and the United States itself. This movement, which affiliates people of widely varied social status and convictions was called into being by the natural desire of human beings to survive, by the most pressing dictate of the times: to prevent nuclear holocaust. Only political dolts or deliberate liars can denounce the mass antiwar movement of today as the work of the "hand of Moscow", the intrigues of communists. The worldwide coalition of forces opposed to the nuclear menace today is as broad as perhaps no movement has been in human history.

The problems of peace are bound up closely and directly with defence of the working people's vital social interests. The Marxists have always regarded them as such. All Leninist communists view them in the same light today. The Soviet people highly appreciate the courageous struggle waged by the fraternal parties against war, for peace, security, and social progress. Allegiant to its internationalist duty, the CPSU has done and will do all in its power to strengthen in the course of this struggle its solidarity and co-operation with its foreign class comrades, to contribute to achieving still closer unity of the communist movement on the basis of the principles of Marxism–Leninism.

Soviet foreign policy, just as in Lenin's day, represents our peaceful interests in relation to all countries and peoples of the world. We will never swerve from this Leninist line.

*   *   *

Leninism has a long and splendid history. Leninism, however, has not and will never become a mere part of the historical past.

Lenin's ideas which illumine the path towards socialism and communism for the working class and all labouring masses are alive and will never die.

Lenin's deeds which ushered in the great era of practical transition to new forms of social life, to socialism are alive and will live on forever.

The Party founded by Lenin, in which his ideas and his work are immortalized, is alive and will live on. Its entire political biography and its development are under the powerful influence of Lenin's personality. Founding our Party Lenin put his whole heart and soul into it.

Raising the party of the new type and defending it in uncompromising struggle against opportunists of every stripe, Lenin pointed out that such a party alone was able "to take over power and to lead the whole people towards socialism, to guide and organize the new system, to be the teacher, guide and leader of all working and exploited people in the cause of organizing their social life without the bourgeoisie and against the *bourgeoisie*. Such was Lenin's idea of a revolutionary proletarian party. And such was the Bolshevik party he had created. The Communist Party of the Soviet Union has remained faithful to Lenin's idea to this day.

Long live the Communist Party of the Soviet Union—the party of Lenin and the Leninists!

Long live Marxism–Leninism, the mainspring of the revolutionary energy and creativity of the masses!

Glory to the great Soviet people building communism!

Speech at the Extraordinary Plenary Meeting of the CPSU Central Committee
12 November 1982

Comrades!

Our Party and country, the entire Soviet people, have suffered a severe bereavement. Leonid Ilyich Brezhnev, the leader of the Soviet Communist Party and the Soviet state, an outstanding leader of the international communist and working-class movement, an ardent communist, a loyal son of the Soviet people, has died.

The greatest political leader of today is no longer with us. He was our comrade and friend, a man with a noble soul and a generous heart, tactful and friendly, responsive and profoundly humane. Utter dedication to our common cause, uncompromising exactingness to himself and to others, wise circumspection in taking important decisions, high-principledness and courage at crucial moments of history, invariable respect for and attention to people—such are the remarkable qualities which won Leonid Brezhnev high prestige and affection in the Party and among the people.

I request you to honour the dear memory of Leonid Brezhnev with a minute's silence. . . .

Leonid Brezhnev used to say that every day of his life was inseparably bound up with the affairs of the Soviet Communist Party and the country as a whole. That was truly so.

The country's industrialization and the collectivization of agriculture, the Great Patriotic War and the postwar economic recovery, virgin land development and space exploration—all of these are great milestones on the path of the Soviet people's work and struggle, as well as on the path traversed by Leonid Brezhnev as a communist.

The growth of the power of the great socialist community of nations and the development of all-round co-operation between them, the active involvement of the world communist movement in accomplishing the historic tasks facing mankind in our epoch, the strengthening of the solidarity of all forces of national liberation and social progress on earth are inseparably associated with his name and his contributions.

Leonid Brezhnev will be always thankfully remembered by mankind as a consistent, ardent and indefatigable fighter for peace and the security of nations, for removing the danger of world thermonuclear war overhanging mankind.

We know full well that peace cannot be secured by begging for it from imperialists. Peace can be defended only by reliance on the invincible power of the Soviet Armed Forces. As the leader of the Party and the head of state, and as Chairman of the USSR Defence Council, Leonid Brezhnev gave unflagging attention to maintaining the country's defence capability at a modern level.

Assembled in this hall are the members of our Party's headquarters, headed continuously by Leonid Brezhnev for eighteen years. Each of us knows how much effort and spirit he put into organizing concerted, collective work for this headquarters in order to map out its correct Leninist policy. Each of us knows of his inestimable contribution to creating the healthy moral and political climate characteristic of our Party's life and work today.

Our Party's high-principled struggle in defence of Marxism-Leninism, the evolvement of the theory of developed socialism, the charting of the ways of fulfilling the most pressing tasks in communist construction, are associated with his name. His activity in the world communist movement has rightly deserved extremely high appreciation from the fraternal parties, our foreign class brothers, our comrades in the struggle for socialism against capitalist oppression, for the triumph of the great communist ideals.

Leonid Brezhnev's life ended at a time when his thoughts and efforts were focused on implementing the great tasks in economic, social and cultural development outlined by the 26th Congress of the CPSU and the subsequent plenary meetings of its Central Committee. It is our prime duty to achieve these tasks, to carry into effect consistently the home and foreign policies of our Party and the Soviet state planned under Leonid Brezhnev's guidance. This will be our finest tribute to the dear memory of our late leader.

Our grief is infinite. The loss we have suffered is severe.

In this situation it is the duty of each of us, of every communist, to close our ranks still more tightly, to rally still more closely around the Party's Central Committee, to do our utmost in our jobs and in our lives for the benefit of the Soviet people, for the consolidation of peace, for the triumph of communism.

The Soviet people have implicit trust in their Communist Party. They know that the Party has never served any interests other than the vital interests of the Soviet people. To live up to this trust means to advance along the path of communist construction, to work for the further prosperity of this great socialist country.

There is a factor which invariably helps us at the most critical junctures and enables us to cope with the most formidable tasks. This factor is the unity of our Party ranks, the Party's collective wisdom and its unity with the people.

We have assembled for this plenary meeting in order to honour Leonid Brezhnev's memory and to ensure the continuation of the cause to which he dedicated his life.

This plenum is to elect a new General Secretary of the Communist Party of the Soviet Union.

Please submit your suggestions on this matter.

Speech at the funeral of Leonid Brezhnev in Red Square

15 November 1982

Comrades!

Our Party and people, all progressive mankind, have lost a great leader. Today we pay our last respects to Leonid Ilyich Brezhnev, a splendid son of this country, a dedicated Marxist–Leninist, an outstanding leader of the Communist Party and the Soviet state, the most prominent figure in the international communist and working-class movement, a tireless fighter for peace and friendship among nations. Allow me first of all to express our heartfelt condolences to his family, his near and dear ones.

Leonid Brezhnev belonged to the constellation of political leaders raised and steeled in the years of the Soviet people's selfless struggle to consolidate the achievements of the Great October Socialist Revolution, to fulfil Lenin's behests, to build socialism in this country, to uphold its freedom and independence.

A worker and soldier, a skilful organizer and a wise political leader, Leonid Brezhnev was linked to the people by vital, inseparable ties. All his life and work were a continuous record of service to the working people. He devoted all his brilliant talent and all his ebulient energy to the cause of socialism—a society of freedom and social justice, the working people's brotherhood.

Leonid Brezhnev's activities in the top Party and government posts marked a crucially important period in the history of our Party and country. It was under his guidance that the Party policy permeated with constant concern for the working people, for improving their well-being, was planned and consistently carried into effect, the Leninist norms of Party life and government work were strongly affirmed and the favourable atmosphere of efficient teamwork was firmly established.

The people will always remember Leonid Brezhnev as an outstanding champion of lasting peace and peaceful co-operation among nations. He struggled consistently and enthusiastically for an easing of international tensions, for delivering mankind from the menace of nuclear war, for strengthening the cohesion of the socialist community of nations, and for unity of the international communist movement.

At this hour of grief, bidding farewell to Leonid Brezhnev, our Party and its Central Committee declare their determination to follow firmly and consistently the strategic line in home and foreign policies charted under Leonid Brezhnev's beneficial influence.

The Soviet people are rallying still more closely behind the Party, its Leninist Central Committee and its collective leadership and are declaring their support for the Party policy and their infinite trust in the Party. The Party will continue to do whatever is necessary for further improving the people's living standards, for developing the democratic foundations of Soviet society, for strengthening the country's economic and defence potentials, for promoting friendship among the sister nations of the Soviet Union. The CPSU Central Committee shall unswervingly implement the resolutions of the 26th Party Congress, abiding by the will of the Soviet people.

We will do our utmost to strengthen further the cohesion of the great community of socialist states, the unity of the world's communists in the struggle for their common goals and ideals. We will maintain and develop our solidarity and our co-operation with the countries which have thrown off the colonial yoke, with the peoples struggling for their national independence and social progress. We will always be allegiant to the cause of the struggle for peace and a relaxation of international tensions.

In the current complicated international situation, where the imperialist forces are attempting to prod nations to a path of hostility and military confrontation, our Party and state will steadfastly uphold the vital interests of this country, and maintain high vigilance and preparedness to give a devastating rebuff to any attempted aggression. They will multiply their efforts in the struggle for the security of nations and strengthen co-operation with all peace-loving forces on earth. We are always prepared for honest and mutually beneficial co-operation based on equality with any state willing to reciprocate.

In these days of mourning we feel especially keenly the support for and solidarity with our Party and the Soviet people on the part of the working people in the socialist countries, the fraternal parties, all fighters for social progress. We are thankful to them for that. We are also grateful to the governments and peoples of many countries in all continents who have honoured Leonid Brezhnev's memory at this time.

The Communist Party of the Soviet Union firmly declares that service of the cause of the working class, all working people, the cause of peace and communism to which Leonid Brezhnev dedicated all his life, constitutes and will constitute the supreme goal and meaning of all its activities.

Farewell, dear comrade and friend! Your memory will live forever in our hearts. Your cause will be continued in the accomplishments of our Party and people!

Speech delivered at the Plenary Meeting of the CPSU Central Committee
22 November 1982

Comrades!

We are completing the discussion of the draft plan and budget for the next year of the Five-year Plan. In the documents submitted to us a number of essential remarks made at the Politbureau meeting have already been taken into account. I expect that in the process of fulfilling the plan the Council of Ministers will also take into consideration the suggestions made by some comrades today.

Judging by what the speakers at this plenary meeting have said we have a consensus: the draft plan and budget correspond on the whole with the guidelines of the 26th Congress of the CPSU and should be approved.

What is characteristic of the draft plan? It is planned to step up the rates of economic development, to increase the absolute increment in national income, the output of industry and agriculture, and the turnover of retail trade. The efforts to advance the efficiency of the national economy are to be continued; the heavy tasks facing it must be accomplished with a relatively smaller increase in material and labour inputs.

It is important to emphasize that the draft follows the Party line of advancing the well-being of the working people. It is planned to secure an accelerated growth of the group "B" industries, to increase consumer goods production. Large material and financial resources have been allocated for the continued development of the agro-industrial complex. The real incomes of the population will continue to grow. The scope of housing construction also corresponds to the assignments of the Five-year Plan.

248

Thus, the draft plan confirms that concern for the Soviet people, their working and living conditions, and their cultural advancement remains the Party's key programme principle.

As usual, the defence needs have been sufficiently taken into account. The Politbureau believe that it is indispensable to give the armed services everything they need, particularly in the present international situation.

The draft budget secures the financing of the national economy and sociocultural development.

The current plenary meeting of the Party's Central Committee is taking place at an important stage in the drive to implement the assignments of the Eleventh Five-year Plan, on the eve of its third, pivotal, so to say, year. We have done a good deal of work. Ahead of us, however, is another period of hard and tense effort.

I wish to draw your full attention to the fact that the assignments for the first two years of the Five-year Plan have not been fulfilled for a number of major indicators. This has naturally affected the draft we are discussing today.

The Central Committee members remember Leonid Brezhnev's last statements and his memoranda on economic development problems submitted to the Central Committee's Politbureau. He posed the question as follows: at Party Congresses and plenary meetings of the Central Committee we have worked out an economic policy on scientific lines and set a course for advancing the efficiency of production, its intensification. However, the transition of the economy to this course, the turn towards efficiency, is being implemented slowly for the time being.

The main indicator of the efficiency of the economy—the productivity of labour—is growing at a rate that cannot satisfy us. The problem of discrepancy in the development of the raw materials and manufacturing branches remains unresolved. Material consumption per unit product practically fails to be reduced.

Plans are being fulfilled as before at the cost of large spending and production outlays. There are still quite a few economic executives who readily quote Leonid Brezhnev's smart expression "the economy must be economical" but are doing practically little to cope with this task.

Evidently the force of inertia, the old habits, are still there. And some probably simply don't know how to get things moving. It is necessary to think of ways to help such comrades. What matters most now is to step up efforts to improve the entire sphere of guidance of the economy: management, planning, the economic mechanism.

It is mandatory to create such conditions—both economic and organizational—that would stimulate high-quality efficient work, initiative and resourcefulness. And conversely, poor work performance, inaction, negligence must directly and inevitably affect the material remuneration, official status and moral prestige of executives.

It is necessary to enhance the responsibility for compliance with the general interests of the state and the people, to resolutely uproot narrow departmental attitudes and parochialism. It is necessary to make it a rule that every new decision on one and the same question may be taken only when the earlier decisions have been fulfilled or some new circumstances have arisen. The struggle against any breaches of Party, state and labour discipline should be waged more vigorously. I am confident that in this matter we shall have full support from the Party and trade union organizations, from all Soviet citizens.

Of late there has been much talk of the need to widen the scope of independence of associations and enterprises, collective and state farms. I believe it is time practical steps were taken to settle this question. Appropriate assignments have been given in this connexion to the Council of Ministers and the State Planning Committee. In this area one should act with circumspectness, to carry out experiments, and if necessary also to assess and take into consideration the experience of the fraternal countries. Greater independence should in all cases be combined with greater responsibility and concern for the general national interests.

We have great latent reserves in the national economy. This has been pointed out in particular by today's speakers. These reserves should be brought into play by accelerating the rates of scientific and technological progress, by broad and prompt application of the achievements of science and technology and advanced experience in the production field. This question, of course, is not a new one. It has

more than once been raised at Party Congresses and plenary meetings of the Central Committee. Nevertheless, progress in this field is
slow. Why is that so? The answer has also been long known: to
introduce a new process or new technology, production should be
reorganized one way or the other, and this affects the fulfilment of
the plan. Moreover, one will be held responsible for failure to fulfil
the plan, while all one will get for inadequate application of new
technology will be just reproach.

If we really want to give a boost to the application of new technology and new methods of work it is necessary to ensure that the
central economic bodies of the State Committee for Science and
Technology and the Ministries should not simply recommend them
but bring to light and deal with the practical difficulties hindering
scientific and technological progress. Combination of science and
production should be facilitated by the planning methods and the
system of material incentives. It is necessary to see to it that those
who boldly introduce new technology will not find themselves at a
disadvantage.

Another large latent reserve is national utilization of material and
labour resources. The plan for 1983 has set increased assignments for
saving them. However, I wish to call your attention to the fact that
now the problem of saving material resources should be regarded in a
new way and not just as follows: "to save" is good and "not to save"
is tolerable.

Economy and a frugal attitude to national wealth today are crucial
to the feasibility of our plans. A solution to this problem should be
secured by a complete system of practical measures, primarily on the
part of the USSR State Planning Committee and the USSR Committee for Materials and Technical Supply, the Ministries and government departments. Great work is in store for all Party committees
and Party organizations.

We have quite a few examples of work with initiative, of a truly
frugal attitude to national wealth. Unfortunately, however, this
experience is not being disseminated adequately, though more often
than not no great spending is required to spread it. This means a
different kind of shortage: a lack of initiative and of a determined
struggle against mismanagement and extravagance.

Needless to say, this task can be accomplished only with the active participation of every worker, every working man and woman employed in our enterprises, every collective and state farmer. It is necessary to ensure that they regard this task as their own vital cause.

On the whole there are many pressing problems in the national economy. Naturally, I have no ready-made prescriptions for their solution. All of us—the Party's Central Committee—must find the answers to these problems. We must find them by summing up our national and world experience, by accumulating the expertise of the best practical workers and scientists. Generally speaking, slogans alone will not get things moving. What is needed is great organizing efforts on the part of Party organizations, economic executives, engineering and technical personnel, so that each of these enormous and important tasks may be examined not only from the angle of every sector of the economy but also from that of every plant, every department and section, and, if you like, every working place.

I wish to emphasize that these are problems of top priority, of vital importance to the country. Their effective solution will give an impetus to further economic development and continued improvement in the people's standards of living.

The measures to implement the Food Programme are at the focus of our plans.

The first steps to carry out the resolutions of the May 1982 plenary meeting of the Central Committee had to be taken in a fairly difficult situation. Also the weather was not favourable to us this year. It is all the more important, therefore, to commend the selfless work of the Soviet farmers. Their efforts as well as the reinforcement of the material and technological facilities of agriculture have yielded fairly good results in a number of regions, territories and Republics. The grain harvest has markedly increased compared with last year's, and a fairly good crop of cotton, vegetables and grapes has been grown. There has been an increment in the production of milk and eggs. The subsidiary farms of industrial plants are gaining strength. Concern for developing individual subsidiary farming has also proved fruitful. For all that, shortages in the supplies of certain foodstuffs have not yet been eliminated.

It is clear to all, of course, that the implementation of the Food

Programme is not a matter of one year. This is clearly so. Nevertheless, we are obliged to say frankly that the implementation of this programme should not be procrastinated. The workers of the agro-industrial complex must step up their efforts day by day, to work in such a way as to make the enormous funds appropriated for the fulfilment of this task yield fruit today and still greater fruit tomorrow.

The Politbureau believe that the forthcoming plenary meetings and meetings of Party committee activists, the sessions of the Soviets of People's Deputies which will discuss the plans for the next year, must also review progress in implementing the resolutions of the Central Committee's plenary meeting of May 1982. It is necessary for us to dovetail all practical efforts in this important area of economic work with the provisions of the Food Programme.

I will not dwell in detail on how important it is to complete the agricultural season in good fashion, to preserve the harvest taken in, to lay the basis for next year's harvest, to secure good winter accommodation for livestock. All this is self-evident. It is necessary to attack without delay new tasks, considering them as being closely bound up with the guidelines for developing the agro-industrial complex and bearing in mind that it is precisely a complex where no problem is of secondary importance.

In the plan for 1983 keen attention is paid to increasing the output and improving the quality of consumer goods, to which Leonid Brezhnev attached special significance. The task is not only to increase production but also to advance significantly the quality of consumer goods. This concerns not only light and local industries but also heavy and defence industry enterprises.

Local party and government bodies should directly concern themselves with consumer goods production, as Comrade Baibakov has quite correctly pointed out here. Indeed, a situation where the question of manufacturing a number of simple items is decided at a level almost as high as the USSR State Planning Committee cannot be accepted as normal. It is necessary for local bodies to take charge of this work and assume full responsibility for its performance.

Now let me dwell on some major problems involved in the development of key industries. This refers primarily to the continued development of the fuel and energy complex. The increment in primary energy resources of about 41 million tons of fuel in conventional units planned for 1983 is a perfectly feasible target. This will ensure trouble-free and regular operation of all energy systems.

It is highly important to make rational use of coal, natural gas, crude, petroleum products, thermal and electrical power. This requires, of course, a certain restructuring in all industries, primarily broad introduction of energy-saving technology and processes, an improvement in normatives, and more effective material and moral incentives in the drive for economy, stricter responsibility for over-expenditure, for overstepping quotas and ceilings.

It is planned to submit to the next session of the USSR Supreme Soviet a proposal to set up at the Soviet of the Union and the Soviet of Nationalities standing commissions for power development to supervise the work of the Ministries and call economic executives of any rank to account for irrational use of resources.

It is necessary to galvanize into action the commissions set up in territories, regions and Republics to supervise the organization of this work at enterprises.

The Politbureau are concerned about the situation in the transport services. The Ministry of Railways fails as before to meet the needs of the national economy in the transportation of fuel, timber, and other freight. The CPSU Central Committee is receiving a large number of complaints on this score from local government and economic organizations. This plenary meeting has also discussed this question today.

The standards of railway services have unfortunately been deteriorating year after year in spite of the important assistance rendered to the Ministry of Railways by the Government. The amount of capital investments in the services run by this Ministry has grown by 43 per cent since 1975, while the fleet of main-line and electric locomotives has grown by 23 per cent. The CPSU Central Committee and the Government have adopted a series of resolutions to improve the social conditions of railwaymen, to perfect the economic mechanism in the transport services. These measures, however, have not yet yielded the desired effect.

In the services under the Ministry of Railways the organization of

repairs and maintenance of the fleet of locomotives and the organization of traffic are of a low standard. Evidently, not only the leadership of this Ministry but also the USSR Council of Ministers and the
CPSU Central Committee will have to draw serious conclusions from
the criticisms expressed at this plenary meeting.

There have been more frequent bottlenecks in the operation of
iron-and-steel plants. Just as last year, this industry has failed to cope
with its plan assignments. The national economy has received a few
million tons of rolled stock less than planned. It is primarily the
Ministry of Ferrous Metallurgy that is to blame for the situation in
this industry. Of course, there are also objective difficulties. A significant share of the basic productive capacities requires reconstruction and modernization. The Ministry is in need of effective help
from the State Planning Committee, the State Committee for
Materials and Technical Supply and the engineering Ministries.

We invest enormous funds in economic development, the
construction of new capacities, housing construction, and the
development of cultural and service establishments. Effective use of
these funds is a task of crucial significance. However, quite a few
problems still exist in the sphere of capital construction. It is mandatory to oppose more resolutely the scattering of material resources
and manpower between numerous building projects. The share of
reconstruction and modernization should be increased, and the number of new construction projects reduced. We are dissatisfied with
many aspects of the organization of construction as such. The shortcomings existing here result year after year in underfulfilment of
plans of commissioning new capacities. A number of construction
Ministries tend to reduce the scope of building and assembly
operations, although the Government provides large financial
resources, machinery and equipment to reinforce the material and
technological facilities of these Ministries. In many instances the
standards of building and assembly work remain low. The mobility of
building organizations is insufficient.

Quite a few resolutions have been adopted to eliminate these
drawbacks. They must be fulfilled. To introduce order in capital
construction is one of the central tasks in the national economy.

I will not dwell today on other spheres and branches of the economy. All of them are important for our society and our people. Every Ministry and government department should again and again analyse the situation thoroughly and devise and implement effective measures to cope with existing problems. The chief criterion they should use to assess their work is the degree to which their respective branches meet the steadily growing needs of society.

Efforts to secure constant economic growth and improvement of public welfare are our duty to the Soviet people and our internationalist duty. Viewing this question in this light, the Party is guided by Lenin's far-sighted statement to the effect that the main influence on the world revolutionary process is exerted by our economic policy.

Leonid Brezhnev's death has caused a plethora of conjectures abroad about the future policy of the CPSU and the Soviet Government on the international scene. Just recall how many attempts have been made in the last years to ascribe to the Soviet Union various malicious intentions, to depict our policy as aggressive and endangering the security of now one state, now another. Today, however, apprehensions are being voiced lest this policy be revised. Its continuation is regarded as crucial to peace and tranquillity in the international arena.

I must declare with the full awareness of my responsibility that Soviet foreign policy has been and will remain as it was laid down in the resolutions of the 24th, 25th and 26th Party Congresses. To secure lasting peace, to defend the right of nations to independence and social progress are invariable aims of our foreign policy. In the struggle to achieve these aims the leadership of the Party and state will pursue a high-principled, consistent and balanced policy.

We believe that the difficulties and tensions characteristic of today's international situation can and must be overcome. Mankind cannot tolerate the arms race and wars indefinitely unless it wants to put its own future at stake. The CPSU is against a contest between ideas turning into a confrontation between states and peoples, against arms and preparedness to resort to arms becoming a criterion of the potentials of social systems.

The aggressive intrigues of the imperialists are compelling us and our allies, the fraternal socialist nations, to concern ourselves seriously with maintaining our defence capability at an adequate level.

However, as Leonid Brezhnev has repeatedly stated, military rivalry is not our choice. A world without arms is an ideal of socialism.

The strengthening of the socialist community of nations will continue to be a matter of prime concern to our Party. Unity is the source of our strength and the guarantee of eventual success even in the most gruelling trials.

All the plans of the community of socialist states are plans of peace and construction. We are striving for relations of comradely co-operation and socialist mutual assistance between the fraternal countries to become even more close and fruitful, in particular in the joint solution of scientific and technological, production, transport, energy and other problems. Further joint steps are already being planned in this context.

The CPSU and the Soviet Government sincerely desire to develop and improve relations with all socialist countries. Mutual goodwill, respect for the lawful interest of each other, common concern for the interests of socialism and peace must suggest the right decisions also where there is not yet for various reasons the necessary trust and mutual understanding.

This refers in particular to our great neighbour, the People's Republic of China. The ideas Leonid Brezhnev expressed in his speeches in Tashkent and Baku and his emphasis on common sense and the need to overcome the inertia of prejudice expressed the convictions of all our Party and its desire to look ahead. It is with keen attention that we respond to every positive response to this from the Chinese side.

The significance of the groups of states which have founded the non-aligned movement is growing in international affairs. The Soviet Union maintains with many of them many-sided friendly ties which benefit both sides and contribute to greater stability in the world. This is exemplified by the Soviet Union's relations with India. Solidarity with the states which have thrown off the colonial yoke and help with defending their independence has been and remains one of the fundamental principles of Soviet foreign policy.

From the early days of Soviet government the Soviet Union has invariably expressed its desire to co-operate sincerely and honestly with all countries willing to reciprocate. The difference between the

ASW-I

social systems should not obstruct this co-operation and do not obstruct it where there is goodwill on both sides. Conclusive evidence of this is the appreciable progress in the development of peaceful co-operation between the USSR and many countries of Western Europe.

It is our profound belief that the seventies, which passed under the beneficial influence of *détente*, were not an accidental episode in mankind's difficult history, as is alleged by some imperialist leaders today. No, the policy of *détente* is by no means a thing of the past. It is the wave of the future.

All have an equal interest in the preservation of peace and *détente*. Therefore, statements in which consent to normalize relations is linked to the demand that the Soviet Union should pay for this with some preliminary concessions in various fields do not sound serious, to say the least. We will not agree to that. As a matter of fact, we have nothing to desist from: we have not introduced sanctions against anybody, nor do we renounce the treaties and agreements we have signed, and we have not broken off any negotiations once started. I wish to re-emphasize that the Soviet Union is in favour of agreement, but it should be sought on a basis of reciprocity and equality.

We see the meaning of the talks with the United States and other Western countries, primarily on arms race limitation, not in fixing our differences. We regard negotiations as a means of pooling the efforts of different states to achieve results beneficial to all parties. Problems will not cease to exist by themselves if negotiations are pursued for their own sake, which, unfortunately, is often the case. We are in favour of quests of a sound basis for a solution to the most complicated problems acceptable to the sides, primarily, of course, to the problems of curbing the arms race, both nuclear and conventional. However, nobody should expect us to disarm unilaterally. We are not naïve.

We are not demanding unilateral disarmament of the West. We are in favour of equality, respect for the interests of both sides, an honest agreement. We are fully prepared for a fair deal.

As regards, in particular, the strategic nuclear arms in possession of the USSR and the USA, the Soviet Union has agreed, as is known, that as a first step towards future agreement the two sides should "freeze" their arsenals, thereby creating a more favourable climate for a continuation of talks on their mutual reduction.

The Soviet Union rejects in general the viewpoint of those who are trying to persuade people that force and arms decide and will always decide everything.

The peoples are now coming to the forefront of the historical arena on a scale unknown before. They have gained the right to voice their opinion which nobody will be able to silence. By their active and determined efforts they can remove the danger of nuclear war, preserve peace and hence life on our planet. The Communist Party of the Soviet Union and the Soviet Government will do everything to this end.

The 26th CPSU Congress detailed the Party's long-term strategy for the period of the Eleventh Five-year Plan and for the eighties as a whole. The aim of this strategy is to secure that the life of the Soviet people is improved year after year, that their work yields ever more tangible fruit, that our socialist system reveals its humane essence and its constructive potentials ever more completely.

Important and largely new tasks have been set in all fields of economic and social progress. Success, of course, depends on many factors, primarily on the purposeful collective work of our Central Committee, on our ability to concentrate the efforts of Party, government and economic bodies and all labour collectives in the key directions.

It is necessary to mobilize all facilities at our disposal, to launch a wide public education campaign to explain the tasks of the plan of 1983. They must be specified in relation to the tasks facing every enterprise, every labour collective. This is our first objective.

Second, it is necessary to ensure correct placement of cadres, so that work in decisive areas can be directed by politically mature and competent people with initiative, organizing talent and a hunch for innovation, without which successful management of modern production is impossible today.

Third, it is necessary to stimulate the activity of the working people themselves. This is the central task facing party committees, government, trade union and YCL bodies today. As is known, the Party's ideas, plans and appeals become a material force only when they have been adopted by the masses. Today it is crucially important and necessary that every working man and woman realize that the fulfilment of the plan depends on their own labour contribution as well, that all understand the simple truth that the better we work, the better we live. As Lenin emphasized, the wider the scope of our plans and our production tasks, the "greater the numbers of people who should be drawn by the millions into independent participation in the fulfilment of these tasks".

This means that it is necessary to ensure the continued development of socialist democracy in its broadest sense, that is ever more active involvement of the working people in the management of the affairs of state and society. Naturally, there is no need to argue here to prove how important it is to display concern for the needs of the working people, for their working and living conditions.

We will always be unswervingly faithful to the Leninist norms and principles which have been securely affirmed in the life of the Party and state.

The tasks facing us are truly enormous and complex. Our Party, however, can measure up to them.

The days when we paid our last respects to Leonid Brezhnev have shown to the whole world that our Communist Party and the Soviet people are linked by indissoluble ties, that they are united by their common determination to follow staunchly and undeviatingly the path charted by Lenin.

The Soviet people have again demonstrated their utter devotion to the ideas of Marxism–Leninism, their profound respect and affection for the Party, their organization, self-control, and confidence in their strength.

We look forward to an important event in the history of our multinational socialist state—the 60th anniversary of the Union of Soviet Socialist Republics. In these days the Soviet people devote their finest thoughts to the Leninist Party which stood at the cradle of the USSR and is wisely leading the peoples of this country along the path of communist construction.

To strengthen the unity of the Party and people, to follow steadfastly the great Lenin's behests—this is the guarantee of our our future triumphs!

Interview with Mr. Joseph Kingsbury-Smith, an American Political Analyst
Pravda, 31 December 1982

Question. What would you like to wish the American people for the New Year, 1983?

Answer. First of all, I wish them a happy New Year, and I extend my sincere wishes of well-being and happiness to every American family. I wish above all peace to the Americans, lasting peace and prosperity based on peaceful work and fruitful co-operation with other nations. Now the Soviet and American peoples have a common enemy — the danger of war and everything that aggravates it. The Soviet Union desires that peace be preserved and strengthened and is doing everything to this end, firmly convinced that no task is more important in international politics today than one of averting the growing danger of nuclear war, of holding in check and ending the nuclear arms race. I wish America also made a contribution worthy of that great nation to promoting peace and friendship among nations, rather than escalating the arms race and fomenting warlike passions.

Question. What crucial steps could the Soviet Union and the United States take jointly in 1983 in the interests of world peace and of improving Soviet-American relations?

Answer. I believe our two countries could jointly do much that would benefit them and other countries and peoples; for instance, implement mutual troop and arms reductions in Central Europe, or co-operate in defusing the most dangerous seats of military conflict, such as the one in the Middle East, and in other areas.

What matters most, of course, is to achieve fair and mutually acceptable agreement on the principle of parity and equal security at the talks on the limitation and reduction of strategic arms and medium-range nuclear weapons in Europe and to take practical steps to carry them into effect.

Question. Do you believe that through continued negotiations the differences between the Soviet and American governments on nuclear arms issues can be sufficiently narrowed to create favourable conditions for reaching a compromise?

Answer. I certainly do. Objectively, this is quite possible, since there are solutions to the problems under discussion that would prejudice the interests of neither party and lead to drastic arms reductions by both sides to the best advantage of universal peace and security. This is precisely the motive behind the Soviet Union's concrete proposals, including those we have put forward recently. Let me remind you of the main idea of these proposals. It is very simple and logical. We have proposed an immediate end to the further arms build-up by both sides, that is, a freeze on the present level of armaments to be followed by a roughly 25 per cent reduction in the existing arsenals, bringing them down to equal levels, and later by further progress towards new reductions.

As far as nuclear weapons in the zone of Europe are concerned, we have proposed different options. Either to have no such weapons there at all — neither medium range nor tactical ones — neither on the Soviet side nor on the side of the NATO powers. That would be a "zero option", so to speak, for both sides. Or else, both sides could reduce their medium-range weapons (missiles, and nuclear-armed aircraft) by more than two thirds. With this settlement there would be no opposing Soviet and American medium-range missiles here at all, while the USSR would retain exactly as many such missiles as Britain and France have. As regards aircraft, we are again in favour of complete parity at a considerably lower level than now. In short, we do not want to have in the zone of Europe a single missile or aircraft more than the NATO powers have.

It is to be hoped that the United States will respond to this fair and constructive stand with a manifestation of good will. This would help secure the success of negotiations. I am confident such success would make 1983 a good year for all mankind.

Question. Ex-President Richard Nixon has appealed for a meeting between you and the US President. What is your response to this?

Answer. The Soviet leadership has always regarded summitry as one of the most effective methods of developing relations between states.

We adhere to this view today as well. It is natural, however, that thorough preparations are necessary for such a meeting to be a success. At any rate, we are in favour of improving Soviet-American relations and of implementing the mutually beneficial treaties and agreements concluded between our two countries, and we will welcome any step in this direction.

Meeting with Moscow's Machine-tool Builders
31 January 1983

The General Secretary of the CPSU Central Committee, Yuri V. Andropov, visited the Moscow Machine-tool Plant named after Sergo Ordjonikidze. He made a round of its departments and inspected its products. Yuri Andropov met workers and foremen at their various working places, and discussed with them the organization of work, training and recreation.

During his visit to the mechanical assembly department Yuri Andropov put questions about manpower supply.

The plant manager, N. S. Chikirev, told him that the plant was plagued by a grave manpower shortage.

Y. V. Andropov: Why?

N. S. Chikirev: We have a shortage of fitters, electrical assemblymen, and a weak influx of fresh blood. This is a problem not only in Moscow but in other cities as well. The plant has difficulties with employment of machine-tool operators, too.

Y. V. Andropov: How much does a machine-tool operator earn?

N. S. Chikirev: Their earnings are quite decent.

Y. V. Andropov: (addressing the planer S. A. Korolev): How long have you worked here?

S. A. Korolev: Seven years.

Y. V. Andropov: All this time at the bench?

S. A. Korolev: Yes, all this time.

Y. V. Andropov: How much do you earn?

S. A. Korolev: Quite enough.

Y. V. Andropov: Could you say how much?

S. A. Korolev: Well, some 250 roubles.

Y. V. Andropov: Does a fitter earn more?

S. A. Korolev: No, roughly the same.

In the next department Y. V. Andropov discussed the reconstruction of the plant and some new products manufactured there. He was interested in the competitive power of the machine-tools on the world market and asked which countries imported them.

Y. V. Andropov: What technical assistance does your plant render to enterprises in the socialist countries?

N. S. Chikirev: We supply products of our plant to COMECON member countries. Specialists and workers come from socialist countries to learn our experience. We maintain direct ties with our counterparts. Our friends come to us, for instance, from Czechoslovakia. We also visit them.

Y. V. Andropov: (addressing an automatic machine-tool fitter B. A. Shunin): How long have you worked at this plant?

B. A. Shunin: Twenty years.

Y. V. Andropov: And at this line?

B. A. Shunin: Six years.

Y. V. Andropov: How long does it take to learn your job?

B. A. Shunin: One has to learn new things all the time.

Y. V. Andropov: Is it difficult?

B. A. Shunin: Yes, it is, but that cannot be helped.

M. F. Skripkin (a veteran fitter joining the conversation): Comrade Andropov, it's not hard work once you have got the knack of it.

Y. V. Andropov: But then you are given something new to learn, aren't you?

M. F. Skripkin: Well, we cope with it. This is our job.

Y. V. Andropov. One question in confidence. How much do you earn?

M. F. Skripkin: Enough.

Y. V. Andropov: How large is your family?

M. F. Skripkin: There are two of us.

N. S. Chikirev: (stopping near a machine-tool manned by a young worker): Here's my son. He's chosen a worker's job after graduating from an institute.

Y. V. Andropov: What institute was that?

V. N. Chikirev: The Institute of Machine-tools and Industrial Implements. I had worked at this plant before I entered the institute. I came to work here straight from school. It's our family tradition; my mother also works at this plant.

ASW-I*

Y. V. Andropov: Why did you choose the job of a machine-tool operator?

V. N. Chikirev: To know better how machine-tools are made, one has to handle them with one's own hands.

V. P. Chaika (a woman veteran drilling-machine operator, coming up to Y. V. Andropov): I have worked 41 years at this plant. I retired on pension and was given a very good send-off. Everything went well in my family, too. But to stay at home all day was boring. It's better to be at work and mingle with one's workmates. I am considered valuable here. I hear many good words about my work. I came to work at this plant at the age of 15 in 1942. As I recall, I was given a little pig as a prize for good work at that time. I am determined to work at this plant as long as I can.

*   *   *

Then, during a break, Yuri V. Andropov had a meeting with representatives of the departments and the plant management — workers, team leaders, technicians, engineers, leading executives, the Party, trade union and Komsomol organizations — at the plant's conference hall.

The meeting was opened by V. M. Kubrin, secretary of the plant's Party Committee.

The plant manager, N. S. Chikirev, described the history of the plant, the progress of the socialist emulation drive, the implementation of the resolutions of the 26th congress of the CPSU, the November plenary meeting of the CPSU Central Committee by the work force of the plant, the techno-economic indicators and the prospects for machine-tool manufacturing.

Since the November plenary meeting of the CPSU Central Committee, he declared, the work collective of the plant has paid keener attention to the problem of discipline. Our plant, along with other enterprises of Moscow, has come forward with the initiative of improving the organization of work and enhancing labour and production discipline. A decision has been taken to increase the productivity of labour by at least 1.5-2 per cent by reducing losses of working time in 1983. I believe that the work we are now doing to strengthen labour discipline is highly important indeed. We are aware of our shortcomings and know how to fight them. We can measure up to the tasks set by the plenary meeting of the CPSU Central Committee. Our work force has taken solemn socialist pledges for this year to secure the successful performance of the plans facing it. They have been discussed within individual departments and at a general meeting. We have undertaken to fulfil the plan for the current year towards December 27.

Yuri V. Andropov was the next to take the floor. He said as follows:

Dear Comrades!

I thank you very much for your warm hospitality. I regard your good attitude as a credit for the future, and I will try to work well to live up to your trust. Naturally, I apply this not only to my own person but to the Central Committee and the Politbureau. I thank you again for your trust.

I would like to express my gratitude on behalf of the Party's Central Committee for your support, along with other Moscow work collectives, for the decisions of its November plenary meeting. It is a pleasure to see that the decisions of the plenum have evoked a lively response among all work collectives throughout the country. This means that what was discussed at the plenary meeting was really a matter of concern to Soviet citizens. We feel the unanimous support of the Soviet working class for the Party's decisions to stimulate this country's further economic progress.

Your remarkable work collective has proved that it is a good support for the city's Party organization and that the Party's city committee and Central Committee can rely upon it.

The speakers here have pointed out the great significance of the November plenary meeting of the CPSU Central Committee. This significance is determined not only by the fact that the plenary meeting outlined the ways of developing this country's national economy in the current year and set great targets in construction and production. Their scope is truly enormous. No other country in the world is producing so much, say, steel, crude oil and other items of output. The decisions of the plenary meeting are important also because they take into account a number of the difficulties which we are facing or may face in implementing the plan of this year.

Here and there, for example, complaints are being voiced about shortages of metal and electric power. These shortages should be offset. However, we also proceed from the assumption that the communists, the management of enterprises, all work collectives and your collective in particular will find latent reserves to secure an effective economy of all kinds of resources.

As you remember, the plenary meeting called attention to work performance in a number of key areas of our economic activities lagging behind the targets set in the Five-year Plan. it was also pointed out that the productivity of labour was growing at a rate that could not satisfy us. Perhaps you know from your own experience that our progress in the economy is not as good as it should be.

I have in mind the following. What we produce often costs us too much. We have on record considerable over-expenditure of material and financial resources, as well as excessive labour inputs. As a result there is a disproportion between the growth of production and the growth of the population's cash incomes.

Here is one of the sources of this disproportion. All of you are familiar with the expression "to adjust the plan". I must admit that I have never heard of such adjustment being made to increase the plan assignment. If they say that "adjustment" is necessary, this normally implies a reduction (laughter in the audience). It is easy to see what this leads to. The output of produce is reduced, but the wages remain the same. What is more, bonuses are often awarded for the fulfilment of a reduced plan. If this is translated into economic terms on a nationwide scale there will be a gap between the mass of marketable goods and the total cash savings available to the population.

Miracles never happen on earth, as they say. You realize, of course, that the state can give the public exactly as many goods as have been manufactured. The growth of wages and salaries, if not secured with the supply of good commodities which are in demand and with consumer services which are adequate cannot of itself give a real improvement in material well-being.

What is the way out of this situation?

One way, of course, is to put up prices. However, this way is generally unacceptable. Although it must be admitted we have certain distortions and inconsistency in prices and are forced to correct them.

What is to be done? The main road for us is to enhance the efficiency of production. It is necessary to make and produce whatever we make and produce at minimum costs, to secure high quality, speed and good workmanship. It is necessary to produce more goods so that shop counters are never empty. I am speaking figuratively, of course. You may say that your machine-tools will not be sold at shops. However, your production contributes in the final analysis to the output of goods made available to the consumer.

As was stated at the plenary meeting, the current year is the key year of the Five-year Plan. We must complete what we have failed, speaking frankly, to complete during the first two years and try to catch up on what has been lost and provide conditions for normal work in the remaining two years of the Five-year Plan.

It is important to improve the quality of work, to accelerate its tempo, and to cheapen the cost of products. Such is the pressing task facing us.

But where is, to use Lenin's phrase, the link that should be seized to pull out the whole chain? Indeed, it is a large and heavy chain. And although we cannot reduce everything to discipline, this is where we have to begin.

The Central Statistical Board has testified that we lose millions of man-hours due to unauthorized absence from work, breaks for smoking, and bungling by individual workers. We must do everything now to ensure that every member of the work force unconditionally copes with his quota, his production assignment. This is by no means an excessive demand.

Indeed, we have front-ranking workers. No praise is too high for them. They are innovators and a model for emulation. But we cannot cope with our tasks relying on the efforts of front-rankers alone. Everyone must fulfil his daily quota unfailingly. Then we shall be able to solve the problem I have discussed above. It should be solved by the working people as a whole.

Therefore, I ask you to look into this matter and find out what should be done to ensure that everyone fulfils his assignment. If somebody needs help, help him.

Why was the question of labour discipline given such a high priority at the plenary meeting of the CPSU Central Committee?

This is primarily a dictate of the times. Indeed, without proper discipline — labour, planning, state discipline — we cannot make rapid progress. Introduction of order really does not require any capital investments but yields an enormous effect. A shirker, a bungler or a loafer cause harm not so much to themselves as to their work collective and to society as a whole.

I wish to emphasise specifically that when we talk of discipline we have in mind the whole production chain involving labour. Of course, all our efforts will come to nothing if the struggle for discipline is conducted superficially, with emphasis on unimportant details: somebody is late for work by a couple of minutes, somebody else takes a break for a smoke too often. Of course, one should not be praised for that. It is necessary to introduce order wherever working time is wasted.

It is the question of a serious attitude to all aspects of production discipline, Including the technological, supply and other aspects. It is necessary to ensure that the effect of enhancing discipline should be felt in all areas of production.

We need conscious labour discipline that will promote production. We must fill the struggle for discipline with a more meaningful content, and link it directly with the performance of production assignments, and then there would be no useless backfiring, as they say. Then what the November plenary meeting of the Party's Central Committee planned would be accomplished.

Yuri V. Andropov further discussed some vital problems of the international situation. You know, he said, that in his report at the 26th Party Congress Leonid Brezhnev emphasised that the situation was being aggravated and the war danger growing. Our Party and the Soviet state are doing everything to avert this danger and to preserve peace.

It is easy to see that the greater our achievements, the stronger our economy and the more effective the performance of our national economy, the stronger our international positions and the more durable peace on earth.

I wish you success in your work for the good of this country and I am confident that you will honourably fulfil your duty.

If you have any questions please put them. I would also like to hear from you what is still being done the wrong way or with mistakes in the efforts to strengthen discipline and what should be done to stimulate production.

The next speaker was K. I. Meschankin, chief of the assembly department. He described the work of his department and its products. We have been given a large plan but we will do our best to fulfil it. We shall supply flowlines to Kharkov's Hammer and Sickle Plant to make engines for the Don-1500 harvesting combines.

Y. V. Andropov: Incidentally, this is a very efficient machine which our whole country is waiting for.

K. I. Meschankin: We will work for all we are worth to cope with our assignment.

We have held a Party meeting to discuss the November plenary meeting of the Central Committee. Our work collective reviews its decisions in its own way.

Y. V. Andropov: What do you mean?

K. I. Meschankin: First of all every member has developed a new awareness of responsibility for the matter in hand and for discipline. In this respect the plenary meeting expressed our thoughts and sentiments. We had expected these decisions. We will continue to enhance our efficiency and awareness and persistently get rid of shortcomings. A Party meeting at our department has instructed us to draw up concrete proposals for improving the performance of all our work collectives. These proposals are now being translated into daily work at our department.

The next speaker was V. G. Komarov, Hero of Socialist Labour, a fitter and assemblyman. I work in the department for assembly of unique machinery. Automatic lines, sophisticated machine-tools, program-controlled ones in particular, are made by the hands of our plant's workers. The discussion we have had today was a much needed, useful discussion. I believe that now we are obliged to work so well nobody could be ashamed of us. We must not simply fulfil, but over-fulfil with enthusiasm, the plans outlined by the 26th Party Congress, and the May and November plenary meetings of the CPSU Central Committee. We must manufacture, as Comrade Andropov has just said, only products of top quality. I am secretary of my department's Party organization. I shall say on behalf of our communists that discipline, as Comrade Andropov has justly pointed out, does not boil down to counting minutes of being late for work. . .

Y. V. Andropov: Yes, the problem should not be reduced to this alone.

V. G. Komarov: At our meeting we have taken a firm decision: to create a climate of intolerance of all breaches of discipline in our department. The main task is to concentrate on implementing proposals for raising the productivity of labour, and reducing losses of working time and production losses. It is also necessary to do everything for the work collective, to provide favourable conditions that would satisfy every worker and make his job pleasant. A worker must feel happy with his labour input every day. Here is one example. Once a young worker, Mikhail Stepanenkov, worked in my team. We made a machine-tool together. And it was a pleasure to see the lively interest with which he looked at the machine-tool when it was assembled and tested. The young man came up to the machine-tool and said: "Look, it is working!" I am very pleased that working along with me in our department are such masters of their trades as Fyodor Bukharev and Alexei Shumilkin. It is good that such people are involved in the training of young workers. These workers will work the way we have taught them when they take over from us. What we invest in them will benefit our favourite plant at a later time.

The next speaker was T. A. Komarova, chief of the department of finishing work. The work force of our department, she said, consists of veteran workers who account for over 50 per cent, and young workers. Therefore, the problem of educating and training young workers in occupational skills is a highly acute problem facing us. We attach great significance to it. For instance, our work teams consist of young workers and veteran workers who serve as instructors. The teams are led by communists. The work force of the department is mainly made up of women. Men are very few here.

Y. V. Andropov: Well, don't you let them in?

T. A. Komarova: You know, men are not very eager to work with us.

Y. V, Andropov: Why?

T. A. Komarova: They come and go. They feel it is hard work since it involves health hazards and they are concerned for their health. It is, of course, rather difficult to work with women alone sometimes. However, there are certain advantages. For instance, with rare exceptions we have no cases of late reporting for work or absenteeism.

We have a different problem. The intra-shift losses are still too large. We have taken vigorous steps to eliminate them.

Y. V. Andropov: What is causing such losses?

T. A. Komarova: The causes are various. At times good lacquers and paints are not available in sufficient amounts, which makes our work very difficult. Sometimes we have to do our work again because we have used materials of poor quality. Occasionally we receive a part after a delay, or its casting is bad. This also makes us extra work. I believe we shall cope with this problem this year, the more so as the lacquers and paint industry intends to improve the quality of its products. At least we have been assured so. We have another problem on our hands: mechanization of minor operations. We have grinding machines which weigh only two kilos but they vibrate so hard that the operator shakes from head to toe.

Y. V. Andropov: Who is in charge of the manufacture of these machines?

N. S. Chikirev: The Ministry of Building and Road Machinery.

T. A. Komarova: All these bottlenecks are a great nuisance and certainly hold back the productivity of labour. Nevertheless, we are determined to fulfil our socialist pledges in 1983.

Since our department is an all-female outfit I want to say a couple of words about social problems. It is very good that all who so desire can accommodate their children in creches. We have a good cafeteria. We can also buy food-stuffs at the plant shop, which is a rather important help to a housewife.

Y. V. Andropov: Incidentally, it's help to men also (laughter in the audience).

T. A. Komarova: It is especially valuable to us. We receive various vouchers. We women workers have enough sanatorial vouchers. Vouchers for accommodation at holiday homes are available at special rates. Working mothers of young children also enjoy privileges.

The next speaker was V. S. Emelyanov, senior foreman of the department and secretary of its Party organization. I have a record of 23 years of work at this plant, he said. My first job here was as a tool fitter and I have worked as foreman for over 15 years. I have witnessed great progress in the advancement of technological equipment, improvement in the quality of products and advancement in the qualification of workers. We manufacture sophisticated accessories for automatic flowlines, complex machine-tools. Our workers efficiently cope with their assignments. Communists are, of course, in the vanguard of this important work. Just witness the work of the boring-machine operator Isakov, the milling-machine operator Polyakov, and the fitter Grechishkin to mention but a few. The whole work force welcomed the decisions of the November plenary meeting of the Party's Central Committee and correctly assessed the significance of the organization of production and labour discipline. We assure you that our department and, as I believe, the whole work force of our plant, will successfully cope with their assignments.

Y. V. Andropov: Can I ask you one delicate question? Have you got many offenders in your department?

V. S. Emelyanov: In January we reduced this problem to nil. Of course, our laws and administrative penalties must play a role in maintaining labour discipline, but, in my opinion, the work collective has the most important role to play in this matter.

Y. V. Andropov: You are certainly right.

V. S. Emelyanov: We are organizing work by the self-sustained brigade method in our department now. Before long we shall change over to this form of work for good. This will open great latent potentials for strengthening labour discipline and enhancing the productivity of labour. Generally speaking, we would like to have fewer words and more business.

Y. V. Andropov: Right you are. This is important not only for your plant but everywhere.

The break in working time had ended. The meeting of the General Secretary of the CPSU Central Committee Yuri V. Andropov with Moscow's machine-tool builders came to a close.

The last speaker was V. V. Grishin, Member of the Politbureau and First Secretary of the Moscow City Committee of the CPSU. He assured the audience that the communists and all working people of Moscow would apply every effort to fulfil the decisions of the 26th Congress of the CPSU, the November 1982 plenary meeting of the CPSU Central Committee. Indeed, he said, it is necessary to introduce order in the maintenance of discipline and in the performance of plans. The plenary meeting clearly outlined the way work must be done and the directions to be followed.

Y. V. Andropov: This is a long-term task. It's important not to peter out.

V. V. Grishin: The decisive role in this work, of course, must be played by the communists, Party organizations and the Party organization of your plant which is called upon to inspire all to a struggle for implementing these tasks. Comrade Andropov has spoken here of strengthening discipline. Indeed, it is a problem of many aspects. And it is important not just to report for work on time and to quit work on time although these also matter very much.

Another important component of the effort to strengthen discipline is provision of favourable conditions in production, so that it can be clearly planned, material and technical supplies secured and equipment adjusted. It is necessary to strengthen both production and plan discipline. It has been correctly pointed out here that the decisive role is to be played by the work collective. When an atmosphere of intolerance is created by public opinion over every case of violation of labour discipline, this will be the most potent remedy, more potent than any other.

Y. V. Andropov: I want to add a few words to what Comrade Grishin has just said. I would like this audience to understand correctly the fact that the problem of enforcing discipline concerns not only workers, engineers and technicians. This is a matter of concern to all, from Ministers downwards.

In conclusion, general secretary Andropov again thanked the machine-tool builders for their good work and cordial welcome. He wished them good health, and success in production, in fulfilling the tasks set by the November plenary meeting of the CPSU Central Committee.

The Teaching of Karl Marx and Some Problems of Socialist Construction in the USSR
Article in the journal Communist, No. 3, 1983

It is 100 years since the death of the man who is known to the world as the originator of the Marxian doctrine. A full century. It was a century of dramatic cataclysms, revolutionary storms, radical changes in mankind's destiny. It was a century that toppled and broke to pieces a host of philosophical conceptions, social theories, and political doctrines. It was a century of triumphs for Marxism, which followed one another in rapid succession, and of its growing influence on social development.

The march of time lends growing clarity to the meaning and greatness of the exploits of Karl Marx.

For thousands of years men had searched for ways to remake society on the principles of justice, to deliver it from exploitation, coercion, material and spiritual impoverishment. Brilliant minds dedicated themselves to these quests. Generations of fighters for a happy life of the people sacrificed their own lives in the name of that lofty ideal. However, it was only in the titanic work of Marx that the theory of a great philosopher merged for the first time into his selfless practical work as a leader and organizer of the revolutionary movement of the masses.

Marx is rightly regarded as the heir to what was best in the achievements of classical German philosophy, English political economy, and French Utopian socialism. However, having exposed their achievements to a critical analysis, he advanced much farther ahead, primarily because he had set himself a task which he formulated with the wisdom of a genius in a profound yet simple way: "Philosophers have only interpreted the world in their various ways, but the point is to change it''.[1] So Marx devoted the full powers of his brilliant mind, all his efforts without exception, to the cause of revolutionary remaking of the world.

The unity of a consistent revolutionary theory and revolutionary practice is a distinctive feature of Marxism. Marx's scientific creativity as such could not have come into play otherwise than in close connection with the independent emergence on the political scene of the proletariat, a class which was historically quite young at the time. Marx had the happy lot to see how his own prophetic words of his youth were coming true: "Just as philosophy finds its material weapon in the proletariat, the proletariat finds its spiritual weapon in philosophy"[2].

The philosophy Marx had given the working class was a revolution in the history of social thought. Mankind had not known about itself even a small fraction of what it learned from Marxism. The teaching of Marx, presented in the organic unity of dialectical and historical materialism, political economy, and the theory of scientific communism, was a genuine revolution in the world outlook and at the same time illumined the path for far-reaching social revolutions.

Marx discovered the objective, essentially material, laws of the process of history, where formerly everything had seemed to be just an event of blind chance, or the arbitrary behaviour of individuals, or had been depicted as a self-expression of a mythical universal spirit. He discerned essence behind what was apparent to the eye, or seemed to be such as a phenomenon. He divested the mystery of capitalist production and the exploitation of labour by capital of its shroud and showed how surplus value was produced and who appropriated it.

Friedrich Engels, his great associate and friend, attached special significance to these two brilliant discoveries of Marx: the materialistic interpretation of history and the theory of surplus value. It is easy to see why. It was precisely these discoveries that turned socialism from a Utopia into a science and gave a scientific definition to the class struggle. They provided the basis for what Lenin described as the core of the Marxian doctrine: "explaining the world historical role of the proletariat as the architect of socialist society"[3].

[1] K. Marx and F. Engels. *Works,* vol. 3, p.4.
[2] K. Marx and F. Engels. *Works,* vol. 1, p. 428.
[3] V. Lenin. *Collected Works,* vol. 23, p. 1.

Marx was indeed a genius of science. However, he was also a great practical revolutionary. One can only wonder in amazement at how much he did for the achievement of the aims he had outlined.

In collaboration with Engels Marx founded the Communist League, the first political organization of the class-conscious, revolutionary proletariat in history. Thus he was the first communist in the most modern sense of the world, the founding father of the worldwide communist movement of today.

"Only an international union of the working class can secure its ultimate victory"[1], Marx wrote. And he himself, as the founder of the First International, worked indefatigably to forge the international unity of the workers. The political behests of Marx and Engels to the communists of the world are inconceivable without their impassioned appeal: "Working men of all countries, unite!"

A convinced internationalist, Marx could analyze better than anybody the distinctions of the situation prevailing in various countries — from Britain to India, from France to China, from the United States to Ireland. At the same time, he thoroughly studied the life of individual nations and constantly searched for the inter-relationships with the life of the rest of the world. Here he invariable sought an answer to this cardinal question; who will be the first to begin the revolutionary abolition of the capitalist order and advance along the road to mankind's communist future?

The answer to this question was given by history. It chose the proletariat of Russia to be the trail-blazer of socialist revolution. In our day some critics of the October Revolution allege that it took place contrary to all Marx's expectations. They further claim that in his revolutionary forecasts Marx ignored Russia altogether. Actually, he showed an enormous interest in Russian affairs. He even studied Russian in order to understand them better. An irreconcilable opponent of czarism, he prophetically assessed the prospects facing the public movement rising in Russia and saw in it the shoots of a "great social revolution"[2], which would have worldwide significance. Indeed, his judgement of future events was more accurate than the judgements on the past that some of our critics today pronounce.

---

[1] K. Marx and F. Engels. *Works,* vol. 16, p. 336.
[2] K. Marx and F. Engels. Works, vol. 32, p. 549.

Engels said that the death of Marx had left a yawning gap in the ranks of the embattled proletariat. It was really an immeasurable loss. The banner of Marx, however, was left in dependable hands. It was raised aloft by Engels himself, who was the acknowledged leader of the growing revolutionary working-class movement. As far back as in Engels's life-time, Vladimir Lenin entered the arena of the class struggle of the proletariat.

Lenin was a loyal follower of Marx and Engels. By his own admission he was intolerant of any denigration of his great teachers. That was only natural for a man who did more than anybody else for the defence of Marxism and for creative development of all its component parts, for its practical application in a new historical situation. Lenin advanced Marxism to a new, higher stage. Lenin's name is inseparable from the name of Marx. Leninism is Marxism of the era of imperialism and proletarian revolutions, the collapse of the colonial system, the era of mankind's transition from capitalism to socialism. Marxism in our day is simply inconceivable without Leninism.

Lenin and the Bolshevik Party he had founded led the first victorious socialist revolution, which radically changed the social and political face of the world. This ushered in a new era, one of epoch-making accomplishments and historic achievements of the working class, the popular masses. In this way the scientific socialism originated by Marx has merged into the practical work of millions of working people building a new society.

Today we can appreciate the rich content of the Marxian doctrine much more widely and deeply than his contemporaries could. Indeed, to accept the idea of the historical necessity of socialism in its theoretical form is by no means the same thing as to take part in and witness the process of translating this idea into reality.

The concrete historical paths of the emergence of socialism have not followed exactly the lines visualized by the founders of our revolutionary theory. Initially socialism triumphed in only one country, which was not in any case the best developed economically. The point is that the October Revolution took place in a new historical situation non-existent in Marx's lifetime — in the era of imperialism, which was reflected in Lenin's theory of socialist revolution now fully borne out by history.

Ideologists of the bourgeoisie and reformism have been coming up with intricate systems of arguments to this day in an effort to prove that the new society created in the USSR and other fraternal countries fails to correspond with the image of socialism envisioned by Marx. They claim that the realities are contrary to the ideal. Wittingly or unwittingly, they overlook the fact that in evolving his theory Marx was by no means guided by some abstract idea of pretty, polished "socialism". He derived his concepts of the future system from an analysis of the objective contradictions of large-scale capitalist production. It was precisely his wise scientific approach to the subject that enabled him to outline faithfully the main features of the society which was yet to be born in the sweeping storms of the 20th-century revolutions.

According to Marx, the corner-stone of the socio-economic system that is to replace capitalism is public ownership of the means of production. A clear-cut phrase in the manifesto of the Communist Party emphasizes the significance Marxism attaches to this indispensable revolution in relations of production: " ...the theory of the communists may be summed up in the single sentence: abolition of private property."[1]

The historical experience of real socialism indicates that it is not a simple matter to convert what is "one's own", private, property into the people's common property. A revolution in relations of ownership by no means boils down to a single act which makes the basic means of production the property of the whole people. Getting the right of ownership is a far cry from becoming a truly wise and prudent owner. The people who have carried out a socialist revolution take a long time to adapt to their new status as the supreme and unchallenged masters of all public wealth — to adapt economically and politically and, if you like, psychologically, adopting collectivist mentality and behaviour. Indeed, the mark of socialist mentality is an individual who is interested not only in his own success in work, his own well-being and prestige but also in the affairs of his colleagues, his work collective, the interests of the whole country and the working people of the whole world.

---

[1] K. Marx and F. Engels. *Works,* vol. 4, p. 438.

In speaking of the conversion of private owner mentality to collectivist mentality it should be borne in mind that this is a long-lasting and many-sided process which should not be oversimplified. Even when socialist relations of production have firmly taken root, some individuals still cannot get rid of their selfish habits and may even develop new ones, a craving for gain at the expense of others and of society. All these are, in Marx's phrase, the ill effects of alienation of labour, which do not vanish into thin air by themselves, although the alienation itself has been abolished.

We know all this well enough from the experience of communist construction. We also know, however, that in complete accordance with Marx's prevision, in all countries where a proletarian revolution has triumphed public ownership of the means of production, which has been established in one form or another, has become the chief factor in the existence of socialism, and serves as its basis and the mainspring of its progress.

On the basis of a socialist ownership of the means of production we have built a powerful economy, which is being developed according to plan, enabling national economic and social problems of great scope and complexity to be attacked and solved effectively. Needless to say, these possibilities of ours do not mean that we can rest on our oars. Problems and grave difficulties can and do arise in this field. They vary in origin but are never associated with the essence of public, collective ownership which has been firmly established and has proved its advantages. On the contrary, some of the bottlenecks interfering at times with normal work in certain fields of our national economy are caused precisely by departures from the norms and requirements of economic life, which is based on the strong foundation of socialist ownership of the means of production.

Let us take, for instance, the question of the economical and rational use of material, financial and manpower resources. Its effective settlement has an important bearing on progress in fulfilling the assignments of the current five-year plan and on the development of the Soviet economy in the long term. Taking a closer look at this question, one will see that it is precisely a question of compliance with that necessary norm of economic management which is prescribed by socialist ownership and consists essentially in a frugal attitude to public wealth, and initiative and energy in augmenting it. The whole society has to pay for violations of this norm, and society is fully entitled to bring to account those who squander its wealth through negligence, mismanagement or for selfish motives.

We are now focusing our minds on enhancing the efficiency of production and the economy as a whole. The Party and the Soviet people are profoundly aware of the importance of this problem. As far as its practical solution is concerned, however, the progress to be seen here is not as successful as it should be. What hinders this progress? Why do we fail to get sufficient returns on the enormous investments we make, and why are the achievements of science and technology applied in production at a rate that cannot satisfy us?

One could list many causes, of course. First of all, one cannot fail to see that our work in perfecting and restructuring the economic mechanism, and the forms and methods of management is lagging behind the requirements made by the level attained by Soviet society in its material, technological, social and cultural development. This is the main thing. At the same time one can also feel the impact of such factors, for instance, as large shortfalls in supplies of farm produce over the last four years, and the need to invest growing amounts of financial and material resources in developing fuel, energy and raw materials resources in the country's northern and eastern areas.

One may again and again reiterate Marx's fundamental idea that acceleration of the progress of productive forces requires corresponding forms of organization of economic work; but matters will be at a standstill until this theoretical principle is translated into the concrete language of practice. Today, first priority is attached to the task of planning and consistently implementing measures capable of lending greater scope to the action of the colossal constructive potentials inherent in our economy. These measures must be thoroughly prepared and realistic, which means that in planning them one must invariably be guided by the laws governing the development of the socialist economic system. The objective character of these laws makes it imperative to abandon all attempts to manage the economy by methods alien to its nature. It would not be irrelevant to recall here Lenin's warning against the danger lurking in the naive faith of some executives that they can fulfil all their tasks by issuing "communist decrees"[1].

On the other hand, once the necessary measures have been agreed upon and the appropriate decisions taken, it is impermissible to stop half-way. Decisions taken must be fulfilled. This is our Party's Leninist tradition, and it would be dishonourable for us to retreat from it.

The interests of society as a whole are a key guideline for developing an economy based on socialist ownership. From this, naturally, it should not be inferred that, in the name of the idea of the common good, socialism suppresses or ignores personal, local interests, or the specific needs of various social groups. By no means so. "An 'idea' ", as Marx and Engels emphasized, "invariably discredited itself as soon as it had isolated itself from an 'interest'."[2] One of the key tasks in perfecting our economic mechanism consists exactly in securing accurate analysis of these interests, and their optimum harmony with the general interests of the people, and thus using them as a motive force to stimulate the growth of the Soviet economy, to enhance its efficiency and the productivity of labour, to consolidate in every way the economic potential and defence capability of the Soviet state.

Of course, the efficiency of the socialist national economy must be judged not only by the economic criteria as such, but also by the social criteria, keeping in one's field of vision the ultimate goal of social production. Under capitalism this goal is profit returns on capital; under socialism, as Marx proved theoretically, this goal is the well-being of the working people, the provision of favourable conditions for the individual's all-round development. Real socialism invests this principle of Marxian theory with flesh and blood.

Indeed, however diverse the tasks facing the Soviet economy may be, all of them eventually merge into the common task of securing improvement in the working people's well-being, providing favourable material conditions for further advancement of their spiritual, cultural life and their social activity. This determines the general line of the economic policy of the CPSU, which is reflected in the documents of its 26th Congress and in the Food Programme being im-

---

[1] V. Lenin. *Collected Works,* vol. 44, p. 173.
[2] K. Marx and F. Engels. *Works,* vol. 2, p. 89.

plemented now, and in Party resolutions on specific national economic problems. It is clear that this also determines very much our approach to rationalizing and intensifying production. In other words, it is not at the expense of the working people but precisely in their interest that the problems of enhancing economic efficiency are being resolved in our society. This does not make our work simpler but, to make up for it, allows us to perform it relying on the inexaustible potentials of the knowledge, creativity and energy of the entire Soviet people.

According to Marx, the historical predestination of the system coming to replace capitalism is to convert labour from an agonizing, oppressive duty into the first vital need of the individual. Now we know from our own experience how much has to be done on the long road towards implementing this idea in full. However, the decisive boundary line has already been crossed. We have done away with that situation, which is normal under capitalism, where the product of labour is opposed to the working man as an alien, even hostile, entity and where it transpires that the more physical and mental power is spent by the worker, the more he increases the power of his oppressors. It is an indisputable achievement of socialism of enormous significance that it has created conditions securing the right to work to every individual. It is precisely work, conscious, conscientious work with initiative for the benefit of society that is recognized in our society as the supreme criterion of the dignity and social prestige of the individual.

It has also been proved in practice that socialization of the means and objects of labour is an indispensable and effective factor in creating the social climate of socialism, in which a human being has no oppressive feeling of uncertainty of his future, in which the spirit of collectivism and comradely mutual assistance, moral health and social optimism reigns supreme. *In toto,* all these mean a fundamentally new quality of life for the working masses, which is by no means confined to material comfort but covers the entire spectrum of full-blooded human life.

Needless to say, all this is not achieved on the day following the establishment of public ownership. Therefore, this progress cannot be immediately proclaimed a "ready-made" perfect socialism. A revolution in the relations of ownership does not by itself dispose of all negative aspects of human community life which have accumulated over the centuries. The question in point is different. The fact is that without such a revolution any "model" of socialism, in whatever attractive clothes it may be dressed, will prove short-lived and will continue to exist only in the imagination of its authors. This is a truism of Marxism. And it is just as valid today as it was a century ago.

One should in general handle with care the so-called fundamental truisms of Marxism, because one guilty of misunderstanding or ignoring them is severely punished by life itself. For instance, the full significance of Marx's views on distribution was only realized at the cost of great pains and even mistakes. He persistently pointed out that in the first phase of communism every worker "receives from society after all deductions exactly as much as he himself gives society", that is, in strict accordance with the quantity and quality of his work[1] which conforms to the basic principles of socialism: "from each according to his abilities, to each according to his work". A consistent democrat and humanist, Marx was a strong opponent of wage levelling and categorically rejected demagogic or naive arguments, which were fairly common in his time, depicting socialism as a society of "universal equality" in distribution and consumption.

Today not only the socio-economic but also the enormous political significance of these ideas of the founders of scientific communism is clear from practice, and from the experience of many socialist countries. Indeed, relations of distribution affect the interests of all and each. The character of distribution is in effect one of the major indicators of the degree of social equality possible under socialism. Any attempt to exceed this possible degree by a voluntary decision, to forestall events in an effort to reach communist forms of distribution without accurate registration of the labour input of each into the production of material and spiritual values, may and do cause undesirable effects.

Thus, the intolerability of violation of the objective economic requirement for priority growth of the productivity of labour has

---

[1] K. Marx and F. Engels, *Works,* vol. 19, p. 18.

revealed itself with full clarity. Without a close link with this decisive factor an increase in wages, which at first produces an outwardly favourable impression, will eventually have a negative impact on all economic life. In particular, it generates a demand that cannot be fully satisfied with a given level of production and interferes with efforts to offset shortages with all their ugly implications, causing just indignation among the working people.

A correct solution to the problems of distribution under socialism implies, of course, compensation in kind for the population's spending in cash with various consumer goods and services. The decisive factor in this matter is the level of development of productive forces. Of course, it is impossible to satisfy demand which exceeds our possibilities. At the same time, it has always been and will be our unquestionable duty to work in these two directions: first, to secure steady growth of social production and advance on this basis the material and cultural standards of life of the people; second, to contribute in every way to the advancement of the material and cultural requirements of Soviet man.

Complete social equality does not appear overnight and in perfect form. Society develops in this direction for a fairly long time, with great difficulty, and reaches this level at the cost of enormous effort. Society must advance its productive forces to build up the material and technological basis of communism. It must cultivate in every working man and woman an acute awareness, culture, professional skills and an ability to enjoy the benefits of socialism sensibly.

As long as these conditions are unavailable, relations of distribution and stringent control over the measure of work and the measure of consumption must be in the focus of attention of the Party guiding socialist society. Therefore the CPSU displays constant concern that the principle of socialist distribution discovered by Marx should be applied in practice unfailingly and everywhere, more effectively and more completely. If this principle is violated, society has to deal with unearned income, the so-called "rolling stones", shirkers, loafers, and botchers who are in effect spongers living off the labours of society, at the expense of the mass of conscientious workers. This is an intolerable phenomenon, a form of parasitism on the humanism of our system.

Work and work alone, its practical results rather than someone's subjective desire or good will, must determine the level of every citizen's well-being. This approach completely accords with the spirit and content of Marx's views on distribution under socialism.

The system of material and moral incentives to labour has long taken shape in our society. It has served well and does serve today the interests of the struggle for socialism and communism. However, today both this system itself and the forms and practice of its application are evidently in need of further improvement. It is important to guarantee not only good remuneration for good work but also the public recognition that it well deserves. It is necessary to ensure that the practice of material and moral encouragement combined with a model organization of labour maintain and develop in individuals an awareness of the usefulness and necessity of their efforts and the products they make. It should, in the final analysis, reinforce their sense of personal involvement in the affairs and plans of their collectives and the entire people. Indeed, this sense has a greater mobilizing effect and maintains discipline better than any persuasion or appeals.

In perfecting relations of distribution one should take into account the entire complex of mutual relations in the process of work. What should one have in mind here in the first place? It is that consistent efforts should be applied in all spheres of the national economy to strengthen, in Marx's phrase, "a state of regulation and order", which he regarded as forms of "social reinforcement of the prevailing mode of production".[1] Work in this direction is severely impaired by formal administration and empty phraseology, by the substitution of idle talk for real business. An executive who fails to understand this, who attempts to substitute impressive but ineffective campaigns for systematic and persistent reorganizing efforts, will not achieve much. The efforts of the Party to improve management, to advance organization and business efficiency, to plan, to improve state and labour discipline, have as their aim not only the elimination of certain shortcomings and difficulties, which is of great significance in itself, but also to consolidate eventually to a still greater extent the foundations on which the socialist way of life is based.

---

[1] K. Marx and F. Engels. *Works,* vol. 25, part 2, p. 356.

Of course, in this work the Party proceeds from the real conditions of labour management existing at the present stage of development of Soviet society. So far these conditions are such that the economic law which Marx considered the first law on the basis of collective production — the law of working time economy — has not yet been brought into full play in our society. The reason for this is largely the existence of a large number of arduous, monotonous, routine jobs, and the slow rate of their mechanization, let alone automation.

However, suffice it to take a look at the manpower shortage and the demographic situation in the country to realize clearly the economic disadvantage of further retention of a large share of manual, non-mechanized work which accounts for 40 per cent in industry alone. This is why it is so vital today to accelerate in every way the rates of scientific and technological progress, to apply its achievements more actively, primarily in those areas where labour inputs are especially great. The basis for this does exist in our society. It is in the high level of development of the socialist national economy. It is in the high occupational skills and know-how of the Soviet working class. It is the large body of competent specialists and managers in the national economy, the powerful scientific and intellectual potential, whose productive force becomes increasingly significant under present conditions. The task is to bring into play all our potentialities in the most efficient way, and as quickly as possible to advance the cultural standards of work and organization of production.

Another reason why it is necessary to make stubborn efforts to accelerate production mechanization and automation is their socio-political implications. Indeed, an individual freed from arduous, fatiguing manual work displays, as a rule, greater initiative and a keener sense of responsibility for his performance results. He enjoys additional opportunities for study and recreation, for participation in public activities, in management of production. Thus he is in a position to exercise more fully his political, democratic rights granted to the working people by the socialist revolution — the rights of the unchallenged masters of their own society and their own state.

Long before the emergence of the society which came to replace capitalism, Marx had revealed the essence of the political forms of its life. Already the Manifesto of the Communist Party proclaimed that "the first step in the revolution by the working class is to raise the proletariat to the position of ruling class, to win the battle of democracy".[1] It is inconceivable to establish socialism without firm political power whose class content was defined by Marx as "the dictatorship of the proletariat".

It is precisely this dictatorship that, according to the Marxian doctrine, opens the way to political development that eventually leads to communist public self-government.

How does the actual history of socialism compare with these forecasts of Marx?

In our country exactly as, incidentally, in any country where the working class, the working people, took over political power, this meant a triumph of democracy in the most literal and precise sense of the word — a genuine triumph of government by the people. The working people finally achieved the rights and freedoms capitalism had always denied them and does deny them today, if not formally, then in fact.

Soviet democracy, which encountered especially fierce opposition on the part of counter-revolutionary forces at home and abroad, openly affirmed itself, without concealing its class character, and went to the length of granting privileges to the working people in relation to members of the exploiter classes who were fighting against the new government. As regards its essence it is and always will be a democracy which guarantees broad rights and defends the interests of the working people and is always prepared to call to account those who raise their hand against the socialist achievements of the people.

In the course of building a new society the content of socialist democracy is enriched, restrictions imposed by historic necessity are lifted, and the forms of the exercise of people's power become more diversified. This process is closely bound up with the development of socialist statehood which itself undergoes qualitative changes. The most important of them is the development of the state of the dictatorship of the proletariat into a state of the whole people. This is a change of enormous significance for the socialist political system. It is recorded in the Constitution of the USSR of 1977 which has provided

---

[1] K. Marx and F. Engels. *Works,* vol. 4, p. 446.

the legislative foundation for the further intensifying of socialist democracy.

We do not idealize what has been done and is being done in this respect in our country. Soviet democracy had in the past, has now and, it may be assumed, will have in the future, difficulties of growth conditioned by the material possibilities of society, and the level of awareness of the masses and their political culture, as well as by the fact that our society does not develop in laboratory conditions, in isolation from a hostile world, but is exposed to the cold winds of the "psychological war" unleashed by the imperialists. Perfection of Soviet democracy requires removal of bureaucratic "over-organization" and formalism — everything that handicaps and under-mines the initiative of the masses, the creativity and enterprise of the working people. We have fought such evils in the past, and we will fight them with still greater energy and persistence.

One may hear at times that the present-day image of socialist statehood and democracy does not conform to the prospect of com-munist self-government envisioned by Marx. The path we have traversed, the experience we have gained, however, give the lie to such allegations.

Let us take, for example, Marx's idea that to govern the new society is a matter for the "people organized in communes", that the essence of new government is "government of the people and by the people".[1] It is known that these ideas were suggested by the realities of life, in the heroic exploits of the Communards of Paris. Never-theless, they contained only the most general outline of a remote goal. Only the revolutionary creativity of the masses themselves could specify the ways to approach this goal. As early as the eve of the October Revolution it had yielded experience which enabled Lenin to plan a practical step towards implementing Marx's formula in the con-ditions of our country: " ... the people united in Soviets — this is the social force that must govern the state".[2]

The people who do not know any other power over themselves but the power of their own association — this idea of Marx, Engels and

---

[1] K. Marx and F. Engels. *Works,* vol. 17, pp. 344, 350.
[2] *Collected Works,* vol. 31, p. 188.

Lenin has been translated into reality in the activities of the Soviets, which integrate the functions of legislation, administration and control. It is also embodied in the work of the trade unions and other public organizations, in the life of work collectives and in the development of the entire political system of our society. So the point is not to seek out its distinctions from the ideal of communist self-government; one can point to quite a few such distinctions which exist if only by virtue of the historical distance in time separating us from the second phase of communism. Far more important is another thing, namely that this system is functioning and advancing, finding ever new forms and methods of developing democracy, widening the proprietary rights and possibilities of the working man in production, in all socio-political activities, ranging from deputies' commissions and people's control to standing production conferences. This is real socialist self-government of the people, which develops in the process of communist construction.

The experience of our democratic development in accordance with the new Constitution of the USSR demands special analysis and summation. This refers, in the first place, to encouraging and using local initiative on a broader scale, to more organic involvement of work collectives in our general work of state administration. In recent years the powers of local Soviets have been substantially widened in relation to enterprises, institutions and organizations located in the areas under their jurisdiction. The possibilities of district, regional, territorial and autonomous republican Soviets will be also increased in the course of implementing the decision of the May 1982 plenary meeting of the CPSU Central Committee to set up agro-industrial associations coming under their terms of reference. Thus, the representative bodies are to play a greater role in implementing the main, economic-organizational function of the socialist state. It is necessary to mention such a primary form of production management invented by the masses themselves as the economically autonomous work team.

Of course, we are strongly opposed to that interpretation of self-government which gravitates towards anarcho-syndicalism, fragmentation of society into independent corporations competing with one another, towards democracy without discipline, towards the concept of rights as rights without duties. The time-tested principle of the organization of all life in socialist society is one of democratic centralism, which allows successful combination of free creativity of the masses with the advantages of the integrated system of scientific direction, planning and management.

The socialist system makes the exercise of the collective rights and duties of the working people the mainspring of social progress. At the same time the interests of the individual are by no means ignored. The Soviet Constitution grants Soviet citizens broad rights and freedoms and at the same time emphasizes the priority of public interests, service to which is the supreme expression of civic awareness.

Soviet society has abolished the gulf between the interests of the state and the citizen existing under capitalism. Unfortunately, there are still a few individuals who attempt to oppose their selfish interests on society and its other members. In this light one can clearly see the need for work in education, and sometimes in the re-education of certain individuals, for struggle against violations of socialist law and order, of the rules of our collectivist community life. This is not a violation of "human rights", as is hypocritically alleged by bourgeois propaganda, but real humanism and democracy which means government by the majority in the interests of all working people.

The CPSU attaches top priority to the interests of the people, society as a whole. It pays daily attention to providing conditions which bring into play the creativity of the working people and their social activity, to extending the scope of independence of industrial enterprises, collective and state farms. This activity and this initiative are crucial to the realistic nature of the Party's plans, the growth of its strength and, in the final analysis, are the guarantee that the programme of communist construction will be implemented.

At the core of the political system of Soviet society, the Party sets an example of democratic organization by all its activity; it lays down and develops democratic principles which are adopted in all the spheres of our socialist life. This is one of the major manifestations of the Party's leading role in the life of society and its inspiring influence on the masses.

Analyzing Marx's method of approach to revealing the main features of the new society, Lenin wrote in his time: "Marx never attempted to invent Utopias or engage in idle guesswork about what could not be learnt.... Instead of scholastically abstruse, 'fabricated' definitions and fruitless arguments over words (what is socialism and what is communism) Marx gives an analysis of what may be called stages of the economic maturity of communism".[1] As is known, it was precisely on the basis of this analysis that Marx evolved his teaching on the two phases of development of the communist formation which has been adopted by the CPSU and other fraternal parties. It was on this foundation that Lenin summed up the new historical experience and comprehensively developed the theory of socialist and communist construction. It is from these principles that we proceed today in solving what Marx, Engels and Lenin regarded as one of the most difficult problems — the concrete forms of transition to communism.

The fundamental features of modern Soviet society are reflected in the conception of developed socialism. It shows conclusively the dialectical unity of the real successes in socialist construction, in implementing many economic, social and cultural tasks in the first phase of communism, the growing shoots of the communist future and the yet unresolved problems we have inherited from the past. This means that it will take some time to bring up the rear which is lagging behind, and go further ahead. We must have a sober idea of where we are. To forestall events means to set tasks which are not feasible; to rest on our laurels means to fail to use our potential to the full. To see our society in its real dynamic progress, with all its possibilities and needs — this is what is required now.

The 26th Congress of the CPSU placed the evolvement of the conception of developed socialism in the forefront of what had been achieved in the field of Marxist-Leninist theory over the few previous years. Relying on this conception, the Party outlined its strategy and tactics for the coming few years and for a longer term, and warned against possible exaggerations in assessing the degree of the country's advancement to the higher phase of communism. All this has made it possible to specify and make more concrete the ways and terms of implementing our programme goals.

Large-scale tasks face the Party and people in the last decades of the 20th century. Viewed as a complex, these tasks boil down to what may

---

[1] V. Lenin. *Collected Works,* vol. 33, pp. 85, 98.

be called perfection of developed socialism to bring about gradual transition to communism. Our country is at the beginning of this long historical stage, which will naturally have its own periods, its own stages of growth. Only experience and daily practice will show how long they will last and what concrete forms they will take. However, one of the biggest and, one may say, qualitative targets on this path was clearly outlined by the 26th Party Congress which formulated the provision for the formation, in its main elements, of the classless structure of society within the historical framework of developed socialism.

Significantly, this conclusion made on the basis of real practice echoes Marx's idea of socialism as a society which knows no class differentiation.[1] This is, incidentally, just more evidence to confirm that the correctness of Marx's views cannot only be verified by the experience of several past decades but also assessed from the viewpoint of a longer perspective.

He who seeks today an answer to the question "What is socialism?" primarily in the works of Marx, Engels and Lenin is absolutely right. However, one should no longer confine himself to this alone. Today the notion of "socialism" cannot be comprehended otherwise than with consideration of the rich practical experience of the peoples of the Soviet Union and other fraternal countries. This experience shows that many problems involved in socialist construction are not simple at all. It also shows that socialism alone can find a solution to the most complicated problems of social life.

It is socialism itself that tears down the centuries-old barriers which separated labour from culture, creates a strong alliance of the workers, peasants, the intelligentsia, and all physical and mental workers, with the working class playing the leading role. It brings the achievements of science and technology, literature and the arts within reach of the working masses, secures unprecedented public recognition for the creative work of the intelligentsia. It is socialism itself that has united in one friendly family the peoples formerly divided by ethnic strife, and secures a just settlement of the nationalities problem generated by the exploiter system. Socialism, by contributing to the

---

[1] K. Marx and F. Engels. *Works,* vol. 19, p. 19.

flourishing of national forms of social life, builds a new type of inter-national, interstate relations, ruling out all inequality and based on fraternal cooperation and mutual assistance.

The most bitter social conflicts in society which are rooted in the final analysis in its division into hostile classes are settled with the completion of the transition from capitalism to socialism, with the consolidation of the new, socialist mode of life. This conclusion, however, has nothing in common with the oversimplified and politically naive concept to the effect that socialism brings deliverance in general from all contradictions and differences, from all setbacks in private life. Incidentally, this concept is exploited in their own way by our ideological opponents seeking to calumniate the new system by references to the fact that people living under it experience difficulties and disillusionments, and that under this system the struggle of the new against the old is sometimes very hard.

Indeed, contradictions and difficulties do exist in our society. To think that some other course of development is possible means to leave the dependable, although at times hard, ground of reality, to break loose from the foundations of Marxist dialectics. On the theoretical plane, this question was cleared up by Lenin relying on Marxist theory. "An antagonism and a contradiction", he wrote, "are by no means one and the same thing. The former will disappear while the latter will remain under socialism".[1]

Today this principle has been borne out by practice. It does not follow from this, however, that non-antagonistic contradictions may be ignored in politics. The realities of life show that with such disregard even contradictions which are not antagonistic by nature may generate serious collisions. Another — and most important — aspect of the matter is to be able to use correctly the contradictions of socialism as a source of and a stimulus to its progress.

Our experience indicates that successes in socialist construction are possible when the policy of the ruling Communist Party rests on a solid scientific foundation. Any underestimation of the role of Marxist-Leninist theory and its creative development, a narrow pragmatic interpretation of its tasks, disregard for the fundamental

---

[1] *Lenin's Miscellany XI*, p. 357.

problems of theory, overemphasis on current expediency or scholastic theorizing, are fraught with the danger of grave political and ideological setbacks. Experience and practice have repeatedly proved the truth of Lenin's statement that "he who undertakes to cope with specific problems without finding a preliminary solution to general problems will inevitably, at every step, come up against these general problems without realizing it. To run into such problems blindly in every particular case means to condemn one's policy to the worst waverings and unprincipledness".[1]

The CPSU attaches great significance to developing Marxist-Leninist theory as is demanded by its creative essence. This is vitally important for solving our practical tasks. We feel, for instance, a growing need for serious research in the field of political economy of socialism. And here Marx's "Capital" has been and remains a brilliant example of profound penetration into the essence of phenomena of economic life to our science.

The many-sided experience of the fraternal socialist countries, which is not identical in all areas, supplies enormous material for theoretical research. One cannot but recall in this context Lenin's statement that "it is only through a series of attempts — each of which taken separately will be one-sided, will suffer from certain incongruity — that complete socialism will be built by revolutionary cooperation of proletarians of all countries".[2] This task is being practically fulfilled in our day in vast areas of the globe, within the framework of the world socialist system, which has become the key factor in mankind's social progress. And it is being fulfilled on those lines of principle which were predicted by Karl Marx.

Lenin used to say that he constantly verified all his activities by the principles laid down by Marx. The CPSU verifies each of its steps by the teachings of Marx, Engels and Lenin.

To verify one's actions by the principles of Marx, of Marxism-Leninism, is by no means to compare mechanically the process of life with certain formulas. We would be worthless followers of our teachers if we satisfied ourselves with a repetition of the truths they

---

[1] V. Lenin. *Collected Works,* vol. 15, p. 368.
[2] V. Lenin. *Collected Works,* vol. 36, p. 306.

had discovered and relied on the magic power of quotations once learned by heart.

Marxism is not a dogma but a living guide to action, to independent work on complicated problems we are faced with at every new turn of history. Not to lag behind the progress of life the communists must advance and enrich Marx's theory in all directions, apply creatively in practice his method of materialistic dialectics which is rightly called the living soul of Marxism. Only such an attitude to our priceless ideological heritage exemplified by the work of Lenin, only such continuous self-rejuvenation of revolutionary theory under the impact of revolutionary practice make Marxism the genuine science and art of revolutionary creativity. This is the clue to the strength of Marxism-Leninism, its eternal vitality.

One may hear at times allegations to the effect that new phenomena of social life do not "dovetail" with the conception of Marxism-Leninism, that it is gripped by a "crisis" and that it should be "revived" by an infusion of ideas borrowed from Western sociology, philosophy or political science. However, this is not a matter of any imaginary "crisis" of Marxism. It is a matter of a different kind: the inability of some theoreticians describing themselves as Marxists to comprehend the true scope of the theoretical thinking of Marx, Engels and Lenin, or to take advantage of the enormous intellectual potential of their teachings in the process of concrete analysis of concrete problems. It would not be irrelevant to add that quite a few bourgeois theoreticians in the fields of philosophy, sociology and political economy have won a name for themselves mostly by dabbling in Marxist ideas and interpreting them in their own style.

Communists should be immune to infatuations with the smart phraseology of various claimants to the improvement of Marxist theory, or with fabrications of bourgeois science. Not to erode Marxist-Leninist theory but, on the contrary, to fight for its integrity, to develop it creatively — this is the high road to learning and solving new problems. Only this approach corresponds to the traditions and spirit of our teaching, to the requirements of the communist movement.

We Soviet communists are proud to belong to the most influential ideological movement in the entire history of world civilization —

ASW-J*

Marxism-Leninism. Fully open to what is best and most advanced in modern science and culture, it is today the focus of the world's intellectual life and reigns over the minds of millions upon millions of people. This is the ideological creed of an ascending class liberating all mankind. This is the philosophy of social optimism, the philosophy of the present and the future.

Today a long stretch has been traversed along the path of social renovation of the world, of implementing the revolutionary goals and ideals of the working class. The political map of the world has changed. Science has made its greatest discoveries and the achievements of technology take one's breath away. At the same time mankind is confronted with many new problems, some of which are by no means simple. It feels growing concern about the aggravation of the raw materials, energy, food, ecological and other problems on a global scale. The most important concern of the peoples today is the need to preserve peace and to prevent thermonuclear catastrophe. Nothing is more important on the international plane for our Party, the Soviet state, all the peoples of the world.

To understand all the complexities of the modern world, to organize and direct the revolutionary socio-historic creativity of the working class, all working people — such is the breathtaking task being fulfilled today by Marxist-Leninist theory and the practical struggle for mankind's progress. That very task which Marx set himself and his ideological and political followers — to interpret and to change the world.

A Pravda Interview
27 March 1983

Question. President Reagan on 23 March made a long statement on US military policy issues. What is your assessment of this statement?

Answer. In recent time a veritable torrent of words has been coming out of Washington on only one subject — war preparations, military programmes, development of new types of weapons. This time the President has again spoken on this subject.

The President's speech was evidently conceived to try and appease the sentiments in the United States, and to lull the growing anxiety of the public about the Administration's warlike policy. It is, of course, a matter for the Americans themselves to assess what the President has said. However, what the President spoke of concerns not only Americans alone. Indeed, the whole purport of his speech can be summed up in the idea that America should arm itself intensively and become the dominating military power of the world. In an effort to substantiate these hegemonistic claims, such shameless distortions of Soviet policy, such foul tricks are used that, frankly speaking, one wonders about the President's ideas of the standards of doing business with other states.

According to the US President, the United States is weaker than the Soviet Union here and there and even near its national territory. All this is due to the Soviet Union's alleged arms build-up during the last two decades while the United States has been sitting on its hands and its armed forces have been deteriorating.

Indeed, the Soviet Union did strengthen its defence capability. In the face of the feverish efforts of the US to deploy military bases near Soviet territory, to develop ever new types of nuclear and other arms, the Soviet Union had to do that to offset the American military superiority they are so nostalgic about in Washington. The military strategic parity attained has deprived the United States of the

299

possibility of blackmailing us with nuclear attack. This parity is a dependable guarantee of peace, and we will do everything to preserve it.

As for the allegations that the United States has been doing nothing in the arms field during the last two decades, this can delude only the naive. To confirm this, let us take a look at some of the more important facts.

It is a fact that precisely over this period a sharp qualitative change has taken place in the US strategic forces. Suffice it to recall that the United States adopted multiple warheads for its ballistic missiles. That was done in defiance of our insistent appeals to abstain from this, so as to avoid a new spiral in the nuclear arms race. If the President had troubled himself to take a look into the negotiations file he would easily have seen exactly how the matter stood.

What has happened as a result is graphically illustrated by the fact that after such modernization one missile mounted on a US submarine is capable of hitting 14 targets simultaneously. Each submarine carries 16 such missiles. Their total yield is almost equivalent to 500 atom bombs like the one dropped on Hiroshima. Overall, in the period of alleged US inaction that the President referred to, the number of nuclear charges in US strategic arms had grown from 4,000 to 10,000-odd units. Can one really describe a 150 per cent increase in the nuclear arsenal as inactivity? No, by no means so.

Now for Europe, where in the words of the US Chief Executive, the position of the United States and NATO in general is difficult. If one looks at the facts, however, one can easily see that the total number of American nuclear weapons alone has increased three times over the period so that it now tops 7,000 units. Is this also the result of inactivity?

The President makes believe that the European zone does not contain almost 1,000 medium-range nuclear weapons of the United States and its NATO allies, that he is unaware that for the total number of nuclear explosives in these weapons NATO outnumbers the USSR by 50 per cent.

In addition to keeping silent on all this, the President tells deliberate falsehoods alleging that the Soviet Union does not observe the unilateral moratorium it has declared on deploying medium-range missiles.

He also passes over in silence the fact that American medium-range weapons are stationed literally on our very threshold and not far away. Incidentally, from this point of view we see no difference between them and strategic weapons deployed in US territory. And this refers not only to Europe. All along the perimeter of the USSR hundreds of American delivery vehicles capable of launching a nuclear strike against Soviet territory are concentrated. According to the Pentagon's officially announced plans their number is to grow many times over. It is planned to deploy over 12,000 long-range cruise missiles alone.

The President showed a photo of a civilian airport in a Latin American country, describing this also as a threat to the United States. However, he didn't show any photos of hundreds of runways thousands of miles away from the United States on which American nuclear-armed aircraft stand in readiness to take off at any moment.

It turns out that all this is not enough for the present US Administration. Trillions of dollars are wrested from the public to be able to have even more arms on land, at sea, in the air and in outer space. A sharp build-up of all types of nuclear weapons has been planned. The President also announced wide-scale measures to develop qualitatively new systems of conventional armaments. Thereby another field of the arms race is to be opened. Persistent fabrications to the effect that all this is being done to meet the "Soviet military challenge", however often repeated, must not delude anybody. Everything the Soviet Union has done or is doing by no means testifies to an ambition to gain military superiority. The treaties and agreements to which we were and are willingly prepared to sign with the American side are aimed at reducing the level of nuclear confrontation without upsetting parity, that is without detriment to the security of either the USSR or the USA.

It is not becoming for those who have derailed the SALT-2 treaty, which clearly formulated precisely this goal, to try now to assume the pose of peacemakers. While rejecting our proposals for the Soviet Union and NATO to have equal numbers of missiles, equal numbers of aircraft in Europe or to have no nuclear weapons there at all — either medium-range or tactical ones — they still talk of the Soviet Union's ambitions for superiority. The methods to which

Washington's present leaders resort to denigrate Soviet policy are impermissible in relations between states.

Question. President Reagan declared that he had invented some new defensive conception. What does this mean in practical terms?

Answer. This deserves to be dwelt upon in greater detail. Having discoursed at length on a "Soviet military menace", President Reagan expressed himself to the effect that it was allegedly time a new approach was used to the problem of securing US strategic interests, and announced in this context the beginning of work to establish a wide-scale and highly efficient anti-missile defence system.

At first glance this may even look attractive to the uninformed since the President spoke of what seemed to be defensive measures. This, however, is only a superficial impression of those who are unfamiliar with these questions. Actually, development and improvement of the US strategic offensive forces will be continued at full speed and along a perfectly definite line for that matter — one of acquiring a first nuclear strike capability. In this situation the intention to achieve the possibility of destroying by means of anti-missile defence the relevant strategic weapons of the other side, that is to deprive it of its capability for a retaliatory strike, is designed to disarm the Soviet Union in the face of an American nuclear threat. This should be clearly seen in order to assess correctly the true meaning of this "new conception".

At one time when the USSR and the USA got down to a discussion of the strategic arms problem they jointly recognized the existence of an inseparable inter-relation between strategic offensive arms and defensive weapons. It was not accidental that in 1972 our two countries concluded simultaneously the treaties on the limitation of anti-ballistic missile systems and the first agreement on the limitation of strategic offensive arms.

In other words, the two sides acknowledged and recorded in the aforesaid documents that only mutual restraint in the field of anti-missile defence would enable progress towards limitation and reduction of offensive arms, that is, would make it possible to hold back and reverse the strategic arms race in general. Now the United States has decided to break this inter-relation. The result of such a conception, should it be carried into effect, would be in fact giving a free hand to a reckless race in all types of strategic weapons, both offensive and defensive. Such is the true meaning, the reverse side, so to speak, of Washington's "defensive conception".

Question. What is the general conclusion to be drawn from the US President's speech?

Answer. My answer will be brief and unambiguous: the present US Administration is going ahead along an extremely dangerous path. The problems of war and peace should not be viewed so lightmindedly. Indeed, all attempts to achieve military superiority over the USSR will come to naught. The Soviet Union will never let this happen and will never find itself unarmed in the face of any danger. Let this be firmly remembered in Washington. It is time they stopped inventing ever new variants of the best way to unleash nuclear war in the hope of winning it. This is not simply an irresponsible pursuit, but sheer insanity.

Although in his speech the President referred primarily to the Soviet Union it affected the interests of all states and peoples. One must be aware of the fact that the American leaders are trying today to convert European countries into nuclear hostages. Washington's actions are threatening the whole world.

All efforts today must be directed to one common goal — to prevent nuclear catastrophe. We emphatically call on the United States to take this path.

Speech at a Conference of First Secretaries of the Central Committees of the Communist Parties of the Union Republics, Territorial and Regional Committees of the Party at the Central Committee of the CPSU[1]
18 April 1983

The Central Committee of the CPSU is carrying out consistent work to intensify the organizing and political activities of the Party in all areas of economic and cultural development and in the guidance of foreign policy.

The Politbureau and the Secretariat keep in the focus of their attention the problems involved in implementing the decisions of the November 1982 plenary meeting of the Central Committee. Emphasis was placed on perfecting the style of work, on increasing control over the fulfilment of decisions, on enhancing Party, government and labour discipline. This has met with approval on the part of Communists, and of all working people, and has had a favourable impact on matters of production. The plan of the first quarter-year for marketing produce has been fulfilled in industry by 102 per cent. The output of industrial goods has grown 4.7 per cent since the corresponding period of last year. In 1982 this indicator was equal to 2.1 per cent. The productivity of labour has grown 3.9 per cent as compared with 1.5 per cent in the first quarter-year of last year.

It is important to lend a stable character to this incipient tendency towards improvement of the main economic indicators. These are the objects of the measures already taken and being drawn up to improve

---

[1] Partly condensed

planning, to perfect the economic mechanism, to provide economic incentives stimulating the interest of work collectives in increasing the output of products and improving their quality.

The Politbureau believes that for this it is mandatory to continue to work actively and to make persistent efforts to achieve the goals set in all areas of the national economy.

One of the key areas of work of the Party is agriculture. The ways of its further advancement were outlined at the 26th Party Congress. The May 1982 plenary meeting of the CPSU Central Committee approved the Food Programme of the USSR. These are decisions of fundamental importance. However, they will not be implemented by their own momentum. We need excellent organization and the mobilization of working people to fulfil them.

The situation in agriculture is still complicated. Of course, among the causes responsible for it is unfavourable weather which has been a veritable curse during the last few years. However, some workers under these conditions seek and find ways of overcoming difficulties and increasing the output of agricultural produce, while others use such conditions to exonerate themselves for grave omissions in their work. The CPSU Central Committee believes that active efforts are necessary to overcome difficulties so as to speed up the rates of developing agriculture and solving the food problem.

A wide range of problems have been discussed in the report and by the speakers in the debate. Although these are not all of the problems facing agriculture their discussion is important because this helps identify what matters most now, and to organize work more efficiently.

It is necessary above all to ensure the stability of crop farming and raise its productivity considerably. Each republic and each region have their distinctive features which should be taken into account in the process of work. Science and practice have proved that a changeover to zonal systems of crop farming are indispensable for obtaining bumper harvests. They have been drawn up practically everywhere but are being introduced slowly, while recommendations of scientists and experts in this field are in some places shelved for years and crop farming follows traditional methods. It is mandatory to accelerate the introduction of crop farming systems on scientific lines. This means that in the coming year or two the system of crop rotation will have to be completed and a changeover will be made to such a structure of crop farming that ensures the largest output per hectare of land, along with a wide introduction of industrial technologies of crop cultivation and efficient methods of soil cultivation. These measures combined with land reclamation on a continually growing scale can secure high and stable yields of grain, fodder and other crops.

Agriculture must keep abreast of scientific and technological progress. The collective and state farms expect more from scientific institutions. Another thing should be emphasised. We have a fairly good record of valuable scientific and technological research and development. The best farms and innovators in production have accumulated vast experience. These results, however, are being applied inadequately, only on individual farms. It is necessary to take advantage of everything that is new and progressive more boldly and actively and on a wider scale.

It is mandatory to improve radically the use of the material and technological facilities available in the countryside. Not infrequently references are made to a shortage of tractors, harvesting combines and other machinery. Of course the collective and state farms have not yet been supplied with everything they need. However, our record of accomplishments should not be played down. Since the March 1965 plenary meeting of the CPSU Central Committee the main assets in agriculture have grown 300 per cent, the power-to-man ratio and deliveries of mineral fertilizers more than 200 per cent, and the areas under reclaimed land 70 per cent.

The Central Committee of the CPSU and the Council of Ministers of the USSR have recently adopted a resolution outlining a broad programme of further equipment of collective and state farms with modern highly productive machinery.

Even the material and technological facilities available, however, make it possible to achieve much better results in agriculture than those on record. These possibilities are not taken advantage of effectively at all times. On many collective and state farms there is a shortage of manpower operating farm machinery. Some of the machinery, in particular costly heavy-duty tractors, have no regular crews. The basis of facilities for repairs and storage of machinery is being set up slowly, and a large number of machines are discarded before the end of their service life.

It is, of course, necessary to improve the standards of farm machinery but, more important, their more efficient maintenance must be organized in the first place. The decisions taken to develop the facilities for storage, repairs and technical servicing are so far being fulfilled unsatisfactorily. This situation must be remedied promptly.

To be able to cope more quickly with the task of effective utilization of the land and of productive potentials in the countryside it is necessary to supply collective and state farms with permanent manpower as a matter of first priority. This is not a simple task. There is need to build much more housing, general and vocational schools and other cultural institutions and every-day service establishments. Enormous investments have been earmarked for these purposes and a decision has been taken to use the capacities of urban building organizations for the development of the infrastructure in the villages. Success in this area depends on the initiative of local bodies and their skill in organizing practical work. Many regional committees of the Party have actively got down to work to fulfil this task. This has been discussed by speakers at the conference in particular. The Politbureau approves of this approach to this important matter.

Today when agro-industrial associations are operating in the countryside to deal with economic problems the Party committees must raise considerably the standards of organizing and political work within rural work collectives. Equally, as in the entire national economy, vigorous efforts to strengthen discipline are required here. It is mandatory to enhance among farmers and other rural workers the sense of a proprietary attitude to the land. Because of this the socialist emulation drive should be made more effective and wider use should be made of time-tested forms of work among the people, of organizing production and stimulating labour, of developing and strengthening the principle of economic autonomy in every way.

In present conditions the question of work among leading executives of collective and state farms assumes special significance. The complex tasks facing agriculture, the growing use of the achievements of science and technology, the changeover to progressive forms of organization of remuneration, make great and largely new demands on management. It is mandatory to ensure that leading executives constantly widen their outlook and special competence. We must take thorough and prompt action to analyze how far the existing system of training and advanced training of personnel meets today's tasks and adopt measures to perfect it.

In many areas one can evidence great fluctuations of manpower which is attributable to shortcomings in the selection and education of personnel. Not infrequently painstaking work among personnel and assistance to and support for its members are replaced with naked administration, which has an adverse effect on the progress of work.

As is known, the CPSU Central Committee and the government have adopted a special resolution to enhance the role and responsibility of leading executives in the rural areas. Its fulfilment must be kept under constant control. The work among personnel must be firmly held in the Party's hands.

The new bodies of management — agro-industrial associations — are called upon to play a major role in implementing the tasks ensuing from the decisions of the May Plenary Meeting and the Food Programme. The Party committees must see to it that the new bodies in the countryside gain strength more rapidly. It is extremely important to help them from the outset to select a correct guideline for their activities, to handle efficiently the main problems involved in the development of agriculture and the agro-industrial complex as a whole.

In securing coordination of the actions of all organizations connected with agriculture, these associations must support and stimulate useful initiatives and enterprise of collective and state farms. The commission of the Presidium of the Council of Ministers of the USSR for the problems of the agro-industrial complex and the Ministry of Agriculture must organize systematic work in the study, summing up and dissemination of the experience of agro-industrial associations.

The tasks facing agriculture now make incomparably greater demands on the activity of not only the central bodies but also the republican, territorial and regional Party organizations and enhance their responsibility for the performance of the Food Programme. It is necessary to emphasise this because individual workers, instead of acting vigorously and solving problems in good time, instead of making better use of latent reserves and possibilities, seek to shift many of their concerns on to the shoulders of the state. This refers primarily to fairly frequent requests from the provinces for deliveries of feed grain from the state reserves. At the same time the problems of increasing the output of crude and succulent feed are not effectively handled in many republics, territories and regions. This is also evidenced by numerous requests for the construction of new livestock farms to be supplied with feed from state reserves.

Practically every year large quantities of the seed for agricultural crops have to be allocated out of government reserves. In principle this is intolerable, since the possibilities for organizing seed production are available practically everywhere.

In a number of regions, territories and republics local resources are not used in full to improve the supply of foodstuffs to the population. This refers, in particular, to the potential of personal subsidiary households. The fact that many families living in villages keep no livestock cannot be accepted as normal. Subsidiary farms of industrial plants and factories can and must be a great help in supplying work collectives with foodstuffs. In many areas, however, this important matter is denied sufficient attention.

The present year 1983 is decisive to the Five-Year Plan as a whole. The main thing to be done this year is to harvest grain in quantities planned, as well as fodder, technical and other agricultural crops, to reinforce the favourable changes which are in evidence in animal husbandry.

From the beginning of the year the Politbureau has kept as its focus of attention all work in the centre and in the provinces in connection with the harvesting plan. Now that the spring fieldwork is in progress in all republics, agro technical work of a high standard is the most important practical task. Special concern should be displayed for effective use of reclaimed and, primarily, irrigated land, and for rational and frugal use of water resources so as to secure high crop yields. It is necessary to institute control over the entire range of operations in irrigated farming and take promptly whatever measures may be necessary.

On behalf of the Politbureau I express my confidence that the Ministries and other government departments, local Party and government bodies will draw the right conclusions and adopt effective measures to intensify organizing and political work and secure success in fulfilling the tasks facing agriculture.

Der Spiegel Interview
Pravda, 25 April 1983

The West German magazine *Der Spiegel* requested the General Secretary of the CPSU Central Committee, Yuri Andropov, to give his replies to a number of questions, as well as to grant an interview to its publisher R. Augstein. As announced earlier, this interview took place on 19 April this year.

Following below are Yuri Andropov's replies and his discussion with R. Augstein.

Question. The Geneva negotiations on medium-range weapons in Europe are clearly making no progress. The American proposal which contains the "zero option" and recently, an "interim solution" appears incompatible with the Soviet proposal to reduce the number of Soviet missiles to the number of West European medium-range missiles. What is, in your opinion, the essence of the differences and do you believe that a compromise is possible?

Answer. We understand the concern about the fact that the problems of limitation of medium-range weapons in Europe which are under discussion at Geneva cannot for the time being be resolved. Speaking frankly, these talks have reached a stalemate.

What was the motive for starting them? The Soviet side proposed negotiations and began to press with determination for a reduction of medium-range nuclear weapons of the USSR and the NATO powers existing in this area, and for a radical mutual reduction of the level of nuclear confrontation. The aim pursued by the United States at the Geneva negotiations, as it has transpired, is to add at all costs new powerful armaments to the already existing vast nuclear arsenal of NATO and to reduce Soviet missiles alone.

As you see, two opposite lines — I would even say two fundamentally different approaches — confront each other at Geneva. We witnessed this line from the Americans even before Geneva. As is known, the United States derailed the SALT-2 Treaty, and withdrew from a series of negotiations which were gaining momentum or approaching a successful conclusion. I can recall that the United States broke off and has been evading to this day a resumption of talks on the total and universal prohibition of nuclear weapons tests, on anti-satellite systems, on the limitation of deliveries and sales of conventional armaments, on restrictions on military activity in the Indian Ocean. I shall add to this that the United States has not yet ratified the treaties with the Soviet Union on the limitation of underground tests of nuclear weapons and nuclear explosions for peaceful purposes. All this speaks for itself. As is common knowledge, the present US Administration went to the Geneva negotiations with great reluctance.

For us achievement of an agreement between the negotiating parties means a settlement of issues to their mutual satisfaction. The US Administration, however, behaves as if the centuries-old history of international relations, the practice of agreements and treaties were non-existent. The recent modification by Washington of its proposal, clearly unacceptable to the USSR, which has been given the false name of a "zero option" does not change the matter, and the US Administration clings to its former one-sided stand without showing the slightest intention to reckon with the lawful interests of the other side, or to reach a fair mutually acceptable agreement. In every particularity, in advancing its proposals the United States seeks   and this is its central aim — to cause damage primarily to the security of the Soviet Union, and to upset the existing balance of forces in its own favour.

This is the main cause of the setbacks for the Geneva negotiations. In response to our clear-cut and fair proposals the Reagan Administration comes forward with either a "zero" or an "interim-zero" option. Both of them are unrealistic and by no means facilitate progress towards agreement. Why? Because they are intended to disarm us and to arm NATO to a still greater extent. We will not agree to that.

In recent time there has been talk in the United States and in some other NATO countries about alleged "uncooperativeness" on the Soviet side. What concessions should we make, after all? We are asked to agree to the reduction of missiles only — of the existing medium-range Soviet missiles and American missiles planned to be brought to Europe. As for other components of intermediate-range nuclear weapons, the Americans simply refuse to agree upon them. They declare that they are unwilling to negotiate on this issue, and that's all.

They want us to make believe that we do not see the over 400 warheads on British and French sea- and land-based missiles targeted on the Soviet Union and other socialist countries. The Americans, who are seconded by representatives of other NATO countries, describe British and French missiles as "deterrent" forces. I am prepared to admit that this is so. Then one may be allowed to ask: Why are France and Britain recognized as entitled to deterrence, whereas we are denied the right to have our corresponding deterrent forces in exactly the same numbers that are available to the French and the British?

It is argued that the nuclear armaments of France and Britain should not be counted in, by virtue of their "independent status". But have these countries ceased to be members of the North Atlantic alliance? Do they conceal the fact that their nuclear forces are directed against the Soviet Union? And is it not symptomatic that the French government, far from dissociating itself from the plans of deploying American nuclear missiles in Western Europe, on the contrary, is zealously supporting them? What kind of "independent status" is that? On the other hand, NATO's well-known decision is depicted as a mandate of its own kind granted to the United States by all members of this alliance and, on the other hand, when the armaments of NATO are counted, it is claimed that British and French missiles have nothing to do with all this, because they are allegedly "independent". There is no logic in this whatsoever.

Just try and look at the situation from the viewpoint of the Soviet Union and its lawful interests: on what grounds and by what right can they insist that we should be left unarmed in the face of these British and French nuclear missiles targeted on our country? It is clear that we cannot agree and will never agree to this. The Soviet people have the same right to security as the peoples of America, Britain, France and other countries.

We are also requested to shut our eyes to the fact that the Americans, in case we accept their proposal, would retain in the zone of Europe all of their land-based and carrier-based aircraft, that is, forward-based forces armed with nuclear weapons capable of reaching the territory of the Soviet Union. And these are quite a few — hundreds of delivery vehicles and thousands of nuclear warheads.

Violations of universally recognized standards of conducting negotiations, and an unwillingness to work for a mutually acceptable agreement are manifest in the US Administration's attempt to secure our unilateral disarmament not only in the west, in Europe, but also in the east, in Asia. Washington would like to dictate its terms to us: that we should not deploy our medium-range missiles in the Asiatic part of the Soviet Union. This, of course, goes far beyond the framework of the Geneva negotiations. The Americans are silent about the fact that they have concentrated numerous nuclear weapons directed against us in Asia, in the Pacific and Indian Oceans, and in the Far East. Incidentally, the American and British press occasionally leaks information concerning the US intention to deploy medium-range missiles in Alaska. Should this ever happen, this would not, of course, be ignored on our side. I mention this fact now to illustrate the conclusion that the American side is demanding from the Soviet Union what the American side itself has evidently no intention of reciprocating.

One wonders which side has greater reason to be concerned about its security.

It is all the more fair to view this question in this light because the Soviet Union, as is well known, has taken a pledge not to be the first to resort to nuclear arms, whereas the nuclear powers of NATO have been flatly refusing to assume such a commitment to this day.

Question. West and East accuse each other of ambitions to gain military superiority. The Americans even allege that the Soviet negotiators at Geneva are seeking to perpetuate Soviet superiority in medium-range missiles on the European continent. What should in your opinion rough parity look like?

Answer. We know of such allegations. American military and political leaders are particularly active in this respect. Some other politicians of the West are not far behind them either. There is not a grain of truth in such allegations. One must stick to the hard facts. In the recent period alone, the Soviet Union, in an effort to break the deadlock in the negotiations, submitted for consideration by the

American side and other NATO countries a series of proposals whose constructive character is obvious.

Suffice it to recall our proposals at the very same Geneva talks on the limitation of medium-range nuclear weapons in Europe. Today each side has roughly 1,000 medium-range nuclear delivery vehicles in Europe. Add to this a few thousand tactical nuclear warheads on either side. Should our most far-reaching proposal which, incidentally, they prefer to keep silent about in the West, be accepted no types of nuclear weapons intended to hit targets in Europe — either medium-range or tactical ones — would remain on the European continent in general. Will Europe and European security gain or lose if this proposal is accepted? The answer is clear and unambiguous.

This also holds true of another proposal of ours. Should it be implemented, a radical reduction would be effected: medium-range weapons would be reduced by two thirds on either side. In other words, we would cover two thirds of the way towards Europe's complete deliverance from these weapons.

Finally, should the West accept the option we proposed in December of last year, the USSR and the NATO powers would have 162 missiles in their arsenals on each side: that is exactly as many as the number now available on the side of NATO, that is, to Britain and France. Each side would also retain 138 medium-range aircraft. I wish to emphasise that these ceilings are not final. They could be reduced on a mutual basis, if NATO agreed to that.

All these Soviet proposals remain valid. They completely guarantee genuine parity and a real balance of forces.

How does this show the Soviet Union's ambition to gain military superiority here?

The complexity and danger of the current situation are caused by the fact that the arms race being escalated by the West proceeds at a faster rate than the negotiations. To offset this discrepancy and create a favourable climate for the progress of negotiations common sense suggests the need to freeze the nuclear arsenals of all sides. This would be the most sensible thing to do as long as no other solutions are found. We proposed a freeze on medium-range weapons, as on strategic armaments. This would be, in our opinion, only the first step. We hear this objection: why talk about a freeze when reductions are necessary? This may sound good, but the trouble is that while such declarations are made armaments are being built. So we have neither freeze nor reduction.

The contrast between the approaches of the USSR and the USA to other problems of arms limitation and reduction is no less striking.

I have already mentioned the pledge we have taken not to be the first to resort to nuclear arms. If a similar commitment were assumed by the United States and other NATO members in possession of nuclear arms, people would heave a sigh of relief throughout the world. Why not do this, one wonders? Our initiative, however, has fallen on deaf ears.

Another example: How can one explain the fact that the West has as yet shown no reaction to the fair proposal dictated by the best intentions, which the Soviet Union submitted along with other socialist countries to conclude a treaty on the non-use of military force and maintaining peaceful relations between the Warsaw Treaty and NATO countries? It is hard to find a reasonable explanation for this silence.

Or let us take a look at the conduct of both sides at the strategic arms negotiations. Let us compare the two positions. We have proposed substantial reductions — by more than a quarter — in the total number of strategic delivery vehicles without any exceptions. The number of nuclear warheads they carry would also be reduced to equal ceilings. What, however, does the United States insist on? It only pays lip-service to reductions while going ahead in effect with a considerable, really "radical" build-up of strategic armaments. It plans to deploy additionally more than 12,000 long-range cruise missiles alone. I refer also to the latest news from Washington: another plan has been put on the President's desk — one of deploying additionally in the coming two years a considerable number of a new generation of ICBMs.

This is a reckless arms race. It cannot be described otherwise.

It is an open secret that the United States is stockpiling and planning to use such a formidable tool of war as chemical weapons. These weapons are already being imported to Europe, while ever new, even more lethal, types of such weapons are being intensively developed in the United States. We, however, propose to ban the development, production and stockpiling of chemical weapons and in general to destroy them. It would seem there is not, and cannot be any question here. However, there are leaders both in the United States and in Western Europe who are extolling these weapons as "useful".

I shall say a couple of words about the problem of verification of arms reduction. It is alleged that the Soviet Union is opposed to such verification and hence it is hard to come to terms with it. To use the pictorial German expression, this is "old hat", a threadbare argument. For us verification is just as important if not more important than for others. We approach the problems of verification on a concrete plane rather than on the plane of general declarations. This approach of ours is embodied in the agreements on the limitation of strategic arms. Our policy towards the problems of verification is a far-reaching policy going as far as general and complete verification when it comes to general and complete disarmament. We are opposed to the problem of verification being converted into a stumbling block at negotiations.

Such is the real picture. I have cited only a few facts. Many more such facts could be listed but it is clear from the aforesaid what positions are held by the Soviet Union and the United States on disarmament issues.

Now judge for yourself which side is seeking military superiority and which side is in favour of parity and of reducing the level of military confrontation.

Question. The US President Reagan intends to raise arms outlays to the enormous sum of 1,600 thousand million dollars over the period until 1987. He is planning development of the MX intercontinental missile, the Pershing-2 missile, the cruise missile and even an anti-missile system deployed in outer space which is expected to make the United States invulnerable. What do you intend to oppose to this?

Answer. Of late it has become fashionable among members of the Reagan Administration to feign injured pride when they are found guilty of militarist, aggressive ambitions. Perhaps a person without much experience in politics may be impressed by such a stance. Evidently it is designed to produce this impression. In such cases, however, it is best to turn to facts. The facts indicate, however, that the United States is determined to escalate the arms race in all directions and on an unprecedented scale, and is whipping up international tension to a high pitch.

Speaking in concrete terms, I have in mind, in particular, the plans of developing a far-flung and highly efficient anti-missile defence system announced in Washington. The adventurism and dangers of all these plans stem from their stake on escaping retaliation, on delivering a first nuclear strike in the hope of securing protection against a retaliatory strike. From here it is a short way to being tempted to pull the trigger. This is the main danger of the new American military doctrine. It can only bring the world closer to the nuclear abyss. As a result, there is talk about defence while actually a mine is being laid under the whole process of limitation of strategic arms.

That this is truly so is declared by the world's most prestigious scientists. We offer the US government: let Soviet and American scientists, specialists in this field, meet and discuss the possible consequences of setting up a wide scale anti-missile defence system. Let scientists express their authoritative opinions.

It becomes increasingly clear that the development of tools of space warfare is a component part of American war preparations. They want to deploy weapons in outer space and threaten mankind from there. This should not be allowed to happen. Outer space should remain free of the tools of war. We have proposed to conclude an international treaty on non-deployment of weapons of any kind in outer space. We are convinced that it is necessary to go further than that: to ban the use of force in general in outer space and from outer space, to attack targets on earth.

Not to begin an arms race where it does not exist and to halt it where it is in progress — this is the essence of our stand, this is the principle we are guided by at negotiations.

The Soviet Union will continue its consistent efforts to find common language with the American side. Our proposals submitted earlier remain in force. If the US Administration submits proposals on a particular problem with a view to its solution in the spirit of equal security, we will certainly examine them in a favourable light.

Question. The Federal Chancellor Helmut Kohl is planning to visit Moscow soon. What is your assessment of the prospects of relations between the USSR and the FRG, and do you believe it would be possible to cooperate if the Kohl cabinet were involved in the so-called complementary armament of NATO?

Answer. The peaceful, businesslike cooperation between the USSR and the Federal Republic is a substantial factor of stability in Europe and in international affairs in general. I believe that to preserve this is in the mutual interest of the FRG and the Soviet Union. There is a basis for this and a good basis at that. This is the Moscow Treaty and a series of other agreements concluded between our two countries in the seventies. This is the experience jointly accumulated in practical cooperation in a variety of fields.

We in the Soviet Union are expecting a visit of Chancellor H. Kohl, which has been arranged in principle. We hope that in the course of this visit it will be possible to reinforce the record of positive achievements in relations between our two countries and outline the prospects for the future. At the same time, reviewing the prospects of our relations we naturally cannot ignore the plans to deploy new American nuclear missiles in the FRG.

Judge for yourself what damage would be caused to these relations if the territory of the FRG were converted into a springboard for delivering a nuclear strike to the USSR and its allies. Should this happen, this would have disastrous consequences for the Federal Republic itself.

I repeat, however, that the Soviet Union is resolutely against developments taking such a turn. We propose a different way out of the current situation, which would strengthen the security of both the FRG and the Soviet Union and enable our two countries to cooperate successfully in the interest of consolidating European and world peace.

*   *   *

R. Augstein. I am very happy to have an opportunity to meet and have a discussion with the top leader of the Soviet Union. We have already formulated some questions to which we have received replies in written form. I should tell you that before this meeting I had read the text of your replies. I wonder if you will hand it over to me officially or if it may be considered already delivered to us.

Y. V. Andropov. I am ready to hand over this text to you. I believe this is the most reasonable and convenient way. Does that satisfy you?

R. Augstein. Yes, of course, Thank you. Since, however, no text can be exhaustive I would like to ask your permission to put a few questions more now.

Y. V. Andropov. You are welcome.

R. Augstein. In the West one may often hear allegations to the effect that during a definite period when the United States was not building up its armaments at the rate it is doing and planning to do now, the Soviet Union was actively building up its own armaments. As a result, according to these allegations, during the seventies Soviet armaments increased while American armaments even decreased.

Y. V. Andropov. These allegations are not new. They are being circulated especially actively by the Americans, helped by their NATO allies. I did not specially prepare to answer this question but it is easy to prove that the allegations you are referring to do not hold water. To begin with, let me remind you that the Soviet Union was not the first power to have invented and adopted nuclear weapons. Indeed, there was a fairly long period when we had no such weapons at all, while the Americans had them and attempted to blackmail us and the whole world for that matter. We were compelled to catch up with them. After a few years the Soviet Union also developed nuclear weapons. We were forced to do that. That's how it was.

R. Augstein. But didn't the top leaders of the Soviet Union themselves admit in 1977 the existence of a rough parity in armaments between the two sides?

Y. V. Andropov. It was exactly so. But I have not yet finished my answer to your earlier question. If one traces developments through a series of stages, one will see that they followed this course: the United States undertook strenuous efforts to perfect its nuclear arms. From single warheads it changed over to multiple warheads. We had to follow suit. Then the Americans adopted into their armaments multiple individually targetable re-entry vehicles (MIRV). In response we had to develop them as well. Then the United States began to install MIRV missiles on submarines. We had no such programme at the time. We had to counter the American move with a similar pro gramme.

A rough balance of forces does exist now, and we do believe there is a rough parity.

Thus, all the time we only followed the Americans in building up armaments, rather than the other way around. Moreover, while gaining on the United States we constantly offered to end this race and to freeze the level of armaments on both sides and then to proceed to their reductions. Unfortunately, we could not obtain consent to our proposals from the American side.

Speaking of the situation in this field at present one may, of course, assess it differently, relying on different methods and approaches. The United States, for instance, believed that its nuclear weapons would be less vulnerable if they were installed on submarines. Therefore it did exactly that. This is understandable since the United States is a maritime power. We are a continental power and the greater part of our nuclear arsenal was deployed on land. Now, however, the Americans make this proposal: let us reduce the nuclear weapons deployed on land leaving sea-based missiles intact. Naturally, this approach cannot satisfy us. We, for our part, take into account all kinds of nuclear weapons available to both sides and propose their equal reductions on either side down to their eventual complete elimination.

As for the detailed data on the balance of forces between the two sides, this subject has recently been discussed in a public statement of the USSR Minister of Defence D. F. Ustinov who adduced detailed facts and figures. Just take a look at these figures to see that what I have just told you is absolutely correct.

R. Augstein. Many in Western Europe feel that the Soviet SS-20 missiles are especially dangerous to them since they are a new and highly effective kind of weapon.

Y. V. Andropov. Properly speaking, this subject is discussed in the text of my replies to your questions. However, I can say the following in addition. I understand that the peoples of Europe are worried and even alarmed. We are in favour of removing the causes of this alarm. We have offered various options. We proposed to dismantle all nuclear weapons, both medium-range and tactical ones, in Europe. The United States did not even respond to this proposal. It continued to cling stubbornly to its so-called "zero option" which does not deserve to be dwelt upon here. We have repeatedly explained its true essence. So as regards public concern about the situation prevailing we are of the same mind as you. The United States, however, would like to deploy its nuclear missiles in the territory of Western Europe and make you, the West Germans, the Belgians and the Dutch its hostages. We are opposed to this. We have offered various ways out of the situation, which would make it possible either to eliminate the danger to both sides for good or to lessen existing tensions appreciably.

R. Augstein. The Soviet Union has declared that if the Geneva negotiations fail to bring positive results and American missiles are finally deployed in Europe, the USSR will deploy its missiles at roughly the same distance from US territory. I would like to ask you, Herr General Secretary, if you really intend to do this and if you do, could you say in what regions of the world your missiles can be deployed?

Y. V. Andropov. I will not tell you that, even between you and me and the lamp-post, for obvious reasons. Speaking of the essence of the matter, however, I wish to reaffirm that we shall find a way to counter the actions of the Americans both in relation to US territory as such and in relation to Europe. Nuclear arms talks are not a game of poker which one may lose but hope to win later. These talks have a bearing literally on the question of life and death for the peoples of the Soviet Union and the United States, the Warsaw Treaty and NATO countries. We cannot take a careless view of the prospect of deployment not far from our borders of more than 500 nuclear missiles in addition to the French and British missiles already targeted upon us. Our counter-measures will be perfectly justified from any point of view, by the loftiest moral standards in particular.

R. Augstein. You have mentioned French missiles here, and this makes me recall another question. The Soviet Union had very good relations with France. It so happened, however, that it was in fact its socialist government, in which Communists are represented, that ordered about 50 Soviet diplomats and other Soviet personnel out of France. What is your opinion of this development?

Y. V. Andropov. What can I tell you about that? First of all, I would not like the blame for this crude act of provocation against the Soviet people to be shifted onto French Socialists, let alone Communists. We are well aware that this act was masterminded by forces opposed to good relations between France and the Soviet Union. It is

ASW-K

not unlikely that these forces operate not only in France itself but elsewhere as well. It is hard to believe that this act meets the national interests of France. This is an act of lawlessness. It has no legal justification whatsoever. All allegations to the effect that these Soviet citizens engaged in illegal activity are fabrications.

I would also like to note the following fact. Among the Soviet citizens ordered to leave France, some left it half a year ago and are now in the Soviet Union. Others have not worked in France for more than a fortnight. Wasn't it absurd to undertake such an act?

We have been told only one thing: Soviet personnel engaged in gathering information. As far as I know, the functions of the diplomatic and other services of any country, of any embassy, include collection of information about the country where they work and its delivery to their government. Is this indeed illegal activity? In fact, it is allowed under the terms of international diplomatic conventions.

This action of French authorities cannot be qualified otherwise than as a deliberate attempt to worsen Franco-Soviet relations.

It has been alleged in some organs of the press in France that the fact that no retaliatory measures have been taken on our part in relation to French personnel in Moscow is an indirect admission of its "guilt" by the Soviet Union. This is nonsense. Such interpretation of our actions certainly demonstrates a misunderstanding of Soviet foreign policy. It would be only too easy to take retaliatory measures in relation to French personnel working in the USSR. Displaying restraint, we are guided by the broader interests of Franco-Soviet relations which we cherish and which have taken shape over a long period of time, as well as by the interests of preserving detente in Europe.

This does not mean, however, that we shall tolerate anywhere acts of lawlessness in relation to Soviet diplomats and other personnel working in Soviet offices abroad.

R. Augstein. Yes, one may say in this case you acted in accordance with the Bible which says: "Whosoever shall smite thee on thy right cheek turn to him the other also".

Y. V. Andropov. Not exactly. We bear little if any resemblance to biblical characters. We were guided by sober political motives, a desire to prevent a deterioration in Franco-Soviet relations, and we took a broader view of what this limited local conflict implied.

R. Augstein. Since we have touched on biblical themes here I would like to say the following. President Reagan speaking to a religious audience described the Soviet Union as the "focus of evil". In your response to this statement you expressed your assessment of it. Do you believe that reasonable and successful negotiations are possible in principle in such an atmosphere?

Y. V. Andropov. We are sober-minded enough to ignore rhetoric. If Mr. Reagan apart from his accusations accepted at least one of our concrete proposals for arms reductions or put forward at least one reasonable, acceptable proposal himself, we would forgive him his unfounded — to put it mildly — statement. The French are evidently right to say that each speaks the language he knows.

R. Augstein. It seldom happens that all evil and all guilt are on one side only, even if the East feels so about the West and the West feels so about the East. I must ask in this context: is it realized in the Soviet Union that the problem of Afghanistan poisons the international atmosphere and are there plans to remedy this situation?

Y. V. Andropov. In reply to the first part of your question I can say: of course, it is realized. Our plans for a political settlement of the Afghan problem are no secret. We have set them out in public repeatedly. Leonid Brezhnev spoke of them in his time. We believe that as soon as interference from the outside in the affairs of Afghanistan is stopped and guarantees are provided that this interference would not be resumed, we shall withdraw our troops from Afghanistan. Our military contingent stays in that country at the request of the lawful Afghan government — the one which was in office at that time — and it continues to stay there at the request of the lawful government of Babrak Karmal. We are seeking nothing for ourselves there. We have responded to a request for assistance from a friendly neighbouring country. Of course, we are by no means indifferent to what is happening right on our southern border. Indeed, Washington even considers itself authorized to judge what government should be in Nicaragua, since this allegedly affects the vital interests of the United States. Nicaragua, however, is more than 1,000 kilometres away from the United States, while the Soviet Union and Afghanistan have a long common border. Thus, rendering assistance to our friends we think at the same time of safeguarding the interests of our own security.

Political negotiations on a settlement of problems connected with Afghanistan are now in progress. They are, it is true, heavy going because the Pakistanis, one may say, are held by the sleeve by their overseas friends. For all that we believe that these negotiations held through the good offices of a representative of the UN Secretary-General have some chances of success.

R. Augstein. I want to return once again to the problem of medium-range missiles. If the Americans finally deploy them in the FRG, will you continue negotiations with the United States on nuclear weapons in Europe?

Y. V. Andropov. It has more than once been emphasised by the Soviet side that such a course of developments would mean a sharp change for the worse in the situation not only in Europe but on a global scale as well. Accordingly we would have to take whatever decisions would be necessary.

R. Augstein. There is another question which is causing concern to very many in the FRG. It is known that the foreign debt of certain socialist countries has now grown to very dangerous proportions. What settlement is possible here to avoid the crisis being brought to a head? Indeed, all of us in Europe depend on one another.

Y. V. Andropov. Since this question concerns sovereign states I can only say that a search for a solution to problems is the sovereign right of each country concerned. If, however, it is a question of what could be done by the FRG for its part, I can give only this advice: carry on trade, develop economic relations and do not waste your time on "sanctions".

Speech in the Kremlin at the Ceremony of Presentation of the Order of Lenin and the Gold Star Medal of Hero of the Soviet Union to Erich Honecker, General Secretary of the SUPG Central Committee, and Chairman of the Council of State of the GDR
3 May 1983

Dear Comrades!

The Presidium of the USSR Supreme Soviet has given me a pleasant assignment — to present the Order of Lenin and the Gold Star of Hero of the Soviet Union to Comrade Erich Honecker, General Secretary of the Central Committee of the Socialist Unity Party of Germany, and Chairman of the Council of State of the GDR.

This supreme Soviet decoration has been awarded to our dear friend and consistent internationalist for his active participation in the struggle against fascism, for his outstanding services to strengthening fraternal friendship and all-round cooperation between the peoples of the German Democratic Republic and the Soviet Union, and for his great contributions to the cause of peace and to consolidating the positions of socialism.

Comrade Honecker has served as General Secretary of the Central Committee of the SUPG for more than ten years now. This period has been characterised by the continued all-round progress of the economy, science and culture of the republic, the improvement of the working people's well-being, and the enhancement of the international prestige of the German Democratic Republic.

We have witnessed how relations between our two countries have multiplied during the last few years and the strong, inviolable friendship between our peoples has grown stronger. It is indisputable that the visit of the Party and government delegation of the GDR which has started today will give a strong impetus to the continued perfection of our cooperation in the interest of the peoples of the USSR and the GDR and the entire socialist community, in the interest of our common communist cause.

Dear Comrade Honecker! Please accept my heartfelt congratulations on this award. As I present it, it is a pleasure for me to emphasise once again that the Soviet people entertain sincere feelings of brotherhood for their loyal friends and allies — the working people of the German Democratic Republic.

We wish you from the bottom of our hearts good health, inexhaustible energy and new successes in your indefatigable activities in building a developed socialist society in the GDR, and in promoting internationalist cooperation between our parties and peoples.

Speech at a dinner in the Grand Kremlin Palace in honour of the Party and Government delegation of the GDR led by the General Secretary of the Central Committee of the Socialist Unity Party of Germany, Chairman of the Council of State of the German Democratic Republic, Erich Honecker
3 May 1983

Esteemed Comrade Honecker!
Esteemed Comrades!

First of all, allow me, on behalf of the Soviet leadership and all our people, to welcome cordially our dear guests — the Party and Government delegation of the German Democratic Republic.

At the negotiations which have just been held we have exchanged detailed information on each other's affairs. The Soviet communists, and all Soviet citizens are glad to know that the working people of the GDR under the leadership of the SUPG, its Central Committee headed by Comrade Honecker, have made appreciable progress in fulfilling the decisions of the 10th Party Congress. We wish wholeheartedly that our dear friends will continue confidently to translate their plans into reality. Please convey our sincere wishes of happiness and prosperity to the entire fraternal people of the German Democratic Republic.

Our discussions focused on the questions of relations between our two countries. In all of the last few years they have been on the upgrade as they are today. This is true of the inter-party links between the CPSU and the SUPG, the cooperation between government bodies, public organizations and work collectives, the exchange of cultural values and other forms of human association.

The USSR and the GDR have been the biggest trade partners for one another over many years. Direct cooperation in the production field plays an ever greater part in our economic ties today.

In our day advances in the key areas of scientific and technological progress have assumed special significance. The Soviet Union, the GDR and other countries of the socialist community possess a vast potential of creativity, a large body of highly qualified scientists, specialists and production workers. The better we combine these forces and bring their unlimited potentials into play, the more quickly and successfully we can cope with the varied economic and social problems our peoples are working to solve.

Today, on the eve of the 165th birthday of Karl Marx, we communists can say proudly: history has followed and is following the course indicated by Marx, Engels and Lenin. Marxism-Leninism, which is being constantly enriched with the practices of the Communist and Workers' parties, the international experience of socialist construction and the struggle for socialism, is the only correct and dependable guide to action today as well.

Our ideological adversaries have responded to the Marx year in their own distinctive way. President Reagan of the United States has even called for a "crusade" against communism, predicting its collapse. Washington does not confine itself to words alone. It is openly making plans to gain military superiority over the USSR and other socialist countries. The United States flagrantly interferes in the affairs of foreign nations, seeking to impose the American way of life upon them, and is aspiring, in effect, towards world supremacy. This is truly the root of evil being bred in the world and threatening the very existence of the human race.

We proceed from the assumption that the historic contest between the two social systems, the battle of ideas, is a perfectly legitimate phenomenon ensuing from the very fact of the existence of socialism and capitalism. However, we are resolutely opposed to this historic confrontation being directed towards curtailment of peaceful co-existence let alone progression towards nuclear war.

In a situation where nuclear catastrophe threatens all mankind it is the duty of all those involved in political decision making to attach top priority to the preservation of peace. Is it not time American leaders displayed greater political restraint, responsibility and common sense?

This refers in the first place to the most pressing demand of today — to prevent another spiral in the nuclear arms race, to prevent war.

The socialist countries approach these problems with a keen sense of responsibility. Our proposals have been set forth in a number of joint documents, in particular in the Prague declaration of the Warsaw Treaty Political Consultative Committee. They provide for both the elimination of the material tools of war and for erecting political barriers against it. They cover both nuclear and conventional armaments. They take into account the lawful security interests of the peoples of Europe and the rest of the world. The NATO powers have so far been evading an answer to the new peace initiatives of the socialist countries.

We have more than once declared our willingness to examine any other initiatives based on the principle of parity and equal security. No attempt to violate this principle has any chance of success. We will not allow ourselves to be deluded.

Now it is a highly crucial moment: one careless step may trigger off a chain reaction. This is precisely what can be provoked by deployment of American Pershing and cruise missile in Western Europe. If, contrary to all voices of reason, matters take such a turn, a chain reaction will follow inevitably. The USSR, the GDR and other Warsaw Treaty powers will be compelled to take counteraction.

We would not like to believe that such a prospect satisfies the American leadership. But how should one then interpret their statements and actions? Indeed, it is clearly realized in Washington that neither the "zero option" nor the "interim solution" designed to secure unilateral disarmament of the Soviet Union and to give the United States military superiority in Europe can become the basis for a fair settlement acceptable to both sides.

The stand taken by the governments of some other NATO countries also leaves one wondering. It is known, for instance, that statesmen of the FRG have more than once expressed their agreement that war should never again be unleashed from German soil. How is one to square this with support for the plans to deploy American missiles on West German soil? These are, indeed, first-strike weapons. Besides, a decision to launch these missiles would be taken on the far side of the Atlantic.

The Soviet Union has declared its readiness to have in Europe not a single missile, not a single aircraft more than the NATO powers have there today. We are told that in such an event the Soviet Union would have more nuclear warheads on missiles. Well, we are prepared to agree on a parity of nuclear potentials in Europe as regards both the delivery vehicles and nuclear explosives, taking account of course, the relevant armaments of Britain and France.

In other words, we are in favour of an agreement whereby the USSR would have no more missiles and warheads upon them than on the NATO side in every mutually stipulated period. With a reduction in the number of warheads on British and French missiles the number of warheads on our Intermediate-range missiles would be reduced to just as many. The same approach would be applied to aircraft of this class deployed in Europe. Thereby a rough parity would be maintained between the USSR and NATO both in intermediate-range nuclear delivery vehicles, that is, missiles and aircraft, and in the number of nuclear explosives they carry, and that parity would be at a considerably lower level than now.

I wish to emphasize specifically that the implementation of this new proposal would have the result that the number of intermediate-range missiles and warheads upon them deployed in the European part of the USSR would be considerably smaller than it was before 1976, when we had no SS-20 missiles.

Those who will again say no in response to this proposal of ours will assume a grave responsibility before the peoples of Europe and the whole world, since every week and every day lost for achieving agreement increases the nuclear danger.

All the peoples and governments must realize the extent of this danger and do everything to preserve peace, to reverse the trend of developments towards detente.

For our part we are doing all in our power to this end. And here — I wish to emphasize this — we have a full consensus of views and intentions with our German comrades.

I propose a toast to the good health of Comrade Honecker and the members of the Party and Government delegation of the GDR.

To the inviolable friendship between the peoples of the Soviet Union and the German Democratic Republic!

To new successes for the cause of socialism!

To peace in Europe and throughout the world!

Replies to Representatives of
Public Organizations of Finland
11 May 1983

Question. What are your proposals for nuclear disarmament and for removing the dangerous situation in Europe, as well as for a nuclear-free Europe?

Answer. The removal of the nuclear danger is the most important aim of Soviet policy. Since the time the first atom bombs were developed we have struggled persistently for a ban on nuclear weapons and for eliminating them. As far back as 1946 we proposed an international convention to ban nuclear weapons and use nuclear energy exclusively for peaceful purposes. Our efforts to this end were frustrated by the opposition of those who were determined to preserve their atomic monopoly.

In later years the Soviet Union persistently came forward as it does today with proposals to halt the build-up of nuclear arsenals, to lessen the risk of nuclear conflict and eventually to make it generally impossible.

I shall mention just a few of them.

We proposed ending production of nuclear weapons to be followed by gradual elimination of their stockpiles. To put this matter on a practical basis, we suggested that a programme of phased nuclear disarmament be drawn up and submitted a relevant document to the Geneva Committee on Disarmament.

Seeking to ease agreement on the limitation of nuclear armaments and to take the first step towards their reduction, the USSR has expressed its willingness to agree on a mutual freeze on nuclear arsenals by all states in possession of nuclear weapons or only by the Soviet Union and the United States for a start. We also propose a freeze on intermediate-range nuclear weapons and strategic armaments of the two sides for the period of Soviet-American negotiations.

At the talks with the United States on strategic armaments we proposed a substantial reduction — by more than one quarter — in the total number of strategic delivery vehicles, which would result in the withdrawal of more than 1,000 units of such weapons from the arsenals of both sides. The number of nuclear explosives would be reduced to equal ceilings, lower than now.

We propose an immediate ban on all experimental explosions of nuclear weapons everywhere, which would hinder development of new kinds and types of nuclear weapons. Pending the conclusion of an agreement to this effect we are prepared, jointly with all states possessing nuclear weapons, to impose a moratorium on any nuclear explosions, including those for peaceful purposes.

Finally, the Soviet Union has assumed a unilateral commitment not to be the first to resort to nuclear arms and called on other nuclear powers to follow suit.

Now for Europe. The best solution to the problem of nuclear weapons here could be provided by complete deliverance of the European continent from nuclear weapons, both intermediate-range and tactical ones. This is a realistic way towards a nuclear-free Europe. Of course, it should be taken by all states which have nuclear weapons in this region. Unfortunately, those to whom our proposal is addressed seem to ignore it.

At the Geneva talks with the United States we proposed the following option: a radical reduction — roughly from 1,000 units to 300 units on each side — of intermediate-range nuclear weapons in Europe. At the same time, the Soviet Union is prepared to retain only 162 missiles after such reductions, that is, as many as NATO — Britain and France — has there now. Equally low ceilings — 138 units on each side — would be established on nuclear-armed aircraft.

We are told that this would leave the Soviet Union with a larger number of nuclear warheads on missiles. Well, we are prepared to agree on a parity of nuclear potentials in Europe, both in delivery vehicles and in explosives, taking account, of course, of the relevant armaments of Britain and France.

In other words, we are in favour of a settlement whereby the USSR would have no more missiles and warheads upon them than NATO has in every mutually stipulated period of time. With a reduction in the number of warheads on British and French missiles, the number of warheads on our intermediate-range missiles would be reduced by just as many. The same approach would be applied to the aircraft of this class deployed in Europe. This would secure a rough parity between the USSR and NATO both in intermediate-range nuclear delivery vehicles, that is, missiles and aircraft, and in the number of nuclear explosives they carry, and at a much lower level than now.

I want to emphasize specifically that the implementation of this new proposal would leave in the European part of the USSR a number of intermediate-range missiles and warheads upon them much smaller than it was before 1976, when we had no SS-20 missiles.

This would bring Europe much closer to complete deliverance from nuclear weapons, both intermediate-range and tactical ones. This proposal is unacceptable only to one intending to deploy new American missiles in Western Europe at all costs, thereby upsetting the existing balance of forces in Europe and on a global scale. Should this happen, the danger of war would draw nearer to the doorstep of Europe. We cannot allow this to happen and we will take whatever measures may be necessary to preserve the parity.

Question. Do you support the idea of setting up a nuclear-free zone, say in Northern Europe, and are you ready to provide guarantees of security for such zones?

Answer. Yes, we are in favour of nuclear-free zones in Northern Europe and in other parts of the European continent, regarding them as an important means of strengthening the security of European nations.

We supported unequivocally Finland's proposal for proclaiming Northern Europe a nuclear-free zone. It is important, of course, that this zone should be really free from nuclear weapons and that any loopholes for their deployment there be closed.

For its part, the Soviet Union is prepared to assume an obligation not to use nuclear weapons against the countries of Northern Europe within this zone. This could be formalized either by a multilateral agreement or bilateral agreements with each of the states within the zone. Naturally, the security of these countries would be guaranteed more dependably if the nuclear powers of NATO also provided the

ASW-L

relevant guarantees. However, we are not making our obligation conditional on this.

In view of the requests expressed in a number of Scandinavian countries the USSR is also prepared to discuss some measures — and substantial ones for that matter — to be applied to its own territory adjoining such a zone that would contribute to strengthening the nuclear-free status of Northern Europe.

Supporting the proposal for a nuclear-free zone in Northern Europe the Soviet Union has also declared its favourable attitude in principle to the Swedish government's idea to set up in Central Europe a zone free from battlefield-range nuclear weapons.

I am convinced that the implementation of the aforesaid proposals for nuclear-free zones would help deliver all Europe from nuclear weapons in the future.

Question. What would be the significance of the commitments of nuclear powers not to be the first to resort to nuclear arms for lessening the risk of nuclear war?

Answer. It is our profound conviction that such commitments would contribute to the prevention of nuclear war by creating an atmosphere of greater trust in relations between states. In the current international situation this is of crucial significance.

As I have already pointed out, the Soviet Union has assumed an obligation not to be the first to resort to nuclear arms. If the Soviet example were followed by the other nuclear powers this would practically be equivalent to a general renunciation of nuclear weapons. Indeed, if these weapons were not used by anyone, there would be no second or third nuclear strike. The assumption of such a commitment would not demand long negotiations or agreements. It requires only good will and a sincere desire of peace. The United States and its NATO allies, however, are clinging to their stake on first use of nuclear weapons, and are evading any step to follow the Soviet example.

Question. Is a broad and effective movement for peace a factor of international security and of support for the disarmament negotiations between the USSR and the USA?

Answer. I am convinced it is. The massive anti-war movements are a crucial factor in favour of peace. It cannot be ignored by statesmen and governments if they reckon with the opinion of their peoples. In this sense the peace movement indisputably exerts an influence on the arms limitation talks.

Speech at a dinner in the Grand Kremlin Palace in honour of President Mauno Koivisto of the Republic of Finland
6 June 1983

Esteemed Mr. President!
Esteemed Mrs. Koivisto!
Esteemed Finnish guests!
Comrades!

I cordially welcome you, Mr. President and Madame Koivisto, Prime Minister Mr. Sorsa, all the statesmen and political leaders, as well as members of the business community of friendly Finland who are accompanying the President.

The visit by the President of the Finnish Republic to the Soviet Union has been marked by important actions to deepen cooperation between our two countries.

Today the record of Soviet-Finnish relations has been supplemented with another vivid page: a Protocol has been signed to prolong the Treaty of Friendship, Cooperation and Mutual Assistance between the USSR and Finland for the next twenty-year period.

For 35 years now this treaty has been serving effectively the development of good neighbourly relations between our two countries and contributing substantially to peace in Northern Europe and on the continent of Europe as a whole. The new, third pre-term extension of the treaty clearly evidences the determination of our two states to continue further the time-tested course of friendship, mutual understanding and cooperation.

The long-term programme of developing and increasing trade, economic, industrial, scientific and technical cooperation spanning the period up to 1995 is being implemented successfully. The Protocol just signed, on cooperation in the field of agriculture and the production of foodstuffs, is a good supplement to it.

Thus, everybody can see that relations of good neighbourliness and friendship between the USSR and Finland are not subject to waverings of the needle of the barometer of international climate, and are clearly directed towards the future.

Soviet-Finnish relations are not to the liking of the champions of aggravating international tension and a reckless arms race; those who praise power politics; those who wish to dominate other peoples, and intimidate them with the spectre of a ''Soviet menace''. This is easy to understand, since our relations are indisputable evidence of the groundlessness of all allegations that those who poison the international climate are trying to make the peoples believe.

The USSR and Finland cooperate as fully equal partners. We do not interfere in any way in each other's internal affairs, and each side strictly respects the sovereignty and interests of the other side. We have established and are developing extensive economic ties which are truly beneficial to both sides. We are cooperating effectively in the noble cause of strengthening peace and international security.

Thus, our traditional cooperation which develops year by year is a conclusive example of how successful and fruitful relations between states with different social systems and different ideologies can be — not just peaceful, courteous ties but relations of true friendship, mutual respect and mutual trust.

In this connection I wish to emphasize specifically the role which has been played in the establishment, strengthening and all-round development of friendly relations between our two countries by such outstanding statesmen as the Presidents of the Finnish Republic Juho Kusti Paasikivi and Urho Kaleva Kekkonen, and now by President Mauno Koivisto. We in the Soviet Union have a profound respect for these statesmen of neighbouring Finland as serious political leaders, solid and honest partners, and patriots of their country sincerely dedicated to the cause of lasting peace. Hence their indisputably high prestige in the international arena.

Finland's foreign policy — the ''Paasikivi-Kekkonen line'' — is widely known and deeply respected.

Finland today is an active member of the international community, and we in the USSR highly appreciate its role, and its initiatives directed to strengthening peace, security and cooperation among the peoples of Europe. Suffice it to recall in this context Finland's proposal for establishing a nuclear-free zone in Northern Europe and the efforts of Finland's diplomacy at the Madrid follow-up conference of the 35 Helsinki nations.

The Soviet Union is not just sympathetic to the idea of a nuclear-free zone in Northern Europe but is prepared to assist in its establishment.

We would not only assume a commitment to respect the status of such a zone but would be prepared to study the question of some measures, and substantial ones for that matter, concerning our own territory adjoining the zone, which would help consolidate its nuclear-free status. The Soviet Union could also discuss with the interested sides the question of lending nuclear-free status to the Baltic Sea area.

The gravest threat to European security now is, of course, the intention to deploy American missiles in Western Europe, to convert its land into a launching pad for delivering a nuclear strike at the Soviet Union and its allies. We have already given warning that if such deployment begins the USSR will take prompt and effective counter-measures in relation to both the areas where the new American missiles will be deployed and the territory of the United States itself. We shall be obliged to take such measures out of concern for the security of the Soviet people and their friends.

However, we would not want matters to go that far. We are in favour of a Europe delivered from the nuclear threat. We are prepared, as before, to reach agreement for a start on drastic reductions of the nuclear arsenals in Europe on both sides. This, however, must be a fair deal based on equality. We will not accept a settlement whereby the Soviet Union would be left unarmed in the face of hundreds of nuclear missiles of NATO countries targeted upon it and without a deterrent equivalent for retaliation. If the principle of parity and equal security is respected it will be always possible to reach agreement with us.

Soviet foreign policy has no aim more important than peace, lasting peace in Europe and the rest of the world. This is why we appreciate so highly the policy of states committed to peace including, of course, Finland.

Mr. President, I believe you will agree that our talks with you and the prolongation of the Treaty of 1948 are not only a long step in the further development of friendship and cooperation between the Soviet Union and Finland but also a very useful contribution to the cause of consolidating peace and security in Europe.

Expressing our gratitude to our guest for this visit I propose a toast to the health of President Mauno Koivisto of the Finnish Republic and Madame Tellervo Koivisto, to the health of all Finnish guests present here!

To relations of good neighbourliness and friendship between the peoples of the Soviet Union and Finland!

To lasting and just peace in Europe and throughout the world!

Speech at a Plenary Meeting of the CPSU Central Committee

15 June 1983

Comrades!

This plenary meeting is discussing one of the key problems of Party activity, a major component of the work to build communism. What are the main tasks facing the Party in its ideological work under present conditions?

First. All our ideological, educational and propaganda work should be radically improved to cope with the great and complex tasks the Party is fulfilling in the process of perfecting a developed socialist society. The Party committees at all levels and every Party organization must realize that for all the importance of other problems they have to handle (economic, organizational and others) ideological work is increasingly assuming first priority. We clearly see the grave damage caused by flaws in this work, by the inadequate civic awareness of citizens whenever it is in evidence. And conversely, we can see today how much faster the rates of our advance become, when our ideological work is more effective, when the masses more clearly understand the Party's policy, regarding it as their own cause meeting the vital interests of the people.

Second. We have at our disposal a wealth of facilities for enlightenment and education. These are the press, the radio broadcasting and television services, and the enormous network of educational establishments of various types. All this has been discussed in detail in the report of Comrade K. U. Chernenko and in the debate. The task is to use all these facilities more efficiently, more actively, more imaginatively, taking account, in particular, of the considerably enhanced level of education and requirements of Soviet citizens. In this field we still have much to learn, and the main obstacles in our way are formalism, stereotypy, over-caution and at times laziness of thinking. We must also proceed from the principle that shaping the consciousness of communists and all citizens of our socialist society is a matter of concern not only to professional ideologists, propagandists, and workers in the mass media. It is a cause for the Party as a whole.

Third. The question of cadres. All Party committees in the republics, territories, regions, cities, towns and districts must have specially trained cadres capable of skilfully organizing ideological work within various population groups — the workers, the collective farmers, the intelligentsia, and young people, and be accountable for the standards of this work. These cadres must be well-educated people enjoying prestige. It is necessary to provide favourable conditions for them, to display concern for regular advancement of their qualifications. The sole criterion for assessment of their performance must always be the level of the political awareness and labour activity of the masses.

Fourth. It is necessary to secure a new, considerably higher level of ideological and theoretical work in the social sciences, primarily in economic sciences, of the work of our research institutions and every scientist individually. It is mandatory to effect a radical turn towards the real, practical tasks which the realities of life pose to our society. The social sciences to the same extent as natural sciences must become an efficient assistant of the Party and the people as a whole in fulfilling these tasks.

Fifth. An important role is to be played by a change in the style of the work of political enlightenment and of the mass political training network. It is necessary above all to do away with formalism, with mechanical repetition or quotations from printed text of general truisms divorced from realities. The purpose of political instruction is to help everyone understand more profoundly the Party's policy under present conditions, use his knowledge practically, have a clearer awareness of his duty and perform it in deed.

Sixth. In all educational and propaganda work it is constantly necessary to take account of the distinctions of the historical period mankind lives in today. Indeed, it is emphasised by a confrontation of two opposite world outlooks, two political lines — those of socialism and imperialism — a confrontation without precedent in intensity and bitterness in all postwar history. A struggle is going on for the minds and hearts of thousands of millions of people on earth. The future of mankind will largely depend on the outcome of this ideological struggle. It is clear, therefore, how important it is to be able to bring the truth about a socialist society, its advantages and its policy of peace in clear and eloquent language to the broad popular masses throughout the world. It is no less important to expose competently fallacious subversive imperialist propaganda. We need a well planned uniform system of counter-propaganda that is both dynamic and efficient.

In short, we have a lot of things to do on the ideological front and this work should be handled without procrastination.

However, even the most eloquent and interesting propaganda, the most skilful and competent instruction, the most talented art will fail to achieve their goal unless they are pervaded with profound ideas closely linked with the realities of life today, which is of crucial importance for ideological work and for all activities of the Party in general.

As it is stated in the resolution of the Congress, the Party Programme now in effect correctly defines on the whole the laws governing world social development, and the aims and basic tasks of the struggle waged by the Party and the Soviet people for communism. Its fundamental principles have been corroborated by the realities of life. Much of what is recorded in the Programme has already been fulfilled. At the same time, some of its provisions — this must be stated frankly — have not stood the test of time in full measure, since they contain elements divorced from realities, forestalling of events and unwarranted specification of details. Of course, during the last two decades many important changes have taken place in the life of Soviet society, of other socialist countries and in world development as a whole. All this requires profound theoretical interpretation and must be taken into consideration in planning the Party's long-term strategy in the field of home and foreign policies.

A realistic analysis of the prevailing situation and clear-cut guidelines for the future which would link the experience of history with the ultimate goals of our Communist party — this is what we would like to see in the new edition of the CPSU Programme. Lenin said in connection with the drafting of the Party's Second Programme: "Without any exaggeration, absolutely objectively, sticking to the facts we must tell in our programme what we are and what we intend to do"[1]. We must also act in this way, comrades.

For a correct understanding of the prospects — in economics, in politics and in ideology — one must have a clear idea primarily of the character of that stage of social development which we witness today. The Party has defined it as the stage of developed socialism. This is a society in which the economic basis, the social structure, the political system corresponding to socialist principles have already been established in full, where socialism is developing on its own collectivist basis and is generally recognized.

All this does not mean, of course, that the society we have built is perfect. It still contains many objectively conditioned difficulties natural for the present level of development. There are also quite a few shortcomings generated by subjective causes, or by the work of people which is not always skilful and well organized. The Party Programme under present conditions must be primarily a programme of planned and comprehensive perfection of developed socialism and hence of further advance towards communism. The text of the Programme must patently contain a detailed characterization of the period of developed socialism.

It is well known that the face of any society is determined in the final analysis by the level of development of its productive forces. In our social development we have now approached a historical boundary where a fundamental qualitative change in productive forces and an advancement of relations of production corresponding to this change have become imminent and inevitable. This is not simply our wish but an objective necessity, and we cannot bypass it in any way. The change in the consciousness of individuals, and in all the forms of social life which are commonly called the superstructure, must take place in close interconnection with this.

In the economic sphere the key task is to secure a radical advancement of the productivity of labour. We must seek to achieve

---

[1] V. Lenin. *Collected Works,* vol. 36, p. 55.

the highest world level in this field. It was not fortuitious that Lenin regarded this in the final analysis as the most important, the chief factor for victory of the new social system[1]. Today in the conditions of the scientific and technological revolution this task has assumed special significance both for our internal development and on the international plane.

What path will be followed in the development of this country's productive forces in the foreseeable future?

The immediate goal is clear: it is necessary first of all to introduce exemplary order in what we have, to secure the most rational use of the country's productive, scientific and technological potential, in particular, to overcome the shortfall of such branches as agriculture, transport and services. The report and the speakers in the debate spoke of the drive to strengthen discipline and order, to enhance the organization and responsibility which has now been launched on the Party's initiative throughout the country. I wish to emphasise that to secure a well-organized and trouble-free operation of the entire economic mechanism is a requirement of today and a programme task for the future. This is a component of the general process of perfecting our social system.

The main road towards a qualitative change in productive forces is, of course, a changeover to intensive development, a combination in practice of the advantages of our socialist system with the achievements of the scientific and technological revolution. Its latest stage holds out an especially rich promise of a technological breakthrough in many spheres of production. I believe that all will agree that this direction in the activities of the Party and people must be duly reflected in the new edition of the Party Programme.

A uniform scientific and technological policy has assumed decisive significance today. Enormous work is in store for us in the development of machines, mechanisms and technologies for both today and tomorrow. We are to implement automation of production, to secure the broadest application of computers and robots, and to introduce flexible technologies enabling rapid and efficient regearing of production to the manufacture of new product items. The future of our power industry depends primarily on the use of the most up-to-

---

[1] *ibid,* vol. 39, p.21.

date nuclear reactors and in the longer term on the practical solution of the problem of controlled nuclear fusion. We also have on the order of the day such tasks as production of materials with pre-set properties, the development of biological technology, and the broad application of waste-free and energy-saving technologies in industry. All this will lead to a veritable revolution in our national economy.

Unfortunately, it is precisely in the area of the practical introduction of scientific and technological achievements that we still have, as you know, many bottlenecks. An economic executive who takes a risk by introducing a new technology at his enterprise, and applying or manufacturing new equipment, not infrequently stands to lose whereas one who avoids innovation loses nothing at all. The task is to devise a system of organizational, economic and moral incentives that will stimulate an interest in the renewal of technology on the part of both managers and production workers and, of course, of scientists and engineers and will make work by outdated methods unprofitable. This is now the subject of research at the State Planning Committee, the Academy of Sciences, the State Committee for Science and Technology. It is necessary to cope with this task more speedily since the loss of time costs the country dearly.

Naturally, in advancing production efficiency it is a task of first priority to curtail drastically the use of manual labour, primarily by means of comprehensive mechanization. The situation in the field of labour productivity is to be radically improved by the broad application of robots, particularly in those areas of production where manual, physically arduous, unskilled and monotonous work operations are still common today. This will improve the working conditions of hundreds of thousands of persons, who will then derive more satisfaction from their work. This is of fundamental significance, since it will bring nearer the solution of one of the basic problems of communist construction, one of overcoming the essential distinctions between physical and mental work.

Generally, the main productive force is, of course, man, his labour activity. Here I have in mind not only conscious discipline and a creative attitude to work, but also a strict and efficient organization of labour processes and remuneration.

Thus, here we come close to the question of improving relations of production. Their foundation is public ownership of the means of production. In our society it has, as is known, a dual form: state ownership and ownership by collective farms and cooperatives. We see in pespective a merger of these two forms of property into the common property of the whole people. Of course, not by means of mechanical conversion of collective farms into state farms. Practical experience has proved that there are different ways, such as agro-industrial integration, the development of inter-collective farm and collective farm–state farm associations. The programme should elucidate this problem profoundly and clearly.

There is yet another important factor. We must not forget that we live in a socialist society whose development must be regulated on the fundamental principles of socialism, including, of course, the principle of distribution according to work. In our society all have equal rights and equal duties to society. Complete equality in the sense of equal availability of material benefits will be possible only under communism. However, a long path will have to be traversed before this is achieved. This requires a much higher level of the economy and of the consciousness of citizens. Today, besides a definite share of the social consumption funds, every Soviet citizen is entitled only to such material benefits that correspond to the quantity and quality of his socially useful work. Only to this share alone. It is important to secure strict accounting and stringent compliance with this principle.

Advancement of relations of production requires also a radical improvement in planning and management. We have built an integrated national economic complex and gained definite experience in comprehensive planning on a regional basis and on key problems facing the economy. The latest examples illustrating this are the Food Programme and the Energy Programme, a major document of long-term significance, a kind of a GOELRO nation-wide electrification programme under present conditions. The implementation of these programmes will require enormous efforts by the Party, the state and the people as a whole. The shortcomings in our planning are well known: these are an unwarranted dispersion of resources, the unbalanced character of plans, and the gap between the mass of commodities and the incomes of the population. To remedy such flaws is a task of both economic and political significance.

The development of relations of production makes new demands on the organization of the socialist emulation drive today. One of its basic forms now is a contest for the overfulfilment of production plans, mainly with regard to quantity indicators. In many instances this is justified as before, particularly in the extractive industries. I believe, however, that it would be useful to focus our attention today on such aims of the emulation drive as improving product quality, better utilization of productive capacities, raw materials, energy and working time. And, of course, reasonable economy, saving on everything, from each ton of metal to each kilo of grain.

It should be said in general that the forms of socialist emulation, just like other public initiatives and mass movements, are not something fossilized and are subject to change. These forms change depending on the level of the material and cultural maturity of society. It is the duty of the Party to notice in good time, and to support and disseminate all useful creative innovations.

At the 26th Party Congress we clearly declared the need for securing a close link between economic and social policies. This is only natural; indeed, the ultimate goal of our efforts in the economic sphere is improvement of the life of the people.

It is necessary for us to learn, in drawing up our economic plans, to analyse comprehensively and reflect in them the major factors in the development of society — social, ethnic and demographic. This must be a uniform policy of the Party, a uniform strategy of social development.

The phrase "improving the standards of life" is often used in our society. Sometimes, however, it is interpreted in an oversimplified manner, having in mind only the growth of the population's income and the production of consumer goods. Actually, however, the notion of the level of life is much wider and richer. It implies a permanent growth in the level of consciousness and culture of citizens, including standards of behaviour in every-day life and also what I would call the culture of reasonable consumption. It implies also exemplary public order and a healthy, rational diet, a high quality of public services (an area in which, far from everything goes smoothly, as we know). It also implies the fruitful use of leisure time, rational from both the moral and aesthetic point of view. In short, everything that *in toto* deserves to be described as civilized socialist living.

An enormous improvement is evident in the housing conditions of the population. Nevertheless, the housing shortage is still felt acutely by many. We are determined to solve this problem in the main in the not too distant future, so that every family will have a separate apartment. It is necessary to ensure that the distribution of apartments, just like other benefits, should be fair and should take account, in particular, of the standards of the individual's work performance. It might also be useful to provide for a broader development of cooperative principles and to encourage investment of enterprises in construction — and not only of apartment houses but also, let us say, boarding houses for the aged wherever possible and necessary. This will be useful not only on the economic plane but also will help to foster in individuals a sense of collectivism, a feeling of direct involvement in the management of the affairs of society.

It is not enough to improve the system of remuneration for work in cash, it is also necessary to produce the required quantity of goods in demand. Moreover, the criteria of quality must be applied with strictness: the best. Today, however, the situation is sometimes very saddening: the raw materials are good, but the products are such that consumers prefer to overpay the profiteer for articles made with good taste. The situation must be remedied and, for that matter, without delay.

It is especially necessary to organize an uninterrupted supply of high-quality foodstuffs, pursuing the goals of achieving a maximum of self-sufficiency in this respect. Our Food Programme is targeted on the solution of this problem.

Questions of health care will indisputably hold a growing place in the Party's social policy. The democratic character of our system of free medical care, which is the first in the world, is generally known. However, its standards of quality far from always meet the requirements of developed socialism. This has more than once been pointed out in Party resolutions during the last few years. To fulfil them, however, fairly great efforts are necessary. Prevention of disease merits special attention and, as one of the ways to achieve this, the introduction of annual medical check-ups of the entire population. Indeed, public health is a matter of crucial importance both on the social and economic plane.

The solution of all these large problems in the home policy of the Party will mean appreciable progress towards the social uniformity of society. This great goal outlined in theory, which has been the cherished dream of several generations of communists, has become a question of immediate practice today. The realities of life suggest that by all indications the classless structure of society in its main and most important features will be ready formed in the stage of mature socialism. This conclusion of the 26th Congress of the CPSU will evidently be reflected in the new edition of the Party Programme.

The Party proceeds from the premise that the coming years and decades will bring considerable changes also in the political and ideological superstructure of the spiritual life of society.

I speak above all of the development of our political system, of the improvement of Soviet statehood, and of widening socialist democracy.

Many provisions to this effect in the existing Party Programme have already been implemented, particularly since the adoption of the new Constitution of the USSR. The links between deputies and Soviets in general and the population have strengthened appreciably. Nation-wide discussion of major draft laws has become a matter of course. The role of the people's control has increased. There is an increase in the activity of the trade unions which now affiliate practically all working people in town and country.

In short, quite a lot has been done, although of course, not all that should and could has been done.

Take, for instance, the procedure of taking decisions on major problems involved in state and social affairs. There are opportunities for its further democratization. I have in mind ever broader discussion of drafts of such decisions within labour collectives; obligatory consideration in the relevant cases of conclusions by trade unions, the Young Communist League, and women's organizations; and the maximum of attention to suggestions from working people.

Greater publicity in work, and regular accountability of leading executives to the public will certainly bring the activities of Party and government bodies closer to the needs and interests of the people.

The Party Programme formulates the task of reduction and simplification of the managerial apparatus. I believe this task should as before be considered urgent. This is a practical and political problem of principle which was emphasised by Lenin in his time. Some efforts are being made for progress in this direction but they are still inadequate. I am convinced that the staffs of many institutions and organizations could be reduced considerably without harm to the running of business. The personnel released could easily find jobs where now we have a manpower shortage.

Of course, in the new edition of the Party Programme the theme of the further development of democratic principles in the management of production should be given considerable space. Tomorrow's session of the USSR Supreme Soviet will discuss the draft of the Law on Labour Collectives, the first in the history of our state. This is an act of great political significance. It is correct and good that this law is to be adopted after its detailed truly nation-wide discussion. And it is highly important to ensure that it is carried into effect completely.

The normal course of our social development is inconceivable without the stringent observance of the laws safeguarding the interests of society and the rights of citizens. It is necessary, In particular, to put an end completely to such evils as cases of misuse of state and public property, and of official positions for purposes of private enrichment. Indeed, taking a more careful look at this evil one will see that this is nothing less than an undermining of the very essence of our system. Here the law must be intransigent and its penalties inevitable. Protection of the interests of the people is one of the foundations of our socialist democracy.

There is yet another problem. We must declare a real war on such practices where our democratic norms and principles are not reinforced with deeds, and where only the form and semblance of business are accepted as sufficient. What is the use, say, of a meeting held, as is not infrequently the case, on the basis of a prepared scenario, if there is no open and interesting discussion, where statements by speakers are edited in advance and initiative, to say nothing of criticism, is toned down and suppressed? What is the use of the work of a trade union organization which does not dare to raise its voice in defence of the working people's interests, against various violations in the sphere of production? Or of the activities of people's controllers, if their complaints are not heeded and no measures to remedy the situation are taken?

It is crucially important to ensure that words should never disagree with deeds, while the essence of the matter should never be sacrificed to form. This is, if you like, one of the major reserves for perfecting our socialist democracy in all areas of state and public activities.

As far as a more distant perspective is concerned, we communists see it in gradual transformation of Soviet state administration into public self-government. This will occur, as we believe, through the further development of the state of the whole people, through broader involvement of the masses in the management of the affairs of society.

Evidently, this process will not take place by itself or simply by somebody's good will. It is conditioned both by the material possibilities of society and the level of political awareness and the cultural standards of the masses. It is highly important to realize and remember this. Not to think up abstractly further ways and forms of developing democracy but to be guided by the realities of life. This is the guarantee of the realism of our programme principles.

Needless to say, the problems involved in the Party's nationalities policy will be given adequate attention in the new edition of the Party Programme. I have had occasion to point out that perfection of developed socialism must indispensably include a thoroughly planned and scientifically grounded nationalities policy. It should be based on the principles bequeathed to us by Lenin: complete equality of all nations and national minorities of the country, their free development within the framework of a fraternal union and a steadfast course towards their convergence and consolidation. Implementation of this policy requires and will require in the future consistent education of all Soviet citizens in the spirit of socialist internationalism, and a profound awareness of the community of the interests of all Soviet nations.

Perfection of developed socialism is inconceivable without vital work to encourage the cultural advancement of citizens.

As it has been rightly pointed out here, the moulding of an individual begins in the early years of his life. The work of our schools and other educational institutions has been discussed at length at this plenary meeting. I wish to emphasize the following: the Party is making efforts to secure that the individual is raised in our society not simply as one in possession of a definite body of knowledge but primarily as a citizen of socialist society, an active builder of communism with firm ideological convictions, morals and interests, with a fine culture of work and behaviour.

The combination of instruction with productive work is an effective means of education. It is necessary to pursue firmly the line of fostering in school children the habit and love of useful work. This may be physical or mental work but of necessity real work, productive work, needed by society.

Work also contributes to physical development. In this area not everything is right in our society. I have in mind not only lessons in physical culture and athletic sports, but also the elements of knowledge of hygiene and medical aid. It is necessary for an individual to know his organism from his youth and to be capable of maintaining it in good shape.

Where else but in school can a person receive the rudiments of aesthetic education, acquire a sense of beauty, an ability to appreciate work of art, or get access to artistic creation?

Naturally, it will take a lot of effort and time to accomplish all these tasks. Apart from other measures, it will be necessary to improve the selection and training of teachers with a view to modern requirements.

Here in the presidium we have exchanged opinions on the following subject. It is evidently time we gave serious thought to the need for a reform of our schools, including the vocational training system.

The Party's strategy in perfecting developed socialist society must rest on the solid foundation of Marxist-Leninist theory. Speaking frankly, we have not yet studied thoroughly enough the society in which we live and work, or fully revealed the laws intrinsic to it, the economic laws in particular. Therefore, at times we have to act empirically, as it were, relying on the extremely irrational method of trial and error.

Unfortunately, science has not yet suggested in practice a solution to a number of important problems conforming to the principles and conditions of developed socialist society. What do I have in mind? Primarily the choice of the most dependable ways of advancing production efficiency, improving the quality of products, and the principles of price formation on scientific lines. And not only this. As our society makes progress, ever new problems appear on the scene.

What is more, there is a record of experience in the socialist development of a few other countries, which requires a thorough study, assessment and summing up. In short, the part played by the social sciences in modern life should certainly be given attention in the new edition of the CPSU Programme.

The effective Programme contains some good words about the significance of literature and the arts in our socialist society. However, some provisions to this effect should perhaps be amplified.

The Party supports everything that enriches science and culture, or helps to educate the working people in the spirit of the norms and principles of developed socialism. It has a solicitous, respectful attitude to talent, and to the creative quests of artists, and does not interfere in the forms and style of their work. The Party, however, cannot be indifferent to the ideological content of art. It will always guide the development of art to help it serve the interests of the people. Naturally, this does not imply administrative injunction. The main method of influence on artistic creativity must be Marxist-Leninist criticism, active, delicate and attentive, as well as intransigent to ideologically alien and professionally inferior works.

All of us can see that the impact of art on the minds of the people grows side by side with their cultural advancement. This increases the possibilities for its active interference in social life, and enhances enormously the responsibility of members of the literary and artistic community for the powerful weapons they hold in their hands being used for the service of the interests of the people, for the communist cause.

The experience of world development over the last quarter-century dictates the need to develop further many provisions of the Programme referring to international problems.

The alignment of forces in the world arena has changed substantially. The struggle betwen the two world social systems has hardened to an unprecedented degree. Obviously, an attempt to settle the historic dispute between these systems by force of arms would be fatal to mankind. The character of the development of relations between them, that is, in effect, the question of preserving peace on earth, is the pivotal problem in the foreign policy of our Party today and will be such in the foreseeable future.

And not only of our Party. The danger of nuclear war threatening mankind necessitates a new assessment of the main purpose of the activity of the entire communist movement. The communists have always been fighters against oppression and exploitation of man by man, and today they are also fighting for the survival of human civilization, for the right of man to life. This must also be reflected in the Programme.

The socialist countries and their policy today are a factor of enormous significance in securing lasting peace on earth. Promoting the co-operation and unity of these countries is, I would say, the key direction of the international activity of the CPSU and the Soviet state.

The CPSU Programme says that a new type of relation between the socialist countries has emerged. The last two decades, however, have enriched our concepts of the socialist world and shown graphically its diversity and complexity. There are great distinctions between individual socialist countries in the field of the economy and culture, and in the ways and methods of solving the tasks in socialist development. We regard this as natural even though at one time we believed that it would be more uniform.

The history of world socialism confirms that the socialist system provides every opportunity for society's confident advance and for harmonious relations between countries. We can witness quite a few examples of how these opportunities are being realized on the principles of socialist internationalism, which imply complete respect for the sovereign rights of each country and for mutual comradely assistance and mutual support. As demonstrated by experience, however, all this does not occur by itself. For these opportunities to be realized a correct political line should be pursued.

One has to pay for mistakes in policy. Where the leading role of a Communist Party weakens, the danger of slipping on to a bourgeois reformist path of development arises. When a Party loses its links with the people a vacuum occurs in which self-styled claimants to the expression of the working people's interest appear. Where no rebuff is given to nationalistic sentiments, inter-state conflicts flare up — conflicts for which there seem to be no basis in the socialist world.

It is particularly important, of course, to ensure that existing differences do not interfere with the development of cooperation. To secure this cooperation is the sacred duty of communists, of the ruling communist parties. In the final analysis, what divides us is immeasurably less than what we have in common as the builders of a new society.

We are in favour of friendship with all socialist countries. As far as our closest friends and allies — the countries of the socialist community — are concerned, we have a consensus to the following effect: the realities of life demand not simply an expansion of cooperation but enhancement of its quality and efficiency.

This implies in the first place a further perfection of political cooperation, of which the major instrument is the Warsaw Treaty Organization. We believe that our cooperation will be increasingly closer in this sphere. Of course, it will continue to develop with a view to the distinctive features of the situation, as well as the specific interests of individual states. At the same time the jointly planned common policy will be an ever stronger alloy of the opinions and positions of the fraternal countries.

We seek, secondly, to achieve a qualitatively new level of economic integration. Without it the life of the socialist community of nations is inconceivable today. In perspective, integration will be ever deeper, all-embracing and effective, firmly ensuring the strengthening of the national economies of the countries involved. This is the objective of our joint efforts.

Finally, in the sphere of spiritual life, we foresee further ideological integration of the fraternal peoples, the growth of their feeling of unity, the community of their historical destinies, an expansion of the exchange of cultural values.

Needless to say, all this entails lengthy processes. These are in progress already today but they will be even more in evidence tomorrow and in the decades to come. We are convinced that the higher the levels of social development of the socialist countries and the closer they are to one another the greater the mutual understanding between them and the more organic, richer and deeper their cooperation.

An objective scientific analysis of the essence of differences whenever they occur on certain issues between individual socialist countries, as well as between some fraternal parties in the world communist movement, and a quest for ways to overcome them on a Marxist-Leninist basis, ways of strengthening the unity of communists — this is indisputably one of the Party's major tasks on the international plane. The programme cannot ignore it, if we want to remain on realistic ground.

One of the cardinal features of the modern world which must be reflected in the new edition of the Programme is the growing role played by the countries of Asia, Africa and Latin America which have liberated themselves from colonial and semi-colonial dependence. The processes taking place within them are complicated and varied, and it is important to interpret them correctly.

In some of these countries the capitalist system has been established. Their objective interests, however, are contradicted by the aggressive policy of domination and dictation pursued by the imperialist powers. In seeking to overcome their economic backwardness these countries need international cooperation based on equality and lasting peace. Many of them see in their ties with the socialist countries a means of consolidating their independence. Naturally, we will continue to follow a policy of mutually beneficial cooperation with these states, with complete respect for their sovereignty and non-interference in their internal affairs.

In the former colonial world the countries which have chosen a path of socialist orientation are the closest to us. We are united with them not only by our common anti-imperialist objectives and commitment to peace but also by our common ideals of social justice and progress. We are aware, of course, of the difficulty of their situation and of their revolutionary development. Indeed, it is one thing to declare socialism as a goal and another thing to build it. For this a definite level of productive forces, culture, and public awareness are necessary. The socialist countries have feelings of solidarity with these progressive states, render assistance to them in the sphere of politics and culture, and help strengthen their national defence. We also help to the extent of our abilities with their economic progress. Basically, however, this progress, like the social progress of these countries, can of course only be the result of the work of their own peoples and the correct policy of their leadership.

As far as the capitalist world is concerned, we are witnessing a considerable aggravation of the general crisis of this social system. The methods by which capitalism managed to maintain the relative stability of its development in the postwar period are becoming increasingly ineffective. It is increasingly clear that imperialism is unable to cope with the social consequences of a scientific and technological revolution of unprecedented depth and scope, where millions upon millions of working people are doomed to unemployment and poverty.

Imperialism has become entangled in its internal and inter-state antagonisms, cataclysms and conflicts. This has a strong and varying impact on the policies of capitalist countries.

On the one hand, as we have seen, the aggressiveness of the ultrareactionary forces led by US imperialism has sharply increased. Attempts are being made to reverse the trend of developments at all costs. Of course, this policy will not bring success for the imperialists but, because of its adventurism, it is extremely dangerous to mankind. Therefore, it is meeting with powerful resistance on the part of the peoples which will indisputably continue to grow.

In today's capitalist world, however, there exist other trends and other politicians who have a more realistic view of the international situation. They realize that irreversible processes have already taken place in the world and are aware of the need for and mutual benefits of lasting peaceful coexistence of states belonging to different social systems. We for our part have stated more than once (and repeat it) that we are prepared for this. We are convinced that it meets the interests of the peoples on both sides of the social barricade dividing the world. Indeed, there are quite a few large problems which concern all countries of the world, and their significance grows steadily. This refers, for instance, to nature conservation on our planet, the search for new energy sources, the exploration of outer space and the utilization of the resources of the World Ocean.

The Communists are convinced that the future belongs to socialism. Such is the trend of history. This does not mean, however, that we intend to engage in the "export of revolution" or to interfere in the affairs of foreign countries. "Export of revolution" is impossible in principle. Socialism grows only on the soil of the objective requirements of social development in each particular country. We firmly believe that socialism will eventually prove its advantages precisely in the conditions of peaceful coexistence and contest with capitalism. However, we are by no means advocates of the competition in the military field which imperialism is imposing upon us.

The military-strategic balance between socialism and imperialism objectively contributes to peaceful coexistence. The attainment of this balance is one of the fundamental results of the last few decades. It has demanded great exertion and resources from our people and the peoples of other countries of the socialist community, and we will not allow it to be upset. We will continue to do everything necessary to guarantee the security of our country, our friends and allies; we will continue to strengthen the efficiency of the Soviet Armed Forces — a powerful factor in holding back aggression, the aggressive ambitions of imperialist reaction. However, if it were possible to reduce the level of armaments and military spending on both sides and to begin disarmament, which we are actively striving for, that would be a great blessing to all countries and peoples.

Our goal is not simply to prevent wars. We are striving for a radical improvement of international relations, and for strengthening and developing all good initiatives in these relations. We will press for securing respect for the sovereign rights of states and peoples, and for strict compliance with the principles of international law which imperialism more and more often attempts to discard and trample underfoot.

In short, in our epoch it is precisely socialism that is acting as the most consistent champion of fair principles to be applied in international relations, a champion of the interests of detente and peace, the interests of every people and all mankind. All this should evidently be clearly expressed in the new edition of the CPSU Programme.

The enormous tasks facing this country will require further enhancement of the Party's leading role. Therefore the Party must constantly perfect the forms and methods of its own work. The CPSU Programme contains a number of provisions to this effect which are yet to be translated into reality. New problems also arise.

It is highly important, for instance, to secure practically a correct distribution of functions between Party and government bodies. It has been stated more than once that Party bodies should not duplicate institutions of state, but this is not always possible to ensure. As a result, this often leads to a lessening of the responsibility of the leading executives of government bodies, and to tendencies towards shifting it onto Party bodies, which generates elements of a departmental approach to the matter in hand on the part of the latter.

A large reserve of latent opportunities in the Party is the further development of intra-Party democracy, and the enhancement of the creativity, initiative and responsibility of communists. The more boldly and more concretely communists discuss the vital problems of the life of the Party and country, the more actively they will take part in fulfilling the decisions taken, and the more successfully our Party will be able to perform its historic mission.

The new edition of the Party Programme is called upon to help all of us to concentrate forces on solving the key problems facing the Party and country. If we cope well with them this will be a new great step in developing the country and in improving the life of the people. Then our socialist sytem will demonstrate its advantages and its force of attraction to the whole world even more conclusively.

It is important not only to set clear and well-considered guidelines for the future but also to bring them to the awareness of millions of communists and unaffiliated people so that they may actively join in the forthcoming work. This is precisely one of the main tasks facing the fighters on the ideological front. Ideological, educational work is primarily the question of ties between the Party and people. This accounts for its significance. I am confident that this plenary meeting will give the Party considerable assistance in all its work.

Speech at the 8th Session of the USSR Supreme Soviet (10th convocation) following Election as President of the Presidium of the USSR Supreme Soviet
16 June 1983

Esteemed comrade deputies!

I thank you cordially from the bottom of my heart for the profound trust you have reposed in me by electing me President of the Presidium of the USSR Supreme Soviet.

I interpret this trust as your confidence in our Leninist Communist Party of which I have been a member for over forty years and to whose ideals I am totally dedicated.

Allow me to assure you that in my post as President of the Presidium of the USSR Supreme Soviet I will apply all my energies, knowledge and experience to honourably live up to your distinguished trust.

Speech at a dinner in the Grand Kremlin Palace in honour of the Party and Government Delegation of the Hungarian People's Republic led by Janos Kadar, First Secretary of the Central Committee of the Hungarian Socialist Workers' Party
20 July 1983

Dear Comrade Kadar!
Dear Hungarian guests!
Comrades!

It is a great pleasure on behalf of the leadership of the CPSU and the Soviet state to welcome to Moscow in a spirit of cordiality and brotherhood the Hungarian Party and government delegation. We greet you as comrades in arms, our allies and our like-minded comrades.

We are especially pleased to see at the head of the delegation Comrade Kadar, the time-tested leader of socialist Hungary, a good friend of the Soviet people.

Our parties and states are linked by long-standing and strong ties of international solidarity. There is every reason to say that relations between the Soviet Union and the Hungarian People's Republic become ever more diversified and fruitful. Literally in every sphere favourable results have been achieved and new, still broader, horizons are opened up for our cooperation.

The political calendar of the socialist countries contains a rich record of mutual relations and meetings on a multilateral and bilateral basis. This is motivated by the objective necessity of further improving the effectiveness of cooperation between our two countries, of advancing it to a considerably higher, I would even say qualitatively new, level.

These questions are the focus of attention at the current Soviet-Hungarian talks. The Central Committee of the CPSU and the Soviet government attach great significance to them. We are profoundly satisfied with the fact that our exchange of opinion has confirmed our common views and intentions.

Strengthening their cooperation and their cohesion, the socialist countries thereby multiply the force of their favourable influence on the course of world development, and this is beneficial to all.

Indeed, it is the socialist countries themselves that are the main bulwark of peace. They act as the vehicles of Lenin's ideas of peaceful coexistence, cooperation based on equality among all states, of strengthening the security of nations, and are at the forefront for preserving the very existence of civilization on earth against the increased danger of nuclear annihilation.

This is the object of their wide-scale, far-reaching proposals and initiatives in recent times, including those put forward at the Prague Conference of the Warsaw Treaty Political Consultative Committee and at the recent meeting of Party and government leaders of seven socialist countries in Moscow.

As is known, the Soviet Union has assumed a unilateral commitment not to use nuclear weapons first, while the Warsaw Treaty nations have proposed to the NATO powers that they conclude an agreement on reciprocal renunciation of the use of nuclear and conventional weapons.

The socialist countries have appealed for a freeze to be imposed on nuclear armaments to create thereby favourable conditions for more radical steps towards their reduction and eventual complete eradication.

Everyone viewing international developments without bias clearly understands that the implementation of the set of measures proposed by the socialist countries would avert the nuclear menace and make it possible to normalize international relations radically, and to remove from them dangerous mistrust and suspicion.

The only cause of the continued growth of tensions in the world is the policy and actions of imperialist circles, primarily those of the United States and its NATO allies. Washington is unwilling to reach a fair and honest agreement and does not conceal the fact that it intends to upset the military balance, to make a breakthrough in the armaments field and thus gain a position of world dominance. The public is deliberately misled and persuaded that the escalation of American strategic arms and the deployment of Pershing and cruise missiles in Western Europe will bring about progress at the negotiations now under way. These allegations have nothing in common with the truth. Progress in the negotiations will be secured not by an increase in the numbers of missiles but by a desire to find mutually acceptable agreements on a substantial reduction of the nuclear confrontation on the basis of reckoning with existing realities, the principle of parity and equal security. This is precisely the desire that pervades the Soviet stand at the talks on strategic arms and nuclear weapons in Europe.

Deployment of new American nuclear missiles in Europe would inevitably lead to consequences of a military and political character that would substantially complicate the world situation as a whole.

Is it possible to avoid such a course of development?

The socialist countries believe it is.

It is significant, for instance, that in the course of a hard and prolonged political struggle at the Madrid follow-up conference the overwhelming majority of states, contrary to the line of certain forces, still made a choice in favour of finding mutually acceptable settlements. This is a hopeful, healthy symptom. It is necessary to secure the successful completion of this conference, and the continuation of positive processes in complete conformity with the spirit and letter of the Helsinki Final Act.

The vital interests of the peoples of the European countries, and not only these peoples, dictate the need to prevent a race in nuclear armaments on the European continent, to reduce the numbers of medium-range nuclear weapons already deployed there. If the United States and NATO finally assess the situation soberly and abandon their one-sided and hopeless approach to negotiations based on a striving to secure the Soviet Union's unilateral disarmament, success in negotiations will be possible.

I am confident, dear comrades, that I express our common opinion if I say that our meeting will give a new impetus to the further development and deepening of all-round fraternal relations between the USSR and Hungary. It will conclusively demonstrate the consistent and high-principled line of the socialist countries in the struggle to preserve and consolidate peace, for the radiant ideals of socialism.

I propose a toast to the health of Comrade Kadar and other members of the Party and government delegation of the Hungarian People's Republic.

To the inviolable Soviet-Hungarian friendship!

To peace in Europe and throughout the world!

Index

365